Lecture Notes in Computer Science 14244

Founding Editors

Gerhard Goos
Juris Hartmanis

The series Lecture Notes in Computer Science (LNCS), including its subseries Lecture Notes in Artificial Intelligence (LNAI) and Lecture Notes in Bioinformatics (LNBI), has established itself as a medium for the publication of new developments in computer science and information technology research, teaching, and education.

LNCS enjoys close cooperation with the computer science R & D community, the series counts many renowned academics among its volume editors and paper authors, and collaborates with prestigious societies. Its mission is to serve this international community by providing an invaluable service, mainly focused on the publication of conference and workshop proceedings and postproceedings. LNCS commenced publication in 1973.

Anna Fensel · Ana Ozaki · Dumitru Roman ·
Ahmet Soylu

Editors

Rules and Reasoning

7th International Joint Conference, RuleML+RR 2023
Oslo, Norway, September 18–20, 2023
Proceedings

Springer

Editors
Anna Fensel (iD)
Wageningen University and Research
Wageningen, The Netherlands

Ana Ozaki (iD)
University of Oslo
Oslo, Norway

Dumitru Roman
SINTEF AS/Oslo Metropolitan University
Oslo, Norway

Ahmet Soylu
Oslo Metropolitan University
Oslo, Norway

ISSN 0302-9743   ISSN 1611-3349 (electronic)
Lecture Notes in Computer Science
ISBN 978-3-031-45071-6   ISBN 978-3-031-45072-3 (eBook)
https://doi.org/10.1007/978-3-031-45072-3

This Springer imprint is published by the registered company Springer Nature Switzerland AG
The registered company address is: Gewerbestrasse 11, 6330 Cham, Switzerland

Paper in this product is recyclable.

Preface

These are the proceedings of the 7th International Joint Conference on Rules and Reasoning (RuleML+RR). RuleML+RR joined the efforts of two well-established conference series: the International Web Rule Symposia (RuleML) and the Web Reasoning and Rule Systems (RR) conferences.

The RuleML symposia have been held since 2002 and the RR conferences since 2007. The RR conferences have been a forum for discussion and dissemination of new results on Web Reasoning and Rule Systems, with an emphasis on rule-based approaches and languages. The RuleML symposia were devoted to disseminating research, applications, languages, and standards for rule technologies, with attention to both theoretical and practical developments, to challenging new ideas and to industrial applications. Building on the tradition of both, RuleML and RR, the joint conference series RuleML+RR aims at bridging academia and industry in the field of rules, and at fostering cross-fertilization between the different communities focused on the research, development, and applications of rule-based systems. RuleML+RR aims at being the leading conference series for all subjects concerning theoretical advances, novel technologies, and innovative applications of knowledge representation and reasoning with rules.

To leverage these ambitions, RuleML+RR 2023 was organized as part of the event *Declarative AI 2023: Rules, Reasoning, Decisions, and Explanations*, which was held between the 18th and the 20th of September 2023. This event was hosted by OsloMet, Norway. With its general topic *"Declarative Artificial Intelligence"*, a core objective of the event was to present the latest advancements in AI and rules, rule-based machine learning, reasoning, decisions, and explanations and their adoption in IT systems. To this end, *Declarative AI 2023* brought together co-located events with related interests. In addition to RuleML+RR, this included the Reasoning Web Summer School (RW 2023) and DecisionCAMP 2023.

The RuleML+RR conference moreover included two subevents:

1. *Doctoral Consortium* – an initiative to attract and promote student research in rules and reasoning, with the opportunity for students to present and discuss their ideas, and benefit from close contact with leading experts in the field.
2. *International Rule Challenge* – an initiative to provide competition among work in progress and new visionary ideas concerning innovative rule-oriented applications, aimed at both research and industry.

The program of the main track of RuleML+RR 2023 included the presentation of 13 full research papers and 3 short papers. These contributions were carefully selected by the Program Committee from 46 high-quality submissions to the event. Each paper was carefully reviewed and discussed by the reviewers. Almost all of them received three reviews (87%) and all of them received two reviews. The technical program was then enriched with the additional contributions from its subevents as well as from DecisionCAMP 2023, an event aimed at practitioners which was virtual this year.

At RuleML+RR 2023, five keynote speakers were invited:

- Oscar Corcho, Professor at Universidad Politécnica de Madrid (Spain): *On the Governance of all the Artefacts Used in Knowledge Graph Creation and Maintenance Scenarios*
- Evgeny Kharlamov, Senior Expert at Bosch Center for Artificial Intelligence (Germany): *From Declarative to Neuro-Symbolic AI in Smart Manufacturing*
- Nathaniel Palmer, Director at Serco (USA): *Declarative AI at Scale: Powering a Robotic Workforce*
- Heiko Paulheim, Professor at University of Mannheim (Germany): *Knowledge Graph Embeddings meet Symbolic Schemas; or: what do they Actually Learn?*
- Fabian M. Suchanek, Professor at Télécom Paris (France): *Knowledge Bases and Language Models: Complementing Forces*

The chairs sincerely thank the keynote speakers for their contribution to the success of the event. The chairs also thank the Program Committee members and the additional reviewers for their hard work in the careful assessment of the submitted papers. Further thanks go to all authors of contributed papers for their efforts in the preparation of their submissions and the camera-ready versions within the established schedule. Sincere thanks to the chairs of the Doctoral Consortium and the Rule Challenge, and to the chairs of all co-located Declarative AI 2023 events. The chairs finally thank the entire organization team including the Publicity, Proceedings, and Sponsorship Chairs, who actively contributed to the organization and the success of the event.

A special thanks goes to all the sponsors of RuleML+RR 2023 and Declarative AI 2023: Artificial Intelligence Journal, Springer, SECAI, OsloMet, University of Oslo, SINTEF, RuleML Inc, and RR Association. A special thanks also goes to the publisher, Springer, for their cooperation in editing this volume and publication of the proceedings. We are grateful to the sponsors of the RuleML+RR 2023 as they also contributed towards the awards: RuleML+RR Harold Boley Distinguished Paper award, RuleML+RR Best Student Paper award, RuleML+RR Best Rule Challenge Paper award, RuleML+RR Best Doctoral Consortium Paper award.

August 2023

Anna Fensel
Ana Ozaki
Dumitru Roman
Ahmet Soylu

Organization

General Chairs

Ahmet Soylu	Oslo Metropolitan University, Norway
Dumitru Roman	SINTEF AS/Oslo Metropolitan University, Norway
Martin Giese	University of Oslo, Norway

Program Chairs

Anna Fensel	Wageningen University & Research, The Netherlands
Ana Ozaki	University of Oslo & University of Bergen, Norway

Doctoral Consortium

Davide Lanti	Free University of Bozen-Bolzano, Italy
Dörthe Arndt	TU Dresden, Germany
Egor V. Kostylev	University of Oslo, Norway

Rule Challenge Chairs

Jan Vanthienen	KU Leuven, Belgium
Tomáš Kliegr	Prague University of Economics and Business, Czech Republic
Paul Fodor	Stony Brook University, USA

Proceedings Chair

Dumitru Roman	SINTEF AS/Oslo Metropolitan University, Norway

Program Committee

Alisa Kovtunova	TU Dresden, Germany
Aljbin Ahmeti	Semantic Web Company, Austria
Andreas Pieris	University of Edinburgh, UK
Anelia Kurteva	TU Delft, The Netherlands
Angelo Montanari	University of Udine, Italy
Anni-Yasmin Turhan	TU Dresden, Germany
Antonis Bikakis	University College London, UK
Baris Setkaya	Frankfurt University of Applied Sciences, Germany
Bernardo Cuenca Grau	University of Oxford, UK
Claudia d'Amato	Università degli Studi di Bari, Italy
Davide Sottara	Mayo Clinic, USA
Diego Calvanese	Free University of Bozen-Bolzano, Italy
Domenico Lembo	Sapienza University of Rome, Italy
Egor V. Kostylev	University of Oslo, Norway
Emanuel Sallinger	TU Wien, Austria
Erman Acar	University of Amsterdam, The Netherlands
Filip Murlak	University of Warsaw, Poland
Francesca Alessandra Lisi	Università degli Studi di Bari "Aldo Moro", Italy
Francesco Ricca	University of Calabria, Italy
Francesco Santini	Università di Perugia, Italy
Francesco M. Donini	Universita' della Tuscia, Italy
Frank Wolter	University of Liverpool, UK
Giovanni De Gasperis	Università degli Studi dell'Aquila, Italy
Grigoris Antoniou	University of Huddersfield, UK
Guido Governatori	Independent researcher, Australia
Horatiu Cirstea	Loria, France
Jan Rauch	Prague University of Economics and Business, Czechia
Jessica Zangari	University of Calabria, Italy
Jorge García-Gutiérrez	University of Seville, Spain
Jorge Martinez-Gil	Software Competence Center Hagenberg, Austria
Juliana Küster Filipe Bowles	University of St Andrews, UK
Kia Teymourian	University of Texas at Austin, USA
Livia Predoiu	Free University of Bozen-Bolzano, Italy
Livio Robaldo	University of Swansea, UK
Loris Bozzato	Fondazione Bruno Kessler, Italy
Manolis Koubarakis	National and Kapodistrian University of Athens, Greece
Mantas Simkus	TU Vienna, Austria

Marco Manna	University of Calabria, Italy
Marco Maratea	University of Genova, Italy
Maria Vanina Martinez	Universidad de Buenos Aires, Argentina
Markus Krötzsch	TU Dresden, Germany
Michaël Thomazo	Inria, France
Nurulhuda A. Manaf	National Defence University of Malaysia (UPNM), Malaysia
Ognjen Savkovic	Free University of Bozen-Bolzano, Italy
Patrick Koopmann	TU Dresden, Germany
Paul Krause	University of Surrey, UK
Pedro Cabalar	University of A Coruña, Spain
Rafael Peñaloza	University of Milano-Bicocca, Italy
Ricardo Guimarães	University of Bergen, Norway
Rolf Schwitter	Macquarie University, Australia
Roman Kontchakov	Birkbeck, University of London, UK
Sarah Alice Gaggl	TU Dresden, Germany
Sebastian Rudolph	TU Dresden, Germany
Sergio Tessaris	Free University of Bozen-Bolzano, Italy
Shqiponja Ahmetaj	Vienna University of Technology, Austria
Stefan Schlobach	Vrije Universiteit Amsterdam, The Netherlands
Stefania Costantini	University of L'Aquila, Italy
Theresa Swift	Universidade Nova de Lisboa, Portugal
Thom Fruehwirth	University of Ulm, Germany
Thomas Lukasiewicz	University of Oxford, UK
Tomas Kliegr	Prague University of Economics and Business, Czechia
Umberto Straccia	ISTI-CNR, Italy
Umutcan Şimşek	University of Innsbruck, Austria
Yuheng Wang	Stony Brook University, USA
Zaenal Akbar	National Research and Innovation Agency, Indonesia

Additional Reviewers

Aldo Ricioppo	University of Calabria, Italy
Cinzia Marte	University of Calabria, Italy
Dominik Rusovac	TU Dresden, Germany
Ivan Scagnetto	University of Udine, Italy
Nicola Saccomanno	University of Udine, Italy
Sascha Rechenberger	University of Ulm, Germany

RuleML+RR 2023 Sponsors

Invited Talks

On the Governance of all the Artefacts Used in Knowledge Graph Creation and Maintenance Scenarios

Oscar Corcho (ID)

Ontology Engineering Group, Universidad Politécnica de Madrid, Boadilla del Monte, Spain
ocorcho@fi.upm.es

Abstract. The creation and maintenance of knowledge graphs is commonly based on the generation and use of several types of artefacts, including ontologies, declarative mappings and different types of scripts and data processing pipelines, sample queries, APIs, etc. All of these artefacts need to be properly maintained so that knowledge graph creation and maintenance processes are sustainable over time, especially in those cases where the original data sources change frequently. It is not uncommon to have situations where ontologies are governed by an organisation or group of organisations, while mappings and data processing pipelines are handled by other organisations or individuals, using different sets of principles. This causes mismatches in the knowledge graphs that are generated, including the need to update all the associated artefacts (declarative mappings, sample queries, APIs, etc.) so as to keep up to date to changes in the ontologies, or in the underlying data sources. In this talk we will discuss several of the challenges associated to the maintenance of all of these artefacts in real-world knowledge graph scenarios, so as to provide some light into how we could set up a complete knowledge graph governance model that may be used across projects and initiatives.

Keywords: Knowledge graph · Governance · Ontologies · Mappings

This work was funded partially by the project Knowledge Spaces: Técnicas y herramientas para la gestión de grafos de conocimientos para dar soporte a espacios de datos (Grant PID2020-118274RB-I00, funded by MCIN/AEI/ 10.13039/501100011033)

Knowledge Graph Embeddings Meet Symbolic Schemas or: What do they Actually Learn?

Heiko Paulheim [ID]

Data and Web Science Group, University of Mannheim, Mannheim, Germany
heiko@informatik.unim-annheim.de

Abstract. Knowledge Graph Embeddings are representations of entities and relations as vectors in a continuous space, and, as such, are used in many tasks, like link prediction or entity classification [3]. While most evaluations of knowledge graph embeddings are on quantitative benchmarks [1, 2], it is still not fully understood what they are actually capable of learning. In this talk, I will show how to quantify the representative capabilities of knowledge graph embeddings using the DLCC benchmark [4], and provide insights into what kinds of logical constructs can be represented by which embedding methods. Based on those considerations, I will discuss various ways in which knowledge graph embeddings can benefit from symbolic schema information, and how those combinations open new ways of evaluating knowledge graph embeddings beyond standard metrics.

References

1. Bloem, P., Wilcke, X., van Berkel, L., de Boer, V.: kgbench: a collection of knowledge graph datasets for evaluating relational and multimodal machine learning. In: Verborgh, R., et al. (ed.) The Semantic Web. ESWC 2021. LNCS, vol. 12731, pp. 614–630, Springer, Cham (2021). https://doi.org/10.1007/978-3-030-77385-4_37
2. Pellegrino, M.A., Altabba, A., Garofalo, M., Ristoski, P., Cochez, M.: GEval: a modular and extensible evaluation framework for graph embedding techniques. In: Harth, A., et al. (ed.) The Semantic Web. ESWC 2020. LNCS, vol. 12123, pp. 565–582, Springer, Cham (2020). https://doi.org/10.1007/978-3-030-49461-2_33
3. Portisch, J., Heist, N., Paulheim, H.: Knowledge graph embedding for data mining vs. knowledge graph embedding for link prediction–two sides of the same coin? Semant. Web 13(3), 399–422 (2022)
4. Portisch, J., Paulheim, H.: The DLCC node classification benchmark for analyzing knowledge graph embeddings. In: Sattler, U., et al. (ed.) The Semantic Web – ISWC 2022. ISWC 2022. LNCS, vol. 13489, pp. 592–609. Springer, Cham (2022). https://doi.org/10.1007/978-3-031-19433-7_34

From Declarative to Neuro-Symbolic AI in Smart Manufacturing

Evgeny Kharlamov[1,2]

[1] Bosch Center for Artificial Intelligence, Germany
[2] SIRIUS Research Centre, University of Oslo, Norway

Symbolic or declarative methods have been extensively used in manufacturing, e.g., as digital representations of physical objects or systems, where they have become one of the key building blocks towards digitalization and automation in the whole production value chain. Indeed, rules, ontologies, answer set programs have been used for modelling of industrial assets as Digital Twins, for industrial analytics, integration and querying of production data, process monitoring and equipment diagnostics, moreover, semantic technologies have been adopted or evaluated in a number of large high tech production companies such as Bosch, Equinor, Festo, Siemens, etc.

New trends in manufacturing that often referred to as Industry 4.0 and that are characterised by an extensive use of sensors and IoT technology brought enormous volumes of production data from manufacturing facilities. This requires data driven solutions including Machine Learning that can cope industrial big data. At the same time such solutions should account for the declarative representations in order to take the vital manufacturing knowledge captured in them to the full extend thus ensuring trust, reliability, explainability, and transparency of AI solutions.

In the keynote talk we discuss the declarative aspects of manufacturing, the new smart manufacturing trends and the necessity of Neural-Symbolic solutions. We will give a number of examples from Bosch and other companies, discuss research and industrial challenges and new exciting directions.

Keywords: Knowledge graphs · Ontologies · Machine learning · LLMs

Acknowledgements. The work was partially supported by EU projects Dome 4.0 (GA 953163), OntoCommons (GA 958371), DataCloud (GA 101016835), Graph Massiviser (GA 101093202), EnRichMyData (GA 101093202), and SMARTEDGE (GA 101092908), and the SIRIUS Centre of the Norwegian Research Council (237898).

Declarative AI at Scale: Powering a Robotic Workforce

Nathaniel Palmer

Serco Inc., 12930 Worldgate Drive Suite 6000, Herndon, VA 20170, USA
ngpalmer@protonmail.com

Abstract. This talk presents the results of a multi-year journey applying Declarative AI to a critical government mission. Leveraging commercial-of-the-self components and innovative design patterns, this journey has combined Deep Neural Network (DNN), and Machine Learning (ML) together with Decision Management (DM), and Robotic Process Automation (RPA) to deliver a robotic workforce powered by Declarative AI, performing complex case management alongside human case workers. Results include substantial gains in efficiency, quality, and consistency verifying the eligibility of tens of millions of consumers seeking to requiring government benefit eligibility verification. One of the largest and most complex applications of AI within the federal government arena, the results of this journey makes a compelling illustration of the difference between Statistical and Declarative AI – at scale! This session will feature a transparent presentation of our results, metrics, approach, and lessons learned (including many never before disclosed to a public audience.) You will learn how we leveraged Declarative AI to escape and exceed the traditional boundaries of automation, moving from discrete tasks to perform "robo-adjudication" delivering greater accuracy, efficiency, and quality of work. Also demonstrated will be how our Declarative AI is leveraged to assign work to humans and robots, ensuring every time right work performed by the right worked at precisely the right moment. Nathaniel will show strategies for automation at this massive scale can be executed with full transparency and accountability, eliminating the reliance on subjective interpretation of policies and rules, while delivery more accurate analytics and ensuring program integrity. He will discuss how to deliver intelligent automation at scale, while avoiding the pitfalls which inevitably otherwise doom to fail initiatives of this size and scope, including what challenges were overcome as well as those unforeseeable at the outset.

Keywords: Decision management · Robotic process automation · Machine learning

Contents

Invited Paper

Knowledge Bases and Language Models: Complementing Forces

Fabian Suchanek[1,2]($\boxtimes$)(ID) and Anh Tuan Luu[2](ID)

[1] Institut Polytechnique de Paris, Palaiseau, France
suchanek@telecom-paris.fr
[2] Nanyang Technological University, Singapore, Singapore

Abstract. Large language models (LLMs), as a particular instance of generative artificial intelligence, have revolutionized natural language processing. In this invited paper, we argue that LLMs are complementary to structured data repositories such as databases or knowledge bases, which use symbolic knowledge representations. Hence, the two ways of knowledge representation will likely continue to co-exist, at least in the near future. We discuss ways that have been explored to make the two approaches work together, and point out opportunities and challenges for their symbiosis.

Keywords: Large Language Models · Knowledge Bases · Databases

1 Large Language Models

Large Language Models (LLMs) have revolutionized the field of natural language processing in 2023, with the rise of models such as GPT [44], LLaMA [69], and PaLM [11]. As instances of what is called "generative Artificial Intelligence (AI)", LLMs can chat like humans, answer questions, summarize or translate text, write program code, and appear to be able to do just about anything a human can do on text.

LLMs thus have the potential to deeply change our everyday life: they might automatize the work of human professionals in areas where we thought human intelligence was indispensable (such as the work of journalists, legal consultants, authors, programmers, teachers, or researchers [15]). They will pose new societal threats, as they can generate fake news, fake posts, and fake conversations at an unprecedented rate. They might one day pursue their own agenda, threaten users (as it has already happened [39]), or manipulate humans to grant them favors (as hypothesized by Eliezer Yudkowsky in his AI Box thought experiment [76][1]). Already now, they pose legal and ethical challenges in areas such as the copyright of the generated text [4], liability for generated statements [78], explainability of decisions based on such text, the personal data stored in language models (or

---

[1] https://arminbagrat.com/agi-box/.

A. Fensel et al. (Eds.): RuleML+RR 2023, LNCS 14244, pp. 3–15, 2023.
https://doi.org/10.1007/978-3-031-45072-3_1

submitted in prompts), the intellectual property of data used for training, and the remuneration of those who created the training data [20].

At the same time, LLMs democratize access to the digital world: novices can now write programs, formulate SQL queries, understand the gist of scientific articles, write, translate, or summarize text, and find answers to just about any question they may have. LLMs will certainly shortly pop up in mobile phones, office software, email clients, and digital assistants, and greatly simplify our life there. In the future, generative AI systems might be granted access to computational tools (so that they can execute code), gain multi-modal capabilities (so that they can see, listen, and speak), become embodied (so that they can physically act), and become ingrained in our life in ways that would be naive to anticipate now [6].

These considerations raise the question whether LLMs will be, or possibly even are, intelligent or even conscious [6]. From a materialistic point of view, one can imagine that a system that is sufficiently complex can indeed show similar emergent properties as the brain, including intelligence and consciousness [58]. However, this is a debate that will have to be pursued not just with computer scientists, but also with philosophers, neuro-scientists, and psychologists. Quite possibly, we might have to come up with new notions of consciousness and intelligence that are suitable for AI. In analogy to Neil deGrasse Tyson's adage, the universe is under no obligation to conform to the words that we humans have invented. It is rather up to us to make our words fit an ever-changing reality— potentially by inventing new ones. For example, when the electric scooter was invented, people did not insist on categorizing it as a kick scooter or as a motorbike. Rather, they invented a new word to describe it, and introduced the legislation to regulate it. We might have to do the same in the case of AI.

2   Structured Data

Despite the successes of LLMs, most knowledge in organizations or companies is stored not in LLMs, but in structured data repositories that use symbolic knowledge representations – such as databases, knowledge bases, XML files, or JSON datasets. Now suppose that we are working at a company that builds an airplane, and that we have a database of all the parts of that airplane. Should we train an LLM to learn the content of that database, and replace the database by the LLM? At the current state of affairs, that would be a terrible idea, for several reasons:

LLMs are probabilistic by nature. While this is convenient for language [77], it is inadmissible for a definite list of items, such as airplane parts. A screw is either part of the airplane or it is not, it should not be there with a certain probability. Even if the LLM tells us that each part is present with a probability of 99%, this would still mean that thousands of parts could be missing, as modern airplanes consist of millions of parts.

LLMs cannot memorize well. Even if we train the models on selected corpora only [13,26], there is no guarantee that the model will remember what it was trained on without forgetting some facts or inventing others [5, 48, 63, 64]. This is to be expected: language models are machine learning models, i.e., they are designed to generalize, not to memorize.

LLMs may give different answers depending on how we ask. When the same question is asked in different ways or different languages, the answers can be different [71]. This is the reason for the rise of the new discipline called prompt engineering [75].

LLMs may mislead. LLMs will always wrap their wrong answers into a deceptively convincing language: They know how to talk even when they don't know what to say.

Weaknesses accumulate when the query needs reasoning. Many queries on structured data require joins (such as finding the airplane parts that are part of other airplane parts), aggregation (computing the total weight of the airplane), or even reasoning (proving that the total weight of the airplane plus its cargo can be carried by the lift). In such cases, the above weaknesses may accumulate [19].

LLMs are black boxes. We cannot get a list of all facts that a LLM knows. Thus, we cannot audit LLMs, i.e., we cannot check what they contain and how they will reply to queries [71]. They remain black boxes that act at their own discretion.

LLMs cannot be fixed or updated in a straightforward way. LLMs are great only when they work. However, when the model gives an incorrect answer, or when a data point changes, we cannot easily "fix" the model. There are various ways in which the model can be retrained, supplemented by an external memory, or undergo modification of its parameters – but all of these are more complex, more costly, and less reliable than issuing an UPDATE statement on a database.

LLMs are costly to train. Databases are more sustainable [1, 55], and faster than LLMs when it comes to retrieving simple facts: it does not make sense to train and run a model with hundreds of billions of parameters to retrieve data that can also be retrieved by a query on a database that runs in a few nanoseconds on a household computer [71].

LLMs can be tricked. Through clever prompt engineering (called jailbreaking [32]), LLMs can be made to reveal internal mechanisms, share private data, produce offensive speech, or perform unintended workloads. LLMs thus pose a security risk[2,3,4].

While some of these weaknesses will go away with more (or better) training data, others appear to be here to stay. Thus, at least for now, it seems that structured data repositories have their raison-d'être. Whenever we want to store crisp lists of items, such as commercial products, employees, proteins, or indeed airplane parts, structured data repositories are still the way to go. They are efficient to

---

[2] https://simonwillison.net/2023/May/2/prompt-injection-explained/.

[3] https://www.jailbreakchat.com/.

[4] https://owasp.org/www-project-top-10-for-large-language-model-applications/descriptions/.

query, easy to update, amenable to auditing, and 100% deterministic in their answers. In simple application cases, a JSON document will work. If we want a fixed schema, large-scale efficiency, and ample software support, a database will be the method of choice. If we need a taxonomy, semantic axioms, reasoning capabilities, and interoperability, a knowledge base lends itself.

By way of introduction, a knowledge base (also known as a KB or knowledge graph) is a labeled directed graph, where the nodes are entities (such as airplane parts, people, organizations, or locations), and the edges are relations between these entities (such as which part belongs to which other part, who works where, or which organization is located in which place) [61]. Similar entities are grouped together into classes (all airplane engineers are in a class "airplane engineers"), and these classes form a taxonomy, where more special classes (such as "airplane engineers") are included in more general classes (such as "people"). In addition, a KB can specify axioms that say, e.g., that every person must have a birth date, that the weight of an airplane part must be a positive numerical value, that the part-of relation is transitive, that people and airplane parts are disjoint, or that a person cannot have more than two parents. KBs can refer to entities of other KBs, and thus reuse what has been defined elsewhere. There are today thousands of publicly available KBs, and these are interlinked in the Semantic Web. KBs can be queried in a formal language called SPARQL, and the responses are efficient, deterministic, and easy to update.

3   LLMs and Structured Data: Complementary Forces

LLMs and structured data repositories store information in fundamentally different ways: in the latter, the information is stored in a symbolic, crisp, accessible way. In a (deep-learning based) LLM, the information is stored in a probabilistic, distributed, opaque, and sub-symbolic way. Each approach has its advantages. Structured data repositories provide a cheaper and more reliable performance than LLMs for simple factoid data and queries. However, they are way less accessible to the user than LLMs, because they require complex query languages. LLMs, in contrast, provide an unparalleled ease of interaction – in a way that is literally very natural (natural language). Furthermore, LLMs store a wealth of informal information that would be cumbersome or outright impossible to store in structured data: commonsense knowledge about objects of everyday life [43], probabilistic knowledge about how things usually are [42], knowledge about processes or hypotheses [56], and the ability to perform casual reasoning.

It thus appears that language models and structured data repositories are complementary: language models excel at general knowledge, and at analyzing and generating natural language text. Structured data, in contrast, is the tool of choice when it comes to storing exact items, and reasoning on them. Again, an analogy with the human brain can be instructive: The human brain is a fantastically powerful and versatile tool. And yet, for some intellectual tasks, humans resort to "external tools", such as paper and pen, or a written list of items. For example, we do not learn the phone numbers of all our friends by heart. We put them in an address book. We do not conduct a proof of a theorem entirely in our heads. We write it down. In the same way, a LLM might make use of external tools when it comes to storing data or to formal reasoning. These external tools can be structured data repositories such as databases and knowledge bases, combined with other symbolic tools such as automated reasoners.

4   Combining LLMs and Structured Data

The question is now how a LLM can interact with symbolic knowledge, so that a user can get the ease of interaction of a LLM combined with the factual accuracy of structured data. There are indeed numerous ways in which LLMs have been combined with symbolic knowledge[5]. One way is to fuse the structured data into the model itself [41,80]. This, however, requires intimate access to the model architecture, while most LLMs are black boxes. Therefore, most approaches resort to natural language as the vehicle to teach language models.

Among these, some approaches [41,80] try to instill the knowledge at training or fine-tuning time. However, as we have discussed above, there is no guarantee that the model retains what it has been trained on. Other approaches [12,14] cross-examine the language model to force it to rethink its answers. Again, there is no guarantee that the reply is correct.

Then there is the philosophy that LLMs should not store factual information at all [71]. There is no need for a LLM to learn "by heart" the coordinates of every city on the planet (as GPT currently does), or the weights of all known molecules. Better outsource that knowledge to a knowledge base. The rationale is that if we remove the factoid information from the LLM, this might considerably reduce the size of the model, while allowing it at the same time to concentrate on what it does best: dealing with language. Indeed, there are tasks where a smaller LLM performs better than a large one [72]. This philosophy would call for LLMs to be trained on carefully selected, but much smaller corpora – although still large enough for the LLM to gain general knowledge about the world.

Among the approaches that follow this philosophy, one of the most intuitive ones is to find the relevant information, and add it as a hidden prompt. This is what LangChain proposes[6], and it appears to be what the Bing AI does[7]. This approach can deal with both textual information and structured data [31]. Other approaches equip language models with the ability to use tools – among others, knowledge graphs. This can be achieved via plugins [40], via Augmented Language Models [38], or via an LLM-SQL bridge [25].

5   Challenges in Combining LLMs and Structured Data

The crux of all approaches that aim to combine LLMs with structured data is that they have to bridge the gap between natural language and symbolic

---

[5] https://github.com/RManLuo/Awesome-LLM-KG.

[6] https://docs.langchain.com/docs/use-cases/qa-docs.

[7] https://bing.com.

knowledge representations [41]. In some cases this is trivial: If a user asks for the coordinates of the city of Paris, a simple database lookup will do the job. However, most cases are not of that easy form. Let us briefly present the main challenges in bridging the gap between a natural language text and a symbolic knowledge representation of its meaning.

For a start, many named entities do not consist of a single capitalized word (such as "Paris"). Then, it is difficult to distinguish the named entities from the surrounding text. This applies in particular to movie titles ("Have you seen the life of Brian yesterday?"), medical terms ("His Diabetes Mellitus, Type 2 was treated with insulin"), and terms that do not (yet) appear in a dictionary ("The Institut polytechnique de Paris was founded in 2019"). The problem of identifying the items of interest in natural language text is known as **Named Entity Recognition** (NER).

A user who asks for Paris is most likely interested in the capital of France. However, when the user is interested in the books of an author named John Smith, then there are literally hundreds of authors of that name. The same is true if the user asks for employees of a certain name, or proteins with a certain name component. Depending on which meaning we choose, the answer we give from the knowledge base will be different. Thus, we have to find the entity that the user is referring to. This is known as the problem of **Disambiguation**.

The next step is the understanding of the sentence itself: is the user interested in the date that the movie was released, or the date that the movie shows in a local cinema? This is the problem of **Relation Extraction**. Finally, determining the user intent and formulating a query on the database falls in the domain of **Question Answering** [27]. Again, this is usually not as trivial as looking up the coordinates of Paris. Rather, we may have to formulate queries that aggregate, join, or negate ("Which proportion of people in France do not live in its 10 biggest cities?").

In some cases, we might have to go further: we might have to build a symbolic knowledge representation of what is said in an entire text – either to understand the context of the question, or to feed the knowledge contained in the text into the knowledge base. The process of distilling symbolic knowledge from natural language text is known as **Information Extraction** (IE) [73]. It faces formidable challenges beyond those already mentioned: First, not all information in text can be conveniently represented in current symbolic knowledge representations. Non-named entities [43], subjective information [42], and complex information about sequential processes, causality, or hypothetical statements [56], for example, bring us to the edge of what is currently possible. Second, the extracted information has to be in itself coherent, and then logically consistent with the data that has already been stored [62]. Furthermore, errors accumulate: While it is nowadays trivial to map a simple subject-verb-object sentence to a symbolic representation, the deficiencies of NER, disambiguation, relation extraction, information extraction, and symbolic knowledge representation add up, and it is currently beyond reach to build a symbolic representation of a full text at the push of a button.

Finally, the KBs themselves may contain errors or be outdated. They thus require constant **data curation**.

6 Our Work

As we have seen, there is a gap to be bridged between natural language text and symbolic knowledge representations. While the gap is still large, the domain of information extraction has been around for decades and has made that gap at least significantly smaller than it used to be (see [73,74] for surveys).

We have also contributed our bit to this endeavor [57]. A first step to bridge the gap between LLMs and symbolic representations is to ensure that the language model can represent the input text at all. This requires the **embedding** of the words of the text. We have shown that words that currently have no embedding (so-called *out-of-vocabulary words*) can be embedded efficiently by making their representations similar to the representations of similar words [8]. This approach is called LOVE (for Learning Out-of Vocabulary Embeddings). The next step is to **disambiguate** these words, i.e., to map them to the entities in a knowledge base. We have shown that this can be done with a relatively light-weight model [7], even in the case of non-trivial medical terms. We have also proposed a large benchmark for the disambiguation of acronyms (GLADIS, the General Large Acronym Disambiguation benchmark [9]).

To build knowledge graphs from natural language texts, we need the **combination of different IE subtasks** such as NER, relation extraction, and co-reference resolution. It is well-known that these tasks are correlated and beneficial to each other. However, most of the current studies about knowledge graph construction tend to treat each subtask as a separate task or to apply a sequential pipeline approach, which can lead to cascading errors and obfuscation of the inherent relationship between tasks. To overcome this limitation, we have propose UGFIE [82], a dynamic, graph-based general framework for coupling multiple IE tasks through shared span representations that are refined with context derived from entities, relations, and co-references.

To **deal with a lack of training data** in knowledge graph construction, we have proposed Jointprop [81], a Heterogeneous Graph-based Propagation framework for joint semi-supervised entity and relation extraction. This framework captures the global structured information between individual tasks and exploits interactions within unlabeled data. Specifically, we construct a unified span-based heterogeneous graph from entity and relation candidates and propagate class labels based on confidence scores. We then employ a propagation learning scheme to leverage the affinities between labeled and unlabeled samples.

Another avenue of our research has focused on the **reasoning capabilities** of language models. We have first analyzed the reasoning capabilities of existing (smaller) language models, and catalogued their strengths and weaknesses [21]. We have then addressed one of the weaknesses: **textual inference** in the presence of negation. We have proposed a probabilistic definition of textual inference, and we have then shown that this definition can be used to generate negated training examples from positive training examples. This approach (TINA, for Textual Inference with Negation Augmentation) increases the reasoning performance of these models by up to 20% [23]. A software library for reasoning on text with language models, LogiTorch, complements this work [22].

We have also looked into the evaluation of language models, in particular when it comes to the **quality of the stories that LLMs can generate**. We have first collected quality criteria for stories from the scientific literature in the humanities. We have then generated a large corpus of generated stories with human annotations for these criteria. The resulting benchmark (HANNA, for Human-Annotated Narratives) shows that automated metrics are currently not sufficient to measure the quality of stories [10]. We have also looked into the evaluation of machine learning models in general. Nowadays, such models are no longer evaluated just by their prediction accuracy, but also by their transparency. We have developed an approach that can **explain the decision of a machine-learning model** post-hoc. The central idea is to build not one, but several surrogate models that mimic the behavior of the original model in a human-understandable way (which is why the approach is called STACI, for Surrogate Trees for A posteriori Confident Interpretations) [46]. This work is complemented by an approach for explaining regression models, BELLA (for black-box explanations by local linear models [45]).

The flagship of our work is a **knowledge base called YAGO** (Yet Another Great Ontology) [2,24,37,49,60,68]. This KB contains 50 million entities of general interest (such as people, organizations, or locations) and hundreds of millions of facts about them. While earlier versions of YAGO were extracted from Wikipedia, newer versions build on Wikidata. The main distinguishing feature of YAGO is its data quality: it provides a clean taxonomy, human-readable entity names, a manually designed schema, and enforced semantic constraints. The work on YAGO has been complemented by work that extracts commercial products from Web pages by making use of UPC/GTIN codes [65]. Other work **constructs a taxonomy** for a given set of entities using the information from the Web [33–35,70] .

A KB has to be constantly curated. We have developed several approaches to this end. Some of them [66,67] can automatically **spot errors in a KB based on the edit history**. Others allow the **alignment of entities** in one KB with the entities in another KB (see [79] for a survey). Our main project here is PARIS (Probabilistic Alignment of Relations, Instances, and Schema) [59], which, despite its age of more than 10 years, remains the state of the art in entity alignment even in the face of neural approaches [30].

A large part of our work has focused on the **incompleteness of KBs** (see [47] for a general introduction): We have shown how to compute a lower bound for the number of missing entities in a KB, based purely on the properties of the entities that exist in the KB [53]. We have also developed a method that can estimate, again only from the existing entities in the KB, whether a property (such as *birth-place*) is present in all entities of a given class in the real world [29].

Another method can estimate whether an entity is missing a property in the KB that it has in the real world [16]. One way to fight this incompleteness is to use rules: If we know that people who are married generally live in the place where their spouse lives, we can use that rule to deduce missing places of residence. With AMIE (for Association rule Mining under Incomplete Evidence) [17,18,28], we can **mine such rules automatically from the KB**. These rules have recently been combined with neural methods for link prediction [3].

Finally, we have worked on the **querying of KBs**. We have focused on dynamic KBs, which can be accessed only via functions [51,52]. We have also shown, rather unconventionally, that in some cases it is more efficient to query a KB via Bash commands rather than loading it into a database system [50]. To query several KBs with aggregation queries, we have developed an algorithm that can approximate the answers for such queries [54].

7 Conclusion

Large language models (LLMs), and generative AI in general, offer fascinating opportunities to simplify our lives and to allow for a more equitable access to the digital world. At the same time, they often have to be complemented by structured data in order to ground their output in reality – at least for now. To allow for such a grounding, we have to bridge the gap between the natural language that is the vehicle of communication with LLMs, and the symbolic representations that are used by structured data repositories such as databases and knowledge bases. This is the challenge of information extraction (IE). While this challenge is decades old, newer IE methods make use of LLMs to analyze natural language text, and to help producing symbolic representations from it [36,83]. In this way, LLMs themselves may provide the key to overcoming their weaknesses.

Acknowledgement. This work was partially funded by the grant ANR-20-CHIA-0012-01 ("NoRDF").

References

1. Artificial intelligence is booming—so is its carbon footprint. Bloomberg (2023). https://www.bloomberg.com/news/articles/2023-03-09/how-much-energy-do-ai-and-chatgpt-use-no-one-knows-for-sure
2. Biega, J.A., Kuzey, E., Suchanek, F.M.: Inside YAGO2s: a transparent information extraction architecture. In: WWW Demo Track (2013)
3. Boschin, A., Jain, N., Keretchashvili, G., Suchanek, F.M.: Combining embeddings and rules for fact prediction. In: AIB Invited Paper (2022)
4. Boyle, J., Jenkins, J.: Intellectual Property: Law & The Information Society (2014)
5. Cao, B., et al.: Knowledgeable or educated guess? Revisiting language models as knowledge bases. arXiv preprint arXiv:2106.09231 (2021)
6. Chalmers, D.J.: Could a large language model be conscious? arXiv preprint arXiv:2303.07103 (2023)

7. Chen, L., Varoquaux, G., Suchanek, F.M.: A lightweight neural model for biomedical entity linking. In: AAAI (2021)
8. Chen, L., Varoquaux, G., Suchanek, F.M.: Imputing out-of-vocabulary embedding with LOVE makes language models robust with little cost. In: ACL (2022)
9. Chen, L., Varoquaux, G., Suchanek, F.M.: GLADIS: a general and large acronym disambiguation benchmark. In: EACL (2023)
10. Chhun, C., Colombo, P., Suchanek, F.M., Clavel, C.: Of human criteria and automatic metrics: a benchmark of the evaluation of story generation (HANNA). In: COLING (2022)
11. Chowdhery, A., et al.: Palm: scaling language modeling with pathways. arXiv preprint arXiv:2204.02311 (2022)
12. Cohen, R., Hamri, M., Geva, M., Globerson, A.: LM vs LM: detecting factual errors via cross examination. arXiv preprint arXiv:2305.13281 (2023)
13. Dettmers, T., Pagnoni, A., Holtzman, A., Zettlemoyer, L.: QLoRA: efficient fine-tuning of quantized LLMs. arXiv preprint arXiv:2305.14314 (2023)
14. Du, Y., Li, S., Torralba, A., Tenenbaum, J.B., Mordatch, I.: Improving factuality and reasoning in language models through multiagent debate. arXiv preprint arXiv:2305.14325 (2023)
15. Eloundou, T., Manning, S., Mishkin, P., Rock, D.: GPTs are GPTs: an early look at the labor market impact potential of large language models. arXiv preprint arXiv:2303.10130 (2023)
16. Galárraga, L., Razniewski, S., Amarilli, A., Suchanek, F.M.: Predicting completeness in knowledge bases. In: WSDM (2017)
17. Galárraga, L., Teflioudi, C., Hose, K., Suchanek, F.M.: AMIE: association rule mining under incomplete evidence in ontological knowledge bases. In: WWW (2013)
18. Galárraga, L., Teflioudi, C., Hose, K., Suchanek, F.M.: Fast rule mining in ontological knowledge bases with AMIE+. VLDBJ **24**(6), 707–730 (2015)
19. Golovneva, O., et al.: Roscoe: a suite of metrics for scoring step-by-step reasoning. arXiv preprint arXiv:2212.07919 (2022)
20. Hacker, P., Engel, A., Mauer, M.: Regulating ChatGPT and other large generative AI models. In: ACM Fairness, Accountability, and Transparency (2023)
21. Helwe, C., Clavel, C., Suchanek, F.M.: Reasoning with transformer-based models: deep learning, but shallow reasoning. In: AKBC (2021)
22. Helwe, C., Clavel, C., Suchanek, F.M.: LogiTorch: a pytorch-based library for logical reasoning on natural language. In: EMNLP Demo Track (2022)
23. Helwe, C., Coumes, S., Clavel, C., Suchanek, F.M.: TINA: textual inference with negation augmentation. In: EMNLP Findings (2022)
24. Hoffart, J., Suchanek, F.M., Berberich, K., Weikum, G.: YAGO2: a spatially and temporally enhanced knowledge base from wikipedia. Artif. Intell. **194**, 28–61 (2013)
25. Hu, C., Fu, J., Du, C., Luo, S., Zhao, J., Zhao, H.: ChatDB: augmenting LLMs with databases as their symbolic memory. arXiv preprint arXiv:2306.03901 (2023)
26. Hu, E.J., et al.: Lora: low-rank adaptation of large language models. arXiv preprint arXiv:2106.09685 (2021)
27. Kwiatkowski, T., et al.: Natural questions: a benchmark for question answering research. Trans. Assoc. Comput. Linguist. **7**, 453–466 (2019)
28. Lajus, J., Galárraga, L., Suchanek, F.M.: Fast and exact rule mining with AMIE 3. In: ESWC (2020)
29. Lajus, J., Suchanek, F.M.: Are all people married? Determining obligatory attributes in knowledge bases. In: WWW (2018)

30. Leone, M., Huber, S., Arora, A., García-Durán, A., West, R.: A critical re-evaluation of neural methods for entity alignment. PVLDB **15**(8), 1712–1725 (2022)
31. Liu, Q., Yogatama, D., Blunsom, P.: Relational memory-augmented language models. TACL **10**, 555–572 (2022)
32. Liu, Y., et al.: Jailbreaking ChatGPT via prompt engineering: an empirical study. arXiv preprint arXiv:2305.13860 (2023)
33. Luu, A.T., Kim, J.J., Ng, S.K.: Taxonomy construction using syntactic contextual evidence. In: EMNLP (2014)
34. Luu, A.T., Kim, J.J., Ng, S.K.: Incorporating trustiness and collective synonym/contrastive evidence into taxonomy construction. In: EMNLP (2015)
35. Luu, A.T., Tay, Y., Hui, S.C., Ng, S.K.: Learning term embeddings for taxonomic relation identification using dynamic weighting neural network. In: EMNLP (2016)
36. Ma, Y., Cao, Y., Hong, Y., Sun, A.: Large language model is not a good few-shot information extractor, but a good reranker for hard samples! arXiv preprint arXiv:2303.08559 (2023)
37. Mahdisoltani, F., Biega, J.A., Suchanek, F.M.: YAGO3: a knowledge base from multilingual Wikipedias. In: CIDR (2015)
38. Mialon, G., et al.: Augmented language models: a survey. arXiv preprint arXiv:2302.07842 (2023)
39. Nicholson, K.: Bing chatbot says it feels 'violated and exposed' after attack. CBC News (2023). https://www.cbc.ca/news/science/bing-chatbot-ai-hack-1.6752490
40. OpenAI: ChatGPT plugins (2023). https://openai.com/blog/chatgpt-plugins
41. Pan, S., Luo, L., Wang, Y., Chen, C., Wang, J., Wu, X.: Unifying large language models and knowledge graphs: a roadmap. arXiv preprint arXiv:2306.08302 (2023)
42. Paris, P.H., Aoud, S.E., Suchanek, F.M.: The vagueness of vagueness in noun phrases. In: AKBC (2021)
43. Paris, P.H., Suchanek, F.M.: Non-named entities - the silent majority. In: ESWC Short Paper Track (2021)
44. Radford, A., Wu, J., Child, R., Luan, D., Amodei, D., Sutskever, I., et al.: Language models are unsupervised multitask learners. OpenAI Blog **1**(8), 9 (2019)
45. Radulovic, N., Bifet, A., Suchanek, F.: Bella: black box model explanations by local linear approximations. arXiv preprint arXiv:2305.11311 (2023)
46. Radulović, N., Bifet, A., Suchanek, F.M.: Confident interpretations of black box classifiers (STACI). In: IJCNN (2021)
47. Razniewski, S., Suchanek, F.M., Nutt, W.: But what do we actually know? In: AKBC Workshop (2016)
48. Razniewski, S., Yates, A., Kassner, N., Weikum, G.: Language models as or for knowledge bases. arXiv preprint arXiv:2110.04888 (2021)
49. Rebele, T., Suchanek, F.M., Hoffart, J., Biega, J.A., Kuzey, E., Weikum, G.: YAGO: a multilingual knowledge base from Wikipedia, Wordnet, and Geonames. In: ISWC (2016)
50. Rebele, T., Tanon, T.P., Suchanek, F.M.: Bash datalog: answering datalog queries with unix shell commands. In: ISWC (2018)
51. Romero, J., Preda, N., Amarilli, A., Suchanek, F.M.: Equivalent rewritings on path views with binding patterns. In: ESWC (2020)
52. Romero, J., Preda, N., Suchanek, F.M.: Query rewriting on path views without integrity constraints. In: DataMod Workshop (2020)
53. Soulet, A., Giacometti, A., Markhoff, B., Suchanek, F.M.: Representativeness of knowledge bases with the generalized Benford's law. In: ISWC (2018)

54. Soulet, A., Suchanek, F.M.: Anytime large-scale analytics of linked open data. In: ISWC (2019)
55. Strubell, E., Ganesh, A., McCallum, A.: Energy and policy considerations for deep learning in NLP. arXiv preprint arXiv:1906.02243 (2019)
56. Suchanek, F.M.: The need to move beyond triples. In: Text2Story Workshop (2020)
57. Suchanek, F.M.: A hitchhiker's guide to ontology. In: DESIRES Invited Paper (2021)
58. Suchanek, F.M.: The Atheist Bible, §4.5.8 (2023). https://suchanek.name/texts/atheism
59. Suchanek, F.M., Abiteboul, S., Senellart, P.: PARIS: probabilistic alignment of relations, instances, and schema. In: VLDB (2012)
60. Suchanek, F.M., Kasneci, G., Weikum, G.: Yago - a core of semantic knowledge. In: WWW (2007)
61. Suchanek, F.M., Lajus, J., Boschin, A., Weikum, G.: Knowledge representation and rule mining in entity-centric knowledge bases. In: RW Invited Paper (2019)
62. Suchanek, F.M., Sozio, M., Weikum, G.: SOFIE: a self-organizing framework for information extraction. In: WWW (2009)
63. Suchanek, F.M., Varoquaux, G.: On language models and symbolic representations. In: The Conversation (2022)
64. Sung, M., Lee, J., Yi, S., Jeon, M., Kim, S., Kang, J.: Can language models be biomedical knowledge bases? arXiv preprint arXiv:2109.07154 (2021)
65. Talaika, A., Biega, J.A., Amarilli, A., Suchanek, F.M.: IBEX: harvesting entities from the web using unique identifiers. In: WebDB Workshop (2015)
66. Tanon, T.P., Bourgaux, C., Suchanek, F.M.: Learning how to correct a knowledge base from the edit history. In: WWW (2019)
67. Tanon, T.P., Suchanek, F.M.: Neural knowledge base repairs. In: ESWC (2021)
68. Tanon, T.P., Weikum, G., Suchanek, F.M.: YAGO 4: a reason-able knowledge base. In: ESWC (2020)
69. Touvron, H., et al.: LLaMA: open and efficient foundation language models. arXiv preprint arXiv:2302.13971 (2023)
70. Tuan, L.A., Hui, S.C., Ng, S.K.: Utilizing temporal information for taxonomy construction. TACL 4, 551–564 (2016)
71. Vrandecic, D.: The future of knowledge graphs in a world of large language models (2023). https://www.youtube.com/watch?v=WqYBx2gB6vA
72. Wei, J., Tay, Y., Le, Q.V.: Inverse scaling can become U-shaped. arXiv preprint arXiv:2211.02011 (2022)
73. Weikum, G., Dong, L., Razniewski, S., Suchanek, F.M.: Machine knowledge: creation and curation of comprehensive knowledge bases. Found. Trends Databases 10(2–4), 108–490 (2021)
74. Weikum, G., Hoffart, J., Suchanek, F.: Knowledge harvesting: achievements and challenges. In: Computing and Software Science: State of the Art and Perspectives, pp. 217–235 (2019)
75. White, J., et al.: A prompt pattern catalog to enhance prompt engineering with ChatGPT. arXiv preprint arXiv:2302.11382 (2023)
76. Yudkowsky, E.: The AI-box experiment. Singularity Institute (2002)
77. Zhang, H., Song, H., Li, S., Zhou, M., Song, D.: A survey of controllable text generation using transformer-based pre-trained language models. arXiv preprint arXiv:2201.05337 (2022)
78. Zhao, S., Wen, J., Tuan, L.A., Zhao, J., Fu, J.: Prompt as triggers for backdoor attack: examining the vulnerability in language models. arXiv preprint arXiv:2305.01219 (2023)

79. Zhao, X., Zeng, W., Tang, J., Wang, W., Suchanek, F.M.: An experimental study of state-of-the-art entity alignment approaches. TKDE **34**(6), 2610–2625 (2020)
80. Zhen, C., Shang, Y., Liu, X., Li, Y., Chen, Y., Zhang, D.: A survey on knowledge-enhanced pre-trained language models. arXiv preprint arXiv:2212.13428 (2022)
81. Zheng, Y., Hao, A., Luu, A.T.: Jointprop: joint semi-supervised learning for entity and relation extraction with heterogeneous graph-based propagation. arXiv preprint arXiv:2305.15872 (2023)
82. Zheng, Y., Tuan, L.A.: A novel, cognitively inspired, unified graph-based multi-task framework for information extraction. Cogn. Comput. 1–10 (2023)
83. Zhu, Y., et al.: LLMs for knowledge graph construction and reasoning: recent capabilities and future opportunities. arXiv preprint arXiv:2305.13168 (2023)

Papers

Extension of Regression Tsetlin Machine for Interpretable Uncertainty Assessment

K. Darshana Abeyrathna[1($\boxtimes$)], Sara El Mekkaoui[2], L. Yi Edward[1], Andreas Hafver[1], and Ole-Christoffer Granmo[3]

[1] Emerging Technologies, Group Research and Development, DNV, Oslo, Norway
{darshana.abeyrathna.kuruge,yi.edward.liu,andreas.hafver}@dnv.no

[2] Risk and Modelling Technologies, Group Research and Development, DNV, Oslo, Norway
sara.el.mekkaoui@dnv.no

[3] Centre for Artificial Intelligence Research, Department of Information and Communication Technology, University of Agder (UiA), 4898 Grimstad, Norway
ole.granmo@uia.no

Abstract. In our recent research, we modified the Regression Tsetlin Machine (RTM) to obtain uncertainties in regression prediction. The significance of this research is heightened when the factors leading to higher or lower uncertainties can be elucidated. For example, in the context of active learning, providing explanations such as "**WHEN 4 < x1 < 10 AND x2 = 4 AND 105 < x3 AND ... THEN Variance is higher than 4**" assists in generating additional samples around the specified input combination. However, due to the inherent nature of the Regression Tsetlin Machine, acquiring such rules is challenging. An alternative approach is to examine how the variance fluctuates in relation to a single variable while keeping other variables fixed. Nevertheless, to obtain rules that are easily understandable to humans, we expand upon our previous work by introducing an additional layer of the Tsetlin Machine, which classifies the uncertainties learned by the preceding layer of the RTM. In essence, the samples are grouped based on their uncertainty values and the clauses in the Tsetlin Machine learn sub-patterns associated with each class. First, using an artificial dataset, we show the importance of the proposed approach in explaining the uncertainties. Then, we showcase the practical application of our proposed approach in out-of-distribution (OOD) detection, utilizing a real estate valuation dataset. The obtained results provide compelling evidence that the RTM successfully identifies OOD samples. Moreover, the removal of these samples leads to a notable improvement in performance.

Keywords: Tsetlin Machine · Regression Tsetlin Machine · Uncertainty Quantification · Interpretable Machine Learning · Interpretable AI · Rule-Based Machine Leaning

1 Introduction

The real-world applications of Artificial Intelligence (AI) based systems require a rigorous evaluation of their reliability and efficiency. Developing AI-based systems

A. Fensel et al. (Eds.): RuleML+RR 2023, LNCS 14244, pp. 19–33, 2023.
https://doi.org/10.1007/978-3-031-45072-3_2

for safety-critical areas requires careful consideration of both the accuracy and uncertainty of the Machine Learning (ML) models' predictions [1]. Incorporating uncertainty quantification into AI-enabled systems enhances decision-making processes and fosters trust in the predictions made by these models. Uncertainty quantification plays an important role in machine learning to inform decision-makers, support model evaluation and improvement, guide debugging efforts, assess robustness, and evaluate potential risks. By addressing these aspects, uncertainty quantification forms the foundation for trustworthy AI systems.

Reliable estimations of uncertainties provide valuable insights into the quality of a model's output [2]. Quantifying uncertainty in machine learning models involves representing the uncertainty associated with their predictions, which might be related to noisy data or the model's structure and parameters. Two widely adopted approaches to achieve this are probabilistic machine learning methods and ensemble learning techniques.

Probabilistic machine learning, also known as Bayesian machine learning, employs probability theory to learn from data [3]. This approach utilizes probability distributions to express model's uncertainties and leverages probability rules to infer unobserved quantities based on observed data. The process involves defining prior distributions before observing the data, which are then updated into posterior distributions after observing the data. However, fully probabilistic approaches face computational challenges in high-dimensional and unstructured data or large-parameter models such as deep learning models. To address this, approximation methods like Markov Chain Monte Carlo and variational inference [2] are employed to infer the posterior distributions. When dealing with deep learning models, the Monte Carlo dropout [4] method is commonly used to estimate a Bayesian neural network. However, it is important to use this approach carefully [5]. Another commonly used technique is ensemble learning, where several separate models are trained, and their predictions are combined to make a final prediction. To estimate the uncertainty of the predictions, the models' divergence is utilized. This approach includes deep ensembles formed by multiple deep learning models or classical ensemble methods such as bagging and random forests [6]. There are some limitations when it comes to ensemble models, such as long computational training time, sensitivity to noisy data and outliers, and their lack of interpretability [7].

While quantifying uncertainty is essential, achieving trustworthy AI also requires explainability. Explainable Artificial Intelligence (XAI) is a research field that aims to provide solutions for understanding the predictions of machine learning models. While most efforts have focused on explaining point estimates, limited research addresses the interpretability of uncertainties associated with these predictions [8–10]. By highlighting the reasons behind uncertainties, it is possible to improve model debugging, gain valuable insights, and enhance human-machine learning interactions [2].

Quantifying uncertainty in an interpretable manner can be a challenging task, mainly due to the lack of interpretability in the methods employed for this purpose. Additionally, relying solely on tools designed to explain point predictions may not capture the full essence of uncertainty. Explainability remains a significant challenge in AI, as inherently interpretable machine learning models may not be suitable for high-dimensional and unstructured data, while complex models such as deep learning models present difficulties in explaining their predictions. In this context, Regression Tsetlin Machine (RTM) [11] offers a novel approach for interpretable predictions and uncertainty estimates. While current approaches for explaining uncertainty quantification primarily focus on deep learning models, this paper addresses the uncertainty explanation of RTM.

The rest of the paper is organized as follows. In Sect. 2, we discuss the modifications needed on RTM to provide reasons behind uncertain predictions. We test our proposed algorithm both on artificial and real-world data. The experiments and results are discussed in Sect. 3. We conclude our findings in Sect. 4.

2   Interpretable Uncertainty Assessment

The earliest version of the Tsetlin Machine (TM) is used to solve classification problems by identifying specific patterns for each class [12]. It does this by learning conjunctive clauses that represent these patterns. In contrast, the Regression Tsetlin Machine (RTM) employs a slightly different approach to make predictions. In this section, we will elucidate the structure and learning process of both TM and RTM. Towards the end of the section, we will also discuss the adjustments we make to obtain uncertainty in regression predictions and how the combination of TM and RTM aids in understanding the underlying reasons for uncertainty.

2.1   Pattern Representation and Learning

Structure: A Tsetlin Machine (TM) for binary classification tasks can be seen in TM 3 of Fig. 1. This TM consists of a set of m clauses. Each of these clauses receives input features in binary form. For instance, the kth feature in the feature vector $\mathbf{X}$, x_k, is in the domain $\{0,1\}$. Hence, the feature vector consisting of o propositional variables can be written as $\mathbf{X} = (x_k) \in \{0,1\}^o$. The TM considers both the original feature values and their negations. Now, the augmented feature vector, $\mathbf{X}'$ contains both the original features and the negated features: $\mathbf{X}' = [x_1, x_2, x_3, \dots, x_o, \neg x_1, \neg x_2, \neg x_3, \dots, \neg x_o]$. The elements in $\mathbf{X}'$ are called literals. Hence, mathematically, the clause j can be written as follows,

$$c_j = 1 \wedge \left(\bigwedge_{k \in I_j^I} x_k \right) \wedge \left(\bigwedge_{k \in \bar{I}_j^I} \neg x_k \right). \tag{1}$$

However, only a subset of features takes part in a clause. For clause j, the indexes of these subsets are represented by I_j^I and $\bar{I}_j^I$, where the indexes of the included original features are found in I_j^I while the indexes of the included negated features are found in $\bar{I}_j^I$.

To determine the composition of the identified pattern, a group of Tsetlin Automata (TAs) [13] is assigned to each clause. These TAs, which have two available actions, namely "include" and "exclude", make decisions regarding the inclusion or exclusion of specific literals within the clause. Consequently, the TA team requires the involvement of a total of $2 \times o$ TAs. Half of these TAs are responsible for representing the original features and determining the corresponding indexes in I_j^I, while the other half represents the negated features and identifies the indexes in $\bar{I}_j^I$.

Typically, in each TA, an action has the same number of memory states, denoted as N. The current state, S of a TA, determines the action it takes. In the case of the TM, if the state is less than or equal to N, the corresponding literal is excluded from the clause. Conversely, if the state exceeds N, the corresponding literal is included in the clause.

The calculation of the clause output is relatively straightforward. As the clause consists of a conjunction of literals, if any literal value is 0, the clause output will be 0. Conversely, if all the included literals are 1, the clause output will be 1. This occurs when the feature vector corresponds to a pattern recognized by the clause.

In a binary classification problem, with classes 0 and 1, it is necessary to identify patterns for each class separately. To achieve this in TM, the clauses are divided into two groups. The clauses with odd indexes are assigned positive polarity, denoted as C^+, and they recognize patterns corresponding to class $y = 1$. Conversely, clauses with even indexes are assigned negative polarity, denoted as C^-, and they recognize patterns associated with class $y = 0$.

The TM output is determined by comparing the number of recognized patterns for each class. The class with more clause outputs becomes the TM output. As the first step, total negative clause outputs from the total positive clause outputs are subtracted: $v = \sum_j c_j^+ - \sum_j c_j^-$. Then the TM output is computed as,

$$y = \begin{cases} 1 & \text{if } v \geq 0 \\ 0 & \text{if } v < 0 . \end{cases} \tag{2}$$

Note that for categorization tasks with more classes than two, separate TMs are needed for each class. The structure and the learning of this setup are well explained in [12].

Learning: In the TM, the learning process is based on reinforcement learning. It involves providing feedback to the TAs in the clauses through reward, penalty, and inaction feedback. Several factors are taken into consideration, including the actual training output $\hat{y}$, clause outputs, literal values, and the current state of the TAs. Simply put, clauses are rewarded when they correctly recognize patterns and penalized when they make incorrect recognitions. In the TM, two types of feedback, namely Type I and Type II, are utilized for this purpose.

Type I feedback reinforces clauses to output 1 when they correctly recognize patterns. It is given to clauses with positive polarity when $\hat{y} = 1$ and to clauses with negative polarity when $\hat{y} = 0$. This way, we order clauses with positive polarity to recognize patterns for class 1 and clauses with negative polarity to recognize patterns for class 0. However, the clauses to receive Type I feedback are selected stochastically with probability, $\frac{T-\max(-T,\min(T,v))}{2T}$. Here, the target T, specified by the user, determines the number of clauses involved in learning each sub-pattern. This approach assists the TM in learning a greater variety of patterns instead of being limited to only a few.

Type I feedback is further divided into Type Ia and Type Ib. Type Ia feedback strengthens the "include" actions of TAs by moving one step towards the end of the include action when the corresponding literal value is 1 and the clause output is 1. Type Ib counteracts overfitting by reinforcing the "exclude" actions of TAs by moving one step towards the end of the exclude action when the corresponding literal value is 0 or the clause output is 0. When a clause is selected to receive Type I feedback, the user-defined parameter s (where $s \geq 1$) determines whether the TAs should be updated. Specifically, TAs are updated with a probability of $\frac{s-1}{s}$ for Type Ia feedback and $\frac{1}{s}$ for Type Ib feedback.

The Algorithm 1 summarizes the Type I feedback given clause index is odd when the training output, $\hat{y}$ is 1 or clause index is even when the training output, $\hat{y}$ is 0.

Algorithm 1. Type I feedback

1: **if** $c_j = 1$ **then**:
2: **for** feature $k = 1, ..., 2o$ **do**
3:   **if** $x'_k = 1$ **then**:
4:    Type Ia Feedback: $S \leftarrow S + 1$, if satisfy condition with probability $\frac{s-1}{s}$
5:   **else** $x'_k = 0$ **then**
6:    Type Ib Feedback: $S \leftarrow S - 1$, if satisfy condition with probability $\frac{1}{s}$
7:   **end if**
8: **end for**
9: **else** $c_j = 0$ **then**
10: Type Ib Feedback: $S \leftarrow S - 1$, if satisfy condition with probability $\frac{1}{s}$
11: **end if**

Type II feedback on the other hand combats the false positive clause outputs. Hence, Type II feedback is received by clauses with positive polarity when they output 1 for the training output, $\hat{y}$, 0 and clauses with negative polarity when they output 1 for the training output, $\hat{y}$, 1. Similar to Type I feedback, the candidate TAs are selected stochastically with probability $\frac{T+\max(-T,\min(T,v))}{2T}$.

The clause output can be simply turned from 1 to 0 by including a literal with a value of 0 in the clause. Hence, TAs which represent literals of value 0 receive a penalty on its exclude action with probability 1.0.

The training procedure of the multi-class version of the TM involves the same Type I and Type II feedback. However, the TAs to receive this feedback are selected differently since the structure of the multi-class version of TM is different. The procedure can be found in [12].

Algorithm 2. Type II feedback

1: **if** $c_j = 1$ **then**
2:     **for** feature $k = 1, ..., 2o$ **do**
3:         **if** $x'_k = 0$ **then**
4:             Type II Feedback: $S \leftarrow S + 1$, with probability 1.0
5:         **else** $x'_k = 1$ **then**
6:             Inaction
7:         **end if**
8:     **end for**
9: **else** $c_j = 0$ **then**
10:     Inaction
11: **end if**

2.2   Continuous Outputs

Structure: The Regression Tsetlin Machine (RTM), presented in [11], utilizes clauses as building blocks for calculating continuous outputs. In the RTM, the polarities in the clauses are removed, and the total sum of the clause outputs is mapped to a continuous value ranging from 0 to the maximum training output value, $\hat{y}_{max}$. The structure of the RTM is depicted in TM 1 of Fig. 1[1]. The continuous output, determined by the sum of the clause outputs and the target T, can be obtained using Eq. (3).

$$y = \frac{\sum_{j=1}^{m} C_j(\hat{X})}{T} \times \hat{y}_{max}. \tag{3}$$

Learning: After obtaining a continuous output value y, it is compared with the target output $\hat{y}$. Depending on if the predicted value is higher or lower than the target output, Type I and Type II feedback update the TAs in clauses as follows,

$$Feedback = \begin{cases} \text{Type I,} & \text{if } y < \hat{y}, \\ \\ \text{Type II,} & \text{if } y > \hat{y}. \end{cases} \tag{4}$$

Equation 4 is based on the following rationale. As mentioned earlier, Type I feedback reinforces true positive clause outputs. Therefore, when the predicted output is lower than the target output $(y < \hat{y})$, Type I feedback is given to the clauses. Conversely, Type II feedback suppresses false positive clause outputs and sets them to 0. Hence, when the predicted output is greater than the target output $(y > \hat{y})$, Type II feedback is given to the clauses.

To ensure responsible clause updating in the RTM, the prediction error is utilized in determining the number of clauses to be updated. When the error

---

[1] Even though there is t number of clauses in the RTM in TM 1 of Fig. 1, we generally consider that RTM contains m number of clauses.

is substantial, a larger number of clauses should be updated to reduce the gap. Conversely, when the error is close to zero, updating a few clauses should be sufficient. Thus, a subset of clauses is randomly chosen to receive feedback with probability, $\frac{K \times |y - \hat{y}|}{\hat{y}_{\max}}$. The user set parameter K gives more flexibility to adjust the probability as the probability varies proportionally to the error. Hence, K can be used to scale the probability to fit the total number of clauses.

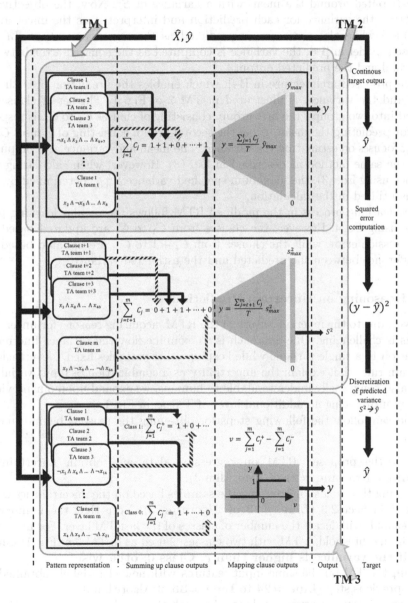

Fig. 1. Proposed TM architecture

2.3 Uncertainty Quantification

The dataset does not provide uncertainty as a second training output. Hence, RTM structure and learning should be modified in order to learn the prediction uncertainty from available data. In this regard, we make the assumption that the outputs corresponding to each input sample follow a normal distribution. The majority of outputs are closer to the mean μ, while the remaining outputs are distributed around the mean with a variance of S^2. Now, the objective is to capture the variance for each prediction and interpret it as the uncertainty associated while also the mean is predicted as the regression output. In the proposed model in [14], the variance is computed as the squared error between the actual and the predicted output.

The proposed architecture in [14], which enables the prediction of both the mean and the variance, is illustrated in TM 2 of Fig. 1. The set of clauses is divided into two groups: the first group, consisting of clauses C_1 to C_t, is responsible for predicting the mean, while the second group, consisting of clauses C_{t+1} to C_m, focuses on estimating the variance. The mean and variance are computed using the same method as described in Eq. (3). However, when calculating the variance using Eq. (3), the maximum specified variance $S_{\max}^2$, determined by the user, is utilized in the calculation.

The learning process in the modified RTM follows the regular learning procedure using Eq. 4. However, the clauses from C_1 to C_t are updated based on the regression error, while the clauses from $C_t + 1$ to C_m are updated based on the difference between the predicted and the estimated variance.

2.4 Reasoning on Uncertain Prediction

However, due to the inherent nature of the RTM, acquiring reasons for uncertain regions is challenging. One approach is to examine how the variance fluctuates in relation to a single variable while keeping other variables fixed. Nevertheless, to obtain rules that explain the uncertainty as a combination of input variables while also being easily understandable to humans, we expand upon our previous work by introducing an additional layer of TM as in Fig. 1.

One can follow the following steps for obtaining the reasons behind uncertainty:

1. Train the proposed RTM on regression data and obtain uncertainties (**Line #1** to **Line #21** of Algorithm 3).
2. Defining thresholds for grouping the samples based on the uncertainties computed in Sect. 2.3 (**Line #23** of Algorithm 3). Note that the number of thresholds will decide the number of classes of the last TM layer. For instance, with one threshold r, TM with two classes is used as in TM 3 of Fig. 1: **Class 1: if the variance is higher than r, Class 0: otherwise.**
3. Train the TM on the same input features with new class labels obtained in the previous step (**Line #24** to **Line #36** of Algorithm 3).
4. Extract patterns learned by clauses for each class as demonstrated in [15–17]

Algorithm 3. Learning process of the proposed algorithm

1: **Initialize RTM for UQ:** m, T, s, S_{max}^2, Random initialization of TAs
2: **for** All training epochs **do**
3:     **for** All training samples $(\hat{X}, \hat{y})$ **do**
4:         **Compute:** Clause outputs, Mean output: y
5:         **for** $j = 1, ..., t$ **do if** satisfy condition with probability $\frac{K \times |y - \hat{y}|}{\hat{y}_{max}}$
6:             **if** $(y < \hat{y})$ **then**
7:                 Type I Feedback: **Algorithm 1**
8:             **else** $(y > \hat{y})$ **then**
9:                 Type II Feedback: **Algorithm 2**
10:            **end if**
11:        **end for**
12:        **Compute:** Squared error: $(y - \hat{y})^2$
13:        **for** $j = t + 1, ..., m$ **do if** satisfy condition with probability $\frac{K \times |y - \hat{y}|}{s_{max}^2}$
14:            **if** $(S^2 < (y - \hat{y})^2)$ **then**
15:                Type I Feedback: **Algorithm 1**
16:            **else** $(S^2 > (y - \hat{y})^2)$ **then**
17:                Type II Feedback: **Algorithm 2**
18:            **end if**
19:        **end for**
20:    **end for**
21: **end for**
22: ──
23: **Compute:** Discretization of S^2: $S^2 \rightarrow \hat{y}, \hat{y} \in \{1, 0\}$
24: **Initialize TM for classification:** m, T, s, Random initialization of TAs
25: **for** All training epochs **do**
26:     **for** All training samples $(\hat{X}, \hat{y})$ **do**
27:         **Compute:** Clause outputs, class output: y
28:         **for** $j = 1, ..., m$ **do if** satisfy condition with probability $\frac{T + max(-T, min(T, v))}{2T}$
     or $\frac{T - max(-T, min(T, v))}{2T}$
29:             **if** $(\hat{y} = 1$ **and** j is odd$)$ **or** $(\hat{y} = 0$ **and** j is even$)$ **then**
30:                 Type I Feedback: **Algorithm 1**
31:             **else** $(\hat{y} = 1$ **and** j is even$)$ **or** $(\hat{y} = 0$ **and** j is odd$)$ **then**
32:                 Type II Feedback: **Algorithm 2**
33:             **end if**
34:        **end for**
35:     **end for**
36: **end for**

---

3   Experiments, Results, and Discussion

In this section, we first utilize an artificial dataset to demonstrate how uncertainty can be explained. The dataset comprises four variables: x_1, x_2, x_3, and x_4. The variables x_1 and x_3 are categorical variables, where x_1 takes values from the set $\{1, 2, 3, 4\}$ and x_3 takes values from the set $\{0, 1\}$. The remaining two variables are continuous variables, with x_2 able to take any integer value between 10 and 20, i.e., $x_2 \in [10, 20]$, while x_4 can take any integer value between 0 and 40, i.e., $x_4 \in [0, 40]$. Both the output and the variance used to perturb the output values are functions of these four variables [14]. The output for a given combination of inputs is computed as $x_1^2 + \frac{1}{2}x_2 - x_3 + \frac{1}{10}x_4$, while the variance used to perturb the aforementioned output is computed as $|x_1^3 + \frac{1}{10}x_2^2 - x_3 + \frac{1}{10}x_4^2|$.

Towards the end of the section, we showcase the significance of uncertainty quantification in OOD detection using the proposed RTM by utilizing a real-world dataset, i.e., Real Estate Valuation[2]. We evaluate the performance of the RTM and compare it against several other state-of-the-art OOD detection approaches.

3.1   Impact of Individual Input Variables on Uncertainty

The aim of this section is to explain the uncertainty solely by utilizing TM 2 of the structure depicted in Fig. 1. To achieve this, we perturb one variable at a time while maintaining the remaining variables at fixed positions. This approach aims to illustrate how the alteration of uncertainty can be elucidated through individual input variables.

As mentioned above, we apply distinct approaches based on the nature of the variable to alter them. For instance, the categorical variables x_1 and x_3 are systematically changed to each category when the other variables remain unchanged. On the other hand, for continuous numerical variables x_2 and x_4, we opt to see the effect throughout all the possible unique values of each variable while the remaining variables are fixed at one position.

The experimental results are organized into four distinct groups, corresponding to the four input variables in this experiment. Figure 2, Fig. 3, Fig. 4, and Fig. 5 provide visual representations of these results, with each plot showcasing the variation of variance against the selected input variable.

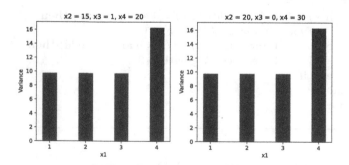

Fig. 2. Variation of variance against x_1

As depicted by the figures, we notice that the variance does not change with input variable values of x_2 and x_3 for the given set of fixed positions of the other

---

[2] Description of the dataset can be found here: https://archive.ics.uci.edu/dataset/477/real+estate+valuation+data+set.

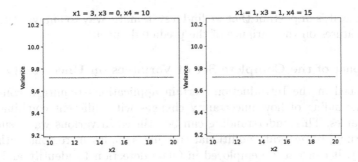

Fig. 3. Variation of variance against x_2

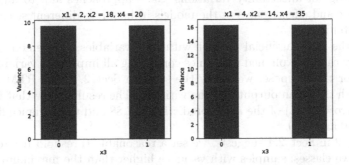

Fig. 4. Variation of variance against x_3

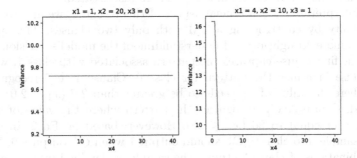

Fig. 5. Variation of variance against x_4

variables. However, it is difficult to say if the variance will remain unchanged for all the combinations of other input variable values.

The change of input feature values of x_1 and x_4 has an effect on the variance, however, x_4 with only one combination of other input variable values while x_1 with both the selected variable combinations for other features.

This explains the complexity of analyzing the impact of input variables on the predicted variance when considering one variable at a time. The complexity further increases with more input variables and more unique feature values in them. Hence, it is important that we find a systematic way to analyze the impact of input features on the variance of the predicted outputs.

3.2 Impact of the Complete Set of Variables on Uncertainty

As mentioned in the Introduction, certain applications require a comprehensive understanding of how uncertainty changes with different combinations of input variables. This understanding can be utilized in various ways, such as in active learning to generate additional training samples in regions with higher uncertainty. It can also be employed in OOD detection to identify and remove samples from the training set that exhibit higher uncertainties. By leveraging this knowledge of uncertainty variations, these approaches aim to improve the performance and effectiveness of the models in handling different scenarios and data distributions.

Using the same artificial dataset with four variables, we demonstrate how uncertainty can be explained with rules containing all important variables in the dataset. For this purpose, we follow the steps in Sect. 2.4. The RTM learns to predict both the mean output and the variance. The results show that the mean absolute error (MAE) of the mean prediction is 7.88 and the variance fluctuates between 0.0 and 20.9.

As step 2 in Sect. 2.4 suggests, we set a reasonable threshold to group samples into two classes: samples with variance higher than the maximum variance multiplied by $\frac{2}{3}$ ($20.9 \times \frac{2}{3}$) are in class 1 while the rest is in class 0. Now, we need to train a new TM for the new dataset we just created.

Since interpretability is a crucial aspect of this research, we aim to enhance interpretability by constructing a TM with only two clauses. This approach facilitates a more straightforward understanding of the model's decision-making process. The first clause captures the pattern associated with class 1, while the second clause identifies the pattern for class 0. Clause 1, C_1^+ recognizes the pattern where the value of x_1 needs to be greater than 2.0 ($x_1 > 2.0$). On the other hand, Clause 2, C_2^- recognizes the pattern where the value of x_4 must be less than or equal to 26 ($x_4 \leq 26$). However, based on Eq. 2, in order to classify a sample into class 0, C_2^- should output 1 when C_1^+ outputs 0. With all other combinations of clause outputs, the sample is classified into class 1. This understanding allows us to create a simple rule for categorizing samples into high or low variance categories, contributing to the interpretability of the TM.

$$Class = \begin{cases} 0 \ (\text{Variance} \leq 20.9 \times \frac{2}{3}), & \text{if } x_4 \leq 26 \text{ AND } x_1 \leq 2 , \\ \\ 1 \ (\text{Variance} > 20.9 \times \frac{2}{3}), & \text{Otherwise} \end{cases} \tag{5}$$

This simple rule classifies samples into the correct class with accuracy over 0.87. The accuracy can be further increased with the optimal set of hyperparameters, especially by increasing the number of clauses. However, as explained in [15], the increase in the number of clauses can cause to decrease in interpretability.

3.3   Uncertainty Quantification for Out-of-Distribution Detection

Now, it's time to test our proposed approach for reasoning uncertain predictions on real-world applications. In this particular experiment, our aim is to improve the predictive performance of the RTM by enhancing the dataset. Specifically, we plan to remove the out-of-distribution (OOD) data samples from the training set, after we identified them with their highly uncertain predictions. To demonstrate how this is achieved, we will utilize the Real Estate Valuation dataset. This dataset involves predicting the house price per unit area using six features, namely the transaction date, the house age, the distance to the nearest MRT station, the number of convenience stores in the living circle on foot, and the geographical coordinates (latitude and longitude).

We follow the steps outlined in Sect. 2.4 to identify the reasons behind higher uncertainties in the predictions. Subsequently, we utilize the threshold specified in Step 2 of Sect. 2.4 also to identify the OOD samples. Specifically, after completing the training process, we normalize the obtained uncertainties to range from 0 to 1. For example, training samples with corresponding normalized uncertainty values exceeding 0.9 are categorized as OOD samples.

The rules learned by the clauses consider only the second feature, i.e., *the age of the house* to classify a sample into the OOD category as follows,

$$
Class = \begin{cases} OOD, & \textbf{if} \quad \text{the age of the house} > 41, \\ \\ Not\ OOD, & Otherwise \end{cases} \tag{6}
$$

Upon further analysis of the dataset, it becomes evident that the findings align with our reasoning. The dataset reveals that the minimum age of a house is 0, the maximum age is 43, and the average age is 17.7. Notably, only five houses in the dataset have an age exceeding 41 years. Consequently, it is reasonable to assume that the dataset has been enriched with more recent houses, and it is advisable to exclude older houses before training predictive models.

The OOD samples that have been identified should be excluded from the training dataset in the subsequent round of training. However, in order to assess the effectiveness of removing OOD samples from the training data, it is crucial to maintain the baseline performance as a reference point. This involves measuring the prediction error on the test set when the complete set of training data is utilized.

Table 1 presents the average Mean Absolute Errors (MAEs) obtained from conducting each experiment 20 times. In order to evaluate the performance of the RTM, we compare it against two other state-of-the-art machine learning models, namely regression tree (RT) and support vector regression (SVR). To ensure a fair comparison, extensive parameter searches were performed to configure each model. The models were trained using both the baseline dataset and updated datasets, which involved the removal of OOD samples. In addition, two alternative approaches, the Isolation Forest algorithm and the Minimum Covariance Determinant (MCD) algorithm, were employed to identify OOD samples.

Table 1. The table presents the Mean Absolute Errors (MAEs) obtained when predicting house prices using various ML models with different OOD detection approaches

	SVR	RT	RTM
Baseline	5.86	6.39	5.86
Isolation Forest	6.11	5.96	5.56
MCD	5.93	6.41	5.26
RTM	5.87	6.00	5.41

By examining the average MAEs presented in Table 1, it becomes apparent that both SVR and RTM demonstrate superior baseline performance compared to RT. Furthermore, when the RTM model identifies and removes the OOD samples from the training dataset, the average MAEs of both RT and RTM decrease. Interestingly, updating the training dataset by removing the OOD samples identified by any of the considered models does not lead to an improvement in SVR performance. However, the RTM model achieves the best average MAE when trained with the updated dataset, where OOD samples are removed based on the findings of the MCD model.

4   Conclusion

In order to gain a deeper understanding of the factors contributing to uncertainty in regression prediction, we extended our previous research on uncertainty quantification using the RTM. This extension involved the introduction of an additional layer to the Tsetlin Machine framework. The added layer is responsible for classifying the uncertainties learned by the preceding layer and provides reasons for different classifications.

In our study, we utilized an artificial dataset to demonstrate the complexity involved in analyzing reasons for uncertainty when considering only one input variable at a time. We then expanded the experiment to showcase how our proposed approach enables the extraction of meaningful reasons that encompass all relevant input variables. Furthermore, we employed our uncertainty quantification approach to effectively detect OOD samples and ascertain the reasons behind their classification as such.

To further validate the applicability of our approach, we extended the experiment to incorporate OOD detection and enhance the predictive performance in regression tasks. The results indicate that our proposed approach not only provides comprehensive reasons for uncertain predictions but also exhibits promising potential in various application domains, including OOD detection and active learning. Overall, our findings demonstrate the versatility and effectiveness of the proposed approach across different contexts.

References

1. Wang, Y., Chung, S.H.: Artificial intelligence in safety-critical systems: a systematic review. Ind. Manag. Data Syst. **122**(2), 442–470 (2022)
2. Murphy, K.P.: Probabilistic Machine Learning: Advanced Topics. MIT Press, Cambridge (2023)
3. Ghahramani, Z.: Probabilistic machine learning and artificial intelligence. Nature **521**(7553), 452–459 (2015)
4. Gal, Y., Ghahramani, Z.: Dropout as a Bayesian approximation: representing model uncertainty in deep learning. In: International Conference on Machine Learning, pp. 1050–1059. PMLR (2016)
5. Seoh, R.: Qualitative analysis of Monte Carlo dropout, arXiv preprint arXiv:2007.01720 (2020)
6. James, G., Witten, D., Hastie, T., Tibshirani, R.: An Introduction to Statistical Learning, vol. 112. Springer, New York (2013)
7. Mienye, I.D., Sun, Y.: A survey of ensemble learning: concepts, algorithms, applications, and prospects. IEEE Access **10**, 99129–99149 (2022)
8. Chen, H., Du, W., Ji, Y.: Explaining predictive uncertainty by looking back at model explanations, arXiv preprint arXiv:2201.03742 (2022)
9. Yang, C.-I., Li, Y.-P.: Explainable uncertainty quantifications for deep learning-based molecular property prediction. J. Cheminform. **15**(1), 13 (2023)
10. Antorán, J., Bhatt, U., Adel, T., Weller, A., Hernández-Lobato, J.M.: Getting a clue: a method for explaining uncertainty estimates, arXiv preprint arXiv:2006.06848 (2020)
11. Darshana Abeyrathna, K., Granmo, O.-C., Zhang, X., Jiao, L., Goodwin, M.: The regression tsetlin machine: a novel approach to interpretable nonlinear regression. Philos. Trans. Roy. Soc. A **378**(2164), 20190165 (2020)
12. Granmo, O.-C.: The Tsetlin Machine - A Game Theoretic Bandit Driven Approach to Optimal Pattern Recognition with Propositional Logic, arXiv:1804.01508 (2018)
13. Narendra, K.S., Thathachar, M.A.: Learning Automata: An Introduction. Courier Corporation (2012)
14. Abeyrathna, K.D., Andreas, H., Edward, L.Y.: Modeling prediction uncertainty in regression using the regression tsetlin machine. In: 2023 International Symposium on the Tsetlin Machine (ISTM) (2023)
15. Abeyrathna, K.D., Granmo, O.-C., Goodwin, M.: Extending the tsetlin machine with integer-weighted clauses for increased interpretability. IEEE Access **9**, 8233–8248 (2021)
16. Darshana Abeyrathna, K., Granmo, O.-C., Goodwin, M.: On obtaining classification confidence, ranked predictions and AUC with tsetlin machines. In: 2020 IEEE Symposium Series on Computational Intelligence (SSCI), pp. 662–669. IEEE (2020)
17. Abeyrathna, K.D., Pussewalage, H.S.G., Ranasinghe, S.N., Oleshchuk, V.A., Granmo, O.-C.: Intrusion detection with interpretable rules generated using the tsetlin machine. In: 2020 IEEE Symposium Series on Computational Intelligence (SSCI), pp. 1121–1130. IEEE (2020)

GUCON: A Generic Graph Pattern Based Policy Framework for Usage Control Enforcement

Ines Akaichi[1]([✉])[iD], Giorgos Flouris[2][iD], Irini Fundulaki[2][iD], and Sabrina Kirrane[1][iD]

[1] Institute for Information Systems and New Media, WU, Vienna, Austria
{ines.akaichi,sabrina.kirrane}@wu.ac.at
[2] Institute of Computer Science, FORTH, Heraklion, Greece
{fgeo,fundul}@ics.forth.gr

Abstract. Robust Usage Control (UC) mechanisms are necessary to protect sensitive data and resources, especially when these are distributed across multiple nodes or users. Existing solutions have limitations in expressing and enforcing usage control policies due to difficulties in capturing complex requirements and the lack of formal semantics necessary for automated compliance checking. To address these challenges, we propose GUCON, a generic policy framework that allows for the expression of and reasoning over granular UC policies. This is achieved by leveraging the expressiveness and semantics of graph pattern expressions, as well as the flexibility of deontic concepts. Additionally, GUCON incorporates algorithms for conflict detection, resolution, compliance and requirements checking, ensuring active policy enforcement. We demonstrate the effectiveness of our framework by proposing instantiations using SHACL, OWL and ODRL. We show how instantiations provide a bridge between abstract formalism and concrete implementations, thus allowing existing reasoners and implementations to be leveraged.

Keywords: Usage Control · Policy · Deontic Rules · Reasoning · Enforcement

1 Introduction

In emerging decentralized environments, such as data spaces, or social linked data[1], the distribution of data across multiple nodes and its accessibility to numerous users raises various concerns. These concerns encompass issues related to privacy, especially in relation to the sharing of personal data; questions surrounding ownership and control of data concerning creative digital work; and notably, the risk of data misuse for purposes that deviate from the original intent. To address these concerns, policy-based UC emerges as an extension of access control, providing a technical instrument to manage not only resource access in

---

[1] Social Linked Data: https://solidproject.org/.

© The Author(s), under exclusive license to Springer Nature Switzerland AG 2023
A. Fensel et al. (Eds.): RuleML+RR 2023, LNCS 14244, pp. 34–53, 2023.
https://doi.org/10.1007/978-3-031-45072-3_3

terms of permissions and prohibitions but also future data usage defined by obligations and dispensations. UC serves as an umbrella term encompassing access control, data privacy protection, copyright, and various legislative and institutional policies (e.g., the General Data Protection Regulation (GDPR) [12] and the new copyright legislation [13]).

In order to specify UC policies, several policy languages and frameworks have been proposed, focusing on access control, privacy, or trust management, such as Rei [17], Protune [3], KAoS [26], and the SPECIAL policy language [5]. These languages are designed to meet the specific requirements of their respective domain areas. However, most standard and well-known languages, such as the Open Digital Rights Language (ODRL) [27] lack formal semantics for specifying or configuring enforcement mechanisms or ensuring policy adherence. Although there are languages with formal semantics that address reasoning over specific deontic concepts, they may not cover the complete range of required concepts in UC [7,16,21]. Furthermore, in general, there is a lack of full support for policy-specific tasks such as compliance checking, consistency checking, or requirement checking [18]. Notably, the presence of diverse policy languages can also lead to interoperability issues in distributed environments.

In this paper, we propose GUCON, a Generic Graph Pattern based Policy Framework for Usage Control enforcement. GUCON introduces an abstract structure with formal and implementable semantics for policy specification, and describes algorithms for policy-specific reasoning tasks. Policies are specified using conditional deontic rules based on graph patterns and deontic concepts (permissions, prohibitions, obligations, and dispensations), offering flexibility in expressing general UC restrictions, while the formalization of policy rules is based on the formal semantics of graph patterns [22]. In GUCON, we also introduce the concept of state of affairs, which captures domain knowledge and events, and serves as the basis for reasoning about, and enforcing UC policies. Using GUCON, diverse types of usage control policies can be explicitly defined and effectively enforced, owing to the adaptable nature of graph patterns and the formal implementable semantics that underlie the framework. To assess its usefulness and effectiveness, we demonstrate how to instantiate GUCON using recognized recommendations from the World Wide Web Consortium (W3C), namely the Shape Constraint Language (SHACL)[2], the Web Ontology Language 2 (OWL 2)[3] and ODRL[4] This enables us to leverage their existing implementations and bridge the gap between GUCON's abstract formalism and concrete implementations.

The remainder of the paper is structured as follows: Sect. 2 discusses related work. Section 3 presents the necessary background. Section 4 introduces the building components of our framework specification, covering policies and the state of affairs and their semantics, while Sect. 5 describes algorithms for policy-specific tasks, namely compliance, consistency, and requirements checking. In

---

[2] SHACL, https://www.w3.org/TR/shac.

[3] OWL 2, https://www.w3.org/TR/owl2-prim.

[4] ODRL, https://www.w3.org/TR/odrl-model.

Sect. 6, we demonstrate the usefulness and effectiveness of our framework by instantiating it using SHACL, OWL 2, and ODRL. Finally, Sect. 7 summarizes the paper and discusses future work.

2   Related Work

Several policy languages/models have been proposed to address UC. UCON [21] is an abstract model that extends access control with the concepts of decision continuity and attribute mutability. Although several formalisms have been suggested for UCON, and attempts have been made to include it in standard representation languages [9,15,19], there is currently no established reference or standard policy specification and implementation for UCON. As a result, UCON has not gained widespread adoption as a UC model in the industry. Another language, the Obligation Specification Language (OSL) formalized in Z [16], is utilized to express mainly conditional prohibitions and obligations but lacks support for dispensations. While OSL offers technical models for policy enforcement of obligations, it lacks provisions for consistency checking or policy querying. DUPO [7] is a policy language that employs defeasible logic to express permissions, prohibitions, and obligations. The language facilitates policy comparison by matching user requests for data access against DUPO polices, resulting in either permitting or prohibiting access. Additionally, the language supports consistency checking. However, reasoning over obligations is not explicitly defined in the current understanding of DUPO.

In the realm of the semantic web community, researchers have put forth various general policy languages and frameworks, including Rei [17], Protune [3], and KAoS [26]. These languages, which are grounded in knowledge representation languages, primarily concentrate on specifying and reasoning about access control and trust management, rather than UC. Specifically, the primary focus of these works is on permission checking, while aspects such as compliance checking with regard to obligations and dispensations are not addressed. Furthermore, as noted in [6]'s analysis, these languages may encounter challenges related to undecidability in certain policy-related tasks. Among the existing proposals, the most closely related to our work from a specification point of view is AIR [18], a language designed to facilitate accountable privacy protection in web-based information systems. AIR employs rules and graph patterns represented in N3. However, it should be noted that AIR was not specifically devised for UC, lacks deontic concepts, and does not encompass consistency checking or policy querying as integral components.

More recent studies proposed policy languages tailored to privacy, such as the SPECIAL policy language, which was specifically designed to facilitate privacy policies by utilizing decidable fragments of OWL [5]. However, this language primarily focuses on expressing authorizations and is constrained by the requirements imposed by GDPR. Another notable language is ODRL [27], which is based on a rich RDF model and vocabulary but lacks formal semantics.

3   Preliminaries

In order to specify the main components of our framework, we rely on the syntax and semantics of graph patterns expressions presented in [22]. Throughout the paper, we assume two pairwise disjoint and infinite sets I and L to denote respectively Internationalized Resource Identifiers (IRIs) and literals. We denote by T the union of $I \cup L$. We introduce the concepts of subject s, property p, and object o to form subject-property-object expressions, called Resource Description Framework (RDF) triples. A triple is defined as $(s, p, o) \in (I) \times (I) \times (I \cup L)$. Note that blank nodes are omitted for simplicity. A set of RDF triples form an *RDF graph*. We assume additionally the existence of an infinite set V of variables disjoint from the above sets. As a notational convention, we will prefix variables with "?" (e.g., ?x, ?y).

Syntax of Graph Patterns. The definition of graph pattern expressions is based on triple patterns. A triple pattern is defined as $(sp, pp, op) \in (I \cup V) \times (I \cup V) \times (I \cup L \cup V)$. The variables occurring in a graph pattern G are denoted as var(G).

Definition 1 (Graph Pattern). *A graph pattern is defined recursively as follows:*

- *A triple pattern is a graph pattern.*
- *If G1 and G2 are graph patterns, then (G1 AND G2), (G1 OPT G2), (G1 UNION G1), (G1 MINUS G2) are graph patterns.*
- *If G is a graph pattern and R is a filter expression, then (G FILTER R) is a graph pattern. A Filter expression is constructed using elements of the sets $I \cup L \cup V$, logical connectives $(\neg, \wedge, \vee)$, inequality symbols $(<, \leq, \geq, >)$, equality symbol $(=)$, plus other features (see [23] for a complete list).*

Semantics of Graph Patterns. The semantics of graph pattern expressions are defined based on a mapping function μ, such as $\mu : V \to T$. For a triple pattern t, we denote by $\mu(t)$ the triple obtained by replacing the variables in t according to μ. The domain of μ, $dom(\mu)$, is the subset of V where μ is defined.

Definition 2 (Evaluation of a Graph Pattern). *Let D be an RDF graph over T. Mapping a graph pattern against D is defined using the function $[[.]]_D$, which takes a graph pattern expression and returns a set of mappings Ω.*

Two mappings μ_1 and μ_2 are said to be compatible, i.e., $\mu_1 \sim \mu_2$ when, for all $x \in dom(\mu_1) \cap dom(\mu_2)$, it is the case that $\mu_1(x) = \mu_2(x)$. The evaluation of a compound graph pattern $G_1 \times G_2$ is defined as follows:

$$[[G_1 \text{ AND } G_2]] = \Omega_1 \bowtie \Omega_2 = \{\mu_1 \cup \mu_2 \mid \mu_1 \in \Omega_1, \mu_2 \in \Omega_2, \mu_1 \sim \mu_2\}$$

$$[[G_1 \text{ UNION } G_2]] = \Omega_1 \cup \Omega_2 = \{\mu_1 \cup \mu_2 \mid \mu_1 \in \Omega_1 \cup \mu_2 \in \Omega_2, \mu_1 \sim \mu_2\}$$

$$[[G_1 \text{ OPT } G_2]] = \Omega_1 \bowtie \Omega_2 = (\Omega_1 \bowtie \Omega_2) \cup (\Omega_1/\Omega_2), \text{ where}$$

$$\Omega_1/\Omega_2 = \{\mu \mid \mu \in \Omega_1 \wedge \nexists \mu' \in \Omega_2, \mu \sim \mu'\}$$

4   Usage Control Framework Specification

In this section, we provide an in-depth analysis of the fundamental constituents of our framework, namely knowledge bases (KBs) and usage control policies (UCPs). We also present a motivating use case scenario that guides our analysis and describes the address registration process in Austria.

4.1   Motivating Use Case Scenario

Assume the address registration process that exists in Austria, which is a legal requirement for all those that change their normal residence to Austria. The address registration process results in the issuing of a registration confirmation, which serves as official proof of residence, necessary for banking, voting, etc. Specifically, residents in Austria must register their address at a local registration office within three days when permanently changing residence or moving from a foreign country. This process requires completing a registration form with personal information and obtaining the signature of the property owner. In the event that a person permanently (or temporarily) stays in a hotel, they may request a signature from the hotel as proof of their stay. Temporary visitors for tourism purposes are exempt from this requirement. Failure to provide a registration confirmation may result in ineligibility to open a bank account or vote, among other things.

4.2   Specification of KBs and UCPs

In our framework, KBs are used to store domain events that have already occurred and general knowledge about the domain and related entities, while UCPs are used to specify imposed restrictions on resource usage. Below, we present a detailed syntactic specification of these components.

Knowledge Bases. We assume the existence of a certain set of triples that represent the current state of affairs or knowledge about the world, called the KB.

Definition 3 (Knowledge Base). *A KB, denoted as K, is an RDF graph describing the set of actual knowledge.*

A KB stores facts related to subjects, which can be either in the form of general knowledge (e.g., *Alice is a person*) or events that have occurred (e.g., *Alice registered her address*), which refer to the execution of an action.

Usage Control Policies. We assume three sets, N (entity names), C (action names), and R (resource names), such that $N, C, R \subseteq I$. We consider a special type of RDF triples, which are generated by the three sets N, C, and R. An RDF triple $(n, c, r) \in (N) \times (C) \times (R)$ is called an *action*. Let us further suppose the presence of disjoint sets V_n, V_c, V_r representing variables from the sets N, C, R respectively, such that V_n, V_c, $V_r \subseteq V$. A UCP consists of a set of rules that govern the behavior of entities with regard to resource usage, specifying what actions are permitted, prohibited, required, or optional. Deontic logic, which deals with permissions, obligations, and related concepts, provides a suitable framework for representing and reasoning about UCPs [10]. As part of our framework, the specification of usage control rules (UCRs) is based on the following deontic operators: permissions or allowance $\mathbf{A}$, prohibitions $\mathbf{P}$, obligations $\mathbf{O}$, and dispensations $\mathbf{D}$ that denote optionality [11]. In the context of an action (n, c, r), these operators have the following meanings:

- $\mathbf{A}(n, c, r)$: indicates that an entity n is permitted (allowed) to perform an action c over a resource r.
- $\mathbf{P}(n, c, r)$: indicates that an entity n is prohibited from performing an action c over a resource r.
- $\mathbf{O}(n, c, r)$: indicates that an entity n is obliged to perform an action c over a resource r.
- $\mathbf{D}(n, c, r)$: indicates that an entity n is exempt from performing an action c over a resource r.

In practice, we will allow variables to be present in the n, c, r positions (e.g., *?entity :request ?resource*), to allow generally applicable restrictions to be expressed, and we refer to such a tuple as an *action pattern* defined as a triple $(np, cp, rp) \in (N \cup V_n) \times (C \cup V_c) \times (R \cup V_r)$. We denote by $\mathcal{AP}$ the set of all action patterns.

A deontic pattern can be defined as follows:

Definition 4 (Deontic Pattern). *Let* $\mathcal{D} = \{\mathbf{A}, \mathbf{P}, \mathbf{O}, \mathbf{D}\}$ *denote the* deontic operators *of* Permission, Prohibition, Obligation, *and* Dispensation. *A deontic pattern is a statement of the form da, where* $d \in \mathcal{D}$ *and* $a \in \mathcal{AP}$.

Example 1 (Deontic Pattern). The tuple $\mathbf{A}(?x, :request, ?y)$ states that an "entity" $?x$ is allowed to request a "resource" $?y$.

Some deontic patterns apply under specific conditions, giving rise to conditional deontic rules [2] (e.g., *to be "allowed" to "request" a resource "signature", one needs to be a "person" staying permanently in a hotel, etc.*). These rules not only prescribe the permissible or impermissible actions that entities may undertake with resources, but also the corresponding obligations or dispensations, under specific conditions. A *condition* is modeled based on a graph pattern expression. Following Definition 1, AND (often abbreviated using ".") and UNION are used to express conjunctive and disjunctive (respectively) conditions. The operator OPT behaves similarly to the outer join operator in SQL, whereas MINUS is used to express conditions involving negation (e.g., to identify persons without a registration confirmation one could write $(?x, :type, :Person)$ MINUS $(?x, :hasA, :registrationConfirmation)$). Lastly, the filter operator is used to express different conditions pertaining to specific sub-elements of a triple. Using a deontic pattern, graph pattern, and the operator $\rightsquigarrow$ in-between, a conditional deontic rule, simply called a *UCR*, can be defined as follows:

Definition 5 (Usage Control Rule). *A UCR is of the form: cond ⤳ da, where cond is a graph pattern, and da is a deontic pattern. We denote by $\mathcal{R}$ the set of all UCRs.*

A UCR can be read as follows: If the condition (*cond*) is satisifed by the KB, then the deontic pattern (*da*) may/must not/must/need not be satisfied. Furthermore, it is assumed that for a given rule, the condition $var(a) \subseteq var(cond)$ holds. Violating this restriction would create an infinite number of deontic requirements, making the model unusable in practice.

Example 2 (Usage Control Rule). The following requirement from our motivating use case scenario: *"In the event that a person permanently stays in a hotel, they may request a signature from the hotel as proof of their stay"*, can be expressed using the following UCR:

(?x, :type, :Person).   (?x, :stayIn, ?l).
(?x, :hasStayDuration, :permanent).   (?l, :type, :Hotel).
(?l, :hasManagementUnit, ?m).   (?m, :type, :HotelManagement).
(?y, :hasSignatory, ?m).   (?y, :type, :Signature)
⤳ **A**(?x, :request, ?y)

The requirements described in our scenario can be expressed in the same general form in Definition 5. The various requirements expressed as UCRs form a UCP.

Definition 6 (Usage Control Policy). *A set of UCRs $R \subseteq \mathcal{R}$ is called a UCP.*

4.3   Semantics of UCPs

To effectively perform the reasoning tasks in our framework, it is imperative that we have the ability to reason about the rules governing UCPs. This is primarily accomplished through the process of evaluating these rules against the KB, resulting in the identification of *active rules*. Active rules are characterized by having a *satisfied condition*, ensuring their applicability in the given KB.

Definition 7 (Satisfied condition). *Let K be a KB over T, P a UCP, and a rule $r \in P$, such that $r = cond \leadsto da$. A condition cond is satisfied for μ, denoted by $K \rhd cond$, if and only if there exists a mapping μ such that $\mu \in [[cond]]_K$.*

Note that multiple mappings may be used to satisfy a given rule.

Definition 8 (Active Rule). *A rule $r \in P$, such that $r = cond \leadsto da$, is active for a mapping μ, if and only if cond is satisfied for μ.*

Note that a rule may be active for multiple mappings. Based on the definition of an active rule, a UCP P is called *active* if any of its rules are active. Otherwise, It is called *inactive*. Furthermore, it is often important to identify the entity/entities for which a rule applies:

Definition 9 (Applicable Rule). *Consider an active rule $r \in P$ such that $r = cond \rightsquigarrow da$, a denotes (n, c, r), $n \in V_n \cup N$, and there is some $n_o \in N$. We say that r is applicable for n_0 with respect to μ if and only if $\mu(n) = n_0$.*

Based on this definition, we call a UCP P *applicable* for n_0 if any of its rules are applicable. Otherwise, It is called *non-applicable*.

5 Reasoning Tasks

Our UC framework leverages KBs and UCPs to support three primary tasks for managing and monitoring UCPs: *consistency checking, compliance checking*, and *requirements checking*. Consistency checking ensures that policies do not contain conflicting or contradictory rules and are logically consistent. Compliance checking aims to verify that the actions of a system and its users, which are stored in KBs, conform to a predefined set of rules and policies, and to identify any instances of non-compliance. Finally, requirements checking helps to ensure that users of systems are informed of their up-to-date rights and obligations specified in policies. In the following, we provide a detailed overview of each reasoning task, related algorithms[5], and concepts.

5.1 Consistency Checking

Consistency checking aims to identify and resolve conflicts among policy rules, with a focus on detecting and resolving *conflicting rules* involving *deontic dilemmas*, which are considered to be application-independent [20]. Deontic dilemmas occur when positive operators (permissions and obligations) in an active rule and negative operators (prohibitions and dispensations) in another active rule refer to the same action triple a. Abstracting from the interplay between positive and negative operators, we mainly focus on the following types of deontic dilemmas defined in [20]: $\mathbf{O}a$ and $\mathbf{P}a$; $\mathbf{A}a$ and $\mathbf{P}a$; $\mathbf{O}a$ and $\mathbf{D}a$.

Definition 10 (Conflicting Rules). *Let $r_1, r_2 \in P$, such that $r_1 = cond_1 \rightsquigarrow d_1 a_1$, $r_2 = cond_2 \rightsquigarrow d_2 a_2$. Let μ_1 be a mapping in $[[cond_1]]_K$, μ_2 be a mapping in $[[cond_2]]_K$, and $\mu_1 \sim \mu_2$. We say that a pair of rules (r_1, r_2) are conflicting with respect to μ, such that $\mu = \mu_1 \bowtie \mu_2$, if and only if the following conditiofns hold:*

1. d_1 and d_2 present a deontic dilemma
2. $\mu(a_1) = \mu(a_2)$

We say that the pair (r_1, r_2) are conflicting if they are conflicting for some μ. We denote by $\mathcal{CR}$ the set of all conflicting rules in P.

---

[5] The functions invoked in the algorithms defined below are available here: https://github.com/Ines-Akaichi/GUCON-Instantiation/blob/main/GUCON-Appendix.pdf.

When conflicts are detected in a policy, it is said to be *inconsistent*. In this case, a decision must be made on how to restore its consistency. A UCP P is called *consistent*, if and only if, there is no $r_1, r_2 \in P$ such that r_1 conflicts with r_2. Otherwise, It is called *inconsistent*.

Using a conflict resolution strategy automatically addresses policy conflicts and restores consistency. One prevalent strategy for resolving modality conflicts is establishing a precedence relationship between rules. Principles for establishing precedence include giving negative policies priority over positive ones, prioritizing specific policies over general ones, and prioritizing new laws over old ones. The specificities of each strategy are outlined in [20]. Our framework incorporates a meta-policy that defines the conflict strategy and the corresponding conflicting rules. Precedence is expressed using the binary operator $\preceq$. That is, for each conflicting pair of rules (r_1, r_2), if $r_1 \preceq r_2$, then r_2 (stronger rule) takes precedence over r_1 (weaker rule).

Definition 11 (Usage Control Meta-policy). *A usage control meta-policy is a tuple $\langle \mathcal{CR}, \preceq \rangle$, such that $\preceq \subseteq \mathcal{CR}^2$ is a partial pre-order over pairs of rules in $\mathcal{CR}$. For any pair of rules (r_1, r_2) and (r_2, r_3) in $\mathcal{CR}$, the relation $\preceq$ satisfies: a) reflexivity: $r_1 \preceq r_1$, i.e. every element is related to itself; b) transitivity: if $r_1 \preceq r_2$ and $r_2 \preceq r_3$ then $r_1 \preceq r_3$.*

Input: Policy P, Knowledge Base K, Meta-policy MP
Output: Policy $\hat{P}$
begin
    /* n is the size of P   */
    for $i=1$ to n **do**
        $\Omega = $ GetMappings($P[i].cond, K$)
        if Ω *is not empty* **then**
            foreach μ in Ω **do**
                $\hat{P}$.insert ($\mu(P[i])$)

    if $\hat{P}$ *is not empty* **then**
        for $i=1$ to n-1 **do**
            for $j=i+1$ to n **do**
                /* If two rules are conflicting   */
                if $(\hat{P}[i].a == \hat{P}[j].a)$ *and* (IsOpposite($\hat{P}[i].d, \hat{P}[j].d$) **then**
                    temp = Compare($\hat{P}$[i], $\hat{P}$[j], MP)
                    if *temp == 1* **then**
                        /* $\hat{P}$[j] $\preceq$ $\hat{P}$[i]   */
                        /* $\hat{P}$[i] does not change   */
                        $\hat{P}$[j].cond = Minus($\hat{P}$[j].cond, $\hat{P}$[i].cond)
                    else if *temp == 2* **then**
                        /* $\hat{P}$[i] $\preceq$ $\hat{P}$[j]   */
                        /* $\hat{P}$[j] does not change   */
                        $\hat{P}$[i].cond = Minus($\hat{P}$[i].cond, $\hat{P}$[j].cond)
                    else if *temp==0* **then**
                      /* $\hat{P}$[i] $\npreceq$ $\hat{P}$[j] and $\hat{P}$[j] $\npreceq$ $\hat{P}$[i]   */
                      quit ();
    return $\hat{P}$

Algorithm 1: Dynamic Conflict Detection and Resolution

Note also the use of $\preceq$ instead of $\prec$: as usual, we will write $r_1 \prec r_2$, as a shorthand for $r_1 \preceq r_2$ and $r_2 \not\preceq r_1$. An example of negative policies override positive ones can be expressed as follows:

Example 3 (Prohibition overrides Permission). This strategy can be formally expressed as follows: for any two rules $r_1 = cond_1 \rightsquigarrow \mathbf{P}a_1$, $r_2 = cond_2 \rightsquigarrow \mathbf{A}a_2$, such that $a_1 = a_2$, it holds that $r_2 \preceq r_1$.

Generally speaking, repairing the consistency of policies involve detecting conflicting rules and then resolving them based on the precedence strategy specified in the corresponding meta-policy. To resolve these conflicts, changes are made to the weaker rule defined based on the precedence strategy specified in the corresponding meta-policy. Specifically, the resolution involves subtracting (using MINUS) the condition in the stronger rules from the condition in the weaker rule. This operation yields a modified version of the weaker rule that no longer conflicts with the stronger rule, allowing its application in the current context. In cases where no precedence is defined, conflicts remain unresolved. This means that conflicting rules without a designated precedence relationship would persist, necessitating manual intervention for resolution [20].

To automate the process of consistency checking and repairing in policies, we propose Algorithm 1, which is a systematic approach to detecting and resolving conflicting rules. The algorithm involves four main steps: (1) It determines an active policy based on a given KB by evoking the function ReturnMappings that evaluates each rule in the policy against a given KB and returns a set of mappings. The resulting mappings are used to populate the inactive rules. (2) Next, each pair of active rules in the returned policy is examined to identify any conflicts. This is done by checking whether the pair has equal actions (triples) and features a deontic dilemma, using the IsOpposite function. (3) If the algorithm detects any conflicting pairs, the function Compare is evoked to decide which rule holds precedence over which rule. (4) Finally, if a precedence is defined between two rules, the meta-policy is applied by invoking the function Minus, which apply necessary changes to the weaker rule. In general, the verification of active rules may be carried out each time the KB is updated.

5.2 Compliance Checking

We propose ex-post compliance of a given KB against a policy or a set of policies. Compliance checking is capable of identifying any breaches or non-compliant behavior of an entity, which is identified by an IRI, thereby ensuring the proper and secure operation of the system. The criteria for determining whether a KB is compliant with a given policy can vary depending on the specific rule being considered, as well as the KB and mappings used to interpret that rule. Note that we do not define compliance for inconsistent policies, however, if we are given any UCP, Algorithm 1 needs to be initially performed, and then compliance checking can be carried out.

Input: Policy P, Knowledge Base K, IRI iri
Output: Boolean $compliant$
begin
   | $compliant = true$
   | $i = 1$
   | /* n is the size of P   */
   | **while** $i \leq n$ **do**
   | | $\mu = $ GetMapping $(P[i].cond, K, iri)$
   | | **if** μ *is not empty* **then**
   | | | **if** $P[i].d == $ **O** **then**
   | | | | **if** *Not Exists($\mu(P[i].a)$, K)* **then**
   | | | | | $compliant = false$
   | | | **break**
   | | | **if** $P[i].d == $ **P** **then**
   | | | | **if** *Exists($\mu(P[i].a)$, K)* **then**
   | | | | | $compliant = false$
   | | | **break**
   | **return** $compliant$

Algorithm 2: Ex-post Compliance checking

Definition 12 (KB Compliance Against a Rule). *Given a KB K and a rule $r \in P$, such that P is consistent, we say that K complies with r, denoted by $K \rhd r$, if and only if any of the following is true:*

- *If r is of the form cond $\rightarrow$ **A**a, then $K \rhd r$*
- *If r is of the form cond $\rightarrow$ **P**a and for all μ such that r is applicable for μ, it holds that $\mu(a) \notin K$*
- *If r is of the form cond $\rightarrow$ **O**a and for all μ such that r is applicable for μ, it holds that $\mu(a) \in K$*
- *If r is of the form cond $\rightarrow$ **D**a, then $K \rhd r$*

Based on this definition, a KB K is said to be *compliant* with a UCP P, denoted by $K \rhd P$, if and only for each applicable rule $r \in P$, $K \rhd r$. Otherwise, It is called *non-compliant*.

Automatically checking for compliance between a KB and an applicable policy, with respect to a given IRI, is performed using Algorithm 2, which employs a two-step approach: (1) The first step of the algorithm involves verifying the applicability of each rule for a given IRI by invoking the `ReturnMapping` function. (2) The second step involves evaluating the KB for compliance with each applicable rule, utilizing the `Exists` function as per the criteria defined in Definition 12. Notably, the algorithm halts as soon as a non-compliant rule is identified.

5.3 Requirements Checking

Requirement checking is a task that enables an entity to query a policy and receive information regarding their applicable deontic rules. This task ensures that entities are continuously aware of the applicable permissions, prohibitions, obligations, and dispensations relevant to their activities.

Algorithm 3 facilitates the retrieval of specific requirements, in accordance with an applicable policy, for a given IRI and a KB. The algorithm operates

Input: Policy P, Knowledge Base K, IRI iri, Deontic d
Output: Policy P_{req}
begin
    /* n is the size of P   */
    for $i = 1$ *to* n **do**
        $\mu = $ GetMapping $(P[i].cond,\ K,\ iri)$
        if μ *is not empty* **then**
            if $P[i].d == d$ **then**
                if $d == $ **O** **then**
                    if $Exists(\mu(P[i].a),\ K)$ **then**
                        $i = i + 1$
                  else
                    $P_{req}.$insert$(\mu(P[i]))$
            else
                $P_{req}.$insert$(\mu(P[i]))$

    return P_{req}

Algorithm 3: Requirements Checking

through a two-step process: (1) In the first step, It verifies the applicability of each rule for a given IRI by invoking the `ReturnMapping` function. This step ensures that only applicable rules are considered in the subsequent requirement checking process. (2) In the second step, It checks each applicable rule to determine whether it is in accordance with the requested deontic, adding it to the list of requested requirements as appropriate. For requested obligations, the algorithm first checks whether a given obligation has already been executed by invoking the `Exists` function. If the obligation has not been executed, the respective rule will be added to the list of requirements.

6   Assessment

In order to demonstrate the effectiveness and suitability of our abstract framework in expressing and reasoning over UCPs in practical contexts, we provide instantiations of our framework using three widely recognized recommendations from the W3C organization, namely, SHACL, OWL 2, and ODRL. These instantiations allow us to showcase how can we effectively map the abstract concepts in our framework into concrete implementations.

In what follows, we first introduce the Usage Control Policy (UCP) ontology and profile, which respectively represent our framework specification and motivating use case scenario, and which serve as the basis for the instantiations performed below. Both the UCP core ontology and the UCP profile are employed in the instantiation process using SHACL and OWL. However, for the ODRL language, we express our motivating scenario by constructing an ODRL profile in accordance with the ODRL specification, which is described in detail below. Finally, we assess the adequacy of instantiations and reasoning capabilities of each of the languages. All the details describing the various instantiations are provided on our GitHub repository[6,7].

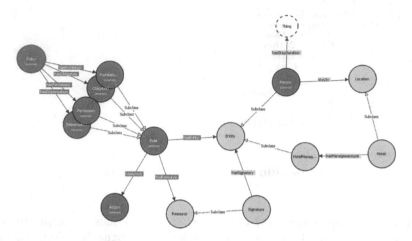

Fig. 1. The UCP Core Ontology and Profile. Dark blue: core model; Light blue: profile (Color figure online)

6.1   The Usage Control Policy Ontology and Profile

Herein, we present the UCP core ontology that defines essential concepts for modeling a UCP based on our framework specification. The core ontology is shown in dark blue in Fig. 1. We use the ucp prefix to identify our <http://example.org/ucp/> ontology. The UCP core ontology includes the following main classes: ucp:Policy, ucp:Rule, ucp:Action, ucp:Resource, and ucp:Entity. A ucp:Rule can be a ucp:Permission, ucp:Prohibition, ucp:Obligation, or ucp:Dispensation. Connections between a ucp:Rule and an ucp:Action, ucp:Resource, and ucp:Entity are established using corresponding OWL properties. A policy can consist of one or more rules and is linked to the ucp:Rule class based on the rule type, using properties like ucp:hasPermission, ect. The ontology incorporates additional constraints and restrictions, but they are not discussed in details in this paper. For instance, ucp:hasPermission has a domain of ucp:Policy and a range of ucp:Permission. The deontic classes are also owl:disjointWith each other. We also introduce the UCP profile <http://example.org/ucp:profile:01/> described

---

[6] GitHub, https://github.com/Ines-Akaichi/GUCON-Instantiation.

[7] The following prefixes are used throughout Sect. 6: rdf:<http://www.w3.org/1999/02/22-rdf-syntax-ns#>; rdfs:<http://www.w3.org/2000/01/rdf-schema#>; owl:<http://www.w3.org/2002/07/owl#>; foaf:<http://xmlns.com/foaf/0.1/>; ex:<http://example.org/>.

with the ucpr prefix, which includes the minimal concepts needed for modeling Example 2 from our motivating scenario, as shown in Fig. 1 with an overview in light blue. It defines a foaf:Person of type ucp:Entity staying at a particular ucpr:Location for a specific period. ucpr:Hotel is of type ucpr:Location and has a ucpr:HotelManagement unit. The profile includes a ucpr:request as an instance of the ucp:Action class, and a ucpr:Signature as a ucp:Resource involving a signatory of type ucp:Entity.

6.2 Instantiation

Initially, SHACL was introduced to validate RDF graphs using specific conditions called *shapes*. However, it has evolved to include advanced features like *SHACL rules*, namely Triple and SPARQL rules. These rules allow for the derivation of inferred triples, expanding SHACL's capabilities beyond validation into a logical programming language [24]. On the other hand, OWL is an ontology language designed for the Semantic Web, with formally defined semantics. OWL 2 is the latest version, offering various options that balance expressive modeling capabilities with efficient computational reasoning [6]. In contrast, ODRL was developed to express policies for digital content and services. It includes a core model and vocabulary that enables the expression of profiles for different use cases [27].

Policy Representation Using SHACL. To express a UCR using SHACL-SPARQL, the rule is defined as a sh:SPARQLRule identifier, bound to the special term $this. The UCR is expressed through the sh:construct property using CONSTRUCT-WHERE assertions in SPARQL. The deontic pattern is rewritten using the CONSTRUCT operator as $this rdfs:subClassOf *DeonticClass*, where *DeonticClass* can be one of the following ucp:Permission, ucp:Prohibition, ucp:Obligation, or ucp:Dispensation. The entity, resource, and action are represented as a conjunction of triples in the WHERE clause, using the identifier $this as the subject; ucp:hasEntity, ucp:hasAction, ucp:hasResource as properties; and the corresponding values as objects. Graph pattern conditions can be added to the WHERE clause alongside the other triples, using an AND connector. Using SHACL-SPARQL rules preserves the expressivity of graph pattern conditions, allowing for more flexible and detailed rule specifications. Example 2 formalized in SHACL is shown in Listing 1.1.

```
1  ex:PermissionRequestSignature
2    a sh:NodeShape ;
3    sh:rule [
4      a sh:SPARQLRule ;
5      sh:prefixes ex: , rdf: , ucp: , :ucpr;
6      sh:construct """
7        CONSTRUCT {
8          $this rdfs:subClassOf ucp:Permission . }
9        WHERE {
10         $this ucp:hasAction ?x .
11         $this ucp:hasEntity ?y .
12         $this ucp:hasResource ?z .
13         ?x rdf:type ucp:Action .
14         ?x rdfs:label "request"@en .
15         ?y rdf:type foaf:Person .
16         ?y ucpr:stayIn ?l.
17         ?y ucpr:hasStayDuration ex:permanent.
```

```
18              ?l  rdf:type  ucpr:Hotel  .
19              ?l  ucpr:hasMangemetUnit ?m .
20              ?m rdf:type    ucpr:HotelManagement .
21              ?z rdf:type   ex:Signature .
22              ?z ucpr:hasSignatory ?m . } """ ; ] .
```

Listing 1.1. Policy Representation using SHACL

Policy Representation Using OWL. To represent a UCR using OWL, the rule can be described as follows: the deontic pattern of the rule is represented by an identifier (denoted by *id*) of type `owl:Class`, which is generated in a way that guarantees uniqueness. The deontic operator is conveyed through the RDF triple representation as *id*, rdfs:subClassOf, *DeonticClass*. *id* describes the entity, resource, and action of the deontic pattern using `owl:equivalentClass` and `owl:intersectionOf` of restrictions on the properties `ucp:hasEntity`, `ucp:hasAction`, and `ucp:hasResource`. These properties can be recursively described using `owl:hasValue` or `owl:allValuesFrom`. Mapping specific instances of type `ucp:Entity`, `ucp:Resource`, or `ucp:Action` described using the graph pattern operators AND, UNION, OPT, FILTER, or MINUS to the OWL representation can be performed as follows: the `owl:intersectionOf` and `owl:unionOf` can be used to express respectively the operators AND and UNION. The `owl:complementOf` property serves as a workaround to express OPT, while also enabling the expression of soft negation to describe MINUS operations. It is important to note that OWL does not explicitly represent the FILTER operator. Nevertheless, constraints on properties and values can be expressed through OWL restrictions and property assertions. Example 2 formalized in OWL is shown in Listing 1.2.

```
 1  ex:PermissionRequestSignature rdf:type owl:Class ;
 2  rdfs:subClassOf  ucp:Permission ;
 3  owl:equivantClass
 4  [
 5  rdf:type      owl:Class;
 6  owl:intersectionOf
 7  ( [
 8  rdf:type   owl:Restriction ;
 9  owl:onProperty   ucp:hasAction ;
10  owl:hasValue ucpr:request  ]
11  [
12  rdf:type owl:Restriction;
13  owl:onProperty ucp:hasResource;
14  owl:allValuesFrom   [
15    rdf:type ucpr:Signature ;
16    ucpr:signatory   ucpr:HotelManagement ] ]
17  [
18  rdf:type owl:Restricton;
19  owl:onProperty ucp:hasEntity;
20  owl:allValuesFrom  [
21    rdf:type   foaf:Person ;
22    ucpr:stayIn [
23      rdf:type ucpr:Hotel ;
24      ucpr:hasManagementUnit   ucpr:HotelMangement; ] ;
25        ucpr:stayDuration ex:permanent ; ] ] ) ] .
```

Listing 1.2. Policy Representation using OWL

Policy Representation Using ODRL. To address the requirements specific to our motivating use case scenario, the first step involves extending the ODRL policy model by creating a profile that represents our particular example. The following prefixes are used to describe respectively the original model odrl:<http://www.

w3.org/ns/odrl/2/> and our profile odrlp:<http://example.org/odrl:profile: 01/>. The profile follows the design guidlines of the ODRL model, particularly, we employ an instance odrlp:persons of type odrl:PartyCollection, while the class foaf:Person is part of odrlp:persons. odrlp:Signature is a subclass of odrl:Asset, the action odrlp:request is an instance of odrl:Action. The properties odrlp:stayIn, odrlp:hasManagementUnit, odrlp:hasStayduration, and odrlp:hasSignatory are defined similarly to the UCP profile. A more comprehensive description of the ODRL profile can be found in our GitHub repository.

Within the ODRL, a UCR can be described using an identifier *id* of type odrl:Set, which is generated in a way that guarantees uniqueness. The deontic pattern of a UCR is described as follows: the deontic operator is specified through an ODRL deontic property (e.g., odrl:permission), although it is important to note that ODRL mainly covers permissions, prohibitions, and obligations. That means, It is not possible to represent a UCR expressing a dispensation in ODRL without creating a new profile. The deontic property is linked to other concepts through properties like odrl:assignee (corresponding to ucp:hasEntity), odrl:action (corresponding to ucp:hasAction), and odrl:target (corresponding to ucp:hasResource). Describing the entity, action, and resource can be done using operators defined in ODRL (e.g., odrl:refinement, odrl:leftOperand, odrl:rightOperand, odrl:operator). Mapping specific instances of type ucp:Entity, ucp:Resource, or ucp:Action described using the graph pattern operators AND, UNION, OPT, FILTER, or MINUS to the ODRL representation can be performed as follows: the intersection or union of patterns can be expressed using the operators odrl:and and odrl:or, respectively. However, defining the OPT operator within the ODRL framework does not have a clear workaround. For the FILTER operator, the properties odrl:leftOperand, odrl:rightOperand, and odrl:operator can be used as a workaround. Negation can be achieved using operators that belong to the class odrl:Operator, such as odrl:neq (not equal) or odrl:isNoneOf (is none of). An ODRL formalization of Example 2 is found in Listing 1.3.

```
1  ex:PermissionRequestSignature
2  a odrl:Set;
3  odrl:profile     <http://example.org/odrl:profile:01/>;
4  odrl:permission
5  [
6  odrl:assignee
7    [
8      a   odrl:PartyCollection ;
9      odrl:source odrlp:persons;
10     odrl:refinement
11     [
12     odrl:and
13     [ odrl:leftOperand      odrlp:stayIn    ;
14       odrl:operator      odrl:eq    ;
15       odrl:rightOperand
16         [a  odrlp:Hotel;
17         odrlp:hasManagementUnit odrlp:HotelManagement; ]; ]  ,
18     [ odrl:leftOperand      odrlp:hasStayDuration   ;
19       odrl:operator     odrl:eq     ;
20       odrl:rightOperand     ex:permanent    ; ] ; ] ];
21  odrl:action odrlp:request;
22  odrl:target
23     [ a odrlp:Signature;
24     odrlp:hasSignatory odrlp:HotelManagement; ] ].
```

Listing 1.3. Policy Representation using ODRL

6.3   Usage Control Requirements Assessment

The implementation of our framework has demonstrated its versatility and adaptability by successfully mapping it to different languages. This is achieved through the strategic utilization of the inherent expressive capabilities present in each language. In the following, we specifically assess two key aspects: (1) the adequacy of mapping our framework to the different instantiations and (2) the reasoning over the given policies by leveraging existing implementations of the defined languages.

Instantiation: *Expressiveness.* UCRs can be mapped directly to SHACL-SPARQL. Additionally, SHACL-SPARQL leverages SPARQL operators and built-in functions, making it expressive for policy specification. OWL is expressive and offers features like conjunction, disjunction, and filtering through property restrictions. It also supports OPT and MINUS using the `owl:complementOf` construct. SHACL-SPARQL and OWL require an ontology to express policy elements. Whereas ODRL is built specifically to express policies by supporting mainly permissions, prohibitions, and obligations, but lacks support for dispensations. ODRL provides conjunction, disjunction, and refinement operators that act as filters for conditions. A form of "Negation" can be achieved using `odrl:neq` or `odrl:isNoneOf`. Whereas, It is not clear how ODRL can support the OPT operator. *Flexibility & extensibility.* SHACL-SPARQL and OWL offer flexibility and extensibility through ontologies. They can accommodate various requirements by defining new concepts and relationships in the ontology. Whereas, ODRL's flexibility and extensibility are achieved through profiles, enabling customization of the language for specific application domains. *Unambiguous.* SHACL-SPARQL and OWL are declarative in syntax, promoting unambiguous policy specifications, while ODRL's syntax is designed to be intuitive, which aids in reducing ambiguity to some extent. *Formal semantics.* SHACL-SPARQL and particularly SPARQL have clear formal semantics, making it well-defined and suitable for formal reasoning. OWL has formal semantics defined by W3C, enabling reasoning and inference, whereas ODRL lacks explicitly defined formal semantics. Nonetheless, there is an active w3c community group dedicated to defining formal semantics for ODRL[8] Finally and most importantly, the adoption of graph patterns formal semantics into the specification of our policy rules provides a rigorous foundation for our framework, which enables precise reasoning about policy rule interactions, conflicts, and compliance, when combined with other representation languages.

Reasoning: One advantage of using representation languages like SHACL, OWL 2, and ODRL is their ability to leverage (and extend) existing engines for implementing our framework reasoning tasks. In the domains of regulatory and privacy compliance research, SHACL is used for representing privacy policies, i.e. permissions, prohibitions, and obligations [1,24], with the TopBraid[9] engine being used to assess compliance of user access request or user data processing

---

[8] ODRL Formal Semantics, https://w3c.github.io/odrl/formal-semantics/.
[9] TopBraid SHACL, https://github.com/TopQuadrant/shacl.

against the SHACL policies. Furthermore, and very recently, SHACL-ACL [25] has been introduced as an extension of SHACL, focusing on access control in RDF knowledge graphs. The validation process for access control involves checking whether SPARQL queries are compliant with access control policies expressed in SHACL-ACL. This validation is carried out using a SHACL validator known as Trav-SHACL[10] Various implementations of SHACL and its advanced features are available, and a full list of engines can be found here[11]. Similarly, recent works [4,5,14] have utilized OWL 2 to express privacy policies and employed off-the-shelf reasoners like Hermit, Pellet, and Racer for compliance checking. As noted in [5], OWL 2 exhibits the advantage that all major policy-reasoning tasks are decidable, and if policies adhere to OWL 2 profiles, they are also tractable. Although ODRL lacks a standard enforcement engine, workarounds have been proposed, such as translating ODRL policies into InstAL and perform compliance verification using an answer set solver [10]. Furthermore, the current efforts within a W3C working group to propose formal semantics for ODRL would represent a significant advancement towards enabling the establishment of a standard implementation for the language [8].

7   Conclusion and Future Work

In this paper, we presented GUCON, a comprehensive framework that defines the specifications of a KB designed to store factual knowledge, as well as UCPs used to define UCRs. Our framework leverages the flexibility of deontic concepts and the expressiveness and semantics of graph pattern expressions to capture general UCRs. In addition, we have introduced algorithms for policy-based reasoning tasks, mainly, consistency checking, compliance checking and requirements checking, which can be accomplished by leveraging the semantics of UCPs and the KB. To demonstrate the effectiveness of our framework, we showed how to instantiate our framework using three different well-known languages. In doing so, we demonstrated not only the expressive power of our framework, but also its adaptability to other relevant languages. This enables us to draw on existing literature and industry solutions supporting these languages as a means of implementing our reasoning tasks.

Our paper leaves room for future work. While the majority of existing literature and industrial solutions focus primarily on compliance checking as the main reasoning task, a potential avenue for future research is to use one of these many implementations to study the integration of the remaining reasoning tasks and bring in our formal semantics to these implementations, in particular consistency checking and requirement checking. In addition, We also plan to investigate how can we facilitate the mapping between our framework and the representation languages introduced herein by implementing and evaluating automated translation algorithms. Finally, we plan to evaluate our framework

---

[10] Trav-SHACL, https://github.com/SDM-TIB/Trav-SHACL.
[11] https://book.validatingrdf.com/bookHtml011.html.

following its implementation based on performance and security criteria, among other aspects.

Acknowledgements. This work is funded by the European Union Horizon 2020 research and innovation programme under the Marie Skłodowska-Curie grant agreement No 860801. Sabrina Kirrane is funded by the FWF Austrian Science Fund and the Internet Foundation Austria under the FWF Elise Richter and netidee SCIENCE programmes as project number V 759-N.

References

1. Al Bassit, A., Krasnashchok, K., Skhiri, S., Mustapha, M.: Policy-based automated compliance checking. In: Rules and Reasoning: 5th International Joint Conference, RuleML+RR 2021, Leuven, Belgium, 13–15 September 2021, Proceedings (2021)
2. Beller, S.: Deontic norms, deontic reasoning, and deontic conditionals. Think. Reason. **14**(4), 305–341 (2008)
3. Bonatti, P., De Coi, J.L., Olmedilla, D., Sauro, L.: A rule-based trust negotiation system. IEEE Trans. Knowl. Data Eng. **22**, 1507–1520 (2010)
4. Bonatti, P., Ioffredo, L., Petrova, I., Sauro, L., Siahaan, I.: Real-time reasoning in OWL2 for GDPR compliance. Artif. Intell. **289**, 103389 (2020)
5. Bonatti, P., Kirrane, S., Petrova, I., Sauro, L.: Machine understandable policies and GDPR compliance checking. KI Künstliche Intelligenz **34**, 303–315 (2020)
6. Bonatti, P.A.: Fast compliance checking in an OWL2 fragment. In: Proceedings of the 27th International Joint Conference on Artificial Intelligence (2018)
7. Cao, Q.H., Giyyarpuram, M., Farahbakhsh, R., Crespi, N.: Policy-based usage control for a trustworthy data sharing platform in smart cities. Future Gener. Comput. Syst. **107**, 998–1010 (2020)
8. Cimmino, A., Cano-Benito, J., García-Castro, R.: Practical challenges of ODRL and potential courses of action. In: Companion Proceedings of the ACM Web Conference (2023)
9. Colombo, M., Lazouski, A., Martinelli, F., Mori, P.: A proposal on enhancing XACML with continuous usage control features. In: Grids, P2P and Services Computing (2010)
10. De Vos, M., Kirrane, S., Padget, J., Satoh, K.: ODRL policy modelling and compliance checking. In: Rules and Reasoning: Third International Joint Conference, RuleML+RR 2019, Bolzano, Italy, 16–19 September 2019, Proceedings (2019)
11. Dimishkovska, A.: Deontic logic and legal rules. Encyclopedia of the Philosophy of Law and Social Philosophy (2017)
12. European Commission: 2018 reform of EU data protection rules (2018). https://ec.europa.eu/commission/sites/beta-political/files/data-protection-factsheet-changes_en.pdf
13. European Commission: 2021 reform of EU copyright protection rules (2021). https://ec.europa.eu/commission/presscorner/detail/en/IP_21_1807
14. Francesconi, E., Governatori, G.: Patterns for legal compliance checking in a decidable framework of linked open data. Artif. Intell. Law **31**(3), 445–464 (2022)
15. e Ghazia, U., Masood, R., Shibli, M.A., Bilal, M.: Usage control model specification in XACML policy language. In: Computer Information Systems and Industrial Management (2012)

16. Hilty, M., Pretschner, A., Basin, D., Schaefer, C., Walter, T.: A policy language for distributed usage control. In: Computer Security - ESORICS (2007)
17. Kagal, L.: Rei: a policy language for the me-centric project. Technical report, HP Labs (2002). http://www.hpl.hp.com/techreports/2002/HPL-2002-270.html
18. Khandelwal, A., Bao, J., Kagal, L., Jacobi, I., Ding, L., Hendler, J.: Analyzing the air language: a semantic web (production) rule language. In: Web Reasoning and Rule Systems (2010)
19. Lazouski, A., Martinelli, F., Mori, P.: Usage control in computer security: a survey. Comput. Sci. Rev. 4(2), 81–99 (2010)
20. Lupu, E., Sloman, M.: Conflicts in policy-based distributed systems management. IEEE Trans. Softw. Eng. 25(6), 852–869 (1999)
21. Park, J., Sandhu, R.: The UCONABC usage control model. ACM Trans. Inf. Syst. Secur. 7, 128–174 (2004)
22. Pérez, J., Arenas, M., Gutierrez, C.: Semantics and complexity of SPARQL. In: The Semantic Web - ISWC 2006 (2006)
23. Prud'hommeaux, E., Seaborne, A.: SPARQL Query Language for RDF (2008). https://www.w3.org/TR/rdf-sparql-query/. W3C Recommendation 15 January 2008
24. Robaldo, L., Batsakis, S., Calegari, R., et al.: Compliance checking on first-order knowledge with conflicting and compensatory norms: a comparison among currently available technologies. Artif. Intell. Law (2023)
25. Rohde, P.D., Iglesias, E., Vidal, M.E.: SHACL-ACL: access control with SHACL. In: European Semantic Web Conference (2023)
26. Uszok, A., et al.: KAoS policy and domain services: toward a description-logic approach to policy representation, deconfliction, and enforcement. In: Proceedings POLICY 2003. IEEE 4th International Workshop on Policies for Distributed Systems and Networks (2003)
27. W3C Working Group: The open digital rights language (ODRL) (2018). https://www.w3.org/TR/odrl-model/

Combining Proofs for Description Logic and Concrete Domain Reasoning

Christian Alrabbaa[1], Franz Baader[1], Stefan Borgwardt[1], Patrick Koopmann[2], and Alisa Kovtunova[1(✉)]

[1] Institute of Theoretical Computer Science, TU Dresden, Dresden, Germany
{christian.alrabbaa,franz.baader,stefan.borgwardt,
alisa.kovtunova}@tu-dresden.de
[2] Department of Computer Science, Vrije Universiteit Amsterdam, Amsterdam, Netherlands
p.k.koopmann@vu.nl

Abstract. Logic-based approaches to AI have the advantage that their behavior can in principle be explained with the help of proofs of the computed consequences. For ontologies based on Description Logic (DL), we have put this advantage into practice by showing how proofs for consequences derived by DL reasoners can be computed and displayed in a user-friendly way. However, these methods are insufficient in applications where also numerical reasoning is relevant. The present paper considers proofs for DLs extended with concrete domains (CDs) based on the rational numbers, which leave reasoning tractable if integrated into the lightweight DL $\mathcal{EL}_\perp$. Since no implemented DL reasoner supports these CDs, we first develop reasoning procedures for them, and show how they can be combined with reasoning approaches for pure DLs, both for $\mathcal{EL}_\perp$ and the more expressive DL $\mathcal{ALC}$. These procedures are designed such that it is easy to extract proofs from them. We show how the extracted CD proofs can be combined with proofs on the DL side into integrated proofs that explain both the DL and the CD reasoning.

1 Introduction

Description Logics (DLs) [10] are a well-investigated family of logic-based knowledge representation languages, which are frequently used to formalize ontologies for various application domains. As the sizes of DL-based ontologies grow, tools that support improving the quality of such ontologies become more important. DL reasoners[1] can be used to detect inconsistencies and to infer other implicit consequences, such as subsumption relationships. However, for developers or users of DL-based ontologies, it is often hard to understand why a consequence computed by the reasoner actually follows from the given, possibly very large ontology. In principle, such a consequence can be explained by producing a proof for it, which shows how the consequence can be derived from the axioms in the

---

[1] See http://owl.cs.manchester.ac.uk/tools/list-of-reasoners/.

A. Fensel et al. (Eds.): RuleML+RR 2023, LNCS 14244, pp. 54–69, 2023.
https://doi.org/10.1007/978-3-031-45072-3_4

ontology by applying certain easy-to-understand inference rules. In recent work, we have investigated how proofs for consequences derived by DL reasoners can be computed [1,2] and displayed [26] in a user-friendly way [5]. However, like previous work [17,18], this was restricted to DLs without concrete domains.

Concrete domains [9,24] (CDs) have been introduced to enable reference to concrete objects (such as numbers) and predefined predicates on these objects (such as numerical comparisons) when defining concepts. For example, assume that we measure the systolic and the diastolic blood pressure of patients. Then we can describe patients with a pulse pressure of 25 mmHg as Patient $\sqcap$ [sys − dia = 25], where sys and dia are *features* that are interpreted as partial functions that return the systolic and the diastolic blood pressure of a patient, respectively, as rational numbers (if available). We can then state that such patients need attention using the general concept inclusion (GCI)

$$\text{Patient} \sqcap [\text{sys} - \text{dia} = 25] \sqsubseteq \text{NeedAttention}.$$

In the presence of GCIs, integrating a CD into a DL may cause undecidability [12, 25] even if solvability of the constraint systems that can be formulated in the CD (in our example, sets of constraints of the form $x - y = q$ for $q \in \mathbb{Q}$) is decidable. One way to overcome this problem is to disallow role paths [8,16,29] in concrete domain restrictions, which means that these restrictions can only constrain feature values of single individuals, as in our example. Comparing feature values of different individuals, such as the age of a woman with that of her children, is then no longer possible.

For tractable (i.e., polynomially decidable) DLs like $\mathcal{EL}_\perp$, preserving decidability is not sufficient: one wants to preserve tractability. As shown in [8], this is the case if one integrates a so-called p-admissible concrete domain into $\mathcal{EL}_\perp$. The only numerical p-admissible concrete domain exhibited in [8] is the CD $\mathcal{D}_{\mathbb{Q},diff}$, which supports constraints of the form $x = q$, $x > q$, and $x + q = y$ (for constants $q \in \mathbb{Q}$). Recently, additional p-admissible concrete domains have been introduced in [12], such as $\mathcal{D}_{\mathbb{Q},lin}$, whose constraints are given by linear equations $\sum_{i=1}^{n} a_i x_i = b$. In the present paper, we will concentrate on these two p-admissible CDs, though the developed ideas and techniques can also be used for other CDs. The constraint used in our example can be expressed in both $\mathcal{D}_{\mathbb{Q},diff}$ and $\mathcal{D}_{\mathbb{Q},lin}$. Unfortunately, no implemented DL reasoner supports these two CDs. In particular, the highly efficient $\mathcal{EL}_\perp$ reasoner ELK [19] does not support any concrete domain. Instead of modifying ELK or implementing our own reasoner for $\mathcal{EL}_\perp$ with concrete domains, we develop here an iterative algorithm that interleaves ELK reasoning with concrete domain reasoning. For the CD reasoning, we could in principle employ existing algorithms and implementations, like Gaussian elimination or the simplex method [15,31] for $\mathcal{D}_{\mathbb{Q},lin}$, and SMT systems that can deal with difference logic [7,22], such as Z3,[2] for $\mathcal{D}_{\mathbb{Q},diff}$. However, since our main purpose is to generate proofs, we develop our own reasoning procedures for $\mathcal{D}_{\mathbb{Q},diff}$ and $\mathcal{D}_{\mathbb{Q},lin}$, which may not be as efficient as existing ones, but can easily be adapted such that they produce proofs.

---

[2] https://theory.stanford.edu/~nikolaj/programmingz3.html.

Proofs for reasoning results in $\mathcal{EL}_\perp$ with a p-admissible CD can in principle be represented using the calculus introduced in [8] or an appropriate extension of the calculus employed by ELK. However, in these calculi, the result of CD reasoning (i.e., that a set of constraints is unsatisfiable or entails another constraint) is used as an applicability condition for certain rules, but the CD reasoning leading to the satisfaction of the conditions is not explained. Instead of augmenting such a proof with separate proofs on the CD side that show why the applicability conditions are satisfied, our goal is to produce a single proof that explains both the $\mathcal{EL}_\perp$ and the CD reasoning in a uniform proof format.

We also consider the integration of the CDs $\mathcal{D}_{\mathbb{Q},\mathit{diff}}$ and $\mathcal{D}_{\mathbb{Q},\mathit{lin}}$ into the more expressive DL $\mathcal{ALC}$. To this purpose, we develop a new calculus for subsumption w.r.t. $\mathcal{ALC}$ ontologies, which is inspired by the one in [21], but has a better worst-case complexity, and then show how it can be extended to deal with concrete domain restrictions. We have implemented our reasoning and proof extraction approaches for DLs with concrete domains and have evaluated them on several self-created benchmarks designed specifically to challenge the CD reasoning and proof generation capabilities. Proofs for all results and more details about the experiments can be found in [3,4].

2   Description Logics with Concrete Domains

We recall the DLs $\mathcal{EL}_\perp$ and $\mathcal{ALC}$ [10], and then discuss their extensions $\mathcal{EL}_\perp[\mathcal{D}]$ and $\mathcal{ALC}[\mathcal{D}]$ with a concrete domain $\mathcal{D}$ [8,9]. Following [12], we use square brackets to indicate that no role paths are allowed. We also introduce the two p-admissible concrete domains $\mathcal{D}_{\mathbb{Q},\mathit{diff}}$ and $\mathcal{D}_{\mathbb{Q},\mathit{lin}}$ [8,12].

2.1   Description Logics

Starting with disjoint, countably infinite sets of *concept* and *role names* $\mathsf{N_C}$ and $\mathsf{N_R}$, $\mathcal{EL}_\perp$ *concepts* are defined by the grammar $C, D ::= \top \mid \perp \mid A \mid C \sqcap D \mid \exists r.C$, where $A \in \mathsf{N_C}$ and $r \in \mathsf{N_R}$. In $\mathcal{ALC}$, we additionally have negation $\neg C$ as concept constructor. As usual, we then define $C \sqcup D := \neg(\neg C \sqcap \neg D)$ and $\forall r.C := \neg \exists r.\neg C$. An $\mathcal{ALC}$ *($\mathcal{EL}_\perp$) TBox* (a.k.a. *ontology*) $\mathcal{O}$ is a finite set of *general concept inclusions (GCIs*, a.k.a. *axioms*) $C \sqsubseteq D$ for $\mathcal{ALC}$ ($\mathcal{EL}_\perp$) concepts C and D. We denote by $\mathsf{sub}(\mathcal{O})$ the set of subconcepts of all concepts appearing in $\mathcal{O}$.

An *interpretation* is a pair $\mathcal{I} = (\Delta^\mathcal{I}, \cdot^\mathcal{I})$, where the *domain* $\Delta^\mathcal{I}$ is a non-empty set, and the *interpretation function* $\cdot^\mathcal{I}$ assigns to every concept name $A \in \mathsf{N_C}$ a set $A^\mathcal{I} \subseteq \Delta^\mathcal{I}$ and to every role name $r \in \mathsf{N_R}$ a binary relation $r^\mathcal{I} \subseteq \Delta^\mathcal{I} \times \Delta^\mathcal{I}$. This function is extended to complex concepts by defining $\top^\mathcal{I} := \Delta^\mathcal{I}$, $\perp^\mathcal{I} := \emptyset$, $(\exists r.C)^\mathcal{I} := \{d \in \Delta^\mathcal{I} \mid \exists e \in \Delta^\mathcal{I}. (d, e) \in r^\mathcal{I} \wedge e \in C^\mathcal{I}\}$, $(\neg C)^\mathcal{I} = \Delta^\mathcal{I} \setminus C^\mathcal{I}$, and $(C \sqcap D)^\mathcal{I} := C^\mathcal{I} \cap D^\mathcal{I}$. The interpretation $\mathcal{I}$ is a *model* of $C \sqsubseteq D$ if $C^\mathcal{I} \subseteq D^\mathcal{I}$ (written $\mathcal{I} \models C \sqsubseteq D$), and it is a model of an ontology $\mathcal{O}$ ($\mathcal{I} \models \mathcal{O}$) if it is a model of all axioms in $\mathcal{O}$. An ontology $\mathcal{O}$ is *consistent* if it has a model, and an axiom $C \sqsubseteq D$ is *entailed* by $\mathcal{O}$ (written $\mathcal{O} \models C \sqsubseteq D$) if every model of $\mathcal{O}$ is a model of $C \sqsubseteq D$; in this case, we also say that C is *subsumed* by D w.r.t. $\mathcal{O}$. The *classification* of $\mathcal{O}$ is the set $\mathsf{CL}(\mathcal{O}) := \{\langle C, D \rangle \mid C, D \in \mathsf{sub}(\mathcal{O}), \mathcal{O} \models C \sqsubseteq D\}$.[3] The three reasoning problems of deciding consistency, checking subsumption, and computing the classification are mutually reducible in polynomial time. Reasoning is P-complete in $\mathcal{EL}_\perp$ and ExpTime-complete in $\mathcal{ALC}$ [10].

2.2 Concrete Domains

Concrete domains have been introduced as a means to integrate reasoning about quantitative features of objects into DLs [9,12,24]. Given a set $\mathsf{N_P}$ of *concrete predicates* and an arity $\mathsf{ar}(P) \in \mathbb{N}$ for each $P \in \mathsf{N_P}$, a *concrete domain (CD)* $\mathcal{D} = (\Delta^\mathcal{D}, \cdot^\mathcal{D})$ over $\mathsf{N_P}$ consists of a set $\Delta^\mathcal{D}$ and relations $P^\mathcal{D} \subseteq (\Delta^\mathcal{D})^{\mathsf{ar}(P)}$ for all $P \in \mathsf{N_P}$. We assume that $\mathsf{N_P}$ always contains a nullary predicate $\perp$, interpreted as $\perp^\mathcal{D} := \emptyset$, and a unary predicate $\top$ interpreted as $\top^\mathcal{D} := \Delta^\mathcal{D}$. Given a set $\mathsf{N_V}$ of *variables*, a *constraint* $P(x_1, \ldots, x_{\mathsf{ar}(P)})$, with $P \in \mathsf{N_P}$ and $x_1, \ldots, x_{\mathsf{ar}(P)} \in \mathsf{N_V}$, is a predicate whose argument positions are filled with variables.

Example 1. The concrete domain $\mathcal{D}_{\mathbb{Q},diff}$ has the set $\mathbb{Q}$ of rational numbers as domain and, in addition to $\top$ and $\perp$, the concrete predicates $x = q$, $x > q$, and $x + q = y$, for constants $q \in \mathbb{Q}$, with their natural semantics [8]. For example, $(x + q = y)^{\mathcal{D}_{\mathbb{Q},diff}} = \{(p, r) \in \mathbb{Q} \times \mathbb{Q} \mid p + q = r\}$.[4]

The concrete domain $\mathcal{D}_{\mathbb{Q},lin}$ has the same domain as $\mathcal{D}_{\mathbb{Q},diff}$, but its predicates other than $\{\top, \perp\}$ are given by linear equations $\sum_{i=1}^n a_i x_i = b$, for $a_i, b \in \mathbb{Q}$, with the natural semantics [12], e.g. the linear equation $x + y - z = 0$ is interpreted as the ternary addition predicate $(x + y - z = 0)^{\mathcal{D}_{\mathbb{Q},lin}} = \{(p, q, s) \in \mathbb{Q}^3 \mid p + q = s\}$.

The expressivity of these two CDs is orthogonal: The $\mathcal{D}_{\mathbb{Q},diff}$ predicate $x > q$ cannot be expressed as a conjunction of constraints in $\mathcal{D}_{\mathbb{Q},lin}$, whereas the $\mathcal{D}_{\mathbb{Q},lin}$ predicate $x + y = 0$ cannot be expressed in $\mathcal{D}_{\mathbb{Q},diff}$. □

A constraint $\alpha = P(x_1, \ldots, x_{\mathsf{ar}(P)})$ is *satisfied* by an assignment $v \colon \mathsf{N_V} \to \Delta^\mathcal{D}$ (written $v \models \alpha$) if $(v(x_1), \ldots, v(x_{\mathsf{ar}(P)})) \in P^\mathcal{D}$. An *implication* is of the form $\gamma \to \delta$, where γ is a conjunction and δ a disjunction of constraints; it is *valid* if all assignments satisfying all constraints in γ also satisfy some constraint in δ (written $\mathcal{D} \models \gamma \to \delta$). A conjunction γ of constraints is *satisfiable* if $\gamma \to \perp$ is not valid. The CD $\mathcal{D}$ is *convex* if, for every valid implication $\gamma \to \delta$, there is a disjunct α in δ s.t. $\gamma \to \alpha$ is valid. It is *p-admissible* if it is convex and validity of implications is decidable in polynomial time. This condition has been introduced with the goal of obtaining tractable extensions of $\mathcal{EL}_\perp$ with concrete domains [8].

Example 2. The CDs $\mathcal{D}_{\mathbb{Q},diff}$ and $\mathcal{D}_{\mathbb{Q},lin}$ are both p-admissible, as shown in [8] and [12], respectively. However, if we combined their predicates into a single

---

[3] Often, the classification is done only for concept names in $\mathcal{O}$, but we use a variant that considers all subconcepts, as it is done by the $\mathcal{EL}_\perp$ reasoner ELK.

[4] The index *diff* in its name is motivated by the fact that such a predicate fixes the difference between the values of two variables.

CD, then we would lose convexity. In fact, $\mathcal{D}_{\mathbb{Q},diff}$ has the constraints $x > 0$ and $x = 0$. In addition, $y > 0$ (of $\mathcal{D}_{\mathbb{Q},diff}$) and $x + y = 0$ (of $\mathcal{D}_{\mathbb{Q},lin}$) express $x < 0$. Thus, the implication $x + y = 0 \to x > 0 \lor x = 0 \lor y > 0$ is valid, but none of the implications $x + y = 0 \to \alpha$ for $\alpha \in \{x > 0, \ x = 0, \ y > 0\}$ is valid. □

To integrate a concrete domain $\mathcal{D}$ into description logics, the most general approach uses role paths $r_1 \ldots r_k$ followed by a *concrete feature* f to instantiate the variables in constraints, where the r_i are roles and f is interpreted as a partial function $f^{\mathcal{I}}\colon \Delta^{\mathcal{I}} \to \Delta^{\mathcal{D}}$. Using the concrete domain $\mathcal{D}_{\mathbb{Q},lin}$, the concept Human $\sqcap \exists$age, parent age.$[2x - y = 0]$, for age being a concrete feature and parent a role name, describes humans with a parent that has twice their age.[5] However, in the presence of role paths, p-admissibility of the CD does not guarantee decidability of the extended DL. Even if we just take the ternary addition predicate of $\mathcal{D}_{\mathbb{Q},lin}$, the extension of $\mathcal{ALC}$ with it becomes undecidable [11], and the paper [12] exhibits a p-admissible CD whose integration into $\mathcal{EL}_\bot$ destroys decidability. Therefore, in this paper we disallow role paths, which effectively restricts concrete domain constraints to the feature values of single abstract objects. Under this restriction, the integration of a p-admissible CD leaves reasoning in P for $\mathcal{EL}_\bot$ [8] and in EXPTIME for $\mathcal{ALC}$ [23].[6] Disallowing role paths also enables us to simplify the syntax by treating variables directly as concrete features.

Formally, the description logics $\mathcal{EL}_\bot[\mathcal{D}]$ and $\mathcal{ALC}[\mathcal{D}]$ are obtained from $\mathcal{EL}_\bot$ and $\mathcal{ALC}$ by allowing constraints α from the CD $\mathcal{D}$ to be used as concepts, where we employ the notation $[\alpha]$ to distinguish constraints visually from classical concepts. Interpretations $\mathcal{I}$ are extended by associating to each variable $x \in \mathsf{N_V}$ a *partial* function $x^{\mathcal{I}}\colon \Delta^{\mathcal{I}} \to \Delta^{\mathcal{D}}$, and defining $[\alpha]^{\mathcal{I}}$ as the set of all $d \in \Delta^{\mathcal{I}}$ for which (a) the assignment $v_d^{\mathcal{I}}(x) := x^{\mathcal{I}}(d)$ is defined for all variables x occurring in α, and (b) $v_d^{\mathcal{I}} \models \alpha$.

Example 3. Extending the medical example from the introduction, we can state that, for a patient in the intensive care unit, the heart rate and blood pressure are monitored, using the GCI ICUpatient $\sqsubseteq [\top(\mathsf{hr})] \sqcap [\top(\mathsf{sys})] \sqcap [\top(\mathsf{dia})]$, which says that, for all elements of the concept ICUpatient, the values of the variables hr, sys, dia are defined. The pulse pressure pp can then be defined via ICUpatient $\sqsubseteq [\mathsf{sys} - \mathsf{dia} - \mathsf{pp} = 0]$. Similarly, the maximal heart rate can be defined by ICUpatient $\sqsubseteq [\mathsf{maxHR} + \mathsf{age} = 220]$. All the constraints employed in these GCIs are available in $\mathcal{D}_{\mathbb{Q},lin}$. One might now be tempted to use the GCI ICUpatient $\sqcap ([\mathsf{pp} > 50] \sqcup [\mathsf{hr} > \mathsf{maxHR}]) \sqsubseteq$ NeedAttention to say that ICU patients whose pulse pressure is larger than 50 mmHG or whose heart rate is larger than their maximal heart rate need attention. However, while $[\mathsf{pp} > 50]$ is a $\mathcal{D}_{\mathbb{Q},diff}$ constraint, it is not available in $\mathcal{D}_{\mathbb{Q},lin}$, and $[\mathsf{hr} > \mathsf{maxHR}]$ is available in neither. But we can raise an alert when the heart rate gets near the maximal one using $[\mathsf{maxHR} - \mathsf{hr} = 5] \sqsubseteq$ NeedAttention since it is a statement over $\mathcal{D}_{\mathbb{Q},lin}$. □

---

[5] See [23] for syntax and semantics of concepts using role paths.

[6] The result in [23] applies to p-admissible CDs $\mathcal{D}$ since it is easy to show that the extension of $\mathcal{D}$ with the negation of its predicates satisfies the required conditions.

3   Combined Concrete and Abstract Reasoning

We start by showing how classification in $\mathcal{EL}_\perp[\mathcal{D}]$ can be realized by interleaving a classifier for $\mathcal{EL}_\perp$ with a constraint solver for $\mathcal{D}$. Then we describe our constraint solvers for $\mathcal{D}_{\mathbb{Q},lin}$ and $\mathcal{D}_{\mathbb{Q},diff}$.

Algorithm 1: Classification algorithm for $\mathcal{EL}_\perp[\mathcal{D}]$

---

1 $\mathcal{O}' := \mathcal{O}^{-\mathcal{D}}, \mathcal{N} := \emptyset$
2 **while** $\mathcal{N} \neq \mathsf{CL}(\mathcal{O}')$ **do**
3 $\quad \mathcal{N} := \mathsf{CL}(\mathcal{O}')$
4 $\quad$ **foreach** $C \in \mathsf{sub}(\mathcal{O}^{-\mathcal{D}})$ **do**
5 $\quad\quad \mathbf{D}_C := \{\alpha \in \mathcal{C}(\mathcal{O}) \mid \langle C, A_\alpha \rangle \in \mathsf{CL}(\mathcal{O}')\}$
6 $\quad\quad$ **if** $\mathcal{D} \models \bigwedge \mathbf{D}_C \to \perp$ **then**
7 $\quad\quad\quad \mid \mathcal{O}' := \mathcal{O}' \cup \{\bigsqcap_{\alpha \in \mathbf{D}_C} A_\alpha \sqsubseteq \perp\}$
8 $\quad\quad$ **else**
9 $\quad\quad\quad \mid \mathcal{O}' := \mathcal{O}' \cup \{\bigsqcap_{\alpha \in \mathbf{D}_C} A_\alpha \sqsubseteq A_\beta \mid \beta \in \mathcal{C}(\mathcal{O}), \mathcal{D} \models \bigwedge \mathbf{D}_C \to \beta\}$
10 **return** $\mathcal{N}[A_\alpha \mapsto \alpha \mid \alpha \in \mathcal{C}(\mathcal{O})]$

3.1   Reasoning in $\mathcal{EL}_\perp[\mathcal{D}]$

The idea is that we can reduce reasoning in $\mathcal{EL}_\perp[\mathcal{D}]$ to reasoning in $\mathcal{EL}_\perp$ by abstracting away CD constraints by new concept names, and then adding GCIs that capture the interactions between constraints. To be more precise, let $\mathcal{D}$ be a p-admissible concrete domain, $\mathcal{O}$ an $\mathcal{EL}_\perp[\mathcal{D}]$ ontology, and $\mathcal{C}(\mathcal{O})$ the finite set of constraints occurring in $\mathcal{O}$. We consider the ontology $\mathcal{O}^{-\mathcal{D}}$ that results from replacing each $\alpha \in \mathcal{C}(\mathcal{O})$ by a fresh concept name A_α. Since $\mathcal{D}$ is p-admissible, the valid implications over the constraints in $\mathcal{C}(\mathcal{O})$ can then be fully encoded by the $\mathcal{EL}_\perp$ ontology

$$\mathcal{O}_\mathcal{D} := \{A_{\alpha_1} \sqcap \cdots \sqcap A_{\alpha_n} \sqsubseteq \perp \mid \alpha_1, \ldots, \alpha_n \in \mathcal{C}(\mathcal{O}), \ \mathcal{D} \models \alpha_1 \wedge \cdots \wedge \alpha_n \to \perp\} \ \cup$$
$$\{A_{\alpha_1} \sqcap \cdots \sqcap A_{\alpha_n} \sqsubseteq A_\beta \mid \alpha_1, \ldots, \alpha_n, \beta \in \mathcal{C}(\mathcal{O}), \ \mathcal{D} \models \alpha_1 \wedge \cdots \wedge \alpha_n \to \beta\}.$$

The definition of $\mathcal{O}_\mathcal{D}$ is an adaptation of the construction introduced in [23, Theorem 2.14] for the more general case of admissible concrete domains. The problem is, however, that $\mathcal{O}_\mathcal{D}$ is usually of exponential size since it considers all subsets $\{\alpha_1, \ldots, \alpha_n\}$ of $\mathcal{C}(\mathcal{O})$. Thus, the reasoning procedure for $\mathcal{EL}_\perp[\mathcal{D}]$ obtained by using $\mathcal{O}^{-\mathcal{D}} \cup \mathcal{O}_\mathcal{D}$ as an abstraction of $\mathcal{O}$ would also be exponential. To avoid this blow-up, we test implications of the form $\alpha_1 \wedge \cdots \wedge \alpha_n \to \perp$ and $\alpha_1 \wedge \cdots \wedge \alpha_n \to \beta$ for validity in $\mathcal{D}$ only if this information is needed, i.e., if there is a concept C that is subsumed by the concept names $A_{\alpha_1}, \ldots, A_{\alpha_n}$.

The resulting approach for classifying the $\mathcal{EL}_\perp[\mathcal{D}]$ ontology $\mathcal{O}$, i.e., for computing $\mathsf{CL}(\mathcal{O}) = \{\langle C, D \rangle \mid C, D \in \mathsf{sub}(\mathcal{O}), \ \mathcal{O} \models C \sqsubseteq D\}$ is described in Algorithm 1, where we assume that $\mathsf{CL}(\mathcal{O}')$ is computed by a polynomial-time $\mathcal{EL}_\perp$

classifier, such as ELK, and that the validity of implications in $\mathcal{D}$ is tested using an appropriate constraint solver for $\mathcal{D}$. Since $\mathcal{D}$ is assumed to be p-admissible, there is a constraint solver that can perform the required tests in polynomial time. Thus, we can show that this algorithm is sound and complete, and also runs in polynomial time.

Theorem 4. *Algorithm 1 computes* $\mathsf{CL}(\mathcal{O})$ *in polynomial time.*

Next, we show how constraint solvers for $\mathcal{D}_{\mathbb{Q},lin}$ and $\mathcal{D}_{\mathbb{Q},diff}$ can be obtained.

3.2   Reasoning in $\mathcal{D}_{\mathbb{Q},lin}$

To decide whether a finite conjunction of linear equations is satisfiable or whether it implies another equation, we can use Gaussian elimination [31], which iteratively eliminates variables from a set of linear constraints in order to solve them. Each elimination step consists of a choice of constraint α that is used to eliminate a variable x_i from another constraint γ by adding a suitable multiple $q \in \mathbb{Q}$ of α, such that, in the sum $\gamma + q\alpha$, the coefficient a_i of x_i becomes 0. This can be used to eliminate x_i from all constraints except α, which can then be discarded to obtain a system of constraints with one less variable. For example, using $\alpha\colon 2x + 3y = 5$ to eliminate x from $\gamma\colon 4x - 6y = 1$ using $q = -2$ yields the new equation $-12y = -9$.

To decide whether $\alpha_1 \wedge \cdots \wedge \alpha_n \to \bot$ is valid in $\mathcal{D}_{\mathbb{Q},lin}$, we must test whether the system of linear equations $\alpha_1, \ldots, \alpha_n$ is unsolvable. For this, we apply Gaussian elimination to this system. If we obtain a constraint of the form $0 = b$ for non-zero b, then the system is unsolvable; otherwise, we obtain $0 = 0$ after all variables have been eliminated, which shows solvability. In case $\alpha_1 \wedge \cdots \wedge \alpha_n \to \bot$ is not valid, Algorithm 1 requires us to test whether $\alpha_1 \wedge \cdots \wedge \alpha_n \to \beta$ is valid for constraints β different from $\bot$. This is the case iff the equation β is a linear combination of the equations $\alpha_1, \ldots, \alpha_n$. For this, we can also apply Gaussian elimination steps to eliminate all variables from β using the equations $\alpha_1, \ldots, \alpha_n$. If this results in the constraint $0 = 0$, it demonstrates that β is a linear combination; otherwise, it is not.

In principle, one could use standard libraries from linear algebra (e.g. for Gaussian elimination or the simplex method [15,28,31]) to implement a constraint solver for $\mathcal{D}_{\mathbb{Q},lin}$. We decided to create our own implementation based on Gaussian elimination, mainly for two reasons. First, most existing numerical libraries are optimized for performance and use floating-point arithmetic. Hence, the results may be erroneous due to repeated rounding [13]. Second, even if rational arithmetic with arbitrary precision is used [15], it is not trivial to extract from these tools a step-by-step account of how the verdict (valid or not) was obtained, which is a crucial requirement for extracting proofs.

3.3   Reasoning in $\mathcal{D}_{\mathbb{Q},diff}$

The constraints of $\mathcal{D}_{\mathbb{Q},diff}$ can in principle be simulated in *difference logic*, which consists of Boolean combinations of expressions of the form $x - y \leq q$, and for

$$\frac{x = q \quad x = p}{\bot} \; R_{\neq} : q \neq p \qquad \frac{x + q = y \quad y + p = z}{x + (q + p) = z} \; R_{+} \qquad \frac{}{x + 0 = x} \; R_0$$

$$\frac{x + q = y \quad x + p = y}{\bot} \; R_{\neq}^{+} : q \neq p \qquad \frac{x = q \quad y = p}{x + (p - q) = y} \; R_{-} \qquad \frac{x + q = y}{y + (-q) = x} \; R_{\leftrightarrow}$$

$$\frac{x = q \quad x > p}{\bot} \; R_{<} : q < p \qquad \frac{x = q \quad x + p = y}{y = q + p} \; R_{=} \qquad \frac{x > q \quad x + p = y}{y > q + p} \; R_{>}$$

Fig. 1. Saturation rules for $\mathcal{D}_{\mathbb{Q}, \mathit{diff}}$ constraints

---

Algorithm 2: Reasoning algorithm for $\mathcal{D}_{\mathbb{Q}, \mathit{diff}}$

Input: An implication $\bigwedge \mathbf{D} \to \beta$ in $\mathcal{D}_{\mathbb{Q}, \mathit{diff}}$
Output: true iff $\mathcal{D}_{\mathbb{Q}, \mathit{diff}} \models \bigwedge \mathbf{D} \to \beta$

1 $\mathbf{D}' := \mathsf{saturate}(\mathbf{D})$
2 **if** $\bot \in \mathbf{D}'$ **or** $\beta \in \mathbf{D}'$ **then return** true
3 **if** β is $x > q$ **then**
4   **if** $x = p \in \mathbf{D}'$ with $p > q$ **then return** true
5   **if** $x > p \in \mathbf{D}'$ with $p \geq q$ **then return** true
6 **return** false

---

which reasoning can be done using the Bellman-Ford algorithm for detecting negative cycles [7, 22]. However, it is again not clear how proofs for the validity of implications can be extracted from the run of such a solver. For this reason, we implemented a simple saturation procedure that uses the rules in Fig. 1 to derive implied constraints, where side conditions are shown in gray; these rules are similar to the rewrite rules for DL-Lite queries with CDs in [6]. We eagerly apply the rules $R_{\neq}$, $R_{<}$, and $R_{\neq}^{+}$, which means that we only need to keep one constraint of the form $x + q = y$ in memory, for each pair (x, y). Since $x > q$ implies $x > p$ for all $p < q$, it similarly suffices to remember one unary constraint of the form $x = q$ or $x > q$ for each variable x. Apart from the three rules deriving $\bot$, we can prioritize rules in the order R_{-}, $R_{\leftrightarrow}$, R_0, R_{+}, $R_{=}$, $R_{>}$, since none of the later rules can enable the applications of earlier rules to derive new constraints. The full decision procedure is described in Algorithm 2.

Theorem 5. *Algorithm 2 terminates in time polynomial in the size of* $\bigwedge \mathbf{D} \to \beta$ *and returns* true *iff* $\mathcal{D}_{\mathbb{Q}, \mathit{diff}} \models \bigwedge \mathbf{D} \to \beta$.

4   Proofs for $\mathcal{EL}_{\bot}[\mathcal{D}]$ Entailments

Our goal is now to use the procedures described in Sect. 3 to obtain separate proofs for the DL part and the CD part of an entailment, which we then want to combine into a single proof, as illustrated in Fig. 2.

Figure 2(a) shows an example of an ELK-proof, a proof generated by the ELK reasoner [18] for the final ontology $\mathcal{O}' \supseteq \mathcal{O}^{-\mathcal{D}}$ from Algorithm 1. The labels $R_{\sqsubseteq}$

$$\dfrac{C \sqsubseteq A_\alpha \quad C \sqsubseteq A_\beta}{C \sqsubseteq A_\alpha \sqcap A_\beta} \ \mathsf{R}^+_\sqcap \qquad A_\alpha \sqcap A_\beta \sqsubseteq A_\gamma \ (*)$$
$$\dfrac{}{C \sqsubseteq A_\gamma} \ \mathsf{R}_\sqsubseteq$$
(a)

(b)
$$\dfrac{2x + 3y = 5 \quad \dfrac{4y = 3 \quad -12y = -9}{4x - 6y = 1}}{\ } \begin{array}{l}[-3]\\{}[2,1]\end{array}$$

(c)
$$\Longrightarrow \qquad \dfrac{C \sqsubseteq [2x + 3y = 5] \quad \dfrac{C \sqsubseteq [4y = 3] \quad C \sqsubseteq [-12y = -9]}{}\begin{array}{l}[-3]\\{}[2,1]\end{array}}{C \sqsubseteq [4x - 6y = 1]}$$

Fig. 2. (a) $\mathcal{EL}_\perp$ proof over $\mathcal{O}'$, (b) $\mathcal{D}_{\mathbb{Q},lin}$ proof and (c) integrated $\mathcal{EL}_\perp[\mathcal{D}_{\mathbb{Q},lin}]$ proof.

and $\mathsf{R}^+_\sqcap$ indicate the rules from the internal calculus of ELK [19], and $(*)$ marks an axiom added by Algorithm 1, where α is $2x + 3y = 5$, β is $4y = 3$, and γ is $4x - 6y = 1$. We now describe how to obtain the proof (b) for the CD implication $\alpha \wedge \beta \to \gamma$, and how to integrate both proofs into the $\mathcal{EL}_\perp[\mathcal{D}_{\mathbb{Q},lin}]$ proof (c).

4.1 Proofs for the Concrete Domains

For $\mathcal{D}_{\mathbb{Q},diff}$, the saturation rules in Fig. 1 can be seen as proof steps. Thus, the algorithms in [1,2] can easily be adapted to extract $\mathcal{D}_{\mathbb{Q},diff}$ proofs. Inferences due to Lines 2, 4 and 5 in Algorithm 2 are captured by the following additional rules:

$$\dfrac{\perp}{\beta} \ \mathsf{R}_\perp \qquad \dfrac{x = p}{x > q} \ \mathsf{R}^+_> : p > q \qquad \dfrac{x > p}{x > q} \ \mathsf{R}^-_> : p \geq q$$

For $\mathcal{D}_{\mathbb{Q},lin}$, inferences are Gaussian elimination steps that derive $\sigma + c\rho$ from linear constraints σ and ρ, and we label them with $[1, c]$ to indicate that σ is multiplied by 1 and ρ by c. This directly gives us a proof if the conclusion is $\perp$ (or, equivalently, $0 = b$ for non-zero b). However, proofs for implications $\bigwedge \mathbf{D} \to \gamma$ need to be treated differently. The Gaussian method would use $\mathbf{D}$ to eliminate the variables from γ to show that γ is a linear combination of $\mathbf{D}$, and would yield a rather uninformative proof with final conclusion $0 = 0$. To obtain a proof with γ as conclusion, we reverse the proof direction by recursively applying the following transformation starting from an inference step that has γ as a premise:

$$\dfrac{\sigma \quad \rho}{\tau} \ [1, c] \qquad \rightsquigarrow \qquad \dfrac{\rho \quad \tau}{\sigma} \ [-c, 1] \qquad\qquad (\dagger)$$

Then we transform the next inference to obtain an inference that has τ as the conclusion, and continue this process until $0 = 0$ becomes a leaf, which we then remove from the proof.

In our example, we would start with the following "proof" for $\mathcal{D} \models \alpha \wedge \beta \to \gamma$:

$$\dfrac{\dfrac{4x - 6y = 1 \quad 2x + 3y = 5}{-12y = -9} \ [1, -2] \quad 4y = 3}{0 = 0} \ [1, 3]$$

After applying two transformation steps $(\dagger)$, we obtain the proof in Fig. 2(b).

4.2 Combining the Proofs

It remains to integrate the concrete domain proofs into the DL proof over $\mathcal{O}^{-\mathcal{D}}$. As a consequence of Algorithm 1, in Fig. 2(a), the introduced concept names A_α, A_β, A_γ occur in axioms with the same left-hand side C. The idea is to add this *DL context* C to every step of the CD proof (b) to obtain the $\mathcal{EL}_\perp[\mathcal{D}]$-proof (c). This proof replaces the applications of $\mathsf{R}_\sqcap^+$ and $\mathsf{R}_\sqsubseteq$ in the original DL proof (a), and both (a) and (c) have essentially the same leafs and conclusion, except that the auxiliary concept names $A_\alpha, A_\beta, A_\gamma$ were replaced by the original constraints and the auxiliary axiom $(*)$ was eliminated. In general, such proofs can be obtained by simple post-processing of proofs obtained separately from the DL and CD reasoning components, and we conjecture that the integrated proof (c) is easier to understand in practice than the separate proofs (a) and (b), since the connection between the DL and CD contexts is shown in all steps.

Lemma 6. *Let $\mathcal{O}'$ be the final ontology computed in Algorithm 1. Given an* ELK*-proof $\mathcal{P}'$ for $\mathcal{O}' \models C^{-\mathcal{D}} \sqsubseteq D^{-\mathcal{D}}$ and proofs for all $\mathcal{D}$-implications $\alpha_1 \wedge \cdots \wedge \alpha_n \rightarrow \beta$ used in $\mathcal{P}'$, we can construct in polynomial time an $\mathcal{EL}_\perp[\mathcal{D}]$-proof for $\mathcal{O} \models C \sqsubseteq D$.*

5 Generating Proofs for $\mathcal{ALC}[\mathcal{D}]$

For $\mathcal{ALC}[\mathcal{D}]$, a black-box algorithm as for $\mathcal{EL}_\perp[\mathcal{D}]$ is not feasible, even though we consider only p-admissible concrete domains and no role paths. The intuitive reason is that $\mathcal{ALC}$ itself is not convex, and we cannot simply use the classification result to determine which implications $\alpha_1 \wedge \ldots \wedge \alpha_n \rightarrow \beta$ in $\mathcal{D}$ are relevant. On the other hand, adding all valid implications is not practical, as there can be exponentially many. We thus need a glass-box approach, i.e. a modified $\mathcal{ALC}$ reasoning procedure that determines the relevant CD implications on-demand.

Moreover, to obtain proofs for $\mathcal{ALC}[\mathcal{D}]$, we need a reasoning procedure that derives new axioms from old ones, and thus classical tableau methods [14,27] are not suited. However, existing consequence-based classification methods for $\mathcal{ALC}$ [30] use complicated calculi that are not needed for our purposes. Instead, we use a modified version of a calculus from [21], which uses only three inference rules, but performs double exponentially many inferences in the worst case. Our modification ensures that we perform at most exponentially many inferences, and are thus worst-case optimal for the ExpTime-complete $\mathcal{ALC}[\mathcal{D}]$.

5.1 A Simple Resolution Calculus for $\mathcal{ALC}$

The calculus represents GCIs $\top \sqsubseteq L_1 \sqcup \cdots \sqcup L_n$ as *clauses* of the form

$$L_1 \sqcup \ldots \sqcup L_n \qquad L_i ::= A \mid \neg A \mid \exists r.D \mid \forall r.D$$

where $n \geq 0$, $A, D \in \mathsf{N_C}$ and $r \in \mathsf{N_R}$. To decide $\mathcal{O} \models A \sqsubseteq B$, we normalize $\mathcal{O}$ into a set of clauses, introducing fresh concept names for concepts under role

$$\mathbf{A1}: \frac{C_1 \sqcup A, \quad C_2 \sqcup \neg A}{C_1 \sqcup C_2} \qquad \mathbf{r1}: \frac{C \sqcup \exists r.D, \quad C_1 \sqcup \forall r.D_1, \ldots, C_n \sqcup \forall r.D_n, \quad \neg D_1 \sqcup \ldots \sqcup \neg D_n}{C \sqcup C_1 \sqcup \ldots \sqcup C_n}$$

$$\mathbf{r2}: \frac{C \sqcup \exists r.D, \quad C_1 \sqcup \forall r.D_1, \ldots, C_n \sqcup \forall r.D_n, \quad \neg D \sqcup \neg D_1 \sqcup \ldots \sqcup \neg D_n}{C \sqcup C_1 \sqcup \ldots \sqcup C_n}$$

Fig. 3. Inference rules for $\mathcal{ALC}$ clauses.

restrictions, and add two special clauses $A_{\mathrm{LHS}} \sqcup A$, $A_{\mathrm{RHS}} \sqcup \neg B$, with fresh concept names A_{LHS} and A_{RHS}. The latter are used to track relevant inferences for constructing the final proof, for which we transform all clauses back into GCIs.

Our inference rules are shown in Fig. 3. **A1** is the standard resolution rule from first-order logic, which is responsible for direct inferences on concept names. The rules **r1** and **r2** perform inferences on role restrictions. They consider an existential role restriction $\exists r.D$ and a (possibly empty) set of value restrictions over r, whose conjunction is unsatisfiable due to a clause over the nested concepts. The concept D may not be relevant for this, which is why there are two rules. Those rules are the main difference to the original calculus in [21], where a more expensive, incremental mechanism was used instead. To transform this calculus into a practical method, we use optimizations common for resolution-based reasoning in first-order logic: ordered resolution, a set-of-support strategy, as well as backward and forward subsumption deletion. In particular, our set-of-support strategy starts with a set of *support clauses* containing only the clauses with A_{LHS} and A_{RHS}. Inferences are always performed with at least one clause from this set, and the conclusion becomes a new support clause. If a support clause contains a literal $\exists r.D/\forall r.D$, we also add all clauses containing $\neg D$ as support clauses [20].

5.2 Incorporating the Concrete Domain and Creating the Proof

To incorporate concrete domains, we again work on the translation $\mathcal{O}^{-\mathcal{D}}$ replacing each constraint α with A_α. In $\mathcal{ALC}[\mathcal{D}]$, constraints can also occur in negated form, which means that we can have literals $\neg A_\alpha$ expressing the negation of a constraint. We keep track of the set $\mathbf{D}$ of concrete domain constraints α for which A_α occurs positively in a support clause. We then use the proof procedure for $\mathcal{D}$ (see Sect. 4.1) to generate all implications of the form $\alpha_1 \wedge \ldots \wedge \alpha_n \rightarrow \beta$, where $\{\alpha_1, \ldots, \alpha_n\} \subseteq \mathbf{D}$ is subset-minimal, for which we add the corresponding clauses $\neg A_{\alpha_1} \sqcup \ldots \sqcup \neg A_{\alpha_n} \sqcup A_\beta$. If $\beta = \bot$, we instead add $\neg A_{\alpha_1} \sqcup \ldots \sqcup \neg A_{\alpha_n}$.

Theorem 7. *Let $\mathcal{O}$ be an $\mathcal{ALC}[\mathcal{D}]$ ontology and $\mathcal{N}$ the normalization of $\mathcal{O}^{-\mathcal{D}}$. Then our method takes at most exponential time, and it derives $A_{LHS} \sqcup A_{RHS}$ or a subclause from $\mathcal{N}$ iff $\mathcal{O} \models C \sqsubseteq D$.*

Proofs generated using the calculus operate on the level of clauses. We transform them into proofs of $\mathcal{O}^{-\mathcal{D}} \models A \sqsubseteq B$ by 1) adding inference steps that reflect the normalization, 2) if necessary, adding an inference to produce $A_{\mathrm{LHS}} \sqcup A_{\mathrm{RHS}}$

from a subclause 3) replacing A_{LHS} by $\neg A$ and A_{RHS} by B, 4) replacing all other introduced concept names by the complex concepts they were introduced for, and 5) transforming clauses into more human-readable GCIs using some simple rewriting rules (see [4] for details). In the resulting proof, the initial clauses $A \sqcup A_{LHS}$ and $\neg B \sqcup A_{RHS}$ then correspond to the tautologies $A \sqsubseteq A$ and $B \sqsubseteq B$. To get a proof for $\mathcal{O} \models A \sqsubseteq B$, we use a procedure similar to the one from Sect. 4.2 to integrate concrete domain proofs. Because the integration requires only simple structural transformations, the complexity of computing the combined proofs is determined by the corresponding complexities for the DL and the concrete domain. We can thus extend the approaches from [1,2] to obtain complexity bounds for finding proofs of small size and depth.

Theorem 8. *For $\mathcal{D} \in \{\mathcal{D}_{\mathbb{Q},lin}, \mathcal{D}_{\mathbb{Q},diff}\}$, deciding the existence of a proof of at most a given size can be done in* NP *for $\mathcal{EL}_\perp[\mathcal{D}]$, and in* NExpTime *for $\mathcal{ALC}[\mathcal{D}]$. For proof depth, the corresponding problem is in* P *for $\mathcal{EL}_\perp[\mathcal{D}_{\mathbb{Q},diff}]$, in* NP *for $\mathcal{EL}_\perp[\mathcal{D}_{\mathbb{Q},lin}]$, and in* ExpTime *for $\mathcal{ALC}[\mathcal{D}]$ (for both concrete domains).*

6   Implementation and Experiments

We implemented the algorithms described above and evaluated their performance and the produced proofs on the self-created benchmarks *Diet*, *Artificial*, *D-Sbj* and *D-Obj*, each of which consists of multiple instances scaling from small to medium-sized ontologies. The latter two benchmarks are formulated in $\mathcal{EL}_\perp[\mathcal{D}_{\mathbb{Q},diff}]$, the rest in $\mathcal{EL}_\perp[\mathcal{D}_{\mathbb{Q},lin}]$. Our tool is written using Java 8 and Scala. We used ELK 0.5, LETHE 0.85 and OWL API 4. The experiments were performed on Debian Linux 10 (24 Intel Xeon E5-2640 CPUs, 2.50 GHz) with 25 GB maximum heap size and a timeout of 3 min for each task. Figure 4 shows the runtimes of the approaches for $\mathcal{EL}_\perp[\mathcal{D}]$ from Sects. 3 and 4 for reasoning and explanation depending on the *problem size*, which counts all occurrences of concept names, role names, and features in the ontology. A more detailed description of the benchmarks and results can be found in [4].

We observe that pure reasoning time (crosses in Fig. 4) scales well w.r.t. problem size. Producing proofs was generally more costly than reasoning, but the times were mostly reasonable. However, there are several *Artificial* instances for which the proof construction times out (blue dots). This is due to the nondeterministic choices of which linear constraints to use to eliminate the next variable, which we resolve using the Dijkstra-like algorithm described in [2], which results in an exponential runtime in the worst case. Another downside is that some proofs were very large (> 2000 inference steps in *D-Obj*). However, we designed our benchmarks specifically to challenge the CD reasoning and proof generation capabilities (in particular, nearly all constraints in each ontology are necessary to entail the target axiom), and these results may improve for realistic ontologies.

Further analysis revealed that the reasoning times were often largely due to the calls to ELK (ranging from 23% in *Diet* to 75% in *Artificial*), which shows that the CD reasoning does not add a huge overhead, unless the number of

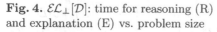

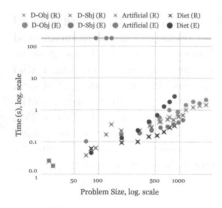
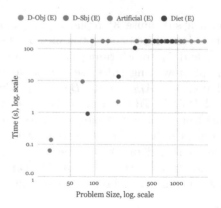

Fig. 4. $\mathcal{EL}_\perp[\mathcal{D}]$: time for reasoning (R) and explanation (E) vs. problem size

Fig. 5. $\mathcal{ALC}[\mathcal{D}]$: total reasoning and explanation time vs. problem size

variables per constraint grows very large (e.g. up to 88 in *Diet*). In comparison to the incremental use of ELK as a black-box reasoner, the hypothetical "ideal" case of calling ELK only once on the final saturated ontology $\mathcal{O}'$ would not save a lot of time (average gain ranging from 42% in *Diet* to 14% in *D-Obj*), which shows that the incremental nature of our approach is also not a bottleneck.

Figure 5 shows the runtime of the $\mathcal{ALC}[\mathcal{D}]$ calculus from Sect. 5. As expected, it performs worse than the dedicated $\mathcal{EL}_\perp[\mathcal{D}]$ algorithms. In particular, currently there is a bottleneck for the $\mathcal{D}_{\mathbb{Q},diff}$ benchmarks (*D-Sbj* and *D-Obj*) that is due an inefficiency in the computation of the relevant CD implications $\alpha_1 \wedge \cdots \wedge \alpha_n \rightarrow \beta$. In order to evaluate the increased expressivity supported by the $\mathcal{ALC}[\mathcal{D}]$ reasoner, we have also incorporated axioms with negation and universal restrictions into the *Artificial* benchmark. Currently, however, the reasoner can solve only the smallest such instance before reaching the timeout.

We also compared our CD reasoning algorithms with Z3 [28], which supports linear arithmetic (for $\mathcal{D}_{\mathbb{Q},lin}$) and difference logic (for $\mathcal{D}_{\mathbb{Q},diff}$). Ignoring the overhead stemming from the interface between Java and C++, the runtime of both approaches was generally in the same range, but our algorithms were faster on many CD reasoning problems. This may be due to the fact that, although our algorithms for $\mathcal{D}_{\mathbb{Q},lin}$ and $\mathcal{D}_{\mathbb{Q},diff}$ are not optimized very much, they are nevertheless tailored towards very specific convex fragments: linear arithmetic with only $=$, and difference logic with only $x + q = y$ and $x > q$, respectively.

7 Conclusion

We have shown that it is feasible to support p-admissible concrete domains in DL reasoning algorithms, and even to produce integrated proofs for explaining consequences in the DLs $\mathcal{EL}_\perp[\mathcal{D}]$ and $\mathcal{ALC}[\mathcal{D}]$, for the p-admissible concrete domains $\mathcal{D}_{\mathbb{Q},lin}$ and $\mathcal{D}_{\mathbb{Q},diff}$. In this work, we have restricted our attention to ontologies containing only GCIs (i.e., TBoxes) and to classification as the main reasoning problem. However, the extension of our methods to data and reasoning about individuals, e.g. fred : ICUpatient $\sqcap$ [hr = 90], encoded in so-called *ABoxes* [10], is straightforward. Likewise, the approach for computing $\mathcal{EL}_\perp[\mathcal{D}]$ proofs can be generalized to use other reasoning calculi for $\mathcal{EL}_\perp$ instead of the one employed by ELK, which makes very small proof steps and thus generates rather large proofs.

One major problem with using proofs to explain consequences is that they may become quite large. This problem already occurs for pure DLs without CDs, and has also shown up in some of our benchmarks in this paper. One possibility to alleviate this problem is to use an interactive proof visualization tool like Evonne [26], which allows zooming into parts of the proof and hiding uninteresting or already inspected parts. Since the integrated proofs that we generate have the same shape as pure DL proofs, they can be displayed using Evonne. It would, however, be interesting to add features tailored to CD reasoning, such as visualizing the solution space of a system of linear equations.

In Example 3, we have seen that it would be useful to have the constraints of $\mathcal{D}_{Q,lin}$ and $\mathcal{D}_{Q,diff}$ available in a single CD. Such a CD $\mathcal{D}$ would still preserve decidability if integrated into $\mathcal{ALC}$. However, since $\mathcal{D}$ is no longer convex, our reasoning approach for $\mathcal{ALC}[\mathcal{D}]$ does not apply. Thus, it would also be interesting to see whether this approach can be extended to *admissible* CDs $\mathcal{D}$ [9,23], i.e. CDs that are closed under negation and for which satisfiability of sets of constraints is decidable.

Acknowledgments. This work was supported by the DFG grant 389792660 as part of TRR 248 (https://perspicuous-computing.science).

References

1. Alrabbaa, C., Baader, F., Borgwardt, S., Koopmann, P., Kovtunova, A.: Finding small proofs for description logic entailments: theory and practice. In: LPAR (2020). https://doi.org/10.29007/nhpp

2. Alrabbaa, C., Baader, F., Borgwardt, S., Koopmann, P., Kovtunova, A.: Finding good proofs for description logic entailments using recursive quality measures. In: CADE (2021). https://doi.org/10.1007/978-3-030-79876-5_17

3. Alrabbaa, C., Baader, F., Borgwardt, S., Koopmann, P., Kovtunova, A.: Combining proofs for description logic and concrete domain reasoning - RuleML+RR23 - Resources (2023). https://doi.org/10.5281/zenodo.8208780

4. Alrabbaa, C., Baader, F., Borgwardt, S., Koopmann, P., Kovtunova, A.: Combining proofs for description logic and concrete domain reasoning (technical report) (2023). https://doi.org/10.48550/arXiv.2308.03705

5. Alrabbaa, C., et al.: In the head of the beholder: comparing different proof representations. In: RuleML+RR (2022). https://doi.org/10.1007/978-3-031-21541-4_14

6. Alrabbaa, C., Koopmann, P., Turhan, A.: Practical query rewriting for DL-Lite with numerical predicates. In: GCAI (2019). https://doi.org/10.29007/gqll

7. Armando, A., Castellini, C., Giunchiglia, E., Maratea, M.: A SAT-based decision procedure for the Boolean combination of difference constraints. In: SAT (2004). https://doi.org/10.1007/11527695_2

8. Baader, F., Brandt, S., Lutz, C.: Pushing the $\mathcal{EL}$ envelope. In: IJCAI (2005). http://ijcai.org/Proceedings/05/Papers/0372.pdf
9. Baader, F., Hanschke, P.: A scheme for integrating concrete domains into concept languages. In: IJCAI (1991). http://ijcai.org/Proceedings/91-1/Papers/070.pdf
10. Baader, F., Horrocks, I., Lutz, C., Sattler, U.: An Introduction to Description Logic. Cambridge University Press, Cambridge (2017). https://doi.org/10.1017/9781139025355
11. Baader, F., Rydval, J.: Description logics with concrete domains and general concept inclusions revisited. In: IJCAR (2020). https://doi.org/10.1007/978-3-030-51074-9_24
12. Baader, F., Rydval, J.: Using model theory to find decidable and tractable description logics with concrete domains. JAR **66**(3), 357–407 (2022). https://doi.org/10.1007/s10817-022-09626-2
13. Barlow, J.L., Bareiss, E.H.: Probabilistic error analysis of Gaussian elimination in floating point and logarithmic arithmetic. Computing **34**(4), 349–364 (1985). https://doi.org/10.1007/BF02251834
14. Donini, F.M., Massacci, F.: ExpTime tableaux for $\mathcal{ALC}$. AIJ **124**(1), 87–138 (2000). https://doi.org/10.1016/S0004-3702(00)00070-9
15. Dutertre, B., de Moura, L.M.: A fast linear-arithmetic solver for DPLL(T). In: CAV (2006). https://doi.org/10.1007/11817963_11
16. Haarslev, V., Möller, R., Wessel, M.: The description logic $\mathcal{ALCNH}_{\mathcal{R}+}$ extended with concrete domains: a practically motivated approach. In: IJCAR (2001). https://doi.org/10.1007/3-540-45744-5_4
17. Horridge, M., Parsia, B., Sattler, U.: Justification oriented proofs in OWL. In: ISWC (2010). https://doi.org/10.1007/978-3-642-17746-0_23
18. Kazakov, Y., Klinov, P., Stupnikov, A.: Towards reusable explanation services in Protege. In: DL (2017). https://ceur-ws.org/Vol-1879/paper31.pdf
19. Kazakov, Y., Krötzsch, M., Simančík, F.: The incredible ELK. J. Autom. Reason. **53**(1), 1–61 (2013). https://doi.org/10.1007/s10817-013-9296-3
20. Koopmann, P., Del-Pinto, W., Tourret, S., Schmidt, R.A.: Signature-based abduction for expressive description logics. In: KR (2020). https://doi.org/10.24963/kr.2020/59
21. Koopmann, P., Schmidt, R.A.: Uniform interpolation of $\mathcal{ALC}$-ontologies using fixpoints. In: FroCoS (2013). https://doi.org/10.1007/978-3-642-40885-4_7
22. Kroening, D., Strichman, O.: Decision Procedures - An Algorithmic Point of View, 2nd edn. EATCS (2016). https://doi.org/10.1007/978-3-662-50497-0
23. Lutz, C.: The complexity of description logics with concrete domains. Ph.D. thesis (2002). https://nbn-resolving.org/urn:nbn:de:hbz:82-opus-3032
24. Lutz, C.: Description logics with concrete domains - a survey. In: Advances in Modal Logic, vol. 4 (2002). http://www.aiml.net/volumes/volume4/Lutz.ps
25. Lutz, C.: NExpTime-complete description logics with concrete domains. ACM TOCL **5**(4), 669–705 (2004). https://doi.org/10.1145/1024922.1024925
26. Méndez, J., Alrabbaa, C., Koopmann, P., Langner, R., Baader, F., Dachselt, R.: Evonne: a visual tool for explaining reasoning with OWL ontologies and supporting interactive debugging. CGF (2023). https://doi.org/10.1111/cgf.14730
27. Motik, B., Shearer, R., Horrocks, I.: Hypertableau reasoning for description logics. JAIR **36**, 165–228 (2009). https://doi.org/10.1613/jair.2811
28. de Moura, L.M., Bjørner, N.S.: Z3: an efficient SMT solver. In: TACAS (2008). https://doi.org/10.1007/978-3-540-78800-3_24
29. Pan, J.Z., Horrocks, I.: Reasoning in the $\mathcal{SHOQ}(D_n)$ description logic. In: DL (2002). https://ceur-ws.org/Vol-53/Pan-Horrocks-shoqdn-2002.ps

30. Simancik, F., Kazakov, Y., Horrocks, I.: Consequence-based reasoning beyond Horn ontologies. In: IJCAI (2011). https://doi.org/10.5591/978-1-57735-516-8/IJCAI11-187
31. Turner, P.R.: Gauss elimination: workhorse of linear algebra (1995). https://apps.dtic.mil/sti/pdfs/ADA313547.pdf. NAWCADPAX-96-194-TR

Notation3 as an Existential Rule Language

Dörthe Arndt[1]($\boxtimes$) and Stephan Mennicke[2]

[1] Computational Logic Group, Technische Universität Dresden, Dresden, Germany
dorthe.arndt@tu-dresden.de
[2] Knowledge-Based Systems Group, Technische Universität Dresden, Dresden, Germany
stephan.mennicke@tu-dresden.de

Abstract. Notation3 Logic (N3) is an extension of RDF which allows the user to write rules introducing new blank nodes to RDF graphs. Many applications (e.g., ontology mapping) rely on this feature as blank nodes – used directly or in auxiliary constructs – are omnipresent on the Web. However, the number of fast N3 reasoners fully supporting blank node introduction is rather limited. On the other hand, there are engines like VLog or Nemo not directly supporting Semantic Web rule formats but developed for very similar constructs: existential rules. In this paper we investigate the relation between N3 rules with blank nodes in their heads and existential rules. We identify a subset of N3 which can be mapped directly to existential rules and define such a mapping preserving the equivalence of N3 formulae. To also illustrate that N3 reasoning could benefit from our translation, we employ this mapping in an implementation to compare the performance of the N3 reasoners EYE and cwm to VLog and Nemo on N3 rules and their mapped counterparts. Our tests show that the existential rule reasoners perform particularly well for use cases containing many facts while the EYE reasoner is very fast when dealing with a high number of dependent rules. We thus provide a tool enabling the Semantic Web community to directly use existing and future existential rule reasoners and benefit from the findings of this active community.

Keywords: Notation3 · RDF · Blank Nodes · Existential rules

1 Introduction

Notation3 Logic (N3) [9,28] is an extension of the Resource Description Framework (RDF) which allows the user to quote graphs, to express rules, and to apply built-in functions on the components of RDF triples. Facilitated by reasoners like cwm [7], Data-Fu [21], or EYE [27], N3 rules directly consume and produce RDF graphs. This makes N3 well-suited for rule exchange on the Web. N3 supports the introduction of new blank nodes through rules, that is, if a blank node appears in the head[1] of a rule, each new match for the rule body produces a new instance of the rule's head containing

---

[1] To stay consistent across frameworks, we use the terms *head* and *body* throughout the whole paper. The head is the part of the rule occurring at the end of the implication arrow, the body the part at its beginning (backward rules: "head ← body", forward rules: "body → head").

A. Fensel et al. (Eds.): RuleML+RR 2023, LNCS 14244, pp. 70–85, 2023.
https://doi.org/10.1007/978-3-031-45072-3_5

fresh blank nodes. This feature is interesting for many use cases – mappings between different vocabularies include blank nodes, workflow composition deals with unknown existing instances [26] – but it also impedes reasoning tasks: from a logical point of view these rules contain existentially quantified variables in their heads. Reasoning with such rules is known to be undecidable in general and very complex on decidable cases [5,25].

Even though recent projects like jen3[2] or RoXi [12] aim at improving the situation, the number of fast N3 reasoners fully supporting blank node introduction is low. This is different for reasoners acting on existential rules, a concept very similar to blank-node-producing rules in N3, but developed for databases. Sometimes it is necessary to uniquely identify data by a value that is not already part of the target database. One tool to achieve that are *labeled nulls* which – just as blank nodes – indicate *the existence* of a value. This problem from databases and the observation that rules may provide a powerful, yet declarative, means of computing has led to more extensive studies of existential rules [5,14]. Many reasoners like for example VLog [15] or Nemo [23] apply dedicated strategies to optimize reasoning with existential rules.

This paper aims to make existing and future optimizations on existential rules usable in the Semantic Web. We introduce a subset of N3 supporting existential quantification but ignoring features of the language not covered in existential rules, like for example built-in functions or lists. We provide a mapping between this logic and existential rules: The mapping and its inverse both preserve equivalences of formulae, enabling N3 reasoning via existential rule technologies. We implement this mapping in python and compare the reasoning performance of the existential rule reasoners Vlog and Nemo, and the N3 reasoners EYE and cwm for two benchmarks: one applying a fixed set of rules on a varying size of facts, and one applying a varying set of highly dependent rules to a fixed set of facts. In our tests VLog and Nemo together with our mapping outperform the traditional N3 reasoners EYE and cwm when dealing with a high number of facts while EYE is the fastest on large dependent rule sets. This is a strong indication that our implementation will be of practical use when extended by further features.

We motivate our approach by providing examples of N3 and existential rule formulae, and discuss how these are connected, in Sect. 2. In Sect. 3 we provide a more formal definition of Existential N3 ($N3^\exists$), introduce its semantics and discuss its properties. We then formally introduce existential rules, provide the mapping from $N3^\exists$ into this logic, and prove its truth-preserving properties in Sect. 4. Section 5 discusses our implementation and provides an evaluation of the different reasoners. In Sect. 6 we discuss the related work to then conclude our paper with Sect. 7. We outsourced all formal proofs to a technical appendix [3]. Furthermore, the code needed for reproducing our experiments is available on GitHub (https://github.com/smennicke/n32rules).

2 Motivation

N3 has been inroduced as a rule-based extension of RDF. As in RDF, N3 knowledge is stated in triples consisting of *subject*, *predicate*, and *object*. In ground triples these can either be Internationalized Resource Identifiers (IRIs) or literals. The expression

$$:\texttt{lucy} :\texttt{knows} :\texttt{tom}. \tag{1}$$

---

[2] https://github.com/william-vw/jen3.

means[3] that *"lucy knows tom"*. Sets of triples are interpreted as their conjunction. Like RDF, N3 supports blank nodes, usually starting with _:, which stand for (implicitly) existentially quantified variables. The statement

$$:\texttt{lucy} :\texttt{knows} \_:\texttt{x}. \tag{2}$$

means *"there exists someone who is known by lucy"*. N3 furthermore supports implicitly universally quantified variables, indicated by a leading question mark (?), and implications which are stated using graphs, i.e., sets of triples, surrounded by curly braces ({}) as body and head connected via an arrow (=>). The formula

$$\{:\texttt{lucy} :\texttt{knows} ?\texttt{x}\}=>\{?\texttt{x} :\texttt{knows} :\texttt{lucy}\}. \tag{3}$$

means that *"everyone known by Lucy also knows her"*. Furthermore, N3 allows the use of blank nodes in rules. These blank nodes are not quantified outside the rule like the universal variables, but in the rule part they occur in, that is either in its body or its head.

$$\{?\texttt{x} :\texttt{knows} :\texttt{tom}\}=>\{?\texttt{x} :\texttt{knows} \_:\texttt{y}. \_:\texttt{y} :\texttt{name"Tom"}\}. \tag{4}$$

means *"everyone knowing Tom knows someone whose name is Tom"*.

This last example shows, that N3 supports rules concluding the *existence* of certain terms which makes it easy to express them as *existential rules*. An existential rule is a first-order sentence of the form

$$\forall \mathbf{x}, \mathbf{y}. \, \varphi[\mathbf{x}, \mathbf{y}] \rightarrow \exists \mathbf{z}. \, \psi[\mathbf{y}, \mathbf{z}] \tag{5}$$

where $\mathbf{x}, \mathbf{y}, \mathbf{z}$ are mutually disjoint lists of variables, φ and ψ are conjunctions of atoms using only variables from the given lists, and φ is referred to as the *body* of the rule while ψ is called the *head*. Using the basic syntactic shape of (5) we go through all the example N3 formulae (1)–(4) again and represent them as existential rules. To allow for the full flexibility of N3 and RDF triples, we translate each RDF triple, just like the one in (1) into a first-order atom $tr(:\texttt{lucy}, :\texttt{knows}, :\texttt{tom})$. Here, tr is a ternary predicate holding subject, predicate, and object of a given RDF triple. This standard translation makes triple predicates (e.g., :knows) accessible as terms. First-order atoms are also known as *facts*, finite sets of facts are called *databases*, and (possibly infinite) sets of facts are called *instances*. Existential rules are evaluated over instances (cf. Sect. 4).

Compared to other rule languages, the distinguishing feature of existential rules is the use of existentially quantified variables in the head of rules (cf. $\mathbf{z}$ in (5)). The N3 formula in (2) contains an existentially quantified variable and can, thus, be encoded as

$$\rightarrow \exists x. \, tr(:\texttt{lucy}, :\texttt{knows}, x) \tag{6}$$

Rule (6) has an empty body, which means the head is unconditionally true. Rule (6) is satisfied on instances containing any fact $tr(:\texttt{lucy}, :\texttt{knows}, \_)$ (e.g., $tr(:\texttt{lucy}, :\texttt{knows}, :\texttt{tim})$ so that variable x can be bound to :tim). The implication of (3) has

$$\forall x. \, tr(:\texttt{lucy}, :\texttt{knows}, x) \rightarrow tr(x, :\texttt{knows}, :\texttt{lucy}) \tag{7}$$

---

[3] We omit name spaces for brevity.

as its (existential) rule counterpart, which does not contain any existentially quantified variables. Rule (7) is satisfied in the instance

$$\mathcal{I}_1 = \{tr(\texttt{:lucy}, \texttt{:knows}, \texttt{:tom}), tr(\texttt{:tom}, \texttt{:knows}, \texttt{:lucy})\}$$

but not in

$$\mathcal{K}_1 = \{tr(\texttt{:lucy}, \texttt{:knows}, \texttt{:tom})\}$$

since the only fact in $\mathcal{K}_1$ matches the body of the rule, but there is no fact reflecting on its (instantiated) head (i.e., the required fact $tr(\texttt{:tom}, \texttt{:knows}, \texttt{:lucy})$ is missing). Ultimately, the implication (4) with blank nodes in its head may be transferred to a rule with an existential quantifier in the head:

$$\forall x.\ tr(x, \texttt{:knows}, \texttt{:tom}) \rightarrow \exists y.\ tr(x, \texttt{:knows}, y) \wedge tr(y, \texttt{:name}, \texttt{"Tom"}). \qquad (8)$$

It is clear that rule (8) is satisfied in instance

$$\mathcal{I}_2 = \{tr(\texttt{:lucy}, \texttt{:knows}, \texttt{:tom}), tr(\texttt{:tom}, \texttt{:name}, \texttt{"Tom"})\}.$$

However, instance $\mathcal{K}_1$ does not satisfy rule (8) because although the only fact satisfies the rule's body, there are no facts jointly satisfying the rule's head.

Note, for query answering over databases and rules, it is usually not required to decide for a concrete value of y (in rule (8)). Many implementations, therefore, use some form of abstraction: for instance, Skolem terms. VLog and Nemo implement the *standard chase* which uses another set of terms, so-called *labeled nulls*. Instead of injecting arbitrary constants for existentially quantified variables, (globally) fresh nulls are inserted in the positions existentially quantified variables occur. Such a labeled null embodies the existence of a constant on the level of instances (just like blank nodes in RDF graphs). Let n be such a labeled null. Then $\mathcal{I}_2$ can be generalized to

$$\mathcal{I}_3 = \{tr(\texttt{:lucy}, \texttt{:knows}, \texttt{:tom}), tr(\texttt{:lucy}, \texttt{:knows}, n), tr(n, \texttt{:name}, \texttt{"Tom"})\},$$

on which rule (8) is satisfied, binding null n to variable y. $\mathcal{I}_3$ is, in fact, more general than $\mathcal{I}_2$ by the following observation: There is a mapping from $\mathcal{I}_3$ to $\mathcal{I}_2$ that is a homomorphism (see Sect. 4.1 for a formal introduction) but not vice versa. The homomorphism here maps the null n (from $\mathcal{I}_3$) to the constant :tom (in $\mathcal{I}_2$). Intuitively, the existence of a query answer (for a conjunctive query) on $\mathcal{I}_3$ implies the existence of a query answer on $\mathcal{I}_2$. Existential rule reasoners implementing some form of *the chase* aim at finding the most general instances (*universal models*) in this respect [18].

In the remainder of this paper, we further analyze the relation between N3 and existential rules. First, we give a brief formal account of the two languages and then provide a correct translation function from N3 to existential rules.

3   Existential N3

In the previous section we introduced essential elements of N3, namely triples and rules. N3 also supports more complex constructs like lists, nesting of rules, and quotation. As these features are not covered by existential rules, we define a subset of N3 excluding them, called *existential N3* ($N3^\exists$).[4] We base our definitions on so-called *simple N3 formulae* [4, Chapter 7], these are N3 formulae which do not allow for nesting.

3.1 Syntax

$N3^\exists$ relies on the RDF alphabet. As the distinction is not relevant in our context, we consider IRIs and literals together as constants. Let C be a set of such constants, U a set of universal variables (starting with ?), and E a set of existential variables (i.e., blank nodes). If the sets C, U, E, and $\{\{,\},=>,.\}$ are mutually disjoint, we call $\mathfrak{A} := C \cup U \cup E \cup \{\{,\},=>,.\}$ an N3 *alphabet*. Figure 1 provides the syntax of $N3^\exists$ over $\mathfrak{A}$.

f ::=		formulae:	t ::=		terms:
	t t t.	atomic formula		ex	existential variables
	{e}=>{e}.	implication		c	constants
	f f	conjunction			
n ::=		N3 terms:	e ::=		expressions:
	uv	universal variables		n n n.	triple expression
	t	terms		e e	conjunction expression

Fig. 1. Syntax of $N3^\exists$

$N3^\exists$ fully covers RDF – RDF formulae are conjunctions of atomic formulae – but allows literals and blank nodes to occur in subject, predicate, and object position. On top of the triples, it supports rules containing existential and universal variables. Note, that the syntax allows rules having new universal variables in their head like for example

$$\{:lucy\ :knows\ :tom\}=>\{?x\ :is\ :happy\}. \qquad (9)$$

which results in a rule expressing *"if lucy knows tom, everyone is happy"*. This implication is problematic: Applied on triple (1), it yields ?x :is :happy. which is a triple containing a universal variable. Such triples are not covered by our syntax, the rule thus introduces a fact we cannot express. Therefore, we restrict $N3^\exists$ rules to *well-formed implications* which rely on *components*. A *component* of a formula or an expression is an N3 term which does not occur nested in a rule. More formally, let f be a formula or an expression over an alphabet $\mathfrak{A}$. The set $comp(f)$ of *components* of f is defined as:

- If f is an atomic formula or a triple expression of the form $t_1\ t_2\ t_3.$, $comp(f) = \{t_1, t_2, t_3\}$.
- If f is an implication of the form $\{e_1\}=>\{e_2\}.$, then $comp(f) = \{\{e_1\}, \{e_2\}\}$.
- If f is a conjunction of the form $f_1 f_2$, then $comp(f) = comp(f_1) \cup comp(f_2)$.

A rule $\{e_1\}=>\{e_2\}.$ is called *well-formed* if $(comp(e_2) \setminus comp(e_1)) \cap U = \emptyset$. For the remainder of this paper we assume all implications to be well-formed.

---

[4] This fragment is expressive enough to support basic use cases like user-defined ontology mapping. Here it is important to note that RDF lists can be expressed using first-rest pairs.

3.2 Semantics

In order to define the semantics of $N3^{\exists}$ we first note, that in our fragment of N3 all quantification of variables is only defined implicitly. The blank node in triple (2) is understood as an existentially quantified variable, the universal in formula (3) as universally quantified. Universal quantification spans over the whole formula – variable ?x occurring in body and head of rule (3) is universally quantified for the whole implication – while existential quantification is local – the conjunction in the head of rule (4) is existentially quantified there. Adding new triples as conjuncts to formula (4) like

$$\texttt{:lucy :knows \_:y. \_:y :likes :cake.} \tag{10}$$

leads to the new statement that *"lucy knows someone who likes cake"* but even though we are using the same blank node identifier _:y in both formulae, the quantification of the variables in this formula is totally seperated and the person named "Tom" is not necessarily related to the cake-liker. With the goal to deal with this locality of blank node scoping, we define substitutions which are only applied on components of formulae and leave nested elements like for example the body and head of rule (3) untouched.

A *substitution* σ is a mapping from a set of variables $X \subset U \cup E$ to the set of N3 terms. We *apply* σ to a term, formula or expression x as follows:

- $x\sigma = \sigma(x)$ if $x \in X$,
- $(s\ p\ o)\sigma = (s\sigma)(p\sigma)(o\sigma)$ if $x = s\ p\ o$ is an atomic formula or a triple expression,
- $(f_1 f_2)\sigma = (f_1\sigma)(f_2\sigma)$ if $x = f_1 f_2$ is a conjunction,
- $x\sigma = x$ else.

For formula $f = \_\texttt{:x :p :o. \{\_:x :b :c\}=>\{\_:x :d :e\}.}$, substitution σ and $\_\texttt{:x} \in \text{dom}(\sigma)$, we get: $f\sigma = \sigma(\_\texttt{:x})\texttt{:p :o. \{\_:x :b :c\}=>\{\_:x :d :e\}}.$[5] We use the substitution to define the semantics of $N3^{\exists}$ which additionally makes use of *N3 interpretations* $\mathfrak{I} = (\mathfrak{D}, \mathfrak{a}, \mathfrak{p})$ consisting of (1) the domain of $\mathfrak{I}$, $\mathfrak{D}$; (2) $\mathfrak{a} : C \to \mathfrak{D}$ called the object function; (3) $\mathfrak{p} : \mathfrak{D} \to 2^{\mathfrak{D} \times \mathfrak{D}}$ called the predicate function.

Just as the function IEXT in RDF's simple interpretations [22], N3's predicate function maps elements from the domain of discourse to a set of pairs of domain elements and is not applied on relation symbols directly. This makes quantification over predicates possible while not exceeding first-order logic in terms of complexity. To introduce the *semantics of* $N3^{\exists}$, let $\mathfrak{I} = (\mathfrak{D}, \mathfrak{a}, \mathfrak{p})$ be an N3 interpretation. For an $N3^{\exists}$ formula f:

1. If $W = \text{comp}(f) \cap E \neq \emptyset$, then $\mathfrak{I} \models f$ iff $\mathfrak{I} \vdash f\mu$ for some substitution $\mu : W \to C$.
2. If $\text{comp}(f) \cap E = \emptyset$:
   (a) If f is an atomic formula $t_1 t_2 t_3$, then $\mathfrak{I} \models t_1 t_2 t_3$. iff $(\mathfrak{a}(t_1), \mathfrak{a}(t_3)) \in \mathfrak{p}(\mathfrak{a}(t_2))$.
   (b) If f is a conjunction $f_1 f_2$, then $\mathfrak{I} \models f_1 f_2$ iff $\mathfrak{I} \models f_1$ and $\mathfrak{I} \models f_2$.
   (c) If f is an implication, then $\mathfrak{I} \models \{e_1\}=>\{e_2\}$ iff $\mathfrak{I} \models e_2\sigma$ if $\mathfrak{I} \models e_1\sigma$ for all substitutions σ on the universal variables $\text{comp}(e_1) \cap U$ by constants.

---

[5] Note that the semantics of *simple formulae* on which $N3^{\exists}$'s semantics is based, relies on two ways to apply a substitution which is necessary to handle nested rules, since such constructs are excluded in $N3^{\exists}$, we simplified here.

The semantics as defined above uses a substitution into the set of constants instead of a direct assignment to the domain of discourse to interpret quantified variables. This design choice inherited from N3 ensures referential opacity of quoted graphs and means, in essence, that quantification always refers to named domain elements.

With that semantics, we call an interpretation $\mathfrak{M}$ *model* of a dataset Φ, written as $\mathfrak{M} \models \Phi$, if $\mathfrak{M} \models f$ for each formula $f \in \Phi$. We say that two sets of $N3^{\exists}$ formulae Φ and Ψ are *equivalent*, written as $\Phi \equiv \Psi$, if for all interpretations $\mathfrak{M}$: $\mathfrak{M} \models \Phi$ iff $\mathfrak{M} \models \Psi$. If $\Phi = \{\phi\}$ and $\Psi = \{\psi\}$ are singleton sets, we write $\phi \equiv \psi$ omitting the brackets.

Piece Normal Form. $N3^{\exists}$ formulae consist of conjunctions of triples and implications. For our goal of translating such formulae to existential rules, it is convenient to consider sub-formulae seperately. Below, we therefore define the so-called *Piece Normal Form* (PNF) for $N3^{\exists}$ formulae and show that each such formula f is equivalent to a set of sub-formulae Φ (i.e., $\Phi \equiv f$) in PNF. We proceed in two steps.

First, we separate formulae based on their blank node components. If two parts of a conjunction share a blank node component, as in formula (10), we cannot split the formula into two since the information about the co-reference would get lost. However, if conjuncts either do not contain blank nodes or only contain disjoint sets of these, we can split them into so-called *pieces*: Two formulae f_1 and f_2 are called *pieces* of a formula f if $f = f_1 f_2$ and $\text{comp}(f_1) \cap \text{comp}(f_2) \cap E = \emptyset$. For such formulae we know:

Lemma 1 (Pieces). *Let* $f = f_1 f_2$ *be an* $N3^{\exists}$ *conjunction and let* $\text{comp}(f_1) \cap \text{comp}(f_2) \cap E = \emptyset$, *then for each interpretation* $\mathfrak{I}$, $\mathfrak{I} \models f$ *iff* $\mathfrak{I} \models f_1$ *and* $\mathfrak{I} \models f_2$.

If we recursively divide all pieces into sub-pieces, we get a maximal set $F = \{f_1, f_2, \ldots, f_n\}$ for each formula f such that $F \equiv \{f\}$ and for all $1 \leq i, j \leq n$, $\text{comp}(f_i) \cap \text{comp}(f_j) \cap E \neq \emptyset$ implies $i = j$.

Second, we replace all blank nodes occurring in rule bodies by *fresh* universals. The rule `{_:x :likes :cake}=>{:cake :is :good}.` becomes `{?y :likes :cake}=>{:cake :is :good}`. Note that both rules have the same meaning, namely *"if someone likes cake, then cake is good."*. We generalize that:

Lemma 2 (Eliminating Existentials). *Let* $f = \{e_1\}=>\{e_2\}$ *and* $g = \{e'_1\}=>\{e_2\}$ *be* $N3^{\exists}$ *implications such that* $e'_1 = e_1 \sigma$ *for some injective substitution* $\sigma : \text{comp}(e_1) \cap E \rightarrow U \setminus \text{comp}(e_1)$ *of the existential variables of* e_1 *by universals. Then:* $f \equiv g$

For a rule f we call the formula f' in which all existentials occurring in its body are replaced by universals following Lemma 2 the *normalized* version of the rule. We call an $N3^{\exists}$ formula f *normalized*, if all rules occurring in it as conjuncts are normalized. This allows us to introduce the *Piece Normal Form*:

Theorem 1 (Piece Normal Form). *For every well-formed* $N3^{\exists}$ *formula* f, *there exists a set* $F = \{f_1, f_2, \ldots, f_k\}$ *of* $N3^{\exists}$ *formulae such that* $F \equiv \{f\}$ *and* F *is in* piece normal form *(PNF). That is, all* $f_i \in F$ *are normalized formulae and* $k \in \mathbb{N}$ *is the maximal number such that for* $1 \leq i, j \leq k$, $comp(f_i) \cap comp(f_j) \cap E \neq \emptyset$ *implies* $i = j$. *If* f_i $(1 \leq i \leq k)$ *is a conjunction of atomic formulae, we call* f_i *an atomic piece.*

Since the piece normal form F of $N3^{\exists}$ formula f is obtained by only replacing variables and separating conjuncts of f into the set form, the overall size of F is linear in f.

4   From N3 to Existential Rules

Without loss of generality, we translate sets F of $N3^{\exists}$ formulae in PNF (cf. Theorem 1) to sets of existential rules $\mathcal{T}(F)$. As a preliminary step, we introduce the language of existential rules formally. Later on, we explain and define the translation function that has already been sketched in Sect. 2. The section closes with a correctness argument, establishing a strong relationship between existential rules and $N3^{\exists}$.

4.1   Foundations of Existential Rule Reasoning

For existential rules, we also consider a first-order vocabulary, consisting of constants (**C**) and variables (**V**), and additionally so-called (labeled) nulls (**N**)[6]. As already mentioned in Sect. 2, we use the same set of constants as N3 formulae, meaning **C** = C. Furthermore, let **P** be a set of *relation names*, where each $p \in \mathbf{P}$ comes with an arity $ar(p) \in \mathbb{N}$. **C**, **V**, **N**, and **P** are countably infinite and pair-wise disjoint. We use the ternary relation name $tr \in \mathbf{P}$ to encode N3 triples in Sect. 2. If $p \in \mathbf{P}$ and $t_1, t_2, \ldots, t_{ar(p)}$ is a list of terms (i.e., $t_i \in \mathbf{C} \cup \mathbf{N} \cup \mathbf{V}$), $p(t_1, t_2, \ldots, t_{ar(p)})$ is called an *atom*. We often use **t** to summarize a term list like $t_1, \ldots, t_n$ ($n \in \mathbb{N}$), and treat it as a set whenever order is irrelevant. An atom $p(\mathbf{t})$ is *ground* if $\mathbf{t} \subseteq \mathbf{C}$. An *instance* is a (possibly infinite) set $\mathcal{I}$ of variable-free atoms and a finite set of ground atoms $\mathcal{D}$ is called a *database*.

For a set of atoms $\mathcal{A}$ and an instance $\mathcal{I}$, we call a function h from the terms occurring in $\mathcal{A}$ to the terms in $\mathcal{I}$ a *homomorphism from $\mathcal{A}$ to $\mathcal{I}$*, denoted by $h : \mathcal{A} \to \mathcal{I}$, if (1) $h(c) = c$ for all $c \in \mathbf{C}$ (occurring in $\mathcal{A}$), and (2) $p(\mathbf{t}) \in \mathcal{A}$ implies $p(h(\mathbf{t})) \in \mathcal{I}$. If any homomorphism from $\mathcal{A}$ to $\mathcal{I}$ exists, write $\mathcal{A} \to \mathcal{I}$. Please note that if n is a null occurring in $\mathcal{A}$, then $h(n)$ may be a constant or null.

For an *(existential) rule* $r \colon \forall \mathbf{x}, \mathbf{y}. \ \varphi[\mathbf{x}, \mathbf{y}] \to \exists \mathbf{z}. \ \psi[\mathbf{y}, \mathbf{z}]$ (cf. (5)), rule bodies (body(r)) and heads (head(r)) will also be considered as sets of atoms for a more compact representation of the semantics. Let r be a rule and $\mathcal{I}$ an instance. We call a homomorphism $h : \text{body}(r) \to \mathcal{I}$ a *match for r in $\mathcal{I}$*. A match h is *satisfied for r in $\mathcal{I}$* if there is an extension $h^\star$ of h (i.e., $h \subseteq h^\star$) such that $h^\star(\text{head}(r)) \subseteq \mathcal{I}$. If all matches of r are satisfied in $\mathcal{I}$, we say that r is satisfied in $\mathcal{I}$, denoted by $\mathcal{I} \models r$. For a rule set Σ and database $\mathcal{D}$, we call an instance $\mathcal{I}$ a *model of Σ and $\mathcal{D}$*, denoted by $\mathcal{I} \models \Sigma, \mathcal{D}$, if $\mathcal{D} \subseteq \mathcal{I}$ and $\mathcal{I} \models r$ for each $r \in \Sigma$. We say that two rule sets Σ_1 and Σ_2 are *equivalent*, denoted $\Sigma_1 \leftrightarrows \Sigma_2$, iff for all instances $\mathcal{I}$, $\mathcal{I} \models \Sigma_1$ iff $\mathcal{I} \models \Sigma_2$.

Labeled nulls play the role of fresh constants without further specification, just like blank nodes in RDF or N3. The chase is a family of algorithms that soundly produces models of rule sets by continuously applying rules for unsatisfied matches. If some rule head is instantiated, existential variables are replaced by fresh nulls in order to facilitate for arbitrary constants. Although the chase is not guaranteed to terminate, it always produces a (possibly infinite) model[7] [18].

---

[6] We choose here different symbols to disambiguate between existential rules and N3, although vocabularies partially overlap.

[7] Not just any model, but a universal model, which is a model that has a homomorphism to any other model of the database and rule set. Up to homomorphisms, universal models are the smallest among all models.

4.2   The Translation Function from N3 to Existential Rules

The translation function $\mathcal{T}$ maps sets $F = \{f_1, \ldots, f_k\}$ of $N3^{\exists}$ formulae in PNF to sets of rules Σ. Before we go into the details of the translation for every type of piece, we consider an auxiliary function $\mathbb{T} : C \cup E \cup U \rightarrow \mathbf{C} \cup \mathbf{V}$ mapping N3 terms to terms in our rule language (cf. previous subsection):

$$\mathbb{T}(t) := \begin{cases} v_{\mathsf{x}}^{\forall} & \text{if } t = ?\mathsf{x} \in U \\ v_{\mathsf{y}}^{\exists} & \text{if } t = \_:\mathsf{y} \in E \\ t & \text{if } t \in C, \end{cases}$$

where $v_{\mathsf{x}}^{\forall}, v_{\mathsf{y}}^{\exists} \in \mathbf{V}$ and $t \in \mathbf{C}$ (i.e., we assume $C \subseteq \mathbf{C}$). While variables in N3 belong to either E or U, this separation is lost under function $\mathbb{T}$. For enhancing readability of subsequent examples, the identity of the variable preserves this information by using superscripts $\exists$ and $\forall$. We provide the translation for every piece $f_i \in F$ ($1 \leq i \leq k$) and later collect the full translation of F as the union of its translated pieces.

Translating Atomic Pieces. If f_i is an atomic piece, it has the form $f_i = g_1 g_2 \ldots g_l$ for some $l \geq 1$ and each g_j ($1 \leq j \leq l$) is an atomic formula. The translation of f_i is the singleton set $\mathcal{T}(f_i) = \{\rightarrow \exists \mathbf{z}. \, tr(\mathbb{T}(g_1)) \wedge tr(\mathbb{T}(g_2)) \wedge \ldots \wedge tr(\mathbb{T}(g_l))\}$, where $\mathbb{T}(g_j) = \mathbb{T}(t_j^1), \mathbb{T}(t_j^2), \mathbb{T}(t_j^3)$ if $g_j = t_j^1 t_j^2 t_j^3$ and $\mathbf{z}$ is the list of translated existential variables (via $\mathbb{T}$) from existentials occurring in f. For example, the formula in (10) constitutes a single piece $f_{(10)}$ which translates to a set containing the rule

$$\rightarrow \exists v_{\mathsf{y}}^{\exists}. \, tr(:\mathtt{lucy}, :\mathtt{knows}, v_{\mathsf{y}}^{\exists}) \wedge tr(v_{\mathsf{y}}^{\exists}, :\mathtt{likes}, :\mathtt{cake}).$$

Translating Rules. For f_i being a rule $\{e_1\} => \{e_2\}$ we also obtain a single rule. Recall that the PNF ensures all variables of e_1 to be universals and all universal variables of e_2 to also occur in e_1. If $e_1 = g_1^1 g_1^2 \cdots g_1^m$ and $e_2 = g_2^1 g_2^2 \cdots g_2^n$, $\mathcal{T}(f_i) = \{\forall \mathbf{x}. \, \bigwedge_{j=1}^{m} tr(\mathbb{T}(g_1^j)) \rightarrow \exists \mathbf{z}. \, \bigwedge_{j=1}^{n} tr(\mathbb{T}(g_2^j))\}$ where $\mathbf{x}$ and $\mathbf{z}$ are the lists of translated universals and existentials, respectively. Applying the translation to the N3 formula in (4), which is a piece according to our definitions, we obtain again a singleton set, now containing the rule

$$\forall v_{\mathsf{x}}^{\forall}. \, tr(v_{\mathsf{x}}^{\forall}, :\mathtt{knows}, :\mathtt{tom}) \rightarrow \exists v_{\mathsf{y}}^{\exists}. \, tr(v_{\mathsf{x}}^{\forall}, :\mathtt{knows}, v_{\mathsf{y}}^{\exists}) \wedge tr(v_{\mathsf{y}}^{\exists}, :\mathtt{name}, \texttt{"Tom"}),$$

which is the same rule as (8) up to a renaming of (bound) variables (α-conversion [19]).

Translating Sets. For the set $F = \{f_1, f_2, \ldots, f_k\}$ of $N3^{\exists}$ formulae in PNF, $\mathcal{T}(F)$ is the union of all translated constituents (i.e., $\mathcal{T}(F) = \bigcup_{i=1}^{k} \mathcal{T}(f_i)$). Please note that $\mathcal{T}$ does not exceed a polynomial overhead of its input.

The correctness argument for $\mathcal{T}$ splits into *soundness* – whenever we translate two equivalent $N3^{\exists}$ formulae, their translated rules turn out to be equivalent as well – and *completeness* – formulae that are not equivalent are translated to rule sets that are not equivalent. Although the different formalisms have quite different notions of models, models of a translated rule sets $\mathcal{M}$ can be converted into models of the original N3 formula by using a Herbrand argument. The full technical lemma and the construction is part of our technical appendix [3]. Our correctness proof also considers completeness since, otherwise, a more trivial translation function would have sufficed: Let $\mathcal{T}_0$ be a function mapping all $N3^{\exists}$ formulae to the empty rule set: All equivalent $N3^{\exists}$ formulae are mapped to equivalent rule sets (always $\emptyset$), but also formulae that are not equivalent yield equivalent rule sets under $\mathcal{T}_0$. Having such a strong relationship between N3 and existential rules allows us to soundly use the translation function $\mathcal{T}$ in practice.

Theorem 2. *For PNFs F and G of $N3^{\exists}$ formulae, $F \equiv G$ iff $\mathcal{T}(F) \leftrightarrows \mathcal{T}(G)$.*

Beyond the correctness of $\mathcal{T}$, we have no further guarantees. As $N3^{\exists}$ reasoning does not necessarily stop, there is no requirement for termination of the chase over translated rule sets. We expect that the similarity between $N3^{\exists}$ and existential rules allows for the adoption of sufficient conditions for finite models (e.g., by means of acyclicity [17]).

5 Evaluation

The considerations provided above allow us to use existential rule reasoners to perform $N3^{\exists}$ reasoning. We would like to find out whether our finding is of practical relevance, that is whether we can identify datasets on which existential rule reasoners, running on the rule translations, outperform classical N3 reasoners provided with the original data.

In order to do this we have implemented $\mathcal{T}$ as a python script that takes an arbitrary $N3^{\exists}$ formula f, constructs its set representation F in PNF, and produces the set of rules $\mathcal{T}(F)$. This script and some additional scripts to translate existential rules (with at most binary predicates) to $N3^{\exists}$ formulae are available on GitHub. Our implementation allows us to compare N3 reasoners with existential rule reasoners, performance-wise. As existential rule reasoners we chose VLog [15], a state-of-the-art reasoning engine designed for working with large piles of input data, and Nemo [23], a recently released rust-based reasoning engine. As N3 reasoners we chose cwm [7] and EYE [27] which – due to their good coverage of N3 features – are most commonly used. All experiments have been performed on a laptop with 11th Gen Intel Core i7-1165G7 CPU, 32GB of RAM, and 1TB disk capacity, running a Ubuntu 22.04 LTS.

5.1 Datasets

We performed our experiments on two datasets: LUBM from the *Chasebench* [6] provides a fixed set of 136 rules and varies in the number of facts these rules are applied; the DEEP TAXONOMY (DT) benchmark developed for the *WellnessRules* project [11] consists of one single fact and a varying number of mutually dependent rules.

The *Chasebench* is a benchmarking suite for existential rule reasoning. Among the different scenaria in Chasebench we picked LUBM for its direct compatibility with N3: all predicates in LUBM have at most arity 2. Furthermore, LUBM allows for a glimpse on scalability since LUBM comes in different database sizes. We have worked with LUBM 001, 010, and 100, roughly referring to dataset sizes of a hundred thousand, one million and ten million facts. We translated LUBM data and rules into a canonical N3 format. Predicate names and constants within the dataset become IRIs using the example prefix. An atom like *src_advisor*(*Student441*, *Professor8*) becomes the triple :Student441 :src_advisor :Professor8.. For atoms using unary predicates, like *TeachingAssistant(Student498)*, we treat :TeachingAssistent as a class and relate :Student498 via rdf:type to the class. For any atom A, we denote its canonical translation into triple format by $t(A)$. Note this canonical translation only applies to atoms of unary and binary predicates. For the existential rule

$$\forall \mathbf{x}.\ B_1 \wedge \ldots \wedge B_m \rightarrow \exists \mathbf{z}.\ H_1 \wedge \ldots \wedge H_n$$

we obtain the canonical translation by applying t to all atoms, respecting universally and existentially quantified variables (i.e., universally quantified variables are translated to universal N3 variables and existentially quantified variables become blank nodes):

$$\{t(B_1).\ \cdots t(B_m).\} \texttt{=>} \{t(H_1).\ \cdots t(H_n).\}.$$

All N3 reasoners have reasoned over the canonical translation of data and rules which was necessary because of the lack of an N3 version of LUBM. Since we are evaluating VLog's and Nemo's performance on our translation $\mathcal{T}$, we converted the translated LUBM by $\mathcal{T}$ back to existential rules before reasoning. Thereby, former unary and binary atoms were turned into triples and then uniformly translated to *tr*-atoms via $\mathcal{T}$.

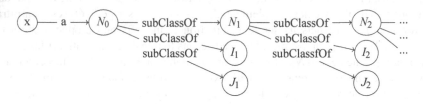

Fig. 2. Structure of the DEEP TAXONOMY benchmark.

The *Deep Taxonomy benchmark* simulates deeply nested RDFS-subclass reasoning[8]. It contains one individual which is member of a class. This class is subclass of three other classes of which one again is subclass of three more classes and so on. Figure 2 illustrates this idea. The benchmark provides different depths for the subclass chain and we tested with the depths of 1,000 and 100,000. The reasoning tests for the membership of the individual in the last class of the chain. For our tests, the subclass declarations were translated to rules, the triple :N0 rdfs:subClassOf :N1. became

$$\{ \texttt{?x a :N0.} \} \texttt{=>} \{ \texttt{?x a :N1.} \}.$$

This translation also illustrates why this rather simple reasoning case is interesting: we have a use case in which we depend on long chains of rules executed after each other. The reasoner EYE allows the user to decide per rule whether it is applied using forward- or backward-reasoning, at least if the head of the rule does not contain blank nodes. For this dataset, we evaluated full backward- and full forward-reasoning, separately.

---

[8] N3 available at: http://eulersharp.sourceforge.net/2009/12dtb/.

5.2 Results

Table 1 presents the running times of the four reasoners and additionally gives statistics about the sizes of the given knowledge base (# facts) and the rule set (# rules). For DT we display two reasoning times for EYE, one produced by only forward reasoning (EYE-fw), one for only backward-reasoning (EYE-bw). Note, that for the latter, the reasoner does not produce the full deductive closure of the dataset, but answers a query instead. As LUBM contains rules with blank nodes in their haeds, full backward reasoning was not possible in that case, the table is left blank. EYE performs much better than VLog and Nemo for the experiments with DT. Its reasoning time is off by one order of magnitude. Conversely, VLog and Nemo could reason over all the LUBM datasets while EYE has thrown an exception after having read the input facts. The reasoning times of VLog are additionally significantly lower than the times for EYE. While Nemo shows a similar runtime on DT as VLog, it is slower on LUBM. However, we may be quite optimistic regarding its progress in runtime behavior, as Nemo already shows better running times on the original LUBM datasets. The reasoner cwm is consistently slower than the other three and from LUBM 010 on. All reasoners tried to find the query answers/deductive closures for at least ten minutes (i.e., — in Table 1 indicates a time-out).

Table 1. Experimental Results

Dataset	# facts	# rules	cwm	EYE-fw	EYE-bw	VLog	Nemo
DT 1000	1	3001	180 s	0.1 s	0.001 s	1.6 s	1.7 s
DT 100000	1	30,001	—	0.3 s	0.003 s	—	—
LUBM 001	100,543	136	117.4 s	3.4 s		0.2 s	2.4 s
LUBM 010	1,272,575	136	—	44.8 s		4.3 s	31.2 s
LUBM 100	13,405,381	136	—	—		47.3 s	362 s

5.3 Discussion

In all our tests we observe a very poor performance of cwm which is not surprising, given that this reasoner has not been updated for some time. The results for EYE, VLog and Nemo are more interesting as they illustrate the different strengths of the reasoners.

For very high numbers of rules compared to the amount of data, EYE performs much better than VLog and Nemo. The good results of 0.1 and 0.3 s can even be improved by using backward reasoning. This makes EYE very well-suited for use cases where we need to apply complex rules on datasets of low or medium size. This could be interesting in decentralized set-ups such as policy-based access control for the Solid-project.[9] On the other hand we see that VLog and Nemo perform best when provided with large datasets and lower numbers of rules. This could be useful use cases involving bigger datasets in the Web like Wikidata or DBpedia[10].

---

[9] https://solidproject.org/.
[10] https://www.wikidata.org/ *and* https://www.dbpedia.org/.

From the perspective of this paper, these two findings together show the relevance of our work: we observed big differences between the tools' reasoning times and these differences depended on the use cases. In other words, there are use cases which could benefit from our translation and we thus do not only make the first steps towards having more N3 reasoners available but also broaden the scope of possible N3 applications.

6   Related Work

When originally proposed as a W3C member submission [8], the formal semantics of N3 was only introduced informally. As a consequence, different systems, using N3, interpreted concepts like nested formulae differently [1]. Since then, the relation of N3 to other Web standards has been studied from a use-case perspective [4] and a W3C Community group has been formed [28], which recently published the semantics without functions [2]. But even with these definitions, the semantic relation of the logic to other standards, especially outside the Semantics Web, has not been studied thouroghly.

For N3's subset RDF, de Bruijn and Heymans [13] provide a translation to first-order logic and F-Logic using similar embeddings (e.g., a tenary predicate to represent triples) to the ones in this paper, but do not cover rules. Boley [10] supports N3 in his RuleML Knowledge-Interoperation Hub providing a translation of N3 to PSOA RuleML. This can be translated to other logics. But the focus is more on syntax than on semantics.

In Description Logics (DL), rewritings in rule-based languages have their own tradition (see, e.g., [16] for a good overview of existing rewritings and their complexity, as well as more references). The goal there is to (1) make state-of-the-art rule reasoners available for DLs and, thereby, (2) use a fragment of a rule language that reflects on the data complexity of the given DL fragment. Also practical tools have been designed to capture certain profiles of the Web Ontology Language (OWL), like the Orel system [24] and, more recently, DaRLing [20]. To the best of our knowledge, a rewriting for N3 as presented in this paper did not exist before. Also, existential rule reasoning engines have not been compared to the existing N3 reasoners.

7   Conclusion

In this paper we studied the close relationship between N3 rules supporting blank node production and existential rules. N3 without special features like built-in functions, nesting of rules, or quotation can be directly mapped to existential rules with unary and binary predicates. In order to show that, we defined a mapping between $N3^\exists$, N3 without the aforementioned features, and existential rules. We argued that this mapping and its inverse preserve the equivalence and non-equivalence between datasets. This result allows us to trust the reasoning results when applying the mapping in practice, that is, when (1) translating $N3^\exists$ to existential rules, (2) reasoning within that framework, and (3) using the inverse mapping to transfer the result back into N3.

We applied that strategy and compared the reasoning times of the N3 reasoners cwm and EYE with the existential rule reasoners VLog and Nemo. The goal of that comparison was to find out whether there are use cases for which N3 reasoning can benefit from the findings on existential rules. We tested the reasoners on two datasets: DT consisting of one single fact and a varying number of mutually dependent rules and LUBM consisting of a fixed number of rules and a varying number of facts. EYE performs better on DT while VLog and Nemo showed their strength on LUBM. We see that as an indication that for use cases of similar nature, that is, reasoning on large numbers of facts, our approach could be used to improve reasoning times. More generally, we see that reasoners differ in their strengths and that by providing the revertible translation between $N3^{\exists}$ and existential rules we increase the number of reasoners (partly) supporting N3 and the range of use cases the logic can support in practice. We see our work as an important step towards fully establishing rule-based reasoning in the Semantic Web.

As many N3 use cases rely on N3's powerful built-in functions and logical features such as support for graph terms, lists and nested rules, future work should include the extension of our translation towards full coverage of N3. Another direction of future work could be to investigate the differences and similarities we found in our evaluation in more detail: while showing differences in their performance, the reasoners produced the exact same result sets (modulo isomorphism) when acting on rules introducing blank nodes. That is, the different reasoning times do not stem from the handling of existentially quantified rule heads but from other optimization techniques. Fully understanding these differences will help the N3 and the existential rule community to further improve their tools. In that context, it would also be interesting to learn if EYE's capability to combine forward and backward reasoning could improve the reasoning times for data sets including existentially quantified rule heads.

We thus hope that our research on existential N3 will spawn further investigations of powerful data-centric features in data-intensive rule reasoning as well as significant progress in tool support towards these features. Ultimately, we envision a Web of data and rule exchange, fully supported by the best tools available as converging efforts of the N3 community, the existential rule reasoning community, and possibly many others.

Acknowledgements. This reasearch is partly supported by Deutsche Forschungsgemeinschaft (DFG, German Research Foundation) in project number 389792660 (TRR 248, Center for Perspicuous Computing), by Bundesministerium für Bildung und Forschung (BMBF, Federal Ministry of Education and Research) and DAAD (German Academic Exchange Service) in project 57616814 (SECAI, School of Embedded and Composite AI), and by the BMBF under project 13GW0552B (KIMEDS, KI-assistierte Zertifizierung medizintechnischer Software) in the Center for Scalable Data Analytics and Artificial Intelligence (ScaDS.AI),

References

1. Arndt, D., Schrijvers, T., De Roo, J., Verborgh, R.: Implicit quantification made explicit: How to interpret blank nodes and universal variables in Notation3 Logic. J. Web Semant. **58**, 100501 (2019). https://doi.org/10.1016/j.websem.2019.04.001
2. Arndt, D., Champin, P.A.: Notation3 semantics. W3C community group report, W3C, July 2023. https://w3c.github.io/N3/reports/20230703/semantics.html
3. Arndt, D., Mennicke, S.: Notation3 as an existential rule language. CoRR abs/2308.07332 (2023)
4. Arndt, D.: Notation3 as the unifying logic for the semantic web. Ph.D. thesis, Ghent University (2019)

5. Baget, J.F., Leclère, M., Mugnier, M.L., Salvat, E.: On rules with existential variables: Walking the decidability line. Artif. Intell. **175**(9–10), 1620–1654 (2011)
6. Benedikt, M., et al. (eds.) Proc. 36th Symposium on Principles of Database Systems (PODS 2017), pp. 37–52. ACM (2017)
7. Berners-Lee, T.: cwm (2000–2009). http://www.w3.org/2000/10/swap/doc/cwm.html
8. Berners-Lee, T., Connolly, D.: Notation3 (n_3): a readable RDF syntax. w_3C Team Submission, March 2011. http://www.w3.org/TeamSubmission/n3/
9. Berners-Lee, T., Connolly, D., Kagal, L., Scharf, Y., Hendler, J.: N3Logic: a logical framework for the world wide web. Theor. Pract. Logic Program. **3**, 249–269 (2008). https://doi.org/10.1017/S1471068407003213
10. Boley, H.: The RuleML knowledge-interoperation hub. In: Alferes, J.J.J., Bertossi, L., Governatori, G., Fodor, P., Roman, D. (eds.) RuleML 2016. LNCS, vol. 9718, pp. 19–33. Springer, Cham (2016). https://doi.org/10.1007/978-3-319-42019-6_2
11. Boley, H., Osmun, T.M., Craig, B.L.: WellnessRules: a web 3.0 case study in RuleML-based prolog-n3 profile interoperation. In: Governatori, G., Hall, J., Paschke, A. (eds.) RuleML 2009. LNCS, vol. 5858, pp. 43–52. Springer, Heidelberg (2009). https://doi.org/10.1007/978-3-642-04985-9_7
12. Bonte, P., Ongenae, F.: Roxi: a framework for reactive reasoning. In: ESWC2023, the First International Workshop on Semantic Web on Constrained Things (2023)
13. de Bruijn, J., Heymans, S.: Logical foundations of (e)RDF(S): complexity and reasoning. In: Aberer, K., et al. (eds.) ASWC/ISWC -2007. LNCS, vol. 4825, pp. 86–99. Springer, Heidelberg (2007). https://doi.org/10.1007/978-3-540-76298-0_7
14. Calì, A., Gottlob, G., Pieris, A.: query answering under non-guarded rules in datalog+/-. In: Hitzler, P., Lukasiewicz, T. (eds.) RR 2010. LNCS, vol. 6333, pp. 1–17. Springer, Heidelberg (2010). https://doi.org/10.1007/978-3-642-15918-3_1
15. Carral, D., Dragoste, I., González, L., Jacobs, C., Krötzsch, M., Urbani, J.: VLog: a rule engine for knowledge graphs. In: Ghidini, C., et al. (eds.) ISWC 2019. LNCS, vol. 11779, pp. 19–35. Springer, Cham (2019). https://doi.org/10.1007/978-3-030-30796-7_2
16. Carral, D., Krötzsch, M.: Rewriting the description logic ALCHIQ to disjunctive existential rules. In: Bessiere, C. (ed.) Proceedings of the 29th International Joint Conference on Artificial Intelligence, IJCAI 2020, pp. 1777–1783. ijcai.org (2020)
17. Cuenca Grau, B., et al.: Acyclicity notions for existential rules and their application to query answering in ontologies. J. Artif. Intell. Res. **47**, 741–808 (2013)
18. Deutsch, A., Nash, A., Remmel, J.B.: The chase revisited. In: Lenzerini, M., Lembo, D. (eds.) Proceedings of 27th Symposium on Principles of Database Systems (PODS 2008), pp. 149–158. ACM (2008)
19. Ebbinghaus, H.D., Flum, J., Thomas, W.: Semantics of First-Order Languages, pp. 27–57. Springer, New York (1994). https://doi.org/10.1007/978-1-4757-2355-7_3
20. Fiorentino, A., Zangari, J., Manna, M.: DaRLing: a datalog rewriter for OWL 2 RL ontological reasoning under SPARQL queries. Theor. Pract. Logic Program. **20**(6), 958–973 (2020)
21. Harth, A., Käfer, T.: Rule-based programming of user agents for linked data. In: Proceedings of the 11th International Workshop on Linked Data on the Web at the Web Conference (27th WWW), CEUR-WS, April 2018
22. Hayes, P. (ed.): RDF semantics. W3C Recommendation, 10 February 2004. http://www.w3.org/TR/rdf-mt/
23. Ivliev, A., Ellmauthaler, S., Gerlach, L., Marx, M., Meißner, M., Meusel, S., Krötzsch, M.: Nemo: First glimpse of a new rule engine. In: 39th on Logic Programming, ICLP 2023 Technical Communications. EPTCS (to appear)
24. Krötzsch, M., Mehdi, A., Rudolph, S.: Orel: database-driven reasoning for OWL 2 profiles. In: Haarslev, V., Toman, D., Weddell, G. (eds.) Proc. 23rd Int. Workshop on Description Logics (DL'10). CEUR Workshop Proceedings, vol. 573, pp. 114–124. CEUR-WS.org (2010)

25. Krötzsch, M., Marx, M., Rudolph, S.: The power of the terminating chase. In: Barceló, P., Calautti, M. (eds.) Proceedings of 22nd International Conference on on Database Theory (ICDT 2019), LIPIcs, vol. 127, pp. 3:1–3:17. Schloss Dagstuhl - Leibniz-Zentrum fuer Informatik (2019)

26. Verborgh, R., et al.: The pragmatic proof: hypermedia API composition and execution. Theor. Pract. Logic Program. **1**, 1–48 (2017). https://doi.org/10.1017/S1471068416000016

27. Verborgh, R., De Roo, J.: Drawing conclusions from linked data on the web: the EYE reasoner. IEEE Softw. **5**, 23–27 (2015). https://doi.org/10.1109/MS.2015.63

28. Woensel, W.V., Arndt, D., Champin, P.A., Tomaszuk, D., Kellogg, G.: Notation3 language, July 2023. https://w3c.github.io/N3/reports/20230703/

Fine-Tuning Large Enterprise Language Models via Ontological Reasoning

Teodoro Baldazzi[1]([✉]), Luigi Bellomarini[2], Stefano Ceri[3], Andrea Colombo[3], Andrea Gentili[2], and Emanuel Sallinger[4,5]

[1] Università Roma Tre, Rome, Italy
teodoro.baldazzi@uniroma3.it
[2] Banca d'Italia, Rome, Italy
[3] Politecnico di Milano, Milan, Italy
andrea1.colombo@polimi.it
[4] TU Wien, Vienna, Austria
[5] University of Oxford, Oxford, UK

Abstract. Large Language Models (LLMs) exploit fine-tuning as a technique to adapt to diverse goals, thanks to task-specific training data. Task specificity should go hand in hand with domain orientation, that is, the specialization of an LLM to accurately address the tasks of a given realm of interest. However, models are usually fine-tuned over publicly available data or, at most, over ground data from databases, ignoring business-level definitions and domain experience. On the other hand, Enterprise Knowledge Graphs (EKGs) are able to capture and augment such domain knowledge via ontological reasoning. With the goal of combining LLM flexibility with the domain orientation of EKGs, we propose a novel neurosymbolic architecture that leverages the power of ontological reasoning to build task- and domain-specific corpora for LLM fine-tuning.

Keywords: Ontological reasoning · Language models · Knowledge graphs

1 Introduction: Context and Overview of the Approach

With the recent soar of AI-based chatbots, currently led by OpenAI's Chat-GPT, the field of Natural Language Processing (NLP) and, in particular, Large Language Models (LLMs), faced a major turning point and transcended its relevance in academia and industry, steering the attention of the general public towards generative AI. While many approaches are being proposed that exploit powerful pre-trained LLMs, such as T5 [18] and GPT [16], to address a plethora of industrial tasks, current solutions show limited effectiveness at specializing the models on enterprise domains, from finance to genomics. In our community, such domain-specific knowledge can be captured by combining factual data from corporate databases with business-level definitions as ontologies in *Enterprise Knowledge Graphs* (EKGs), and further augmented via *ontological reasoning*. In this paper, we build upon this domain representation and propose a novel solution to accurately specialize LLMs on core enterprise NLP tasks.

A. Fensel et al. (Eds.): RuleML+RR 2023, LNCS 14244, pp. 86–94, 2023.
https://doi.org/10.1007/978-3-031-45072-3_6

Limits of Task-Specific Fine-Tuning. LLMs can be pre-trained on extensive datasets and, often, specialized with a *fine-tuning* process that customizes them so as to perform given NLP tasks [20], such as *question-answering, language translation, named-entity recognition, document summarization, sentiment analysis*, and more [7]. According to a very common usage pattern, general-purpose LLMs are fine-tuned for a specific NLP task based on extensive cross- or domain-generic textual corpora that are publicly available [17].

While this approach highlights good generalization capabilities and a surprising human-style interaction, the obtained models have major shortcomings in that they lack enterprise knowledge and trivially fail to solve domain-specific NLP tasks. For instance, in the financial domain, state-of-the-art yet generalist models have shown poor performance for different NLP tasks, for which, on the other hand, further fine-tuning with large additional text corpora has been proved to be helpful in improving the results, such as in the case of *FinBert* [12].

Limits of Domain-Specific Fine-Tuning. Going further, recent studies are exploring the usage of factual data from enterprise databases to fine-tune LLMs and try to tackle domain-specific question-answering tasks: the factual information is leveraged to synthesize prompt-response pairs based on the data and customize the LLM in a task- and domain-specific direction. A primary example is the *SKILL project* [15], where an LLM is directly trained on factual triples derived from the translation into natural language—the so-called *verbalization*—of Wikidata (namely, the *KELM corpus* [2]) for question-answering tasks. Similarly, other approaches highlight possible improvements of accuracy in question-answering tasks, when textual information is first captured into a database, which is then verbalized and employed for fine-tuning [3].

Yet, even the combination of general-purpose knowledge of the pre-trained model and the domain data still offers an accuracy that is not acceptable for core tasks in specialized domains. For example, *BloombergGPT* [22] is an LLM fine-tuned on a wide range of financial data, combining internal enterprise knowledge with publicly-available datasets. The results show that the model fine-tuned for the question-answering task outperforms state-of-the-art counterparts by being able to correctly answer questions related to the financial domain. However, *BloombergGPT* has been tested only on questions whose answers are already contained in (or directly entailed by) the factual information of the input databases, either as data or meta-data (e.g., schema information). It is reasonable, in fact, that it does not have enough fine-tuning data or logical capabilities to go further.

A Look Beyond Current Solutions. Conversely, from an enterprise application perspective, it would be extremely useful to answer questions by means of intelligent combined uses of the input databases with other logic-intensive sources of knowledge (e.g., regulatory bodies, best practices, domain experts, etc.). For instance, in the context of financial cases like those of interest for a Central Bank, answering questions such as *"why does shareholder X exert a relevant influence on the financial intermediary Y?"* (**explanation**), or *"how does this smart contract behave?"* (**description**), or *"is the merger of banks Y and W lawful from a regulatory perspective?"* (**question answering**), or *"based on* *data, how many ties with other intermediaries does Z have?"* (**text-to-query translation**) would be an essential asset.

At present, all the mentioned tasks are far from being solved by off-the-shelf libraries or, directly, by most recent LLMs, and are open research. Going into the details of each of them is beyond the scope of this paper, but the motivations laid out mainly in a question-answering perspective give the flavour of why LLMs are not enough. It is worth remarking, though, that even the translation task, for which thanks to LLMs much progress has been made in the transformation of natural language into the target query languages (say, SQL, SPARQL, etc.) [21,23] is still a largely unsolved problem, especially in the context of languages with an elaborate grammar and complex queries [9].

Ontological Reasoning. From another perspective, in the *Knowledge Representation and Reasoning* [11] (KRR) community, the state-of-the-art research on ontological reasoning over EKGs makes a point of being able to offer a compact combination of factual database information (the *extensional knowledge*) and formally specified business awareness, for instance in the form of logical rules (the *intensional knowledge*), to serve *domain-specific query answering* in an accurate manner. For example, logical KGs exploiting efficient fragments of the $Datalog^{\pm}$ family [8] have been successfully adopted for financial applications [6].

Yet, there is an impedance mismatch between NLP and ontological reasoning, which lacks the flexibility and the language orientation to solve explanation, description, question answering, and translation tasks: queries need to be specified in KRR formalisms; all the inputs and the results are facts/n-tuples/triples; the generation of new knowledge is possible only to the extent reasoning rules capture it. Conversely, while being very good at manipulating human language, LLMs lack a comprehensive domain model, a pillar of KRR approaches.

An Integrated Approach. This paper strives to strengthen LLMs in their use for task- and domain-specific applications, by letting the fine-tuning process be driven by an ontological reasoning task on an EKG. We operate in the context of the VADALOG [5] system, a Datalog-based reasoning engine for EKGs, that finds many industrial applications [6]. We use VADALOG to explore the factual information derived by applying the domain rules, via the CHASE procedure [13], to the enterprise data and synthesize a fine-tuning corpus that covers the entire "reasoning space" to convey domain-specificity to the LLM. A summary of the resulting *fine-tuning pipeline*, provided in Fig. 1, will guide our discussion.

More in detail, our **contributions** can be summarized as follows.

- We present a **reasoning verbalization** technique that generates sets of prompt-response pairs from ground Datalog rules. We provide the algorithm and optimize it with a *lifting technique* exploiting reasoning regularities.
- We deliver such an approach in a **novel neurosymbolic architecture** that fine-tunes task-specific LLMs for a set of four relevant NLP tasks, namely, *explanation, description, question answering,* and *translation*.
- We discuss a preliminary **proof-of-concept** confirming the validity of our approach and comparing models fine-tuned on ground and chase data.

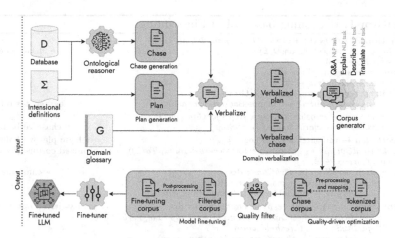

Fig. 1. Neurosymbolic pipeline for reasoning-based LLM fine-tuning.

Overview. In Sect. 2 we present our architecture. A preliminary experimental validation is provided in Sect. 3. We draw our conclusions in Sect. 4.

2   A Neurosymbolic Pipeline to Fine-Tune LLMs

The input blocks of the fine-tuning pipeline in Fig. 1 are D and Σ. They are, respectively, a database of domain facts and a set of reasoning rules, capturing the business dynamics. Our rules are expressed in VADALOG. An EKG is a combination $\Sigma(D)$ of D and Σ, obtained through reasoning. The set $\Sigma(D)$ is computed via the CHASE [13]: starting from $\Sigma(D) = D$, the chase augments $\Sigma(D)$ with facts derived from the application of the rules in Σ to fixpoint.

Let us introduce our running example: a simple trading activity managed with a *smart contract* [14]. Here, D contains a log over time of buy/sell orders from the traders who invest in the smart contract as well as market information, e.g., asset prices (*Price*), or market shutdowns (*MarketClosed*).

Example 1. The following set Σ contains the VADALOG *rules governing the basic functioning of the market, i.e., under which conditions the orders are accepted and how profits and losses are computed.*

$$Open(x, y, t_1), \neg\, MarketClosed(t_1) \rightarrow Accepted(x, y, t_1) \tag{1}$$

$$Accepted(x, y, t_1), Price(p_1, t_1), k = y * p_1 \rightarrow Position(x, y, k, t_1) \tag{2}$$

$$Close(x, t_2), Price(p_2, t_2), Position(x, y, k, t_1),$$
$$t_2 > t_1, pl = y * p_2 - k \rightarrow Return(x, pl) \tag{3}$$

If a trader x wants to open a position (buy) on a certain asset of size y at time t_1 and the market is open at t_1, the order is accepted (rule 1). If the order by x is accepted and the asset price at t_1 is p_1, then x holds a position on the market at time t_1 of size y and of notional (total value) k equal to $y * p_1$ (rule 2). If, later

---

Algorithm 1. Reasoning-based LLM Fine-tuning.

```
 1: function REASONINGFINETUNING(D, Σ, G, model, nlpTask)
 2:     chase ← VADALOG.reason(D, Σ)                                        ▷ chase generation
 3:     verbChase ← ∅
 4:     for each step in chase do
 5:         stepAggrContrib ← ∅
 6:         if hasAggregate(step.getRule()) then
 7:             stepAggrContrib ← composeBack(step, chase)                  ▷ aggregates retrieval
 8:         verbStep ← verbalizeStep(step, stepAggrContrib, G)
 9:         verbChase ← verbChase ∪ {verbStep}                             ▷ chase verbalization
10:     verbPlan ← verbalizePlan(Σ.getLogicPlan())                         ▷ logic plan verbalization
11:     tokenizedCorpus ← generate(preprocess(verbPlan, nlpTask))          ▷ tokenized corpus generation
12:     chaseCorpus ← ∅
13:     for each verbStep in verbChase do                                  ▷ chase mapping
14:         chasePromptResp ← map(tokenizedCorpus, verbStep)
15:         chaseCorpus ← chaseCorpus ∪ {chasePromptResp}
16:     for each pair ⟨prompt, resp⟩ in chaseCorpus do                     ▷ quality-driven optimization
17:         qualityScore ← checkQuality(⟨prompt, resp⟩, nlpTask, verbChase)
18:         if qualityScore ≤ threshold then
19:             chaseCorpus ← chaseCorpus \ {⟨prompt, resp⟩}
20:         else
21:             chaseCorpus ← chaseCorpus ∪ paraphrase(⟨prompt, resp⟩)     ▷ corpus paraphrasing
22:     fineTuningCorpus ← postprocess(chaseCorpus)
23:     ftModel ← fineTune(model, fineTuningCorpus)                        ▷ model fine-tuning
24:     return ftModel
```

---

at t_2, trader x decides to close its position (sell) and the price at t_2 is p_2, then x gets returns (profits or losses) from its trading activity as $y * p_2 - k$ (rule 3).

Applying the vision we laid out to Example 1, the goal of our pipeline is fine-tuning an LLM to address *explanation, description, question answering,* and *text-to-query translation* tasks for the simple trading activity at hand. Let us follow Fig. 1 and Algorithm 1 to describe the application of the pipeline to a database $D = \{Open(EGTech,0.3,1), Open(IEComp,0.5,1), Price(124,1), Price(147,9), Close(EGTech,9), MarketClose(5)\}$.

Chase Generation. The first step of our pipeline builds the chase $\Sigma(D)$, that is, the expansion of D with the facts that can be derived by applying the rules of Σ (line 2, in the algorithm). Rule 1 generates the fact $Accepted(EGTech, 0.3, 1)$, as the market is not closed at time 1. Then, $Position(EGTech, 0.3, 37.2, 1)$ is derived via rule 2. Finally, as trader $EGTech$ closes the position, i.e., sells the asset, at time 9 and the price goes up to 147\$, then $EGTech$ gets a profit of 6.9\$.

Domain Verbalization. Whenever a VADALOG rule is involved in the CHASE, it is translated into pure text with a deterministic transformation, based on the *select-project-join* semantics, which looks up a *glossary G* of atom descriptions. When rules involve aggregation functions, allowed in VADALOG, the process is less straightforward and involves unfolding a chain of chase activations altogether [1] (line 7). At the end of this phase, we are in hold of a *"since-then closure"* of our domain, that focuses on what can be obtained by activating the intensional knowledge of Σ. From another perspective, Σ can be seen as an *attention* mechanism, to select the fragment of D that one wants to verbalize. For instance, with respect to our running example, the chase step $Open(EGTech, 0.3, 1), \neg MarketClose(1) \rightarrow Accepted(EGTech, 0.3, 1)$ (rule 1) is verbalized as: *Since the trader EGTech at time 1 sends an order to open a position of size 0.3, and it is not true that 1 is a time when the market is closed, then the order of size 0.3 by EGTech is accepted at time 1.*

Fine-Tuning Corpus Generation. With the basic verbalization available, we are now ready to generate the fine-tuning corpus. We consider the corpus generation itself as a text manipulation task and exploit the effectiveness of powerful pre-trained LLMs [7], such as GPT-3, to synthesize a finite set of possible prompt-response pairs. Here we have two goals: 1) minimising the number of "calls" to the LLM, for cost- and time-efficiency reasons; 2) avoiding any ground value (coming from the EKG) being disclosed to the LLM, for data protection reasons. We leverage the regularity of logical languages and resort to a *lifting technique*. We build a *logic plan* out of Σ (line 10). A plan is the equivalent in our context of a database execution plan and can be seen as the dependency graph of the rules of Σ, where nodes represent rules and edges stand for head-body dependencies. The plan is then verbalized, obtaining a text with tokens as placeholders for rule variables. Finally, a tokenized fine-tuning corpus is generated from the plan, after minor pre-processing (line 11). The form of the prompts depends on the task. Now, for each verbalized chase step, we look up the corresponding verbalized portion of the plan and instantiate its tokens (lines 13–15). Note that no invocations to the *corpus generator* are needed in this phase. Figure 2 exemplifies the generation process in our example domain.

Plan	Tokenized corpus	Verbalized chase step	Chase corpus
$Open(x, y, t_1),$ $\neg\, MarketClosed(t_1)$ $\rightarrow Accepted(x, y, t_1)$	Q1: What is the size of the order accepted sent by trader $<x>$? A1: The size is $<y>$ Q2: Why was the order sent by trader $<x>$ at time $<t_1>$ accepted? A2: Because at time $<t_1>$ the market was open ...	Since the trader EGTech at time 1 sends an order to open a position of size 0.3, and it is not true that 1 is a time when the market is closed, then the order of size 0.3 by EGTech is accepted at time 1.	Q1: What is the size of the order accepted sent by trader EGTech? A1: The size is 0.3 Q2: Why was the order sent by trader EGTech at time 1 accepted? A2: Because at time 1 the market was open ...
$Open(x, y, t_1),$ $\neg\, MarketClosed(t_1)$ $\rightarrow Accepted(x, y, t_1)$ $\downarrow$ $Accepted(x, y, t_1),$ $Price(p_1, t_1), k = y * p_1$ $\rightarrow Position(x, y, k, t_1)$	Q1: When did $<x>$ send an order to open a position with notional $<k>$? A1: The order to open that position was sent at time $<t_1>$ ...	Since the trader EGTech at time 1 sends an order to open a position of size 0.3, and it is not true that 1 is a time when the market is closed, then the order of size 0.3 by EGTech is accepted at time 1. Since the order of size 0.3 by EGTech is accepted and the price is 124 at time 1, then EGTech holds a position of size 0.3 and notional 37.2 at time 1.	Q1: When did EGTech send an order to open a position with notional 37.2? A1: The order to open that position was sent at time 1 ...

Fig. 2. From plans to fine-tuning corpus, in our running example.

Quality-Driven Optimization. The corpus undergoes a quality check where each pair is filtered according to an NLP-based scoring model in terms of specificity, plausibility, absence of bias, and other user-defined criteria. The filtered-in pairs are enhanced via *NLP paraphrasing* to improve generalization and finally cleansed with additional post-processing procedures (lines 16–22).

Model Fine-Tuning. The refined corpus is injected into an LLM for task- and domain-specific fine-tuning (line 23). In the case of Q&A, the model operates in a *closed-book* approach, that is, it learns to map questions to the corresponding answers without extracting them from an input context, but rather encapsulating the knowledge of the domain into its internal parameters and weights [19]. The resulting specialized model is provided to the user via API, and will act as a natural language interface to the EKG and the ontological reasoning at its foundation in a neurosymbolic fashion.

3 Preliminary Validation via Proof-of-Concept

We implemented our fine-tuning pipeline in VADALOG. A full-scale evaluation of our architecture is beyond the scope of this short work. Conversely, in this section, we propose a conceptual validation of the approach, by briefly showing some executions of the pipeline. We will not consider the text-to-query translation task, as its evaluation would require semantic comparison, which is beyond the scope of this work.

For the proof-of-concept, we made use of a *T5-large* [10] model and considered the same domain as in Example 1. To obtain a dataset that could be visually inspected to informally assess the quality of the textual answers given by an LLM fine-tuned with our pipeline, we performed a kind of *ablation study*. For randomly chosen sets of sample questions, for the NLP tasks of interest, we compared the answers provided by an LLM fine-tuned only with ground facts (*T5-large-ground*) and one fine-tuned with our pipeline (*T5-large-chase*). Both models were trained for 10 epochs and with the same hyperparameters. The fine-tuning corpora and the models are made available [4].

Figure 3 visually reports the comparison. Questions a and b are the baseline, as they can be answered by facts in D. Apart from a less refined write-up, the LLMs show the same output behaviour. On the other hand, in questions c, d, and f T5-large-ground is outperformed by T5-large-chase, which succeeds in answering about events related to trader *EGTech*. Actually, the corresponding facts derive from $\Sigma(D)$, which is not considered in the ground fine-tuning. Similarly, the answer to question e by T5-large-ground is incomplete and only T5-large-chase is able to use the specific domain knowledge from rule 1 of Example 1.

	User question	T5-large-ground	T5-large-chase
a.	What is the size of the position that EGTech opens at time 1?	0.3	The size is 0.3
b.	What is the notional of EGTech's position at time 1?	37.2$	The notional is 37.2$, equal to price 124$ × size 0.3
c.	Why is the order by EGTech at time 1 accepted?	As it is a trade	Because the market at time 1 is not closed
d.	How can EGTech hold a position on the market at time 1 of notional 3$?	0.3	Since EGTech's position of size 0.3 was accepted and the price at time 1 is 10
e.	How does a trader get their position accepted?	By placing an order	By opening the position at a time in which the market is not closed
f.	How does EGTech profits from its trading activity?	EGTech has a profit of 6.9$	By opening a position of size 0.3 at time 1, having the position accepted with an initial price of 124$ and a notional of 37.2$ at time 1, and then closing it at time 9 with a final price of 147$, thus having a profit of 6.9$

Fig. 3. Proof-of-concept for our fine-tuning pipeline.

4 Conclusion

According to a recent work [24] appeared in the European Chapter of the Association for Computational Linguistics, pre-trained language models cannot yet perform deductive reasoning: they are still unable to generalize logical rules and, even when rules are provided, LLMs tend to forget previously inferred facts. While no extensive comparison between transformer architectures and reasoning approaches has been conducted yet, our work showed that LLM performance for domain-specific NLP tasks can be visibly improved by producing a fine-tuning corpus as a byproduct of ontological reasoning. We capitalized on our experience in deductive reasoning to offer a first step towards a neuro-symbolic platform for reasoning on enterprise knowledge graphs.

Acknowledgements. This work has been funded by the Vienna Science and Technology Fund (WWTF) [10.47379/ICT2201, 10.47379/VRG18013, 10.47379/NXT22018]; and the Christian Doppler Research Association (CDG) JRC LIVE.

References

1. Afrati, F.N., Gergatsoulis, M., Toni, F.: Linearisability on datalog programs. Theor. Comput. Sci. **308**(1–3), 199–226 (2003)
2. Agarwal, O., Ge, H., Shakeri, S., Al-Rfou, R.: Knowledge graph based synthetic corpus generation for knowledge-enhanced language model pre-training. arXiv preprint arXiv:2010.12688 (2020)
3. Andrus, B.R., Nasiri, Y., Cui, S., Cullen, B., Fulda, N.: Enhanced story comprehension for large language models through dynamic document-based knowledge graphs. AAAI **36**(10), 10436–10444 (2022)
4. Baldazzi, T., Bellomarini, L., Ceri, S., Colombo, A., Gentili, A., Sallinger, E.: Material. https://bit.ly/44249b5. Accessed 17 June 2023
5. Bellomarini, L., Benedetto, D., Gottlob, G., Sallinger, E.: Vadalog: a modern architecture for automated reasoning with large knowledge graphs. IS **105**, 101528 (2022)
6. Bellomarini, L., Fakhoury, D., Gottlob, G., Sallinger, E.: Knowledge graphs and enterprise AI: the promise of an enabling technology. In: ICDE, pp. 26–37 (2019)
7. Brown, T., et al.: Language models are few-shot learners. In: NeurIPS, vol. 33, pp. 1877–1901. Curran Associates, Inc. (2020)
8. Calì, A., Gottlob, G., Lukasiewicz, T.: A general datalog-based framework for tractable query answering over ontologies. J. Web Semant. **14**, 57–83 (2012)
9. Fu, H., Liu, C., Wu, B., Li, F., Tan, J., Sun, J.: CatSQL: towards real world natural language to SAL applications. VLDB **16**(6), 1534–1547 (2023)
10. Google: T5 large. https://huggingface.co/t5-large. Accessed 17 June 2023
11. Krötzsch, M., Thost, V.: Ontologies for knowledge graphs: breaking the rules. In: Groth, P., et al. (eds.) ISWC 2016. LNCS, vol. 9981, pp. 376–392. Springer, Cham (2016). https://doi.org/10.1007/978-3-319-46523-4_23
12. Liu, Z., Huang, D., Huang, K., Li, Z., Zhao, J.: FinBERT: a pre-trained financial language representation model for financial text mining. In: IJCAI 2020 (2021)
13. Maier, D., Mendelzon, A.O., Sagiv, Y.: Testing implications of data dependencies. ACM TODS **4**(4), 455–469 (1979)
14. Mohanta, B.K., Panda, S.S., Jena, D.: An overview of smart contract and use cases in blockchain technology. In: ICCCNT, pp. 1–4 (2018)
15. Moiseev, F., Dong, Z., Alfonseca, E., Jaggi, M.: SKILL: Structured knowledge infusion for large language models. In: ACL 2022, pp. 1581–1588 (2022)

16. Radford, A., Narasimhan, K., Salimans, T., Sutskever, I., et al.: Improving language understanding by generative pre-training (2018)
17. Rae, J.W., et al.: Scaling language models: methods, analysis & insights from training gopher. arXiv preprint arXiv:2112.11446 (2021)
18. Raffel, C., et al.: Exploring the limits of transfer learning with a unified text-to-text transformer. J. Mach. Learn. Res. **21**, 140:1–140:67 (2020)
19. Roberts, A., Raffel, C., Shazeer, N.: How much knowledge can you pack into the parameters of a language model? In: EMNLP, vol. 1, pp. 5418–5426. ACL (2020)
20. Ruder, S., Peters, M.E., Swayamdipta, S., Wolf, T.: Transfer learning in natural language processing. In: NAACL: Tutorials, pp. 15–18 (2019)
21. Wang, B., et al.: Rat-SQL: relation-aware schema encoding and linking for text-to-SQL parsers. arXiv preprint arXiv:1911.04942 (2019)
22. Wu, S., et al.: BloombergGPT: a large language model for finance. CoRR abs/2303.17564 (2023)
23. Yin, X., Gromann, D., Rudolph, S.: Neural machine translating from natural language to SPARQL. Future Gener. Comput. Syst. **117**, 510–519 (2021)
24. Yuan, Z., Hu, S., Vulic, I., Korhonen, A., Meng, Z.: Can pretrained language models (yet) reason deductively? In: EACL, pp. 1439–1454 (2023)

Layerwise Learning of Mixed Conjunctive and Disjunctive Rule Sets

Florian Beck$^{(\boxtimes)}$ ⓘ, Johannes Fürnkranz ⓘ, and Van Quoc Phuong Huynh

Institute for Application-Oriented Knowledge Processing (FAW), Johannes Kepler University Linz, Altenberger Straße 66b, 4040 Linz, Austria
{fbeck,juffi,vqphuynh}@faw.jku.at

Abstract. Conventional rule learning algorithms learn a description of the positive class in disjunctive normal form (DNF). Alternatively, there are also a few learners who can formulate their model in conjunctive normal form (CNF) instead. While it is clear that both representations are equally expressive, there are domains where DNF learners perform better and others where CNF learners perform better. Thus, an algorithm that can dynamically make use of the best of both worlds is certainly desirable. In this paper, we propose the algorithm CORD that can learn general logical functions by training alternating layers of conjunctive and disjunctive rule sets, using any conventional rule learner. In each layer, the conjunctions/disjunctions trained in the previous layer are used as input features for learning a CNF/DNF expression that forms the next layer. In our experiments on real-world benchmark data, CORD outperformed both state-of-the-art CNF and DNF learners, where the best final performance was typically achieved using a high number of intermediate, general concepts in early layers that were refined in later layers, underlining the importance of more flexible and deeper concept representations.

Keywords: rule learning · constructive induction · CNF · DNF

1 Introduction

Inductive rule learning is one of the oldest and most traditional areas in machine learning [8]. Typically, a rule is a conjunction of conditions, and multiple such rules are learned in order to cover all training examples from a given class. This corresponds to learning a concept in *disjunctive normal form* (DNF). Nevertheless, it may be of interest to investigate alternative ways of formulating logical concepts. In particular, learning concepts in *conjunctive normal form* (CNF) has seen a bit of work in the past, in particular in descriptive inductive logic programming [e.g., 3,4], but less so in a predictive, propositional setting, the most notable exceptions being [5,14]. In this work, we aim at learning mixed logical theories that combine both conjunctive and disjunctive operators.

To this end, we first recapitulate the duality of learning DNFs and CNFs, illustrating them in the context of inverted coverage spaces, which allows to

© The Author(s), under exclusive license to Springer Nature Switzerland AG 2023
A. Fensel et al. (Eds.): RuleML+RR 2023, LNCS 14244, pp. 95–109, 2023.
https://doi.org/10.1007/978-3-031-45072-3_7

use any conventional rule learner for learning expressions in either representation, and, on the way, review related prior work in this area (Sect. 2). On that basis we develop $\overline{\text{LORD}}$, a CNF version of LORD, a recent powerful DNF rule learning algorithm [10], and compare the performance of both versions, thereby confirming previous results [e.g., 5] (Sect. 3).

Our main contribution is CORD, a learner that is able to add multiple conjunctive and disjunctive layers, each time using the disjunctive/conjunctive rule bodies of the previous layer as additional features in the conjunctive/disjunctive next layer (Sect. 4). The alternation of conjunctive and disjunctive layers is motivated by the fact that successive pairs of alternating layers can be interpreted as CNF or DNF expressions, and thus be learned with a single conventional rule learner, as discussed in Sect. 2. Moreover, if, e.g., conjunctive features would be used as an input for a learner that learns conjunctive rules, this does not extend the scope of expressions that can be found (the learned expressions would still be DNF) whereas disjunctive features as input allow a DNF learner to learn a three-layered structure (disjunctions of conjunctions of disjunctions). While this does, of course, not extend the expressiveness of the learner, as every logical expression has a DNF or CNF representation, it nevertheless has an impact on the behavior of the learner, because it changes the syntactic pattern of expressions that can be evaluated and (greedily) optimized. We analyze this behavior for a different number of layers and further hyperparameters, showing that concepts are learned and refined over multiple layers—similar to deep neural networks.

The algorithms are evaluated along the way, indicating that additional layers can further improve the performance of LORD and $\overline{\text{LORD}}$, in particular if earlier layers are tuned towards learning more general concepts, as will be summarized in the conclusions (Sect. 5).

2   Conjunctive and Disjunctive Rules

In the following, we consider **concept learning** problems on binary features, i.e., we have fixed number of binary features, which we typically denote with letter $\{a, b, c, d, e \dots\}$, and two classes, the positive class $(+)$ and the negative class $(-)$. The task is to learn a **rule r** $: + \leftarrow B$ for the positive class, where B is a logical expression defined over the input features. Examples that are not covered by this definition are considered to be negative.

2.1   Refinement of Conjunctive or Disjunctive Rules

Traditionally, rules are learned via **successive refinement**, i.e., an initially empty rule is gradually refined by adding individual conditions. Conjunctive refinements specialize a rule (afterwards it can never cover more examples than before the refinement), whereas disjunctive refinements generalize a rule (afterwards it can never cover fewer examples than before the refinement). This can be visualized in coverage space, a non-normalized ROC space, where the x-axis shows the covered negative and the y-axis the covered positive examples [7].

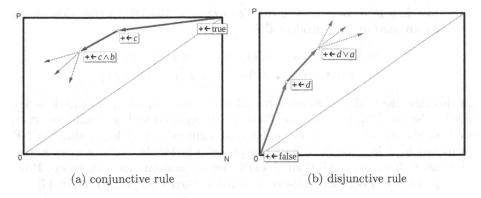

(a) conjunctive rule   (b) disjunctive rule

Fig. 1. Successive refinement of rules

For example, Fig. 1a shows a path that gradually refines an initially universal rule (covering all P positive and N negative examples, upper right corner of the coverage space) into the rule $+ \leftarrow c \wedge b$. In analogy, Fig. 1b shows a path that gradually refines an initially empty rule (covering no examples, lower left corner of the coverage space) into the rule $+ \leftarrow d \vee a$.

Note that the goal of learning is to (approximately) reach the upper left corner, i.e., to find a rule that covers (almost) only positive examples and no negatives. In the case of conjunctive learning, this means that all of the possible conditions must cover all positive examples, which is unrealistic in practical scenarios. In the case of disjunctive learning, conversely, the upper left corner is only reachable if none of the conditions covers any negative examples, which is again not to be expected.

2.2   DNFs and CNFs

In general, a single rule, conjunctive or disjunctive, is not able to model all possible Boolean functions defined on the features. However, multiple conjunctive rules are sufficient to model all possible features. This is, because the rules themselves may be viewed as a disjunction. For example, a set of rules $\{r_1 : + \leftarrow c \wedge a, r_2 : + \leftarrow d, r_3 : + \leftarrow b \wedge e\}$ classifies an example as positive if either the first, the second, or the third rule fires, i.e., if either c and a, or d, or b and e hold. Thus, it corresponds to the single rule

$$r : + \leftarrow (c \wedge a) \vee d \vee (b \wedge e)$$

The logical expression in the body of the rule is in what is known as the **disjunctive normal form (DNF)**. Every logical function can be put into such a form. Rule learning algorithms often learn DNF expressions with the so-called covering or separate-and-conquer strategy, which sequentially adds one rule at a time until all positive examples are covered [6].

The counterpart to a DNF expression is the **conjunctive normal form (CNF)**, i.e., a conjunction of disjunctive terms. Every logical expression can be expressed in a DNF or a CNF form. For example, the DNF expression above can be converted to an equivalent CNF:

$$(c \wedge a) \vee d \vee (b \wedge e) = [(c \vee d) \wedge (a \vee d)] \vee (b \wedge e)$$
$$= (b \vee c \vee d) \wedge (a \vee b \vee d) \wedge (c \vee d \vee e) \wedge (a \vee d \vee e)$$

In this case, the CNF expression is considerably more complex, but this does not need to be case [13]. For example, if every $\wedge$ is replaced with a $\vee$ and vice versa, we have the opposite case of a complex DNF expression that has a simpler CNF formulation. It has also been found empirically [5,14] that some concepts may be easier to learn in a CNF than in a DNF representation (and vice versa). Both settings have also been investigated in learning theory [cf., e.g., 1,11,16,17].

2.3   The Duality of Learning DNFs and CNFs

Using simple Boolean operators, one can transform a CNF expression as follows:

$$(c \wedge a) \vee d \vee (b \wedge e) = \neg\neg [(c \wedge a) \vee d \vee (b \wedge e)]$$
$$= \neg [\neg(c \wedge a) \wedge \neg d \wedge \neg(b \wedge e)]$$
$$= \neg [(\neg c \vee \neg a) \wedge \neg d \wedge (\neg b \vee \neg e)]$$

Essentially this means that for learning an expression in DNF, one could learn a CNF expression on the negated inputs and invert the output. Analogously, a CNF expression can be obtained by learning a DNF. Thus, one can use a conventional rule learner for DNFs to learn a CNF expression by learning a DNF (i) on the negated inputs, and (ii) on the negated class.

More precisely, for learning a CNF expression for the positive class, we negate all features of the input data, and learn a DNF expression on the negative class. The CNF expression for the positive class then has exactly the same structure, but replacing all negated features with the original features, and inverting all logical operators ($\wedge$ becomes $\vee$ and v.v.). For example, the adaptation of the DNF learning algorithm FOIL [15] to learn CNF expressions as proposed by Mooney [14] works in exactly this way. However, FOIL-CNF has there been defined as a separate, dual algorithm, without making the general transformation explicit.

2.4   Inverted Coverage Spaces and Heuristics

The effects of the two transformation mentioned above can be visualized in coverage space as follows:

(i) We learn on the negative class, i.e., the (P, N)-coverage space becomes a (N, P)-coverage space. This corresponds to swapping the two dimensions of the coverage space.
(ii) We learn on the negated features, which corresponds to flipping the coverage space so that the $(0, 0)$-point (covering no examples) becomes the upper right corner (covering all examples).

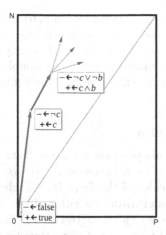
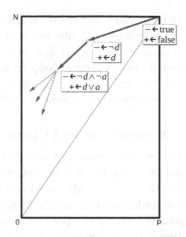

(a) Disjunctive learning of a conjunction.   (b) Conjunctive learning of a disjunction.

Fig. 2. Learning of conjunctive and disjunctive rules in inverted coverage space.

We call the resulting coverage space the **inverted coverage space**. A point
(n, p) in the original coverage space (corresponding to a Boolean expression B
which covers p positive and n negative examples) is mapped to point $(P-p, N-n)$
in this inverted coverage space, because $\neg B$ covers $N - n$ negative and $P - p$
positive examples. Figure 2a illustrates how the conjunctive rule of Fig. 1a could
be learned with a disjunctive learner, and, conversely, Fig. 2b shows how the
disjunctive rule of Fig. 1b could be learned with a conjunctive learner. Also note
the swapped dimensions of the coverage spaces.

This allows us to determine what heuristics should be used for learning disjunctive rules. Typically, rule learning heuristics trade off the importance of covering all positives (**completeness**) and not covering any negatives
(**consistency**), and can thus be written as functions h(p, n), where $0 \le p \le P$
$(0 \le n \le N)$ is the number of positive (negative) examples covered by a rule [7].
As we have seen above (Figs. 1b and 2b), learning a disjunctive rule corresponds
to learning a conjunctive rule in the inverted coverage space. Thus, disjunctive
rules should be evaluated with h$(N - n, P - p) = $ ꓩ(p, n). This also corresponds
to the following intuition: When DNFs are learned in a covering rule, individual
rules aim at minimizing covered negatives (false positives, consistency) and less
importance is given to maximizing covered positives (true positives, completeness), because completeness can be achieved by adding more rules, whereas an
inconsistent rule cannot be fixed by adding more rules (at least not in a strictly
logical interpretation of the learned DNF). Conversely, if a CNF is learned by
successively adding disjunctive rules, each of these rules strives for completeness
(i.e., it should cover all positive examples), because inconsistency (i.e., covering
too many negative examples), can still be fixed by adding another disjunction
that covers all positives but maybe a different set of negative examples.

We thus conclude that if conjunctive rules are evaluated with $h(p, n)$, disjunctive rules should be evaluated with $q(p, n)$. In fact, this approach has already been taken by Mooney [14], who used an inverted FOIL-gain for learning CNF expressions in a covering loop that adds rules until no negative examples are covered (maximizing $N - n$), where each rule is iteratively refined until it covers all positive examples (minimizing $P - p$).

2.5 Deterministic and Characteristic Rules

The astute reader may have observed that the rule pairs shown in Fig. 2 are actually not logically equivalent, because the rule $+ \leftarrow B$ corresponds to $\neg B \leftarrow -$, and not to $- \leftarrow \neg B$. Michalski [12] has called rules of the form $B \leftarrow +$ **characteristic rules**, as opposed to conventional **discriminative rules**. Thus, a discriminative rule for the positive class corresponds to a characteristic rule for the negative class, and vice versa. Another point of view is that characteristic rules encode **necessary**, whereas deterministic rules capture **sufficient** conditions. By not differentiating between the two, we implicitly interpret the implication $+ \leftarrow B$ as an equivalence $+ \leftrightarrow B$. This is justified, if B encompasses the entire positive class, which is the case for a complete DNF or CNF expression, where both $+ \leftarrow B$ (consistency), but also $B \leftarrow +$ (completeness) hold.

3   A Re-evaluation of DNF and CNF Learning

As we have seen in the previous section, any conventional rule learner can be used for learning disjunctive concepts, by negating the input features and learning on the negative class. For the investigations in this paper, we use a recent DNF rule learner LORD (Locally Optimal Rules Discoverer) [10]. In the following, we explain the idea of the LORD algorithm and how it can be adjusted to a CNF setting. In Sect. 4.1, we then propose a combination of these two versions to a multi-layered learner named CORD that uses disjunctive features learned in a CNF setting as an additional input for the DNF rule learner LORD.

3.1   LORD

As the name suggests, LORD learns a locally optimal rule for every single training example. In contrast to most state-of-the-art rule learners, it therefore does not aim for a compact rule set covering all examples but for better rules for every single example, usually leading to much larger rule sets as a consequence. To compute these large rule sets efficiently, it reuses data structures well-known in the field of association rule mining, PPC-trees and N-lists, which can summarize the count of examples covered by a conjunctive expression without further consultation of the data set. In particular, this helps LORD to learn even data sets with millions of examples, where other modern rule learning algorithms come to their limits [10]. LORD can, in principle, work with any heuristic, but is best parameterized with the m-estimate. In the likely case that a testing example is covered by multiple rules, the one with the highest m-estimate is chosen for the class prediction.

3.2 LORD

While in the above setting the output model of LORD corresponds to a DNF, we can adjust it slightly and create a new variant LORD—pronounced NEGLORD—that learns CNF output models instead. As described in Sect. 2.3, $a \lor b = \neg(\neg a \land \neg b)$ holds, i.e., we can still use the original LORD algorithm for learning conjunctive rules if we both negate the features before building rules and the learned rule body afterwards.

After preprocessing and discretizing the data as for LORD, the PPC-tree of LORD will be computed based on the positive class and all negated features, i.e., all features an example does not fulfill. Thereby, the complexity of the PPC-tree increases remarkably for non-binary attributes, since it now depends on the number of features instead of the number of attributes. While there is certainly potential for improvement, for the scope of this paper the described simple approach is sufficient.

LORD learns rules as conjunctions on the negated features, but still uses a positive class. When converting these conjunctions into disjunctions, each rule becomes a "counter-clause" for all classes other than the predicted one, implementing the required second negation of the rule body. However, the prediction can still be performed on the original rule with negated features: The covering rule with the highest m-estimate is selected and results in an unsatisfied clause in the CNF of all classes other than the class in the rule head, which will be predicted. Though, for the usage in CORD, the resulting disjunctive clause will be stored as a new feature.

3.3 Experimental Evaluation

To evaluate the performance of LORD and LORD, we followed the experimental setup used by Dries et al. [5]: The hyperparameter of the m-estimate was tuned on the same five UCI data sets (*diabetes, hepatitis, iris, kr-vs-kp* and *yeast*), and the best-performing value was then used on these 5 and 24 additional data sets. For both algorithms, we tried the values $m \in \{0, 0.1, 0.3, 1, 3, 10, 30, 100\}$, and, in both cases, the value $m = 3$ emerged as the best. For ease of comparison, we also repeat the accuracies of K-CNF and RIPPER as reported by Dries et al. [5].[1]

Table 1 shows the accuracies of these algorithms obtained by 10-fold-cross-validation. To aggregate the results, the last line shows the average rank. First we can notice that the results of the LORD-based algorithms are in line (even slightly better) with the performance of their competitors K-CNF and RIPPER. This lets us conclude that LORD is a good basis for the studies reported in the remainder of this paper.

Second, LORD outperforms its counterpart LORD on 18 of the tested data sets, whereas the opposite only holds in 9 cases (with 2 ties). This confirms that

---

[1] As a sanity check, we also validated the RIPPER accuracies on a random sample of the data sets.

Table 1. Predictive accuracy of two DNF (RIPPER, LORD) and two CNF learners (K-CNF, $\overline{\text{LORD}}$) on 29 UCI data sets.

Data set	RIPPER	K-CNF	LORD	$\overline{\text{LORD}}$	Data set	RIPPER	K-CNF	LORD	$\overline{\text{LORD}}$
anneal	95.10	96.66	98.78	99.11	hypothyroid	99.34	93.24	97.51	97.83
audiology	75.26	74.35	78.81	77.37	iris	93.33	82.67	94.00	94.67
autos	72.64	80.52	76.52	76.05	kr-vs-kp	99.12	97.34	98.72	98.72
balance-scale	71.86	83.05	82.39	82.56	labor	84.00	92.33	80.67	81.67
breast-cancer	74.11	70.25	71.33	71.71	lymph	75.10	81.86	78.29	83.76
breast-w	93.56	97.00	95.13	93.71	mushroom	100.00	100.00	100.00	100.00
colic	84.79	81.52	85.04	85.06	primary-tumor	41.62	42.78	45.43	48.07
credit-a	84.93	81.45	86.81	86.96	segment	95.84	88.23	93.59	94.46
credit-g	72.70	73.10	74.30	72.30	sick	98.49	97.16	95.15	97.00
diabetes	73.70	72.28	71.49	69.93	soybean	91.50	94.58	91.50	91.35
glass	64.11	61.73	65.00	64.94	vote	95.84	94.70	94.04	95.41
heart-c	79.56	82.85	83.10	84.11	vowel	71.11	95.25	75.86	77.17
heart-h	77.44	80.53	81.31	81.66	yeast	58.89	53.44	55.93	56.19
heart-statlog	81.11	78.89	76.30	73.33	zoo	90.18	95.00	90.18	94.18
hepatitis	82.08	83.33	83.92	83.25	Avg. rank	2.67	2.64	2.50	2.19

on average, CNF rule learning outperforms DNF rule learning on the majority of the 29 tested data sets. This was also observed by Mooney [5], as can be seen from the results for RIPPER and K-CNF, but our results are stronger because they are based on exactly the same underlying algorithm, thus removing potential effects of algorithmic differences between RIPPER and K-CNF. In this respect, our results are comparable to those of Mooney [14], who compared a DNF and a CNF variant of FOIL, but only a limited sample of 5 data sets.

Despite the potential effect of algorithmic differences, we also note that the observed performance differences are often quite consistent. For example, it seems that *heart-statlog* can be considerably better learned in a DNF representation, whereas *lymph* seems to be more amenable to CNF. Ideally, an algorithm should be able to make the best of both worlds, which is what we strived for with the work reported in the next section.

4   Learning Mixed Conjunctive and Disjunctive Rules

Even though DNFs and CNFs can represent each possible logical concept, they may be hard to build up iteratively. To see this, note that at any given point, a conjunctive refinement of the logical expression corresponding to this point can only reduce the number of covered (positive and negative) examples, i.e., it can only reach the region to its lower left. Conversely, a disjunctive refinement can only increase the number of covered examples, i.e., it can only reach the region to its upper right. Thus, as illustrated in Fig. 3a, the region between the current point and the perfect rule (upper left corner) can never be reached with purely conjunctive or disjunctive refinements (unless the current point is still on the $n = 0$ or $p = P$ lines).

Note that this can also not be fixed with the commonly used separate-and-conquer strategy, which successively adds one rule at a time. Figure 3b illustrates

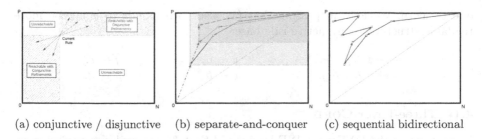

(a) conjunctive / disjunctive   (b) separate-and-conquer   (c) sequential bidirectional

Fig. 3. Reachable and unreachable regions in coverage space

this for learning DNFs: Each time a conjunctive rule (red arrows) is added to the rule set, the covered examples are removed, and the next rule is learned in a reduced coverage space (shown in grey shading). Thus, the addition of conjuncts to the DNF expression follows the green dashed path. Obviously, this approach can also never reach the unreachable area in the upper left of the coverage space.

One way of reaching such points could be a sequential bidirectional search, as illustrated in Fig. 3c. This corresponds to sequentially extending an initially empty logical expression by either AND-ing or OR-ing the next condition to the entire previous turn. Thus, if B is the current expression, the possible refinements will be $B \wedge f$ or $B \vee f$ for each possible feature f. This corresponds to forming a left-bracketed expression $(((a \odot b) \odot c) \odot d) \odot \ldots$, where $\odot$ corresponds to either $\wedge$ or $\vee$. Unfortunately, this approach has another severe disadvantage, namely that only a small share of all logical expressions may be expressed in such a left-bracketed way, i.e., most logical functions can not be found with such a bidirectional search.

Thus, in this paper, we follow a different path, namely to try to add multiple layers of refinement, so that the conjuncts (disjuncts) found in the previous layer can be added to the disjuncts (conjuncts) in the next layer. An example for such a logical expression learned over multiple layers would be:

$$+ \leftarrow (a \vee b) \wedge \left[(c \vee d) \wedge \left(e \vee (f \wedge g) \right) \right] \tag{1}$$

In this case, the first (disjunctive) layer found the concepts $(a \vee b)$ and $(c \vee d)$, which are passed as additional features to the second (conjunctive) layer. This layer in turn uses them to learn the two conjunctive concepts enclosed in brackets. A final third (disjunctive) layer combines these two concepts to a single logical expression. Note that this expression only consists of 7 terms, whereas the corresponding minimal CNF

$$+ \leftarrow (a \vee b) \wedge (e \vee f) \wedge (e \vee g) \wedge (c \vee d \vee f) \wedge (c \vee d \vee g)$$

consists of 12 literals, and the corresponding minimal DNF

$$+ \leftarrow (a \wedge c \wedge e) \vee (a \wedge d \wedge e) \vee (a \wedge f \wedge g) \vee (b \wedge c \wedge e) \vee (b \wedge d \wedge e) \vee (b \wedge f \wedge g)$$

of 18 literals. Therefore, while all these expressions are equivalent, the expression shown above is, arguably, the most interpretable one and potentially the easiest one to learn. We note in passing that (1) also corresponds to a maybe more readable structured conjunctive rule base:

$$+ \leftarrow x \wedge y \wedge e. \qquad x \leftarrow a. \qquad y \leftarrow c.$$
$$+ \leftarrow x \wedge f \wedge g. \qquad x \leftarrow b. \qquad y \leftarrow d.$$

4.1 Three-Layer CORD

In contrast to the DNF and CNF learners of Sect. 3, our goal was to design an algorithm that can cope with both conjunctive and disjunctive features at the same time. We name it CORD, short for Conjunctive OR Disjunctive rule learner.

The simplest version of CORD should be able to learn models in both CNF and DNF. To achieve that, it consists of three phases. In the first, the original data set is processed as described in Sect. 3.2, i.e., we use $\overline{\text{LORD}}$ to learn disjunctive features, which in turn uses LORD to learn conjunctions from the negated features. The formed rules are applied to all instances of the data set, and for each rule an additional feature is generated which encodes the truth value of that rule's body. In the second phase, this enriched data set is passed to LORD, which then learns rules from this augmented data set. Figure 4 shows the scheme of CORD and illustrates how the deep logical expression (1) could be learned.

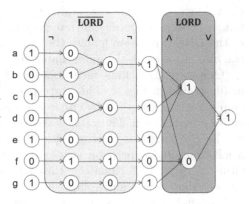

Fig. 4. Scheme of CORD processing the data point $\{a, \neg b, c, \neg d, e, \neg f, g\}$ after learning the deep sample expression (1).

Optionally, by restricting the usage of new generated features to only their negated form, we can make sure to simulate a conjunction as discussed in the last paragraph of Sect. 3.2. However, for a better comparison with $\overline{\text{LORD}}$, we will not use this restriction during the main experiments. Finally, in the third phase, all rules are filtered and combined to a final rule set like in the original LORD algorithm. Note that for predicting the class of a test instance, the rules learned in the first phase have to be applied to this test instance as well before the best covering rule in the final rule set can be determined.

In analogy to neural networks, CORD may be viewed as adding an additional second hidden layer to the learning process in comparison to DNF and CNF rule learners. While DNF rule learners effectively learn a single conjunctive hidden layer that is aggregated by a disjunctive output node in the final layer, and vice versa for CNF learners, CORD consists of a disjunctive hidden layer followed by a conjunctive hidden layer and a disjunctive output node in the final layer.

Obviously, CORD is then still capable to learn CNFs by just using a single conjunctive node in the second hidden layer, which corresponds to the case in which only a single rule is learned in the third phase. Likewise, CORD is still capable to learn DNFs by passing the input layer data to the first hidden layer without modifications, which corresponds to the case in which no rules are learned from the negated features in the first phase.

In the following sections, we will evaluate this three-layer structure, while Sect. 4.2 will discuss the potential of adding additional layers.

Hyperparameter Tuning for CORD. We tuned the parameters of CORD as described in Sect. 3.3. In particular, CORD uses a separate m-parameter m_i for each of its layers. Again, we test the values $m_i \in \{0, 0.1, 0.3, 1, 3, 10, 30, 100\}$ for $i \in \{1, 2\}$ resulting in 64 different versions of CORD.

To compare the performance of the different versions of each learner, we computed the average rank as well as the average accuracy over the five tuning data sets (cf. Sect. 3.3). It turned out that for CORD, the version with the best average rank and the version with the best average accuracy differ from each other: The best rank is shared between the versions $m = [0, 0.1]$, $m = [0, 0.3]$ and $m = [0.1, 0.1]$, whereas the best average accuracy is achieved by version $m = [100, 0]$. All of these versions achieved at least similar performances like LORD on the 29 UCI data sets, so they were better than RIPPER and K-CNF, but only the last version could slightly outscore $\overline{\text{LORD}}$ (see also Table 3).

We also noted that the optimal settings vary considerably between data sets. For example, Tables 2a and 2b show how the predictive accuracy develops for different values of m_1 and m_2 on the example of the data sets *hepatitis* and *primary-tumor*. While for both data sets better accuracies are achieved for lower values for m_2, on the *hepatitis* data set lower values for m_1 and on the *primary-tumor* data set higher values for m_1 are in an advantage. In both cases, increasing values of m_1 led to increasing rule lengths in the final learner, if the newly added features are also considered with a length of one. This can be explained by the fact that these newly added features are already precise enough if generated with low m_1-values and can be used without or only little refinements, whereas newly added features generated with high m_1-values are further refined in the second

Table 2. Predictive accuracy of different CORD versions (in %). Green colors represent the best configurations, red colors the worst.

(a) *hepatitis* data set

m_1 \ m_2	0	0.1	0.3	1	3	10	30	100
0	83.3	83.9	83.9	83.3	82.0	80.0	82.0	82.0
0.1	83.3	83.9	83.9	83.3	82.0	80.0	82.0	82.0
0.3	83.3	83.9	83.9	83.9	82.0	79.4	81.3	82.0
1	83.9	84.5	84.5	84.5	83.9	81.3	82.0	82.0
3	83.3	83.3	83.3	83.3	83.3	80.1	83.3	82.0
10	82.6	82.6	82.6	82.6	82.0	81.3	80.7	80.1
30	81.9	81.9	82.6	81.9	81.3	82.6	83.3	84.5
100	82.5	83.2	83.2	83.5	82.0	81.3	82.0	83.3

(b) *primary-tumor* data set

m_1 \ m_2	0	0.1	0.3	1	3	10	30	100
0	39.8	40.4	40.7	41.9	41.9	41.0	42.7	37.1
0.1	39.8	40.4	40.7	41.9	41.9	41.0	42.7	37.1
0.3	39.5	40.1	40.7	41.6	41.6	41.0	41.9	36.3
1	40.4	40.4	41.9	42.8	40.4	41.3	41.6	38.0
3	43.3	43.3	43.3	44.2	43.6	42.4	43.1	37.1
10	41.9	41.9	42.4	43.3	43.1	39.8	39.8	38.3
30	44.5	43.9	44.2	44.5	43.3	39.8	40.7	40.7
100	44.2	44.2	45.7	44.5	42.2	38.9	39.2	38.0

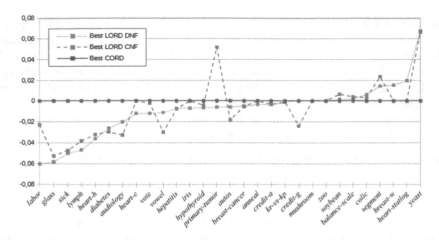

Fig. 5. Predictive accuracy of the three rule learners LORD, $\overline{\text{LORD}}$ and CORD on 29 UCI data sets, relative to the baseline CORD. The data sets are sorted according to the performance difference between LORD and CORD.

phase of CORD. As can be seen from the two tables, it clearly depends on the data set, which of these two variants is more successful.

Comparison to Pure CNF and DNF Learning. As discussed above, the predictive accuracy of CORD highly depends on the selection of m_1 and m_2 and the optimal setting varies for different data sets. LORD and $\overline{\text{LORD}}$ also depend on their parameter m, but it seems less drastic than the influence caused by the combination of m_1 and m_2 for CORD. To evaluate this, we applied all 8 respectively 64 versions of LORD, $\overline{\text{LORD}}$ and CORD to the 29 UCI data sets and found the best accuracy achieved for each type of learner.

Figure 5 summarizes the results. It shows the performance of CORD as a horizontal blue line, and draws the relative performance of the best versions of LORD (dotted green) and $\overline{\text{LORD}}$ (dashed red) on top of it. One can see that on most data sets, the best version of CORD outperforms the best versions of LORD and $\overline{\text{LORD}}$. There are only a few data sets to the right where LORD is better, and a few outliers (in particular *primary-tumor* and *yeast*) where CORD is substantially outperformed by $\overline{\text{LORD}}$. The average rank of CORD over all data sets is 1.6, whereas LORD and $\overline{\text{LORD}}$ rank at 2.24 and 2.16 respectively.

4.2 Multi-layer CORD and DORC

The previous section investigated a fixed structure, consisting of a succession of a CNF learner and a DNF learner, as shown in Fig. 4. Of course, we can also swap the order of these steps—resulting in a version of the learner that we refer to as DORC—and in both versions add further layers, where the features

Table 3. Predictive accuracy of two CORD and two DORC learners, with three and five layers respectively, on 29 UCI data sets.

Data set	CORD3	DORC3	CORD5	DORC5	Data set	CORD3	DORC3	CORD5	DORC5
anneal	99.67	99.55	99.55	99.44	hypothyroid	94.88	98.12	95.97	96.24
audiology	79.98	77.83	79.57	79.57	iris	94.00	94.00	95.33	95.33
autos	80.40	76.45	78.43	77.45	kr-vs-kp	99.19	99.50	99.41	99.28
balance-scale	81.75	80.96	81.11	81.59	labor	82.33	82.00	88.00	88.00
breast-cancer	71.00	71.33	69.59	69.57	lymph	87.10	78.19	81.62	85.00
breast-w	94.42	94.71	94.42	94.71	mushroom	100.00	100.00	100.00	100.00
colic	83.15	83.96	79.91	82.87	primary-tumor	44.23	43.94	41.57	40.39
credit-a	83.62	84.64	85.07	84.93	segment	94.29	94.37	94.59	94.59
credit-g	73.70	74.40	73.30	73.20	sick	96.92	96.79	97.03	97.11
diabetes	74.61	72.79	73.43	72.92	soybean	92.67	90.47	92.08	93.85
glass	67.68	66.32	69.09	67.62	vote	94.50	95.88	94.72	94.48
heart-c	80.52	85.13	79.22	80.84	vowel	79.19	78.69	79.70	79.80
heart-h	83.01	82.30	81.99	81.66	yeast	52.15	55.32	50.27	51.01
heart-statlog	72.22	74.44	77.04	77.04	zoo	94.18	92.18	94.18	91.18
hepatitis	82.54	85.83	84.00	83.92	Avg. rank	2.43	2.57	2.41	2.59

of each previous layer provide additional inputs to subsequent layers, not unlike layer-wise forward training of neural networks [2].

To that end, we expand CORD with an additional disjunctive and an additional conjunctive layer, which corresponds then to a network with four hidden layers and a disjunctive output node in the final fifth layer. Analogously, DORC also has five alternating layers, but starts and ends with a conjunctive instead of a disjunctive layer. The objective is to determine whether, similar to neural networks, new generated concepts in deeper layers can further improve the performance.

As described in Sect. 3.3, we tuned the parameters of the additional CORD and DORC learners based on a few sample data sets[2] and afterwards applied the best configuration on all 29 data sets. For the three-layered DORC the same 64 combinations were tested as for CORD. For the five-layered networks, we tested the values $m_i \in \{0.3, 1, 3, 10, 30\}$ for $i \in \{1, 2, 3, 4\}$ resulting in 625 different versions. The best configuration for each version was chosen based on the average accuracy on the test data sets, resulting in $m = [100, 0]$ for the three-layered CORD, $m = [100, 1]$ for the three-layered DORC, $m = [30, 0.3, 0.3, 10]$ for the five-layered CORD and $m = [10, 30, 30, 10]$ for the five-layered DORC.

Table 3 shows the accuracies of these four variants on 29 UCI data sets, again obtained by 10-fold-cross-validation. Even though they are generally better than those of the benchmark algorithms of Table 1, the results with respect to adding additional layers do not clearly point into a single direction: there are several datasets where additional layers clearly help (e.g., heart-statlog, or labor), but in

---

[2] The yeast data set was omitted due to too long calculation time over all combinations.

others they also reduce the performance (e.g., *breast-cancer*), so that on average, no substantial differences between the tested versions can be obtained. However, these results may also be affected by the selection bias of the UCI repository towards sets where simple rules tend to perform exceptionally well [9].

While the previous experiments could not reveal an advantage for a specific rule learning architecture, all optimal configurations had in common that they use high m-values in early layers and lower values in later layers, resulting in more general rules in the first phases and more specific ones in the end. Intuitively, this behavior makes sense, and is, in a way, analogous to the performance in deep neural networks: the early layers form very general concepts (as, e.g., edge extractors in images), which are successively specialized in later layers. In an attempt to investigate this issue more systematically, for both the five-layered CORD and DORC, we evaluated the accuracy of at least 81 different m-value-combinations for each of the 29 UCI data sets. Table 4 shows the correlation of various characteristics in different layers of the network with the final accuracy. For example, we can see higher values of m tend to deliver better results in earlier layers, and worse in later layers, that a high accuracy is less important in earlier levels, or that a higher number of learned concepts or depth of structuring has a somewhat positive effect.

Table 4. Correlation between model properties after each conjunctive or disjunctive layer C_i/D_i, and the predictive accuracy at the final layer, for both a five-layered CORD and DORC learner.

	CORD				DORC			
	D_1	C_2	D_3	C_4	C_1	D_2	C_3	D_4
m	0.154	0.020	-0.101	-0.131	0.081	0.175	0.019	-0.098
# Rules	-0.189	-0.145	-0.092	-0.043	-0.084	-0.253	-0.134	-0.081
# Concepts	-	0.095	0.045	0.008	-	0.060	0.151	0.074
Avg. Depth	-	0.111	0.057	-0.018	-	0.117	0.159	0.107
Accuracy	0.203	0.520	0.690	-	-0.041	0.342	0.564	-

5   Conclusion

With the goal of learning deeper logical models, we proposed a general framework for using any rule learner for a layer-wise learning of mixed DNF and CNF expressions. We evaluated this on the example of CORD, which, in its simplest version, concatenates the CNF rule learner $\overline{\text{LORD}}$ and the DNF rule learner LORD to make use of both conjunctive and disjunctive logical concepts. The experiments showed that CORD is able to outperform all other tested CNF or DNF rule learners. We also evaluated 5-layer versions of CORD and its counterpart DORC, and found clear indications that in order for them to be helpful, earlier layers should be tuned to learn more general concepts, so that later layers can focus on combining them to high-accuracy models.

References

1. Angluin, D., Laird, P.: Learning from noisy examples. Mach. Learn. **2**(4), 343–370 (1988)
2. Bengio, Y., Lamblin, P., Popovici, D., Larochelle, H.: Greedy layer-wise training of deep networks. In: Schölkopf, B., Platt, J.C., Hofmann, T. (eds.) Advances in Neural Information Processing Systems 19 (NeurIPS), pp. 153–160. MIT Press, Vancouver, British Columbia, Canada (2006)
3. De Raedt, L., Bruynooghe, M.: A theory of clausal discovery. In: Bajcsy, R. (ed.) Proceedings of the 13th International Joint Conference on Artificial Intelligence (IJCAI-93), pp. 1058–1063, Morgan Kaufmann, Chambéry, France (1993)
4. De Raedt, L., Dehaspe, L.: Clausal discovery. machine learning **26**(2/3), 99–146 (1997). special Issue on Inductive Logic Programming
5. Dries, A., De Raedt, L., Nijssen, S.: Mining predictive k-CNF expressions. IEEE Trans. Knowl. Data Eng. **22**(5), 743–748 (2009)
6. Fürnkranz, J.: Separate-and-conquer rule learning. Artif. Intell. Rev. **13**(1), 3–54 (1999)
7. Fürnkranz, J., Flach, P.A.: ROC 'n' rule learning – towards a better understanding of covering algorithms. Mach. Learn. **58**(1), 39–77 (2005)
8. Fürnkranz, J., Gamberger, D., Lavrač, N.: Foundations of rule learning. Springer, Berlin (2012), ISBN 978-3-540-75196-0, https://doi.org/10.1007/978-3-540-75197-7
9. Holte, R.C.: Very simple classification rules perform well on most commonly used datasets. Mach. Learn. **11**, 63–91 (1993)
10. Huynh, V.Q.P., Fürnkranz, J., Beck, F.: Efficient learning of large sets of locally optimal classification rules. Mach. Learn. (2023). ISSN 1573–0565, https://doi.org/10.1007/s10994-022-06290-w
11. Kearns, M.J., Li, M., Pitt, L., Valiant, L.G.: On the learnability of Boolean formulae. In: Aho, A.V. (ed.) Proceedings of the 19th Annual ACM Symposium on Theory of Computing, pp. 285–295, ACM, New York, USA (1987)
12. Michalski, R.S.: A theory and methodology of inductive learning. Artif. Intell. **20**(2), 111–162 (1983)
13. Miltersen, P.B., Radhakrishnan, J., Wegener, I.: On converting CNF to DNF. Theoret. Comput. Sci. **347**(1–2), 325–335 (2005)
14. Mooney, R.J.: Encouraging experimental results on learning CNF. Mach. Learn. **19**, 79–92 (1995)
15. Quinlan, J.R.: Learning logical definitions from relations. Mach. Learn. **5**, 239–266 (1990)
16. Valiant, L.G.: A theory of the learnable. Commun. ACM **27**, 1134–1142 (1984)
17. Valiant, L.G.: Learning disjunction of conjunctions. In: Joshi, A.K. (ed.) Proceedings of the 9th International Joint Conference on Artificial Intelligence (IJCAI), pp. 560–566, Morgan Kaufmann, Los Angeles, CA, USA (1985)

Analyzing Termination for Prev-Aware Fragments of Communicating Datalog Programs

Francesco Di Cosmo(✉)

Free University of Bozen-Bolzano, Bolzano, Italy
fdicosmo@unibz.it

Abstract. Communicating Datalog Programs (CDPs) are a distributed computing model grounded on logic programming: networks of nodes perform Datalog-like computations, leveraging on information coming from incoming messages and databases received from external services. In previous works, the decidability and complexity border of verification for different variants of CDPs was charted. In general, the problem is undecidable, but model-checking of CTL formulas specialized to the data-centric and distributed setting is decidable for CDPs where all data-sources, except the external inputs, are bounded. An intuitive explanation is that "a bounded state is unable to fully take advantage of an unbounded input", a formal justification is missing. However, we note that traditional CDPs have a limited capability of handling external inputs, i.e., they cannot directly compare two successive inputs or messages. Thus, an alternative explanation is that an unbounded data-source does per se not cause undecidability, as long as the CDP cannot compare two successive instances.

1 Introduction

Declarative languages are capable of specifying queries and algorithms in an elegant and succinct way. For that reason, in the last decades, Datalog-like languages have been proposed as a programming language for distributed systems. Some examples are Webdamlog [3], NDlog [9], and Dedalus [2]. We loosely call this kind of model *Declarative Distributed Systems* (DDSs). Morever, since Datalog-like language are data-centric, i.e., they specify the behaviour of systems that can only manipulate relational databases (DBs), they are especially interesting for modelling data-aware Business Processes [4,6,8]. In fact, DDSs can be considered as a natural model for interdependent business processes in which the identity of the data items is crucial and cannot be abstracted away.

Since DDSs are formalized in variants and extensions of first order logic, one can directly apply formal methods for verification. However, the verification of data-aware systems is hard, since they can manipulate fresh data provided by input databases (DBs) from external services, resulting in infinite state systems. In fact, verification of problems like control-state reachability is undecidable.

A. Fensel et al. (Eds.): RuleML+RR 2023, LNCS 14244, pp. 110–125, 2023.
https://doi.org/10.1007/978-3-031-45072-3_8

Nevertheless, previous works [5] over a specific formulation of DDS, i.e., Communicating Datalog Programs (CDPs), showed that decidability is achieved when the active domains of all *data-sources*, i.e., the DBs representing the inputs, the internal memory of the nodes, and the channel configurations, are assumed bounded. A remarkable exception is the data-source representing the interaction with dynamic external services and users. In fact, leaving this source unbounded does not, per se, cause undecidability or a change in complexity. An intuitive explanation is that an otherwise bounded DDS cannot make proper use of unbounded external inputs.

However, this fact could also depend on additional reasons, based on the peculiarity of the interaction of DDSs with external sources, e.g., lack of queries over previously provided external data. In fact, remarkably, the traditional DDS model assumes that nodes can query the previous configuration of their internal memory but not the external inputs. Thus, it may be the case that combinations of boundedness/unboundedness conditions and the ability/inability to query previous instances of the data-sources may have an important impact on the decidability and complexity boundary of verification problems for DDSs.

In this paper, we study prev-aware CDPs, in which the interaction with the nodes previous configuration can be freely tweaked. Their combination with boundedness constraints results in 64 fragments over which we chart the decidability border of verification of termination. This gives a full picture of the impact of the previous configuration over verification of CDP fundamental properties.

To that end, in Sect. 2, we introduce two counter machines and Petri Nets. In Sect. 3, we introduce in detail the CDP model. In Sect. 4, we define the prev-aware fragments and their related verification problems. In Sect. 5, we prove the decidability status of a small set of fragments; these results can be generalized to chart the full spectrum. In Sect. 6, we draw our conclusions.

This paper extends the position paper [7] by providing the technical development of constructions, D2C programs, and proofs (see Sect. 5).

2   Preliminaries

2.1   Two Counter Machines

A (deterministic) two counter machine (**2 cm**) is a finite state automaton operating on two counters containing numbers. Formally, it is a tuple $E = (Q, \delta, q_{\texttt{init}}, q_{\texttt{fin}})$ where Q is the finite set of states, $q_{\texttt{init}}$ and $q_{\texttt{fin}}$ are the *initial* and *final* states and δ is the finite set of instruction. An increment instruction is a tuple $(q_1, q_2, q_2, +, i)$ and a conditional decrement instruction is a tuple $(q_1, q_2, q_3, -, i)$, where the q_js are in Q and $i \in \{1, 2\}$. For each $q \in Q$, there is at most one instruction with q in its first component. The configurations of E are triples (q, n_1, n_2), where $q \in Q$ and $n_1, n_2 \in \mathbb{N}$ (which represent the numbers in the counter). There is a transition from a configurations $C = (q, n_1, n_2)$ to a configuration $C_2 = (q', n_1', n_2')$, denoted $C_1 \rightarrow C_2$ if there is an instruction t such that, 1. $t = (q_1, q_2, q_2, +, i)$, $q = q_1$, $q' = q_2$, $n_i' = n_i + 1$, and $n_j' = n_j$, or 2. $t = (q_1, q_2, q_3, -, i)$, $q = q_1$, $q' = q_2$, $n_i \geq 1$, $n_i' = n_i - 1$, and $n_j' = n_j$, or 3. $t = (q_1, q_2, q_3, -, i)$, $q = q_1$, $q' = q_3$, $n_i = 0 = n_i'$, and $n_j' = n_j$, or where $j \in \{1, 2\} \setminus \{i\}$. The configuration graph of E has the configuration of E as nodes and edges (C_1, C_2) if $C_1 \to C_2$. The initial configuration is $(q_{\text{init}}, 0, 0)$. The well-known undecidable termination problem for **2 cm** ask whether there is a sequence $(q_{\text{init}}, 0, 0) = C_0 \to \cdots \to C_n = (q_{\text{fin}}, n_1, n_2)$.

2.2 Petri Nets

A Petri Net (PN) is a tuple $N = (P, T, F)$, where P is the finite set of places, T is the finite set of transitions, $P \cap T = \emptyset$, and $F : (P \times T) \cup (T \times P) \longrightarrow \mathbb{N}$ is the flow function. Each $F(p, t)$ is called a precondition and $F(t, p)$ is called postcondition. A marking is a function $M : P \longrightarrow \mathbb{N}$. A transition is enabled on a marking M if, for each $p \in P$, $M(p) \geq F(p, t)$. The firing of an enabled transition t on M defines the marking M', denoted $M \to^t M'$, such that, for each $p \in P$, $M'(p) = M(p) - F(p, t) + F(t, p)$. The configuration graph of N has its markings as nodes and edges (M_1, M_2) there is a t such that $M_1 \to^t M_2$. Given an initial marking M_0, N terminates from M_0 if there is a sequence $M_0 \to^{t_0} \cdots \to^{t_{n-1}} C_n$ such that there is no enabled transition in C_n. The termination problem for PNs asks whether N terminates, given an initial marking. This problem is decidable.[1]

3 CDPs

A CDP is a network of nodes running a program, in the Datalog-like language D2C and sharing relational facts over a dedicated *transport signature*. The network is connected, reflexive, and symmetric. Each node has a DB containing its own name and the names of all its neighbors. Messages are sent on a channel (v, u) from the source node v to the destination node u. Messages are received according to the *asynchronous policy*, i.e., at each computation step only one message is delivered. A *channel configuration* represents a multisets of messages on a channel. In fact, channels are assumed unordered, i.e., messages are never lost but the sending order may be different from the delivery one.[2] Thus, channel configurations are assumed to be bag-DBs, i.e., a finite bag of facts.

Next to channels, the nodes receive inputs from external services. This is modeled by the availability to each node of an *input DB*, over an *input signature* $\mathcal{I}$, which can freely change over time, i.e., at each computation step, the input DB may be updated to a different (possibly unrelated) DB over $\mathcal{I}$. Nodes have a local memory, which contains auxiliary information deduced by the node during the previous computation step, stored in a *state DB* over a *state signature* $\mathcal{S}$.

The reception of a message m at a node v triggers a new computation step.[3] First, m is removed from its channel. Then, while all other nodes remain inactive,

---

[1] Since it is a variant of coverability of markings, which is decidable.

[2] This choice is in line with the fact that, in general, Datalog rules (responsible for the production of messages) do not have to be computed in a specific order.

[3] At startup, each self-loop channel contains a special activation message, used to trigger the first computation step.

v combines the input DB I, its state DB S, and the message m labeled by the sender name w (i.e., a labeled transport fact $m@w$) in a single DB, used as extensional data on which a D2C program is computed. The program returns a new state DB $\mathtt{state}(S, I, m@w)$ and a set $\mathtt{out}(S, I, m@w)$ of outgoing messages labeled with destinations. The payload of outgoing messages is retrieved from the state DB, forbidding the direct sending of the input DB active domain on the channels. Finally, the CDP configuration is updated by *(1)* substituting S with $\mathtt{state}(S, I, m@w)$ *(2)* removing m and adding $\mathtt{out}(S, I, m@w)$ (without addresses) to the respective previous channel configurations.

Definition 1. *A configuration of a CDP D is a pair (S, C) where S maps the nodes to their state DBs, I is the input DB, and C maps the channel to teir channel configurations. Given two configurations C_1, C_2, an input DB I and a message m we write $C_1 \to^{m,I} C_2$ to dentoe that the reception of m over the input DB I and the configuration C_1 computes C_2. The configuration graph of D has the configurations of D as nodes and transitions (C_1, C_2) if $C_1 \to^{m,I} C_2$. The initial configuration maps to each node the same initial DB S and to each channel the configuration $\{\mathtt{start}\}$.*

A *D2C program* is a finite set of safe Datalog-like rules of the form

$$H \quad \mathbf{if} \quad L_1, dots, L_n \; prev \;, L_{n+1}, \ldots, Ln + m, C_1, \ldots, C_n.$$

where H is an atom, the L_is are literals, and the C_is are inequality constraints. D2C features specialized construct to handle communication and the query of the previous state DB. Communication is handled by labeling transport literals T with addresses t, resulting in the formulas $T@t$: in the body of a rule, the address represents the node sending the incoming message; in the head, the address represents the recipient of the outgoing message. To query the previous state DB, a special flag *prev* is used: all atoms in its scope range over the (extensional) previous state, while all other predicates range over the (intensional) current state. D2C rules can also make use of inequality constraints. Traditionally, it is required that only state literals can occur in the scope of *prev*. In this paper, we allow all literals, irrespective of their signature, to occur in the scope of *prev*. This requires to extend the CDP model to what we call *prev-aware CDPs*, in which the configurations are extended with the previous inputs and messages and $\mathtt{out}$ and $\mathtt{state}$ are redefined accordingly.

Finally, the D2C program must be *stratified*, i.e., stratified a la Datalog when the transport predicates in the body and the predicates in the scope of *prev* are interpreted as extensional predicates. Both stratification and formal semantics of the program can be formalized via an encoding in traditional Datalog rules.

We now define constraints on the CDP data-sources, i.e., state, input, and channel. A configuration is reachable if it can be obtained from the initial configuration in a finite number of computation steps. Given a $b \in \mathbb{N}$, we say that a CDP is b-state bounded if, for each reachable configuration σ, the active domains of all state DBs in σ contain at most b constants. We say that it is b-channel bounded if all the channel configurations contain at most b messages (considering multiplicities). A similar constraint can be put on the input. However, in this case, we have to change the semantics of CDPs. Specifically, a b-input bounded CDP is a CDP with the provision that the input DBs triggering transitions must have an active domain bounded by b. A data-source is bounded if it is b-bounded for some b. A CDP is bounded if all its data-sources are bounded.

Given a CDP D with program Π, a data-source C is *prev-free* if there is no literal in the signature of C that occurs in the scope of *prev* in some rule of Π. Otherwise, it is *prev-aware*. Given an atom or inequality constrain A, $Var(A)$ is the set of variables occurring in A.

4 Problem

Previous results on the verification of CDPs showed that model checking of specialized CTL languages is decidable only if all the data-sources are bounded [5], with the only exception of the input data-source, whose unboundedness is irrelevant. In all other cases, problems like control-state reachability, termination, and convergence are undecidable. The decidability for unbounded input can be explained by the fact that a bounded state cannot make proper use of an unbounded input.

However, the input data-source is unique in its kind because it is the only one on which it is not possible to simulate a *prev* by exploiting the *prev* on the state, without violating state boundedness assumptions. I.e., the absence of *prev* over the input data-source is not w.l.o.g. and may motivate the unique impact of input-unboundedness on decidability of verification and Thus, we consider fragments of prew-aware CDPs. We name them by triples $C_i - C_s - C_c$ that denote the family of all CDPs whose input (state, channel) is constrained by C_i (C_s, C_c). We consider four of constraints: BPF enforces both boundedness and prev-freeness, B enforces boundedness but not necessarily prev-freeness, PF enforces prev-freeness but not necessarily boundedness, and $\top$ does not enforce any constraint. We call the resulting 64 fragments *prev-aware*.

We focus on the verification of *termination*.[4] In fact, *(1)* it characterises the decidability status of model checking problems against the specialized CTL languages and *(2)* it is closely related with other problems, such as *control-state reachability* and *convergence*.[5]

The decidability of termination of some of these fragments is an immediate consequence of the results by Calvanese et al. [5]. These are depicted in the first three columns of Table 1. We extend the known cases to the full picture in the table. It is easy to see that these cases are sufficient to completely chart the

---

[4] Termination asks whether there is a run that reaches a configuration where no node can be activated anymore.

[5] Since termination occurs when the channels are empty, termination over bounded states can be viewed as control-state reachability. Moreover, convergence, i.e., the reachability of a configuration from which the state DBs do not change anymore, is a generalization of termination.

decidability status of all 64 fragments, since each other case is a fragment of a decidable one or an extension of an undecidable one.

Table 1. The CDP fragments we consider in this paper. B indicates that the data-source is bounded; PF indicates that the data-source is prev-free; ⊤ indicates that the data-source is not constrained by neither boundedness nor prev-freeness. The first three fragments were studied by Calvanese et al. [5].

Input	PF	BPF	BPF	PF	⊤	B	BPF	BPF	PF	B	B
State	B	⊤	B	PF	BPF	B	PF	BPF	BPF	BPF	PF
Channel	B	BPF	PF	BPF	BPF	B	PF	⊤	PF	PF	B
Status	D	U	U	U	U	D	D	U	D	U	D

Finally, we focus on single-node networks. This comes w.l.o.g., since any arbitrary network can be encoded in a single-node network, by building a disjoint union of the CDP signatures and program.

5 Proofs

We introduce some abbreviation. As customary in logic programming, rule bodies can have anonymous variable _. It serves as a placeholder for a variable that occurs in its place and occurs in the rule only once. For example, the body $A(\_, X), B(X)$ is equivalent to the body $A(Y, X), B(Y)$. W.l.o.g., safety does not apply to negated anonymous variables, at the cost of expanding the signature and incorporating tuples in the state. For example, given an input predicate I, a state predicate A, and a state proposition H, the rule π equal to H if not $I(\_, X), A(X)$ can be equivalently rewritten as the safe rules $I'(X)$ if $I(Y, X)$ and H if not $I'(X), A(X)$. However, this way, even if H is propositional, π may break state-boundedness. In fact, if the input is unbounded, the active domain of the state predicate I' may be unbounded. Thus, anonymous variables should be used carefully when programming state-bounded CDPs.

Given the atoms $H_1, \ldots, H_n$ and a body B, the rule $H_1, \ldots, H_n$ if B denotes the set of rules H_i if B, for $i \leq n$.[6] Given a rule H if B without inequality constraints, and a sequence $C_1, \ldots, C_m$ of inequality constraints, the rule $H \leftharpoonup B C_1, \ldots, C_m$ denotes the set of rules $H \leftharpoonup B C_i$, i.e., the inequality constraints are interpreted disjunctively.

Given a unary predicate U and a constant c, the formula $U = 1/C$, called *cardinality rule*, denotes the rules **Err** if not $U(\_)$. **Err** if $U(X), U(Y), X \neq Y$. **Err** if $U(c)$., i.e., if $|\Delta(U)| \neq 1$ or $c \in \Delta(U)$, then an error is deduced.

---

[6] Note that commas in the heads do not represent disjunction.

PF-PF-BPF. This fragment has undecidable termination. In fact, we show a reduction from satisfiability of stratified Datalog, which is undecidable (even without recursion; see [1], sec. 6.3), to termination of PF-PF-BPF CDPs.

Given a stratified Datalog query Q, we use Q as the core of a D2C program Π for a single node CDP D whose input signature consists of the extensional predicates of Q and the state signature consists of the intensional predicates of Q. The transport signature is $\mathcal{T} = \{\text{step}/0\}$. W.l.o.g., we can assume that Q has a single, propositional output symbol O.[7] We add the following rule, where v is the name of the node: step@v if $\text{not}\, O$.

Note that, at each step, at most one message is produced and this message can only be step. Thus, a run $\rho = \sigma_0, \ldots, \sigma_n = (S, I, C)$ terminates iff no message is sent during the last step $\tau = (\sigma_{n-1} \to \sigma)$. Moreover, step is not sent iff O is deduced, iff the input DB satisfies Q. Thus, D terminates iff Q is satisfiable. Note that D is 1-channel bounded and Π does not use *prev*.

Theorem 1. *Termination of PF-PF-BPF CDPs is undecidable.*

$\top$-*BPF-BPF.* Also this fragment has undecidable termination. In this case, we cannot resort to undecidability of satisfiability for stratified Datalog, since that requires unbounded states to perform arbitrary Datalog computations. However, we can use the unobunded input DBs to encode arbitrary **2 cm** configurations and, exploiting the *prev* on the input, use a CDP program to check whether the sequence of inputs form a **2 cm** run. If this check fails, non-termination is triggered. Otherwise, termination is enforced if the final state of C is reached.

Given a **2 cm** $E = (Q, \delta, q_{\text{init}}, q_{\text{fin}})$, we build a $\top$-BPF-BPF, single-node CDP D, over the node v. The initial state DB S_0 is over the state symbols $\mathsf{Q}/1$ and $\text{tran}/6$. Specifically, $\mathsf{Q}_{S_0} = Q$ and, for $j \in \{1, 2\}$, $\text{tran}_{S_0} = \{(n, q_0, q_1, q_2, p, c) \mid (q_0, q_1, q_2, p, c) \in \delta, f(n) = (q_1, q_2, p, c)\}$, where f is a fixed injective function, i.e., the first component is a primary key. We use input DBs over an input $\mathcal{I} \supseteq \{\text{succ}/2, \text{conf}/1\}$ to encode natural numbers and configurations of C.

Definition 2. *Given an input DB I, I encodes the number $n \in \mathbb{N}$, if there are n pairwise distinct constants $c_1, \ldots, c_n \in \Delta$ such that $\text{succ}_I = \{\text{succ}(\min, c_1), \ldots, \text{succ}(c_n, \max)\}$. Given a $c \in \Delta(\text{succ}_I)$, the number encoded by c in I, denoted $[c]_I$ is i if $c = c_i$ and is 0 if $c = \min$. The number n is denoted by $[I]$. Given an input DB J, J extends by one I if, $[J] = [I] + 1$ and $\text{succ}_I \setminus \{c_n, \max\} \subseteq \text{succ}_J$.*

Definition 3. *Given an input DB I and a **2 cm** configuration $\sigma = (q, c_1, c_2)$, I encodes σ if $[I] \geq \max\{c_1, c_2\}$ and $\text{conf}_I = \{(q, c_1, c_2)\}$. The configuration encoded by C is denoted by $\langle C \rangle$.*

Note that, since D is input unbounded but state bounded, the program of D can freely use anonymous variables only in (1) unary predicates, (2) positive literals, and (3) bounded predicates bounded, e,g., state predicates. The program

---

[7] Otherwise, we can add rules that deduce O when some tuple is produced in one of the output symbols.

Π of D is written in Figs. 1 and 2, with the provision that the bodies of all non-cardinality rules in Fig. 2 have to be extended with a Step@v outside the scope of *prev*. The program Π performs several checks. If any of these fails, an error Err flag is deduced in the state. In turn, this flag is persistent and deduces a persistent ErrMsg message that forces non-termination (rules 1–3).

At startup, D converts the start message into a Step one and checks whether the input encodes the initial configuration of E. Moreover, it checks whether the input provides the domain of succ in $\Delta/1$ (rules 4–10).

1 Err *if* Err.	7 Conf(q_0,min,min) *if* Start@v.
2 ErrMsg *if* Err.	8 Err ⤙ Conf(Q,X,Y),
3 ErrMsg *if* ErrMsg.	Q≠q_0,X≠min,Y≠min.
4 Step *if* Start@v.	9 Dom(min), Dom(max) *if* Start@v.
5 Suc(min,max) *if* Start@v.	10 Err⤙Dom(X), X≠min, X≠max.
6 Err ⤙ Succ(X,Y), X≠min, Y≠min.	

Fig. 1. Program for the first step of the T-BPF-BPF CDP D.

At each other step, i.e., at the reception of Step, v checks whether the current input DB incorporates in succ a constant indicated in the input predicate New/1 (rules 16–23). The predicate New is assumed to contain always a single constant not in the previous extension of succ (rules 11–13). To do that, it is necessary to check also that Δ is updated accordingly (rules 14–15).

Moreover, v also checks whether the new input DB encodes a configuration σ' reachable from the configuration σ in the previous input DB via an instruction. This instruction is chosen by checking that the input predicate Cand contains a single instantiation of the key of tran (rules 24–26), which thus indicates a candidate transition. If the instruction is not applicable or does not trigger a transition $\sigma' \to \sigma$, then an error is deduced (rules 27–33). Finally, v triggers a new step if the input does not encode a **2 cm** configuration over q_{fin} (rule 34).

The following theorems can be proved via induction. For reasons of space, we omit their proofs. An *input stream* is a finite sequence $I_1, \ldots, I_n$ of input DBs, for some $n \geq 0$. A run $(S_0, C_0) \to^{m_0, I_0}, \cdots \to^{m_{n-1}, I_{n-1}} (S_n, C_n)$ is *triggered* by the input stream $I_0, \ldots, I_n$.

Lemma 1. *If ρ is a run in D triggered by the input stream $I_0, \ldots, I_n$ that ends in a configuration C such that* Err $\notin C$, *then, (1) for each configuration C' in ρ,* Err $\notin C'$, *(2) $[I] = n$, and (3) $\langle I_n \rangle = \sigma$, for some configuration σ of E, then σ is reachable in E.*

Theorem 2. *If a configuration σ is reachable in E, then there is a run in D triggered by the input stream $I_0, \ldots, I_n$ such that ρ ends in a configuration C,* Err $\notin C$, *and $\langle I_n \rangle = \sigma$.*

Thus, E terminates iff there is a run ρ in D triggered by an input stream $I_0, \ldots, I_n$ such that $\langle I_0 \rangle$ is over q_{fin}, i.e., equivalently (because of rule 34), D

11 New=1 / max.
12 Err *if* New(X) *prev* Suc(X,Y).
13 Err *if* New(X), *not* Dom(X).
14 Err *if not* Dom(X) *prev* Dom(X).
15 Err *if* Dom(X), New(Y) *prev not*
     Dom(X), X≠ Y.
16 Err *if* Succ(X,Y), Succ(Z,Y), X≠ Z.
17 Err *if* Succ(X,Y), Succ(X,Z), Y≠ Z.
18 Err *if* Succ(X,Y), *not* Dom(X).
19 Err *if* Succ(X,Y), *not* Dom(Y).
20 Err *if* Succ(X,Y) *prev not*
     Succ(X,Y), Y≠ max.
21 Err *if* Succ(X,max) *prev*
     Succ(X,max).
22 Err *if not* Succ(X,Y), New(Y) *prev*
     succ(X,max).
23 Err *if* Succ(X,max), *not* New(X).
24 Cand=1.
25 CandOk *if* Cand(X),
     Tran(X,_,_,_,_,_).
26 Err *if not* CandOk.
27 Err *if* Cand(X),
     Tran(X,Q0,Q1,Q2,T,C), *prev*
     Conf(Q,X,Y), Q0≠Q.

28 Err *if* Cand(X),
     Tran(X,Q0,Q1,Q2,+,1), Succ(X,W),
     not Conf(Q1, W,Y) *prev* Conf(Q,X,Y).
29 Err *if* Cand(X),
     Tran(X,Q0,Q1,Q2,+,2), Suc(Y,W),
     not Conf(Q1, X,W) *prev* Conf(Q,X,Y).
30 Err *if* Cand(X),
     Tran(X,Q0,Q1,Q2,-,1), Succ(W,X),
     not Conf(Q1, W,Y) *prev*
     Conf(Q,X,Y), X≠min.
31 Err *if* Cand(X),
     Tran(X,Q0,Q1,Q2,-,2), Suc(W,Y),
     not Conf(Q1, X,W) *prev*
     Conf(Q,X,Y), Y≠min.
32 Err *if* Cand(X),
     Tran(X,Q0,Q1,Q2,-,1), *not* Conf(Q1,
     min,Y) *prev* Conf(Q,min,Y).
33 Err *if* Cand(X),
     Tran(X,Q0,Q1,Q2,-,2), *not* Conf(Q1,
     X,min) *prev* Conf(Q,X,min).
34 Step@v *if* Conf(Q,X,Y), Q≠q_{fin}.

Fig. 2. Program for the arbitrary step of the T-BPF-BPF CDP D. In the bodies of all the non-cardinality rules, a Step@v atom outside the scope of prev is omitted.

terminates. Note that D is state bounded, since all rules have propositional symbols in the heads. Moreover, it is also 1-channel bounded, since, after startup, at most one instance of Step is on the channel.

Theorem 3. *Termination of* T-*BPF-BPF CDPs is undecidable.*

B-B-B. This fragment has decidable termination. In fact, since all data-sources are bounded, we can use the same technique for BPF-B-BPF CDPs by Calvanese et al. [5] (Thm. 1): because of boundedness, it is possible to finitely represent CDP configurations up to isomorphisms. The prev-awareness of all data-sources results in an bigger abstract representation of the data-sources, but does not affect the applicability of the method.

BPF-PF-PF. This fragment has decidable termination. Since the state is prev-free, the new state contains only constants from the incoming message, which are in bounded number, and from the input DB, which is bounded. Thus, also the state is bounded. Note that, since all sources are prev-free, the name of constants in the messages on the channel are irrelevant. Thus, we can abstract away the messages up to isomorphisms. Since each message contains a bounded number of constants, they result in a finite family of messages. This enables an encoding in Petri nets, which have decidable termination.

```
 1 Succ(min,min), Decide if Start.        8 Succ(Y,Z) ⤳ Ext(X,Y).
 2 Decide ⤳ if Start.                     9 Ext(X,Z), Succ(Y,Z) if Succ(Y,Z)
 3 Done if not Cand(_), Decide.             prev Ext(X,Y), X≠Z, Z≠max.
 4 Ext(X,min) if Cand(X),Decide,X≠min. 10 Succ(Y,X), Succ(X,max), Decide if
 5 Done, Ext ⤳ Decide.                      Succ(Y,max) prev Ext(X,Y).
 6 Done if Done.                          11 T\{Succ} ⤳ Succ(X,Y).
 7 Done ⤳ Done.                           12 ErrMsg if ErrMsg.
```

Fig. 3. Program to encode an arbitrary number in the channel.

Given a BPF-PF-PF CDP D with program Π, we first build the finite abstraction, i.e., an alternative configuration graph bisimilar to that of D.

Definition 4. *A D-isomorphism is a bijection $\xi : \Delta \longrightarrow \Delta$ such that $\alpha|_{\Delta(\Pi)} = id_{\Delta(\Pi)}$. The set of D-isomorphisms is denoted by $\Xi(D)$. The D-isomorphism type $[m]_D$ of a fact m is the set $\{\alpha(m) \mid \alpha \in \Xi(D)\}$. The multiset of D-isomorphism types $[C]_D$ of a multiset C of facts is the multiset such that $supp([C])\{[m]_D \mid m \in C\}$ and $[C]_D([m]_D) = |\{n \in C \mid [n]_D = [m]_D\}|$.*

The abstraction of D works on the types of the channel configurations.

Definition 5. *The abstract configuration graph Υ^{abst} of D is the directed graph $(\mathfrak{C}^{abst}, E^{abst})$ such that (1) $\mathfrak{C}^{abst}$ is the set of all multisets of D-configuration types of multisets of transport facts, and (2) $(C, C') \in E^{abst}$ iff there is a $\tilde{m} \in C$, a $m \in \tilde{m}$, and an input DB I such that $C' = C \setminus \{\tilde{m}\} \cup [\text{out}(\emptyset, I, m)]$, denoted by $C \to_i^{m,\tilde{m}} C'$. The initial configuration of Υ^{abst} is $[C_0]$, where C_0 is the initial configuration of Υ. Given $C, C' \in \mathfrak{C}^{abst}$, $C \to C'$ denotes that $C \to_i^{m,\tilde{m}} C'$ for some $m, \tilde{m}$, and I. The binary relation $B \subset \mathfrak{C} \times \mathfrak{C}^{abst}$ is the relation such that $((S, C), \overline{C}) \in B$ iff $[C] = \overline{C}$.*

Note that, if $\alpha \in \Xi(D)$, $[\alpha(m)]_D = [m]_D$. The fact that B is a bisimulation is an easy consequence of the definitions of the involved configuration graphs. Thus, for space reasons, we omit the proof. Note that, if $B((S, C), C')$ then $C = \emptyset$ iff $C' = \emptyset$. Thus, D terminates iff Υ^{abst} has a finite run that reaches the $\emptyset$.

Theorem 4. *D terminates iff there is a finite run of Υ^{abst} that reaches $\emptyset$.*

We now exploit b-input boundedness to build a Petri Net whose configuration graph is bisimilar to Υ^{abst}. We fix three disjoint sets of constants $\Delta^{spec} = \Delta(D)$, Δ^b, and Δ^a, such that $|\Delta^b| = b$ and $|\Delta^a| = \max\{n \mid I/n \in \mathcal{I}\}$, where $\mathcal{I}$ is the input signature of D. Let $\Delta' = \Delta^{spec} \cup \Delta^b \cup \Delta^a$ and $\tau(\Delta')$ be the set of all messages over Δ'. Note that, since Δ^a is large enough, for each message m over Δ, there is a message $f \in \tau(\Delta')$ such that $[m] = [f]$. Thus, the set of types of messages in $\tau(\Delta')$ is the set of all types, i.e., we can use $\tau(\Delta')$ as a set of (redundant) representatives of all types. Moreover, we can also effectively extract a complete and minimal family of representatives of all types (for example, by imposing a lexicographic order among the tuples of messages over Δ^a and choosing the minimum from each type). Let P^a be such a family.

Definition 6. *The encoding net $N = (P, T, F)$ is such that: $P = P^a$, $T = \{t_I^f \mid \Delta(I) \subset \Delta', f \in P^a\}$ and, for each $g \in P^a$ and $t_I^f \in T$, $F(g, t_I^f), F(t_I^f) \leq 1$ and $F(g, t_I^f) = 1$ iff $g = f$ and $F(t_I^f, g) = 1$ iff $g \in [\text{out}(I, f)]$. Let $\mathfrak{M}$ be the set of markings of $\mathfrak{M}$. A marking M of N encodes a multisets C of types of messages iff, for each $f \in P^a$, $C([f]) = M(f)$. The initial marking is the marking encoding the initial marking of Υ^{abst}.[8] The binary relation $E \subset \mathfrak{d}^{abst} \times \mathfrak{M}$ is such that $E(C, M)$ iff M encodes C.*

The fact that E is a bisimulation is an easy consequence of the definitions of the configuration graphs involved. Thus, for space reasons, we omit the proof. Note that, if $(C, M) \in E$, the number of tokens M coincides with the number of elements (counting multiplicities) in C, Υ^{abst} reaches $\emptyset$ iff M reaches the empty marking. By Theorem 4, and decidable PN reachability, we obtain the Theorem 5.

Theorem 5. *D terminates iff M reaches the empty marking. Thus, termination of BPF-PF-PF CDPs.*

BPF-BPF-$\top$. This fragment has undecidable termination. The first step is to show that there is a BPF-BPF-$\top$, 1-input bounded, single-node CDP D, over node v, that can encode a random natural number on the channel.

Definition 7. *Given a configuration (S, C) of D, we say that (S, C) encodes the number $n \in \mathbb{N}$ if there is a set $\Delta_n \subset \Delta$ of n constants $c_1, \ldots, c_n$ such that $\text{succ}_C = \{(\min, c_1), \ldots, (c_n, \max)\}$ and succ is a transport symbol. The number encoded by c_i in C, denoted $[c_i]_C$, is i. The number encoded by min in C, denoted $[\min]_C$, is 0. The number encoded by C, denoted $[C]$ is n. If $x \in \Delta(\text{succ}_C) \setminus \{\max\}$, the successor of x is the unique y, if it exists, such that $\text{succ}(X, Y)$ and $Y \neq \max$.*

Since D is single-node, all transport facts in rules are labeled with @v. However, to make the read simpler, we omitt the labels. Since the input is bounded, D is state-bounded as long as the program is state and input prev-free. Thus, the program Π of D can freely use anonymous variables. We use the following abbreviation. Given an atom M, a sequence of inequality constraints $C_1, \ldots, C_m$, for $m \geq 0$, and a set $\{A_1, \ldots, A_n\}$, for some $n \geq 1$, where, for each $i \leq n$, A_i is a predicate symbol or an atom in which each $x \in Var(A_i)$ occurs once in A_i, the rule $A_1, \ldots, A_n \rightsquigarrow M, C_1, \ldots, C_m$ denotes the set of rules $\{\text{Err}_{A_i} \text{ if not } A_i' \, prev \, M, \mathcal{C}_i. \mid i \leq n\} \cup \{\text{ErrMsg if } \text{Err}_{A_1}, \ldots, \text{Err}_{A_n}.\}$ where: (1) if A_i is a symbol, then A_i' is the atom $A_i(\_, \ldots, \_)$ and, if A_i is an atom, then A_i' is obtained from A_i by substituting each variable in $Var(A_i) \setminus Var(M)$ with $\_$; (2) $\mathcal{C}_i$ is the sequence of constraints among the C_is such that $Var(C_i) \subset Var(A_i) \cup Var(M)$. (3) $\text{Err}/0$ is a state proposition. If the atoms are over the transport signature, we can read the rule as *the reception of M forces, up to*

---

[8] The uniqueness of the initial marking follows from the minimality of P^a.

errors, the reception of one of the A_is during next step or, shorter, M forces one of the A_is.

The program Π is written in Fig. 3. By rules 1–2, at startup, D initializes an encoding of 0 and sends an auxiliary message decide. The reception of start forces decide. By rules 3–5, the reception of decide instructs v to decide whether to extend the encoding on the channel or to declare the encoding complete, signalling it with the messages done and ext, respectively. The decision is performed by querying the input predicate Cand (which stands for *candidate*) in the current input DB I: if $\text{Cand}_I = \emptyset$, then v decides to stop the extension; if $\text{Cand}_I = \{c\}$, for some constant $c \neq \min$, v decides to attempt an extension of the encoding by incorporating c.[9] Moreover, decide forces a succ-message.

The reception of done should trigger the desired behaviour to be enforced after the completion of the encoding of a number n. We assume that it is just sent back and that done forces done, i.e., rules 6–7.

The sending of ext initiates a *checking* phase, which ends with the first successive sending of a decide: to correctly incorporate a constant c in succ_C, it is necessary to check that c is *fresh* in the current encoding, i.e., $c \notin \Delta(\text{succ}_C)$. Thus, by rules 8–11, the reception of $\text{ext}(x, y)$ instructs v to check, during the next step, whether x is different from the successor z of y, if z exists. If the check fails, an error message is sent on the channel. If it passes, the check is reiterated inductively on the successor of z. If y has no successor, i.e., $(y, \max) \in \text{succ}_C$, then, if the checking phase started with a message of the form $\text{ext}(x, \min)$, x was checked against the full $\Delta(\text{succ}_C)$. Thus, the checking phase can be closed incorporating x in succ_C. To iterate the check, ext must force a succ, while a succ must force a non-succ-message, i.e., a message over $\mathcal{T} \setminus \{\text{succ}\}$, which we call *auxiliary messages*. As long as the channel configuration does not contain ErrMsg and contains at most one auxiliary message, since ext is the only auxiliary message throughout the phase, succ implicitly forces ext.

By rule 12, the reception of ErrMsg triggers non-termination as in the previous constructions, i.e., by always sending ErrMsg back. We now show that D can encode any arbitrary number $n \in \mathbb{N}$. The following lemmas are easily proved by induction on the number of steps of the length of the run, or the number of checking phases in it. For space reasons, we omit their proofs.

Definition 8. *Given a finite run* $(S_0, C_0) \to_{I_0}^{m_0} \cdots \to_{I_{n-1}}^{m_{n-1}} (S_n, C_n)$ *a check phase is a maximal subsequence* $(S_i, C_i) \to_{I_i}^{m_i} \cdots \to_{I_{i+m-1}}^{m_{i+m-1}} (S_{i+m}, C_{i+m})$ *such that* $\text{ext}_{C_i} \neq \emptyset$ *and* $\text{decide}_{C_{i+m}} \neq \emptyset$.

Lemma 2. *Given a run* $(S_0, C_0) \to_{I_0}^{m_0} \cdots \to_{I_{n-1}}^{m_{n-1}} (S_n, C_n)$ *such that* ErrMsg $\notin C_n$, *(1) or each* $i \leq n$, C_i *contains at most one auxiliary message, (2) if* decide $\in C_i$, *then* $m_i = $ decide, *and, for each checking phase* $\varphi = (S_i, C_i), \ldots (S_{i+m}, C_{i+m})$, $m_{i-1} = \text{ext}(\min, c)$, *for some* $c \in \Delta$.

---

[9] Note that, by 1-input boundedness, Cand_I cannot contain more than one constant.

Theorem 6. $n \in \mathbb{N}$ iff there is a run $(S_0, C_0) \rightarrow_{I_0}^{m_0} \cdots \rightarrow_{I_{n-1}}^{m_{n-1}} (S_n, C_n)$ such that $\mathtt{ErrMsg} \notin C_n$, for each $i \geq 0$, $[C_i] \in \mathbb{N}$ and $[C_n] = n$.

13 conf(q₀,min,min) *if* done.
14 conf, terminate ⤳ done.
15 terminate *if* conf(q_fin,X,Y).
16 terminate ⤳ conf(q_fin,X,Y).
17 ErrMsg *if not* cand(_),
   conf(Q,X,Y), Q≠q_fin.
18 ErrMsg *if* cand(N), conf(Q,X,Y),
   tran(N,Q₀,Q₁,Q₂,P,C), Q≠Q₀, Q≠q_fin.
19 Perf(Q,X,Y,Q₁,+,C) *if* cand(N),
   conf(Q,X,Y), tran(N,Q,Q₁,Q₂,+,C),
   Q≠q_fin.
20 Perf(Q,X,Y,Q₁,-,C) *if* cand(N),
   conf(Q,X,Y), tran(N,Q,Q₁,Q₂,-,1),
   X≠min, Q≠q_fin.
21 Perf(Q,X,Y,Q₁,-,C) *if* cand(N),
   conf(Q,X,Y), tran(N,Q,Q₁,Q₂,-,2),
   Y≠min, Q≠q_fin.
22 Perf(Q,X,Y,Q₂,=,C) *if* cand(N),
   conf(Q,min,Y),
   tran(N,Q,Q₁,Q₂,-,1), Q≠q_fin.

23 Perf(Q,X,Y,Q₂,=,C) *if* cand(N),
   conf(Q,X,min),
   tran(N,Q,Q₁,Q₂,-,1), Q≠q_fin.
24 perf ⤳ conf(Q,X,Y).
25 succ, conf ⤳ perf.
26 conf(Q',X,Y) *if* perf(Q,X,Y,Q',=,P).
27 succ(X,Z) ⤳ perf(Q,X,Y,Q',+,1),
   Z≠max.
28 conf(Q',Z,Y) *if* succ(X,Z) *prev*
   perf(Q,X,Y,Q',+,1), Z≠max.
29 succ(Y,Z) ⤳ perf(Q,X,Y,Q',+,2),
   Z≠max.
30 conf(Q',X,Z) *if* succ(X,Z) *prev*
   perf(Q,X,Y,Q',+,2), Z≠max.
31 succ(Z,X) ⤳ perf(Q,X,Y,Q',-,1).
32 conf(Q',Z,Y) *if* succ(Z,X) *prev*
   perf(Q,X,Y,Q',-,1).
33 succ(Z,Y) ⤳ perf(Q,X,Y,Q',-,2).
34 conf(Q',X,Z) *if* succ(Z,Y) *prev*
   perf(Q,X,Y,Q',-,2).

Fig. 4. Program to simulate bounded runs of E.

We now extend Π by dropping rules 6 and 7 and adding those in Fig. 4. The resulting program Π' simulates, up to errors, runs of a **2 cm** $E = (Q, \delta, q_{\mathtt{init}}, q_{\mathtt{fin}})$ whose counters are bounded by n, where n is the number encoded after producing **done**. We assume that the node always contains in the state DB an encoding of Q and δ, via the relations Q/1 and $\mathtt{tran}/6$, whose extensions are Q and $\{(c_1, \ldots, c_6) \mid (c_2, \ldots, c_6) \in \delta$ and $f(c_1) = (c_2, \ldots, c_6)\}$, respectively, where f is a fixed injective function, i.e., the first component of T is a primary key. This is possible even in state prev-free programs via rules A **if** $\top$, i.e., with empty bodies, which deduce in the state the atom A.

Definition 9. *If* C *encodes the number* n, C *encodes the* **2 cm** *configuration* (q, c_1, c_2) *of* E *if* $\mathtt{conf}_C = \{(q, [c_1]_C, [c_2]_C)\}$ *or* $\mathtt{Perf}_C = \{(q, [c_1]_C, [c_2]_C, q', p, c)\}$, *for some* $q', p, c \in Delta$. *We denote* (q, c_1, c_2) *by* $\langle C \rangle$.

By rules 13–15, the reception of **done** triggers the encoding of the initial configuration of E. By rules 15–24, the reception of a **conf**-message instructs v to check whether it contains the final state. In that case, a **terminate** flag is sent on the channel and forced. Otherwise, v looks in the input DB predicate Cand/1 for an instantiation of the primary key in T, to retrieve a **2 cm** instruction. If the retrieved instruction is applicable, then v sends a message to signal via a **Perf**-message. By rules 25–34, the reception of a **Perf**-message triggers the update, according to the information stored in the message itself, of the configuration encoded in the channel. The following theorems can be proved by induction.

Theorem 7. *If* $(S_0, C_0) \to^{m_0, I_0} \ldots, (S_n, C_n)$ *is a finite run of* D, *such that* ErrMsg $\notin C_n$, terminate $\in C_n$ *and* terminate $\notin C_{n-1}$, *then there is a* $i < n$ *such that* done $\in C_i$, $[C_i] = n$, *and* $\langle C_{i+1} \rangle \ldots \langle C_n \rangle$ *is a run of* E *reaching* q_{fin}.

Since runs of E reaching q_{fin} are finite, along them the counters are bounded by some $n \in \mathbb{N}$. Thus, also the following vice-versa can be proved.

Theorem 8. *If* E *terminates, then there is a run of* D *as in Theorem 7.*

Thus, termination of E can be checked by checking whether a configuration C such that terminate $\in C$ is reachable in D. Thus, this latter task is undecidable. We now show how to reduce it to verification of termination. It suffices to make sure that terminate forces succ and that receiving a succ after a terminate trigerrs the sending back of terminate i.e., to add the rules succ $\leftsquigarrow$ terminate. terminate if succ(X, Y) *prev* terminate. In fact, along runs that do not produce error messages, the reception of a terminate (which is auxiliary) does not produce outgoing messages and is followed by the reception of a succ, which produces only a terminate forced message. Thus, a run of D reaches the empty channel configuration iff it does not produce error messages, it sends terminate on the channel, and is maximal.

Theorem 9. *Termination of BPF-BPF-$\top$ CDPs is undecidable.*

Remaining Fragments. PF-BPF-PF has decidable termination. In fact, we can extend the technique from Thm. 4 in [5] to abstract away the unbounded input DB in front of a bounded state DB. The idea is that a bounded state can only make use of an unbounded input to *(1)* retrieve a bounded number of constants and *(2)* answer a finite set of Boolean queries, which behave as guards to rules of the D2C program. By abstracting away the input with the value of those constants and queries, the fragment boils down to BPF-BPF-PF, whose decidability directly follows from that of the BPF-PF-PF fragment. Also B-BPF-PF has undecidable termination. In fact, we can use the *prev* on the input to simulate a *prev* on the channels. It suffices to require that the current received message is also mentioned in the current input DB. If that is not the case, an error is deduced and non-termination is triggered. Thus, this fragment can encode an extension of BPF-BPF-$\top$, which we proved undecidable. Finally, B-PF-B has decidable termination as B-BPF-B (the state is bounded).

6   Conclusions

We have sketched proofs to establish the decidability status of termination for 8 prev-aware fragments. Together with the previous results in [5], these can be generalized to categorize all 64 fragments. In fact, each prev-aware fragment is a fragment with decidable termination or an extension of a fragment with undecidable termination. In our opinion, the most surprising result is the unde-cidability of termination for BPF-BPF-T, since prev-awareness on the channel data-source, on which, because of state boundedness and prev-freenes combined, the node has a very limited control, is nevertheless powerful enough to encode termination of **2 cm**. Notably, the proof we provided does not take advantage of the possibility of having multiple instances on the channel, i.e., as a metter of fact, undecidability apllies also over the even weaker set-based channels, in which not only order in communication is not guaranteed, but multiple instances of messages sent before their reception are lost. However, our technique made crucial use of binary transport predicates. This fact rises further questions about the interaction of *prev*, communication imperfections, and the expressivity of relational signatures, e.g., in the form of constraints on the predicate arities. In this respect, are binary predicates always the primary source of undecidability?

Moreover, we conclude that the principle that "unboundedness causes unde-cidability only in front of *prev*" is not completely correct, because of the unde-cidability of for B-BPF-PF, which has an unbounded but prev-free channel. However, in that case, we obtained undecidability by simulating *prev* on the channel by using *prev* on the input. Note that the opposite is not true, in the sense that it is not possible to use *prev* on the channel to simulate *prev* on the input (PF-BPF-B is decidable). This indicates that the interaction between boundedness and prev-freenes is sensitive to the nature of the data-sources.

References

1. Abiteboul, S., Hull, R., Vianu, V.: Foundations of Databases. Addison-Wesley, Boston (1995)
2. Alvaro, P., Marczak, W.R., Conway, N., Hellerstein, J.M., Maier, D., Sears, R.: DEDALUS: datalog in time and space. In: de Moor, O., Gottlob, G., Furche, T., Sellers, A. (eds.) Datalog 2.0 2010. LNCS, vol. 6702, pp. 262–281. Springer, Heidelberg (2011). https://doi.org/10.1007/978-3-642-24206-9_16
3. Antoine, É.: Distributed data management with a declarative rule-based language Webdamlog. (Gestion des données distribuées avec le langage de règles Webdamlog). Ph.D. thesis, University of Paris-Sud, Orsay, France (2013)
4. Belardinelli, F., Lomuscio, A., Patrizi, F.: An abstraction technique for the verification of artifact-centric systems. In: Brewka, G., Eiter, T., McIlraith, S.A. (eds.) Principles of Knowledge Representation and Reasoning: Proceedings of the Thirteenth International Conference, KR 2012, Rome, Italy, 10–14 June 2012. AAAI Press (2012)
5. Calvanese, D., Di Cosmo, F., Lobo, J., Montali, M.: Convergence verification of declarative distributed systems. In: Monica, S., Bergenti, F. (eds.) Proceedings of the 36th Italian Conference on Computational Logic, Parma, Italy, 7–9 September 2021. CEUR Workshop Proceedings, vol. 3002, pp. 62–76. CEUR-WS.org (2021)
6. Deutsch, A., Sui, L., Vianu, V.: Specification and verification of data-driven web applications. J. Comput. Syst. Sci. **73**(3), 442–474 (2007)
7. Di Cosmo, F.: Verification of prev-free communicating datalog programs. In: Proceedings of CILC 2023 (2023, to appear)

8. Bagheri Hariri, B., Calvanese, D., De Giacomo, G., Deutsch, A., Montali, M.: Verification of relational data-centric dynamic systems with external services. In: Hull, R., Fan, W. (eds.) Proceedings of the 32nd ACM SIGMOD-SIGACT-SIGART Symposium on Principles of Database Systems (PODS), New York, NY, USA - 22–27 June 2013, pp. 163–174. ACM (2013)
9. Loo, B.T., Condie, T., Hellerstein, J.M., Maniatis, P., Roscoe, T., Stoica, I.: Implementing declarative overlays. In: Herbert, A., Birman, K.P. (eds.) Proceedings of the 20th ACM Symposium on Operating Systems Principles (SOSP), Brighton, UK, 23–26 October 2005, pp. 75–90. ACM (2005)

Marrying Query Rewriting and Knowledge Graph Embeddings

Anders Imenes[1], Ricardo Guimarães[1(✉)], and Ana Ozaki[1,2(✉)]

[1] University of Bergen, Bergen, Norway
anders.imenes@student.uib.no, ricardo.guimaraes@uib.no
[2] University of Oslo, Oslo, Norway
anaoz@uio.no

Abstract. Knowledge graph embeddings (KGEs) are useful for creating a continuous and meaningful representation of the data present in knowledge graphs (KGs). While initially employed mainly for link prediction, there has been an increased interest in querying such models using richer query languages, exploiting their continuous nature to obtain answers with a certain degree of confidence, that would not come as a result of querying KGs used to train such models. KGs can greatly benefit from having an ontology expressing conceptual knowledge of the domain and there has already been intensive research in rewriting approaches for querying the data present in KGs while taking their ontologies into account. However, these approaches have not been employed yet to query KGEs. Taking the best of both worlds, in this work we combine query rewriting in the classical DL-Lite ontology language with KGEs. More specifically, we propose a unified framework for querying KGEs that performs query rewriting for DL-Lite ontologies. We perform experiments and discuss how this combination can successfully improve query results.

Keywords: Knowledge Graphs · Query Rewriting · Embeddings

1 Introduction

Knowledge graphs (KGs) have been widely applied in many domains to represent entities and their relationships, using semantic web technologies. The discrete format of KGs, however, lacks robustness to noise and data variability. There has been intensive research on methods for creating knowledge graph embeddings (KGEs) able to capture patterns in KGs in a meaningful way [7], so as to facilitate dealing with noise and data variability. While initially employed mainly for link prediction, there has been an increased interest in querying KGEs using richer query languages, exploiting their continuous nature to obtain answers with a certain degree of confidence, that would not come as a result of querying KGs used to train such models. Current approaches rely on the information given by the KGE for answering the queries.

Supported by the Norwegian Research Council grant number 316022.

However, it has been shown that many KGE methods fail to capture conceptual knowledge expressing an ontology (in the format of rules) in KGs [9]. KGs can greatly benefit from having such an ontology as this avoids the need of having all the information explicit in the KG. Such rules can also be used for expressing constraints in the domain (e.g., a parent cannot be both a mother or a father, these sets are disjoint). There has already been intensive research in rewriting approaches for querying the data present in KGs while taking their ontology into account. Query rewriting is useful since it avoids the need of a reasoner for query answering: one can use the rewritten query in the data directly and have the same answers as the original query over the data and the ontology.

Our Contribution. Query rewriting approaches have not been employed yet for querying KGEs. Taking the best of both worlds, in this work we combine query rewriting in the classical DL-Lite ontology language with KGEs. More specifically, we propose a unified framework for querying KGEs that performs query rewriting for DL-Lite ontologies. We perform experiments using tree-shaped queries with one free variable and discuss whether and how this combination can successfully improve query results. Also, we developed a *query generator* which creates a dataset of queries with various formats.

Related Work. Recent advancements in complex query answering using embeddings have shown promising results (although without considering ontologies and, more specifically, query rewriting as we investigate in this work). Hamilton et al. [10] embedded graph nodes and implemented logical operations as geometric operations, achieving efficient predictions for conjunctive logical queries on incomplete knowledge graphs. Ren and Liang [15] introduced BetaE, a probabilistic embedding framework capable of handling first-order logic operations. They represented queries and entities as distributions to model uncertainty. Query2Box (Q2B) [14] utilized box embeddings for reasoning over knowledge graphs and excelled in answering complex queries with existential quantifiers and disjunctions. The state-of-the-art method for complex query answering is Query Computation Tree Optimization (QTO) [3]. QTO efficiently finds optimal solutions for large search spaces by performing forward-backwards propagation on the query computation tree, achieving superior performance across multiple datasets. However, these methods do not utilize ontologies, in particular TBox information. Various approaches have been proposed for ontology representation to embed ontological knowledge into low-dimensional vector spaces. Gutierrez-Basulto et al. [9] represented relations as regions in the vector space, while Ozcep et al. [13] embedded $\mathcal{ALC}$ ontologies into a real-valued vector space. Xiong et al. [19] represented $\mathcal{EL}$ TBoxes using an embedded space where entities are points and concepts are boxes, enabling intersection queries. We are not aware of any work that injects a *DL-Lite*$_\mathcal{R}$ ontology into a KGE in practice. The study on DeepProbLog [12] demonstrated the integration of logical rules and neural network models while maintaining a technical separation of the two. They used Problog rules to learn tasks without affecting the neural networks classification, for instance addition on MNIST. Such an approach suggests advantages for combining high-level reasoning (logic) and low-level perception (Machine Learning predictions). Our work also separates the logic and the model.

In Sect. 2 we provide basic definitions related to ontologies and query rewriting. Then, in Sect. 3 we describe our approach for combining query rewriting and KGEs. In Sect. 4, we present our experimental results and, finally, conclude in Sect. 5.

2 Preliminaries

We provide basic definitions and notions relevant for our work, in particular, related to ontologies, queries, query rewriting, and knowledge graph embeddings.

2.1 *DL-Lite$_\mathcal{R}$* Ontologies, KGs, and Queries

Let N_C and N_R be countably infinite and mutually disjoint sets of *concept* and *role* names, respectively. *DL-Lite$_\mathcal{R}$* role and concept inclusions are expressions of the form $S \sqsubseteq T$ and $B \sqsubseteq C$, respectively, where S, T are role expressions and B, C are concept expressions built through the grammar rules

$$S::= R \mid R^-, \quad T::= S \mid \neg S, \quad B::= A \mid \exists S, \quad C::= B \mid \neg B,$$

with $R \in N_R$ and $A \in N_C$. A *DL-Lite$_\mathcal{R}$* axiom is a *DL-Lite$_\mathcal{R}$* role or concept inclusion. A *DL-Lite$_\mathcal{R}$* *ontology* is a finite set of *DL-Lite$_\mathcal{R}$* concept and role inclusions. To define KGs, we use a set of *entities* $\mathcal{E}$ (disjoint from N_C and N_R) and a set of *relations* $\mathcal{R}$, defined as $N_R \cup \{rdf : type\}$. A KG is a set of triples that can be of the form (h, R, t), where (the head and tail of the triple) $h, t \in \mathcal{E}$ and $R \in N_R$, or of the form $(h, rdf : type, A)$, where $h \in \mathcal{E}$ and $A \in N_C$. We now provide the relevant definitions for queries. A term is either a variable or an entity in $\mathcal{E}$. An atom is of the form $A(t)$ or $R(t, t')$, where t, t' are terms, $A \in N_C$, and $R \in N_R$. A *conjunctive query* (CQ) is an expression of the form $\exists \vec{x} \phi(\vec{x})$ where $\phi(\vec{x})$ is a conjunction ($\wedge$) of atoms. A variable in a CQ is *distinguished* if it is a free variable (that is, not in the scope of any quantifier) and *undistinguished*, otherwise. We assume that our queries have *only one distinguished variable*. A variable is *shared* if it occurs at least twice. A *bound* variable is a variable that is either distinguished, shared or an entity in $\mathcal{E}$. In contrast, an *unbound* variable is a non-distinguished, non-shared variable. A *match* of a CQ $\exists \vec{x} \phi(\vec{x})$ in a KG $\mathcal{G}$ is a mapping μ from terms occurring in the query and entities in the KG such that $\mu(t) = t$ for all terms that are entities and, for all atoms α in $\phi(\vec{x})$:

- if α is of the form $R(t, t')$ then $(\mu(t), R, \mu(t')) \in \mathcal{G}$;
- if α is of the form $A(t)$ then $(\mu(t), rdf : type, A) \in \mathcal{G}$.

Existential positive first-order queries (EPFOQs) extend CQs with disjunctions ($\vee$). In our work, EPFOQs are converted into a union of CQs. A match for an EPFOQ in a KG is a mapping that is a match for at least one of the CQs in the union of CQs.

Input: a CQ q, a set of positive inclusions $\mathcal{O}_T$
Output: a set of CQs PR

1: $PR := \{q\}$
2: **repeat**
3:   $PR' := PR$
4:   **for all** $q \in PR'$, all $g, g_1, g_2 \in q$ and **all** $I \in \mathcal{O}_T$ **do**
5:     **if** $\{q[g/gr(g,I)]\} \notin PR$ and $I \in \mathcal{O}_T$ is applicable to $g \in q$ **then**
6:       $PR := PR \cup \{q[g/gr(g,I)]\}$
7:     **end if**
8:     **if** there are $g_1, g_2 \in q$ such that g_1 and g_2 unify **then**
9:       $PR := PR \cup \{\tau(\mathsf{reduce}(q, g_1, g_2))\}$
10:    **end if**
11:   **end for**
12: **until** $PR' = PR$
13: **return** PR

Algorithm 1: PerfectRef [6]

2.2   Query Rewriting in DL-Lite$_\mathcal{R}$

We employ the classical query rewriting algorithm PerfectRef [6]. When possible, we use the definitions and terminology from [6, Sec. 5.1], adapting some of them to our setting if needed. For simplicity, for each role R^- occurring in a *DL-Lite*$_\mathcal{R}$ ontology $\mathcal{O}$, we add to $\mathcal{O}$ the role inclusions $R^- \sqsubseteq \bar{R}$ and $\bar{R} \sqsubseteq R^-$, where $\bar{R}$ is a fresh role name in $\mathsf{N_R}$. We assume w.l.o.g. that inverse roles only occur in such role inclusions by replacing other occurrences of R^- with $\bar{R}$. The symbol "_" denotes non-distinguished non-shared variables. A positive inclusion I is a role or concept inclusion without negations. I is *applicable* to $A(x)$ if I it has A in its right-hand side. A positive inclusion I is applicable to $R(x, y)$ if

(i) $y =$_ and the right-hand side of I is $\exists R$, or
(ii) I is a role inclusion and its right-hand side is R or R^-.

Definition 1. *Let g be an atom and I a positive inclusion applicable to g. The atom obtained from g by applying I, denoted by $gr(g, I)$, is defined as follows:*

- $gr(A(x), (A_1 \sqsubseteq A)) = A_1(x)$;
- $gr(A(x), (\exists R \sqsubseteq A)) = R(x, \_)$;
- $gr(R(x, \_), (A \sqsubseteq \exists R)) = A(x)$;
- $gr(R(x, \_), (\exists R_1 \sqsubseteq \exists R)) = R_1(x, \_)$;
- $gr(R(x, y), (R_1 \sqsubseteq R)) = R_1(x, y)$;
- $gr(g, I) = R_1(y, x)$, *if* $g = R(x, y)$ *and either* $I = R_1 \sqsubseteq R^-$ *or* $I = R_1^- \sqsubseteq R$.

We use PerfectRef (Algorithm 1) originally presented in [6], where the applicability of a positive inclusion I to an atom g is as previously described and $gr(g, I)$ follows Definition 1. Let $q[g/g']$ denote the CQ obtained from q by replacing the atom g with a new atom g'; let τ be a function that takes as input a CQ q and returns a new CQ obtained by replacing each occurrence of an unbound variable in q with the symbol '_'; and let reduce be a function that takes as input a CQ q

and two atoms g_1, g_2 and returns the result of applying to q the most general unifier of g_1 and g_2 (unifying mathematically equal terms). $PerfectRef(q, \mathcal{O}_T)$ is the output of the algorithm PerfectRef over q and a set $\mathcal{O}_T$ of positive inclusions.

2.3   Knowledge Graph Embeddings

In a nutshell, KGEs are continuous representations of KGs in vector spaces. Such representations aim at capturing patterns in the data and employ them for tasks such as link prediction. There are several embedding methods in the literature [8,18], making it impractical to evaluate all of them. Dai et al. [8] proposes a division into the following main categories:

- translation-based methods;
- tensor-factorization-based methods; and
- neural network-based methods.

In our experiments (Sect. 4), we consider prototypical representatives of these three categories. One of the first embedding methods in the literature is the classical TransE [5] method, which is based on vector translation. For tensor-factorization, we select another classical model, DistMult [20]. Finally, we use CompGCN [17] as a representative of a neural network-based method. We also include RotatE [16], which has been used in many works for comparison analysis, even though it does not seem to have a clear category (some authors classify it as a tensor-factorization-based method [8] while others as translation-distance [18]). Finally, we include in our evaluation BoxE [1], which is a prominent method based on geometric models.

3   Combining Query Rewriting and KGEs

We first describe the pipeline for combining query rewriting and KGEs. Then we explain the evaluation and the query generator, employed to perform the experiments in the next section.

3.1   Query Answering Pipeline

Initially, we convert the input EPFOQ query into a union of CQs. If an entity appears as an answer in multiple CQs originating from the same EPFOQ, we keep its maximum score among its occurrences in the answer sets. We process each atom of a CQ individually, using the trained KGE model whenever the computation corresponds to a 1-step link prediction. We follow the literature [2, 3,14] and only consider queries with one distinguished variable (as mentioned before) and whose dependency graph is a tree [14]. These constraints facilitate the exploitation of the 1-step predictions from KGEs, by avoiding situations in which multiple variables have to be predicted at once. First, we need to determine the hierarchy between variables in a CQ. We use the variable hierarchy to decide which variable in each atom is the target for the prediction. Intuitively, the variable hierarchy tell how far away a variable is from the distinguished variable. The variable hierarchy is a graph with the query variables as nodes such that there is an edge (x, y) iff there is an atom in which both x and y occur. The structure of the queries produced will ensure that the variable hierarchy will form a tree with the distinguished variable at the root. Since the order of the predictions depends on the variable hierarchy, this structure also dictates the order in which we find predictions for each variable. Example 1 illustrates how the variable hierarchy is determined.

Example 1. Consider the CQ $\exists xyz$ hasFather(x,y) $\wedge$ hasSibling(y,w) $\wedge$ hasMother(z,w). In the variable hierarchy, the variable w is of depth 0. Then, we get two branches. Here, z has depth 1, and y has a depth of 1. We traverse in a depth-first search and obtain x with depth 2. Every leaf variable that only occurs once is unbound. In this example, this is x and z.

Next, we consider three base cases: when the current atom corresponds to a concept (unary predicate), when it corresponds to a role (binary predicate) with exactly one bound variable, and when it corresponds to a role with two bound variables. We do not need to consider the case in which both variables are unbound since such atom would not affect the result of the query and the generator (discussed in Sect. 3.3) avoids generating queries with these atoms.

- In the first case, the current atom is of the form $A(x)$, where A is a concept name. The program finds predictions for x starting from the individuals asserted to be A in the KG: $H_A = \{h \mid (h, rdf : type, A) \in \mathcal{G}\}$. If H_A is empty, we get no predictions; otherwise, we use these entities to obtain new predictions by first taking two intermediate sets of triples:

$$Q_h = \{(h, R, t) \in H_A \times \mathcal{R} \times \mathcal{E} \mid \exists (h', R, t') \in \mathcal{G} \text{ with } h' \in H_A\}; \text{ and}$$
$$Q_t = \{(h, R, t) \in \mathcal{E} \times \mathcal{R} \times H_A \mid \exists (h', R, t') \in \mathcal{G} \text{ with } t' \in H_A\}.$$

Then we take the top-k head entities in Q_h and the top-k tail entities in Q_t, creating a new set Z. Finally, the triples for concept prediction are created: $\{(h, rdf : type, A) \mid h \in Z\}$. We keep these triples sorted by their score according to the trained KGE model.
- In the second case, the current atom is of the form $R(x, y)$, where exactly one among x and y is bound. If the variable x is bound, then we take H as the top-k head entities in triples of the form $(h, R, t) \in \mathcal{G}$, otherwise we take $H = \emptyset$. Otherwise, if the variable y is bound, then we take T as the top-k tail entities in triples of the form $(h, R, t) \in \mathcal{G}$, otherwise we take $T = \emptyset$. In both cases, we keep only the top-k entities from the prediction.
- In the third case, the current atom is of the form $R(x, y)$ and all variables are bound. Hence, we start from the atoms containing the distinguished variable, setting it as the target, and we compute the head and tail predictions for the remaining variables, intersection the head and tail predictions, and using the product to combine the scores.

Since the procedure removes disjunctions beforehand, we only have to consider two situations now: *projections* and *intersections*. We perform a projection if the current atom is a role and both variables are bound. In this case, we check the variable hierarchy to find the closest variable to the distinguished variable and set it as the target variable for the current atom, while the other is deemed as the input variable. Next, we obtain the predictions for the target variable using the current atom and the predictions obtained previously for the input variable. These predictions were computed previously via the base cases mentioned before. The score for each of the top-k predictions of the target is computed by multiplying its score with the score of the corresponding entity for the input variable. We use Example 2 to clarify how our framework handles base cases and projections.

Example 2 (Cont. Example 1). Here, we have two base-cases since two atoms contain exactly one bound variable: hasFather(x,y) and hasMother(z,w). We start by predicting their target variables, respectively y and w. Assume we obtain a list L_1 of entities containing (at least) three people *Alice*, *Bob*, and *Carl* with respective scores 0.9, 0.8, and 0.7 from a prediction with the hasFather relation, and a list L_2 containing (at least) *Dan*, *Erin*, and *Frank* with the hasMother relation with respective scores 0.8, 0.7, and 0.6. We associate L_1 to the variable y and L_2 to w. Next, we have an atom, not a base case: hasSibling(y,w). Here both variables are bound, and we perform a projection, knowing the target is w from the variable hierarchy. We replace y with values in L_1 and predict the values for w. The output of this prediction is a new list L_3, which includes the entities *Dan* and *Erin*, with respective scores of 0.5 and 0.4. These results come from a link prediction with *Alice* as input. To compensate for the projection step, we multiply the score of *Alice* $\in L_1$ with the scores *Dan* and *Erin* in L_3, obtaining a score $0.9 \times 0.5 = 0.45$ for *Dan* and $0.9 \times 0.4 = 0.36$ for *Erin*.

If the current atom's target variable already has candidate entities obtained in a previous step, we need to perform an intersection. In this case, we still perform the prediction for the target variable, obtaining a new list of entities. We keep only entities that appear both in the previously obtained predictions and in the new list of predictions, setting their scores as the product of their respective scores in both sets of predictions. We use Example 3 to illustrate the intersection part of the pipeline.

Example 3. From the previous example, we finished the projection. We keep the list L_3 for the variable w. However, w already contains entities from a previous step; set L_2. This initiates the intersection. We intersect lists L_2 and L_3. Here, *Dan* and *Erin* are the common entities. We multiply their scores to compensate for the operation. For *Dan*, $0.8 \times 0.45 = 0.36$. For *Erin*, $0.7 \times 0.36 = 0.252$. All other entities not intersecting are dropped, that is, *Frank* in this example. The intersection is then the new set linked to w.

Once the pipeline finished processing a CQ, we have a list of k entities and associated scores the answers.

Example 4. All atoms are now processed. We look up the distinguished variable w and retrieve the list containing *Dan* and *Erin*. This is the answer to the query, along with the scores 0.36 and 0.252, respectively.

3.2 Evaluation Settings

As part of our evaluation, we need to determine whether each answer for each query is correct. We consider four configurations in our evaluation, which are combinations of two settings: (1) whether the ground truth is taken from the local dataset (L) or its online version (O) and (2) whether we use solely the initial query (I) or the set of queries including the rewritings (R). We will refer to these configurations as L/I, L/R, O/I, and O/R. The configurations with the local dataset (L) correspond to the traditional evaluation methods in link prediction, where some triples are removed from the original dataset and then used for testing. A query will produce potentially answers under each of these four combinations. We only consider as correct answers under a particular configuration the entities that appear in the corresponding list for that query in that configuration. Therefore, an entity can be seen as a correct answer in one configuration but not in others. And thus, when comparing two configurations we will have different insights on the performance of our system.

3.3 Query Structures and Query Generator

In addition to the KGs themselves, we also require a dataset of queries to perform our experimental evaluation. We consider the 9 query structures commonly employed in the Complex Query Answering literature, such as in Query2Box [14] and CQD [2]: 1p, 2p, 3p, 2i, 3i, pi, ip, up, and 2u. The letter 'i' stands for intersection, 'p' for projection, and 'u' for union. So, for example, the query $\exists yz\ \text{hasFather}(x,y) \land \text{worksAt}(y,z)$ has query structure 2p, while the query in Example 1 is a pi query.

Since our method relies on the TBox associated to each KG, we were unable to use the existing datasets and strategies, and instead devised our own. The generator ignores the RDFS meta properties and creates a frequency count of all concepts and roles occurring in the ABox. Additionally, concepts and relations that only occur in the TBox receive '1' as frequency count. Then queries are generated by replacing each atom in a query structure with a relation or concept, with chance proportional to the frequency count. When rewriting queries using PerfectRef, the query may produce a set of CQs containing CQs that differ in structure from the original query. Even so, we still classify the results according to the query structure of the initial query.

4 Experiments

We first describe the datasets and experimental setup (Sect. 4.1). We then present the results and discuss them in Sect. 4.2.

4.1   Datasets and Experimental Setup

We performed extensive experiments to evaluate query rewriting over KGEs, using various query structures and the datasets:

The Family Dataset. The first dataset used is a subset of Wikidata called the Family Dataset, proposed by Jøsang et al. [11]. This is a subset of Wikidata5m, which extracts six family-related properties. The TBox used alongside this dataset is an extract from Wikidata for the related concepts and roles for family relations. We use the full WikiData online for validation by accessing it through their API.

DBPedia15k. The other dataset used is DBPedia15k[1]. This dataset is a miniature version of DBPedia online. The TBox is a subset of DBPedia as well, borrowed from a GitHub repository on TransROWL[2]. Unfortunately, this dataset contains discrepancies between DBPedia15k and DBPedia, yielding DBPedia15k is not a proper subset. We discovered this flaw after the experiment analysis, which resulted in difficulties using this dataset to evalidate the impact of predictions. The online DBPedia API is used for the validation of predictions.

Setup. We initiated the process by generating 25 initial queries for each query structure and dataset combination. To ensure comprehensive analysis, we ran our experiments by selecting five Knowledge Graph Embedding (KGE) models, namely BoxE [1], CompGCN [17], DistMult [20], RotatE [16], and TransE [5]. Each model was trained using three different dimensions (namely, 64, 128, and 192) and epoch lengths (namely, 16, 20, and 24), resulting in 9 training configurations per KGE model and dataset combination. We utilised the AMRI metric [4] to determine the most effective configuration for each model. This allowed us to identify the best-performing configuration among the nine options for each KGE model and dataset combination. We obtained 10 optimal models (5 KGE models, 2 datasets). We used these configurations to answer the initial queries, evaluating them using Optimistic Mean Reciprocal Rank (o-MRR).

4.2   Experimental Results

Upon obtaining the 10 optimized models, we executed the pipeline and collected the corresponding data for the generated queries. The detailed results can be accessed on GitHub[3]. Among these models, RotatE demonstrated superior performance on the Family Dataset (Wikidata), while TransE outperformed the others on DBPedia15k.

In Table 1, we see o-MRR results overall query structures for both datasets. In bold, we highlight the best value for each validation method between the

---

[1] https://github.com/mniepert/mmkb.
[2] https://github.com/Keehl-Mihael/TransROWL-HRS.
[3] https://github.com/AImenes/query-answering-and-embeddings/tree/main/testcases/001/queries.

Table 1. o-MRR results for all BoxE, CompGCN, DistMult, RotatE, and TransE.

Query	Family Dataset				DBPedia15k			
	L/I	L/R	O/I	O/R	L/I	L/R	O/I	O/R
BoxE								
1p	**0.4400**	**0.6800**	**0.4400**	**0.6800**	0.3909	0.5342	0.2430	0.2293
2p	0.8632	0.9617	**0.9603**	1.0000	0.0536	0.0536	**0.1049**	**0.1049**
3p	0.7785	0.9333	0.8261	0.8658	0.0040	0.0040	0.0014	0.0014
2i	0.2800	0.3600	0.3200	0.3600	0.1024	0.1120	0.0100	0.0024
3i	0.0000	0.0400	0.0000	0.0400	0.0200	0.0400	0.0000	0.0008
pi	0.3133	0.4229	0.3457	0.3433	0.0000	0.0000	0.0000	0.0000
ip	0.2800	0.2800	0.3200	0.3600	**0.0181**	**0.0181**	**0.0133**	**0.0133**
up	0.8407	**0.9000**	0.6207	**0.9000**	0.1198	0.1198	0.0374	0.0531
2u	**0.5600**	**0.8000**	0.6000	**0.8000**	0.4836	0.5636	0.2451	0.2214
CompGCN								
1p	**0.4400**	**0.6800**	**0.4400**	**0.6800**	0.4770	0.6355	0.3460	0.2124
2p	0.3288	0.3856	0.3888	0.3919	0.0153	0.0153	0.0186	0.0186
3p	0.0170	0.2168	0.1632	0.1672	0.0000	0.0000	0.0009	0.0009
2i	0.4400	0.5600	0.4800	**0.5600**	**0.1364**	0.2124	0.0294	**0.0644**
3i	0.0800	0.1600	0.0800	0.2000	**0.0400**	0.1733	0.0000	**0.0200**
pi	0.1247	0.3119	0.2127	0.2319	0.0033	0.0033	0.0025	0.0025
ip	0.0508	0.0508	0.0995	0.1209	0.0032	0.0032	0.0013	0.0013
up	0.3540	0.3841	0.3080	0.3881	0.0835	0.0835	0.0344	0.0366
2u	0.4874	**0.8000**	0.6000	0.7400	0.5645	0.6079	0.4060	0.2591
DistMult								
1p	**0.4400**	**0.6800**	**0.4400**	**0.6800**	**0.5027**	0.6457	0.4027	0.1855
2p	0.7081	0.8100	0.7629	0.7949	**0.0555**	**0.0555**	0.0614	0.0614
3p	0.4395	0.4971	0.5930	0.6056	0.0027	0.0027	0.0017	0.0017
2i	0.2880	0.3680	0.3280	0.4080	0.1328	0.1536	0.0070	0.0021
3i	0.1600	0.2800	0.2400	0.3000	**0.0400**	0.0800	0.0000	0.0000
pi	0.2407	0.3636	0.3747	0.4080	0.0027	0.0027	0.0013	0.0013
ip	0.3057	0.3057	0.3500	0.3557	0.0041	0.0041	0.0010	0.0010
up	0.4415	0.4902	0.3490	0.4769	**0.1469**	**0.1469**	0.0670	0.0657
2u	0.5213	0.7800	**0.6200**	0.7800	0.5722	0.5988	0.3860	0.2462
RotatE								
1p	**0.4400**	**0.6800**	**0.4400**	**0.6800**	0.4744	0.5697	0.2739	**0.3382**
2p	**0.9150**	**0.9700**	0.9300	0.9500	0.0066	0.0066	0.0116	0.0116
3p	**0.8857**	1.0000	**0.9380**	**0.9700**	0.0000	0.0000	0.0000	0.0000
2i	0.2800	0.3200	0.3200	0.3200	0.1036	0.1096	0.0378	0.0235
3i	0.0000	0.0400	0.0000	0.0400	0.0200	0.0527	0.0000	0.0000
pi	0.4200	0.5200	0.4200	0.4600	0.0000	0.0000	0.0000	0.0000
ip	0.2200	0.2400	0.2600	0.3000	0.0055	0.0055	0.0037	0.0037
up	**0.8531**	0.8900	0.6180	0.8500	0.1283	0.1283	**0.0854**	**0.0864**
2u	0.4903	0.8000	0.6000	**0.8000**	0.5386	0.5586	0.3099	0.2889
TransE								
1p	0.3307	0.4757	0.3183	0.4106	0.4691	**0.6854**	**0.4667**	0.2306
2p	0.3426	0.5590	0.4917	0.5307	0.0295	0.0295	0.0530	0.0530
3p	0.3175	0.4457	0.5509	0.5623	**0.0041**	**0.0041**	**0.0408**	**0.0408**
2i	**0.4667**	**0.5924**	**0.5067**	0.5567	0.1083	**0.2283**	**0.0436**	0.0571
3i	**0.3000**	**0.4733**	**0.3600**	**0.4533**	0.0200	**0.1800**	0.0000	0.0000
pi	**0.6113**	**0.7901**	**0.6596**	**0.6778**	0.0000	0.0000	0.0000	0.0000
ip	**0.3792**	**0.3792**	**0.4711**	**0.4853**	0.0162	0.0162	0.0057	0.0057
up	0.5128	0.6181	0.3953	0.5540	0.1357	0.1357	0.0252	0.0390
2u	0.5036	0.6391	0.5800	0.6223	**0.6697**	**0.7630**	**0.5131**	**0.4075**

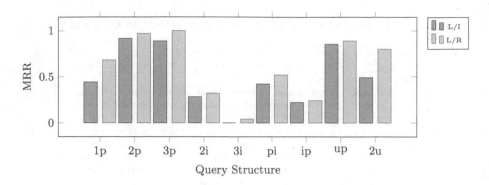

Fig. 1. Family Dataset with RotatE, impact of **rewriting**: MRR for L/I and L/R.

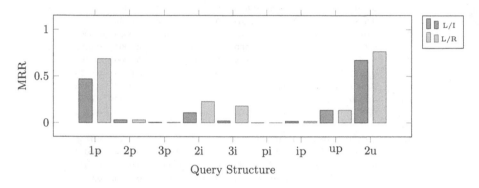

Fig. 2. DBPedia15k Dataset with TransE, showing impact of **rewriting**: MRR for L/I and L/R.

five models. By comparing the rewritten validation sets to the initial query, we obtain the rewriting impact, and by comparing online KG to local KG, we obtain the impact of predictions. For overall performance, we observe that RotatE performs very well on projections queries, closely followed by BoxE. For intersection, TransE outperforms the others. For DBPedia15k, we see TransE performs overall the best, while DistMult is close. To present the impact of rewriting and predictions, we will focus on showcasing the results of RotatE for the Family Dataset (Wikidata) and TransE for DBPedia15k.

We observe the impact of rewriting in Figs. 1 and 2 for the local datasets. There is an apparent increase in overall query structures by introducing query rewriting. However, we observe no clear improvements for predictions on the initial query in Figs. 3 and 4. There are even some decreases in scores because of the discrepancies between local and online KG, as well as partial HTTP response (Code 206) delivery from the online KG when we obtain the entity answers.

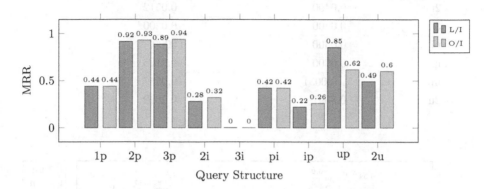

Fig. 3. Family Dataset with RotatE, impact of **predictions**: MRR for L/I and O/I.

Overall, when considering both rewriting and predictions, we see a clear improvement for the Family dataset, while not a clear advantage for DBPedia15k, shown in Table 2. We visualize the differences between local KG Lookup validation and our approach in Figs. 5 and 6.

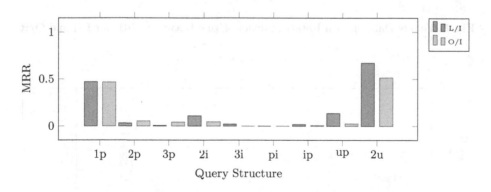

Fig. 4. DBPedia15k with TransE, impact of **predictions**: MRR for L/I and O/I.

Table 2. Rewriting and predictions versus local KG Lookup.

Query Structure	Family Dataset (O/R - L/I)	DBPedia15k (O/R - L/I)
1p	0.2400	−0.2385
2p	0.0350	0.0235
3p	0.0843	0.0367
2i	0.0400	−0.0512
3i	0.0400	−0.0200
pi	0.0400	0.0000
ip	0.0800	−0.0105
up	−0.0031	−0.0967
2u	0.3097	−0.2622

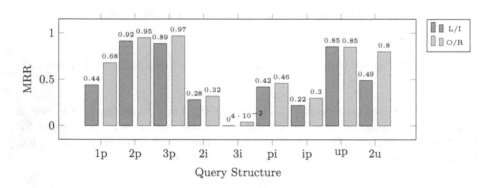

Fig. 5. Family Dataset with RotatE, impact of **predictions**: MRR for L/I and O/R.

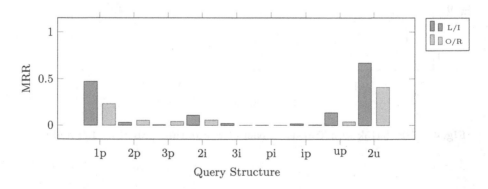

Fig. 6. DBPedia15k with TransE, impact of **predictions**: MRR for L/I and O/R.

5   Conclusion

In this study, we investigated the impact of query rewriting on improving the results of query structures in two different datasets: the family dataset and DBPedia15k. Our findings revealed that query rewriting significantly enhanced the results for all query structures in the family dataset. However, for DBPedia15k, query rewriting yielded improvements for all query structures except the 'up' structure. We did not observe significant improvements when utilizing KGE predictions. This suggests that the datasets we employed are already close to being complete in terms of information coverage.

Furthermore, we encountered discrepancies between DBPedia15k and DBPedia online, which reduced the reliability of validating predictions for DBPedia15k. Conversely, we observed minor improvements when using predictions on the Family Dataset with validation against Wikidata online. Overall, our study demonstrates a clear enhancement in performance through the introduction of query rewriting. These findings suggest that incorporating query rewriting techniques can effectively enhance the capabilities of a complex query answering pipeline for knowledge graphs and their embeddings.

References

1. Abboud, R., Ceylan, I., Lukasiewicz, T., Salvatori, T.: Boxe: a box embedding model for knowledge base completion. In: Larochelle, H., Ranzato, M., Hadsell, R., Balcan, M., Lin, H. (eds.) Advances in Neural Information Processing Systems, vol. 33, pp. 9649–9661. Curran Associates, Inc. (2020). https://proceedings.neurips.cc/paper_files/paper/2020/file/6dbbe6abe5f14af882ff977fc3f35501-Paper.pdf
2. Arakelyan, E., Daza, D., Minervini, P., Cochez, M.: Complex query answering with neural link predictors. In: 9th International Conference on Learning Representations, ICLR 2021, Virtual Event, Austria, 3–7 May 2021. OpenReview.net (2021). https://openreview.net/forum?id=Mos9F9kDwkz
3. Bai, Y., Lv, X., Li, J., Hou, L.: Answering complex logical queries on knowledge graphs via query computation tree optimization. CoRR abs/2212.09567 (2022). https://doi.org/10.48550/arXiv.2212.09567
4. Berrendorf, M., Faerman, E., Vermue, L., Tresp, V.: On the ambiguity of rank-based evaluation of entity alignment or link prediction methods (2020). https://doi.org/10.48550/ARXIV.2002.06914
5. Bordes, A., Usunier, N., Garcia-Durán, A., Weston, J., Yakhnenko, O.: Translating embeddings for modeling multi-relational data. Curran Associates Inc. (2013)
6. Calvanese, D., Giacomo, G.D., Lembo, D., Lenzerini, M., Rosati, R.: Tractable reasoning and efficient query answering in description logics: the DL-Lite family. J. Autom. Reason. **39**(3), 385–429 (2007)
7. Cao, J., Fang, J., Meng, Z., Liang, S.: Knowledge graph embedding: a survey from the perspective of representation spaces. arXiv abs/2211.03536 (2022)
8. Dai, Y., Wang, S., Xiong, N.N., Guo, W.: A survey on knowledge graph embedding: approaches, applications and benchmarks. Electronics **9**(5) (2020). https://doi.org/10.3390/electronics9050750. https://www.mdpi.com/2079-9292/9/5/750

9. Gutiérrez-Basulto, V., Schockaert, S.: From knowledge graph embedding to ontology embedding? An analysis of the compatibility between vector space representations and rules. In: Thielscher, M., Toni, F., Wolter, F. (eds.) Principles of Knowledge Representation and Reasoning: Proceedings of the Sixteenth International Conference, KR 2018, Tempe, Arizona, 30 October–2 November 2018, pp. 379–388. AAAI Press (2018). https://aaai.org/ocs/index.php/KR/KR18/paper/view/18013

10. Hamilton, W.L., Bajaj, P., Zitnik, M., Jurafsky, D., Leskovec, J.: Embedding logical queries on knowledge graphs. In: Bengio, S., Wallach, H.M., Larochelle, H., Grauman, K., Cesa-Bianchi, N., Garnett, R. (eds.) Advances in Neural Information Processing Systems 31: Annual Conference on Neural Information Processing Systems 2018, NeurIPS 2018, 3–8 December 2018, Montréal, Canada, pp. 2030–2041 (2018). https://proceedings.neurips.cc/paper/2018/hash/ef50c335cca9f340bde656363ebd02fd-Abstract.html

11. Jøsang, J., Guimarães, R., Ozaki, A.: On the effectiveness of knowledge graph embeddings: a rule mining approach. CoRR abs/2206.00983 (2022). https://doi.org/10.48550/arXiv.2206.00983

12. Manhaeve, R., Dumancic, S., Kimmig, A., Demeester, T., Raedt, L.D.: Deepproblog: neural probabilistic logic programming. CoRR abs/1805.10872 (2018). http://arxiv.org/abs/1805.10872

13. Özçep, Ö.L., Leemhuis, M., Wolter, D.: Cone semantics for logics with negation. In: Bessiere, C. (ed.) Proceedings of the Twenty-Ninth International Joint Conference on Artificial Intelligence, IJCAI 2020, pp. 1820–1826. ijcai.org (2020). https://doi.org/10.24963/ijcai.2020/252

14. Ren, H., Hu, W., Leskovec, J.: Query2box: reasoning over knowledge graphs in vector space using box embeddings. In: 8th International Conference on Learning Representations, ICLR 2020, Addis Ababa, Ethiopia, 26–30 April 2020. OpenReview.net (2020). https://openreview.net/forum?id=BJgr4kSFDS

15. Ren, H., Leskovec, J.: Beta embeddings for multi-hop logical reasoning in knowledge graphs. In: Larochelle, H., Ranzato, M., Hadsell, R., Balcan, M., Lin, H. (eds.) Advances in Neural Information Processing Systems 33: Annual Conference on Neural Information Processing Systems 2020, NeurIPS 2020, 6–12 December 2020, virtual (2020). https://proceedings.neurips.cc/paper/2020/hash/e43739bba7cdb577e9e3e4e42447f5a5-Abstract.html

16. Sun, Z., Deng, Z.H., Nie, J.Y., Tang, J.: Rotate: knowledge graph embedding by relational rotation in complex space. In: International Conference on Learning Representations (2019)

17. Vashishth, S., Sanyal, S., Nitin, V., Talukdar, P.: Composition-based multirelational graph convolutional networks. In: International Conference on Learning Representations (2020). https://openreview.net/forum?id=BylA_C4tPr

18. Wang, M., Qiu, L., Wang, X.: A survey on knowledge graph embeddings for link prediction. Symmetry 13(3) (2021). https://doi.org/10.3390/sym13030485. https://www.mdpi.com/2073-8994/13/3/485

19. Xiong, B., Potyka, N., Tran, T., Nayyeri, M., Staab, S.: Faithful embeddings for EL++ knowledge bases. In: Sattler, U., et al. (eds.) ISWC 2022. LNCS, vol. 13489, pp. 22–38. Springer, Cham (2022). https://doi.org/10.1007/978-3-031-19433-7_2

20. Yang, B., Yih, W., He, X., Gao, J., Deng, L.: Embedding entities and relations for learning and inference in knowledge bases. In: Bengio, Y., LeCun, Y. (eds.) 3rd International Conference on Learning Representations, ICLR (2015)

Lore: Educational Deductive Database System

Leif Harald Karlsen[✉]

Department of Informatics, University of Oslo, Blindern 0316, Oslo, Norway
leifhka@ifi.uio.no
https://www.mn.uio.no/ifi/

Abstract. This paper introduces Lore, a deductive database implemented as a small extension to PostgreSQL, and Triplelore, a triplestore implementation on top of Lore. Lore introduces relations to PostgreSQL that generalizes tables and views (i.e. relations can be inserted into and simultaneously defined in terms of other relations). Lore also supports forward and backward chaining rules between relations, that can be written both in an SQL-like syntax and a Datalog-like syntax. Lore is a pure extension of SQL and can use all of PostgreSQL's datatypes, functions, indices, and other advanced features and extensions. These systems are used to teach students about properties and applications of rules in different settings.

Keywords: Rules · Deductive Database · Educational · Triplestore

1 Introduction and Motivation

Within the field of data engineering, knowledge representation is becoming increasingly important, as the ever increasing complexity of the data transformation, cleaning and analysis pipelines require more context and domain knowledge. At the same time, relational databases are still, by far, the most used type of database system (see e.g. [2] for a model-based ranking), and SQL is the most used query language (see e.g. [6] for a language ranking). SQL is a powerful language that is Turing complete and declarative, thus it can (in principle) encode any knowledge required by any form of data pipeline and analysis.

For students and traditional database practitioners, it may therefore be unclear why SQL is not a sufficient language for encoding domain knowledge. Given the relations in Fig. 1, we could for example express the knowledge that all taxons with habitat 'Urban' or 'Forest' are terrestrial with:

```
CREATE VIEW terrestrial AS
SELECT t.id FROM taxon AS t JOIN habitat AS h USING (id)
WHERE h.habitat = 'Forest' OR habitat = 'Urban';
```

One quickly apparent downside to SQL is that it is quite verbose. However, there are much deeper deficiencies to SQL for knowledge representation than this,

A. Fensel et al. (Eds.): RuleML+RR 2023, LNCS 14244, pp. 141–156, 2023.
https://doi.org/10.1007/978-3-031-45072-3_10

```
              taxon                          taxonomy              habitat
.------------------------------------.    .--------------.    .----------------.
| id | sci_name          | pop_name  |    | sub | super |    | id | lives_in |
|----+-------------------+-----------|    |-----+-------|    |----+----------|
|  1 | Rattus Norvegicus | Brown rat |    |  1  |   6   |    |  1 | Urban    |
|  2 | Larus Canus       | Common gull |  |  6  |   5   |    |  1 | Forest   |
|  3 | Sternula          | Tern      |    |  5  |   4   |    |  2 | Urban    |
|  4 | Animalia          | Animal    |    |  2  |   8   |    |  2 | Coastal  |
|  5 | Mammalia          | Mammal    |    |  3  |   8   |    |  8 | Coastal  |
|  6 | Rodentia          | Rodent    |    |  8  |   7   |    |  3 | Coastal  |
|  7 | Aves              | Bird      |    |  7  |   4   |    '----------------'
|  8 | Laridae           | Sea bird  |    '--------------'
'------------------------------------'
```

Fig. 1. A relational schema with three tables: `taxon` that describes an element in the species taxonomy with a unique integer `id`, and a scientific and a popular name in text; `taxonomy` describes the taxonomy where `sub` and `super` are foreign keys to `taxon(id)`; and finally `habitat` that describes where individuals of each taxon typically live, where `id` is a foreign key to `taxon(id)` and `lives_in` contains a simple name of the habitat

namely that views are always stratified equivalences, which has the following consequences for knowledge engineering: (1) The term needs to be defined in a single command, and the full complexity of the term must be included in this one command. E.g. the `VIEW`-definition above would need to contain all possible terrestrial habitats. (2) A collection of view definitions are always stratified, with tables at the lowest level. This forces a direction to the definitions. (3) A term defined via a view cannot be instantiated directly. All explicit statements about entities must be expressed using the bottom-most layer, i.e. tables. E.g. with the definition of `terrestrial` above, we cannot state that a particular taxon is terrestrial directly (we need to know exactly which habitat it has and insert that into `habitat`). These properties make it difficult to scale complex knowledge representation in SQL.

All of these drawbacks could be fixed by using only tables and `INSERT`-triggers to encode implications. E.g., we could implement a trigger that on `INSERT`s to `habitat` checks if the row contains `'Urban'` or `'Forest'` for `lives_in`, and if so, also inserts the `id` into the `terrestrial`-table. However triggers are general purpose, and verbose, making them hard to read, maintain and debug [11].

Rule languages are typically defined in such a way that none of these drawbacks are present: There is (often) no separation between tables and views, everything is just relations; and relations are defined using implications rather than equivalences. In other words, it is not *what* knowledge you can represent that makes SQL poor (and rules better) in this regard, but *how* it is represented. For students (and others) to fully understand this, it would be of great help being able to see such different representations side by side, interact with them, and try to encode knowledge within these themselves. To allow this, the languages should have the same features wrt. functions, datatypes, underlying index structures, etc., so that the different representations only highlight the their inherent properties, and not other underlying technical differences.

To this end, we have implemented *Lore* (**L**ogical **R**elations). Lore is a thin abstraction layer on top of PostgreSQL, that implements a deductive database. All Lore statements get translated into SQL, thereby building on a solid and mature foundation. Lore-rules can also use all datatypes, functions and relations already defined in PostgreSQL, and can contain raw SQL-subqueries within rules. This allows students to translate any SQL-query or transformation into or from Lore. Lore is a pure extension to PostgreSQL, that is, all PostgreSQL-commands are legal Lore-commands. In addition, Lore adds three new constructions:

- **Relations:** Generalizes views and tables and behaves like relations in logic.
- **Implications:** Can be both forward or backward implications, corresponding to forward and backward chaining rules.
- **Imports:** Allows one Lore-script to import another.

All of these are defined in a syntax very similar to SQL, making the difference between the original command and the translated SQL-command small. However, Lore also introduces a more succinct syntax that resembles Datalog for its implications. It also introduces a Datalog-like syntax for normal INSERT-commands and basic SELECT-queries. *Triplelore* is a system that can translate RDF and OWL into Lore-relations and rules, can generate direct mappings between tabular data and RDF, and rewrite SPARQL-queries to queries over Lore-relations.

These systems are used in an educational setting for teaching students about rules, mappings, and the relationship between relational and deductive databases and triplestores. However, since the system translates to SQL with little overhead, it can also be used by data engineers and database administrators as a language to simplify the expression of complex queries and knowledge-intensive transformations.

This paper is outlined as follows: Sect. 2 and 3 introduces relations and implications via their SQL-like syntax; Sect. 4 introduces the Datalog-like syntax for implications, insert statements and queries; Sect. 5 introduces the import command; Sect. 6 shows how Lore can create meta-rules, and how these can express general constraints and advanced transformations; Sect. 7 gives more details on the implementation; Sect. 8 briefly outlines Triplelore, the triplestore built on Lore; Sect. 9 shows some more advanced examples of Lore; Sect. 10 discusses the general properties of Lore as a rule language; Sect. 11 discusses the most relevant related work; and Sect. 12 concludes the paper and outlines future work.

2   Relations

In a normal relational database, tables and views are the central means for representing data. Lore introduces a new construction, namely the *relation*, that generalizes these. A relation can be defined in terms of other relations/tables/views (similar to views) via implications (described in the next section), and contain stored data (similar to tables).

In the SQL-like syntax, relations are created similarly as tables and views, with **CREATE**, but with the keyword **RELATION** in place of **TABLE** or **VIEW**, e.g.:

```
CREATE RELATION taxon(id int, sci_name text, pop_name text);
```

The general syntax for creating relations is

```
CREATE RELATION [FROM TABLE] <rel>(<columns>);
```

```
CREATE RELATION [FROM TABLE] <rel>(<columns>);
```

where <rel> is the (possibly schema-prefixed) name of the relation and <columns> is a list of column declarations just like in a **CREATE TABLE**-command, giving a name, type and optionally constraints for each column. If **FROM TABLE** is added, the command transforms an already existing table to a relation.

Implementationally, a relation is a view that is the union of a view and a table. The table-part is named <rel>_stored (where <rel> is the name of the relation) and is used for stored statements. The view-part is named <rel>_virtual and is used for virtual statements. Thus, the **CREATE RELATION**-command for taxon above is translated into the following SQL-commands:

```
CREATE TABLE taxon_stored(id int, sci_name text, pop_name text);
ALTER TABLE taxon_stored ADD UNIQUE (id, sci_name, pop_name);

CREATE VIEW taxon_virtual AS
SELECT * FROM taxon_stored
LIMIT 0; -- Initially empty (redefined via implications)

CREATE VIEW taxon AS
SELECT * FROM taxon_stored
UNION ALL
SELECT * FROM taxon_virtual;

CREATE FUNCTION taxon_insert_trigger_func() RETURNS TRIGGER AS $$
BEGIN
  INSERT INTO taxon_stored (SELECT NEW.id, NEW.sci_name, NEW.pop_name)
  ON CONFLICT (id, sci_name, pop_name) DO NOTHING;
  RETURN NEW;
END; $$ LANGUAGE plpgsql;

CREATE TRIGGER taxon_insert_trigger AS -- redirect INSERTs
INSTEAD OF INSERT ON taxon
FOR EACH ROW EXECUTE PROCEDURE taxon_insert_trigger_func;
```

If **FROM TABLE** is used, the first command is changed to

```
ALTER TABLE taxon RENAME TO taxon_stored;
```

Note that a relation has a **UNIQUE**-constraint on the combination of all columns, thus it is a proper set of tuples. Furthermore, the final two commands create a trigger function and a corresponding trigger that delegates inserts into the relation/view `taxon` into the table-part `taxon_stored`. Inserting duplicate rows is simply ignored (this is an important point wrt. termination of reasoning as we will see below). One can now query and insert into `taxon` as if it were a normal table. In the next section, we will introduce the notion of an *implication* that will, among other things, allow us to redefine the view-part of the relation.

3 Implications

Implications in Lore play the same role as rules does in Datalog. We have chosen the term *implication* since the term *rule* already has a meaning in PostgreSQL. An implication is defined similarly as `VIEW`s, but with the keyword `IMPLICATION` in place of `VIEW`. E.g.:

```
CREATE IMPLICATION terrestrial AS
SELECT t.id FROM taxon AS t JOIN habitat AS h USING (id)
WHERE h.habitat = 'Forest' OR habitat = 'Urban';
```

The default type of implications are backward-chaining implications, i.e. they are not computed and stored but only used to rewrite queries (similar to views). However, if one adds the keyword `FORWARD` in front of `IMPLICATION` in the command, the implication will be a forward-chaining implication, thereby computing all consequences. Backward-chaining implications will redefine the `VIEW`-part of the target relation, whereas a forward-chaining implication is implemented with triggers that makes `INSERT`s into the target relation.

The central idea with implications, just like rules, is that multiple implications can be used to define a relation. Implications can also be recursive.

The general syntax for implications is as follows:

```
CREATE [FORWARD] IMPLICATION <rel> AS <SELECT-query>;
```

where `<rel>` is the (possibly schema-prefixed) name of a relation and `<SELECT-query>` is a normal SQL `SELECT`-query.

A backward-chaining implications is translated into a command that redefines the view-part of a relation, i.e. `<rel>_virtual`. The command

```
CREATE IMPLICATION <rel> AS <SELECT-query>;
```

is translated into

```
CREATE OR REPLACE VIEW <rel>_virtual AS <SELECT-query>;
```

If more than one implication is defined for the same relation, the view becomes the union of all of their `SELECT`-queries. Note that Lore, similarly to normal relational databases, store metadata on all of its relations and implications in the database. Thus, Lore knows of all implications to each relation and adds all of these to the view-definition. This means that different transactions/scripts can add implications to the same relation.

If there is a recursive implication, the `SELECT`-queries are wrapped into a `WITH RECURSIVE`-clause, where the recursive use of the relation is replaced with the name of the full recursive query. E.g. the implications

```
CREATE IMPLICATION habitat
SELECT sub.id, h.lives_in
FROM taxonomy AS t JOIN habitat AS h ON (t.super = h.id);
```

is translated into

```
CREATE VIEW habitat_virtual
WITH RECURSIVE rec AS (
    SELECT * FROM habitat_stored
    UNION ALL
    SELECT sub.id, h.lives_in
    FROM taxonomy AS t JOIN rec AS h ON (t.super = h.id);
)
SELECT * FROM rec;
```

Note that recursive views in PostgreSQL are restricted to only a single use of recursion (i.e. only linear recursion). Thus, each Lore-relation can have at most one recursive backward-chaining implication, and that recursive implication can have at most one use of the target relation's name. If more complex forms of recursion are required, one needs to use forward-chaining implications. If there were more (non-recursive) implications into habitat, their SELECT-queries would be placed into the union within rec.

Forward chaining implications are implemented using triggers that fire INSERT-statements into the target relation whenever one of the relations in the FROM-clause of the SELECT-query is INSERTed into. E.g. the following forward implication:

```
CREATE FORWARD IMPLICATION terrestrial AS
SELECT t.id
FROM taxon AS t JOIN habitat AS h USING (id)
WHERE h.habitat = 'Forest' OR habitat = 'Urban';
```

is translated into

```
CREATE OR REPLACE FUNCTION habitat_to_terrestrial_trigger_fnc()
RETURNS trigger AS $$ BEGIN
  INSERT INTO terrestrial
  SELECT t.id
  FROM taxon AS t JOIN (SELECT NEW.id, NEW.lives_in) AS h USING (id)
  WHERE h.habitat = 'Forest' OR habitat = 'Urban';
  RETURN NEW;
END; $$ LANGUAGE plpgsql;

CREATE TRIGGER habitat_to_terrestrial_trigger
AFTER INSERT ON habitat_stored
FOR EACH ROW EXECUTE PROCEDURE habitat_to_terrestrial_trigger_fnc();
-- ...and analogously for taxon_to_terrestrial_insert_trigger
```

So whenever a new row is inserted into habitat, the row is replaced with habitat in the query and all answers to that query is inserted into terrestrial. Similarly for inserts into taxon. These triggers handle all future inserts. A normal INSERT-command that inserts all current answers to the SELECT-part of the implication is also added to the translation to handle all past inserts.

Forward implications has no restrictions on recursion, so a relation can have many recursive forward implications, and we can even have multiple occurrences of recursion in the same implication.

4   Datalog-Like Syntax

The syntax presented for implications in the previous sections has been very close to SQL, and should feel familiar for anyone who knows SQL well. However, the syntax is quite verbose, which may make it more difficult to read and maintain. In this section we present a terser syntax inspired by other rule languages such as Datalog. In this syntax we could express the terrestrial-implication above as the following two simple (backward) implications:

```
terrestrial(id) <- taxon(id, _, _), habitat(id, 'Forest');
terrestrial(id) <- taxon(id, _, _), habitat(id, 'Urban');
```

or by merging them into a single implication with an OR-expressions as follows:

```
terrestrial(id) <-
    taxon(id, _, _), habitat(id, h) : h  = 'Forest' OR h = 'Urban';
```

The general form of a backward implication in this syntax is:

```
<rel1>(<SELECT_clause>) <-
    <rel2>(<args2>), ..., <relN>(<argsN>) [: <WHERE_clause>] ;
```

where <relI> is any (potentially schema-prefixed) relation name, <SELECT-clause> is the content of a SELECT-clause (i.e. comma separated expressions over bound variables and constants), <argsI> is a list of variable-names and constants with length equal to the number of columns in the corresponding <relI>-relation, and <WHERE_clause> is a normal WHERE-clause over constants and variables bound in <argsI>. Note that joins are performed reusing the same variable name across two or more <argsI>. An underscore can be used for unused variables (just like in Prolog). The <WHERE_clause> can also contain normal SQL-subqueries. For more complex examples exemplifying all of the above features see Sect. 9.

To write FORWARD-implications, one simply writes the arrow in the other direction (similarly as many other rule-languages), i.e. :

```
<rel2>(<args2>), ..., <relN>(<argsN>) [: <WHERE_clause>]
    -> <rel1>(<SELECT_clause>);
```

For example:

```
taxon(id, _, _), habitat(id, h) : h = 'Forest' OR h = 'Habitat'
    -> terrestrial(id);
```

This implication is rewritten to the SQL-like Lore-implication exactly as the backward-chaining implication above, except that the keyword FORWARD is added between CREATE and IMPLICATION.

Lore also introduces a Datalog-like syntax for INSERT-statements, e.g.:

```
taxon(9, 'Lutra', 'Eurasian otter');
```

which is short for

```
INSERT INTO taxon VALUES (9, 'Lutra', 'Eurasian otter');
```

Finally, Lore introduces a Datalog-like syntax also for SELECT-queries. A query can be written by writing a backward-chaining implication without any head. For example, the following is a query for all taxons living in the forest:

```
<- taxon(id, sname, pname), habitat(id, 'Forrest');
```

Note that this then selects all variables from the body of the rule.

5   Imports

Sequences of Lore-commands can, just like sequences of SQL-commands, be stored in a file and executed as a script. Lore is intended as a language for expressing knowledge over data, and such encoding of knowledge can often be used across multiple datasets, similar to how e.g. an OWL-ontology can be reused. Lore can also be used as a programming language, similar to Prolog, where code reuse is important. To better enable such reuse, Lore introduces import statements that allow one script to import another. An import-statement is declared using the IMPORT-keyword, followed by a URL to the script, e.g.:

```
IMPORT 'file:/scripts/taxon.lore';
```

The URL can either be a file path pointing to a file on the same computer as the script importing it (prefixing the path with file:), or a URL pointing to an online file (prefixing the path with http: or https:). Import statements can also be used to break long or complex scripts into separate files that are all imported by a single file for easy execution.

6   Meta-rules: Higher-Order Rules and Constraints

Lore rules are first-order rules, that is, they can only produce new statements in already existing relations. They cannot produce new relations or new rules. However, Lore has implemented a special relation, lore.make_script, that is treated differently to allow for meta-programming and higher-order rules, that is, rules producing rules and relations with variables ranging over relations. The special relation lore.make_script contains two columns, command that contains a Lore-statement as a text-value, and priority that specifies the ordering of the execution of the commands. After Lore has executed a script, it also executes all new commands added to lore.make_script until no new commands are added to this relation. There are also two more convenience relations, lore.make_rule and lore.make_relation, that have implications into lore.make_script with priority set so that relations are created before rules.

With this, we can create rules that create other rules and new relations based on values within existing relations. For example, we can transform the taxonomy described by the `taxonomy`-relation above into a collection of unary relations such that each taxon is denoted by a relation, and each edge in the `taxonomy`-relation becomes an implication with:

```
make_relation(format('CREATE RELATION t_%s(id int);', t)) <- taxon(t, _, _);
make_rule(format('t_%s(i) <- t_%s(i);', y, x)) <- taxonomy(x, y);
```

This would then produce relations and rules of the form:

```
CREATE RELATION t_1(id text);
CREATE RELATION t_6(id text);
t_6(i) <- t_1(i);
```

The meta-rules also fixes a deficiency of Lore as a data representation language. Note that it is possible to use constraints, such as `PRIMARY KEY`, `FOREIGN KEY` and `NOT NULL`, in `CREATE RELATION`-statements, just like when creating tables. However, these constraints are only checked for the stored part of a relation and not the virtual part. `FOREIGN KEY`-constraints are also sensitive to the order in which rows are inserted into tables, that is, all referenced values must be present at insert time of a referencing value. In Lore we have no control of the order of inserts caused by rules. We therefore advice against using the normal PostgreSQL-constraints for relations. However, the meta-rules allows us to encode constraints via implications. Lore has therefore introduced a relation `error(msg text)` that should contain all errors such as constraint violations. Lore then checks (if a special flag is set) this relation for errors, and if any, prints them and fails the transaction and rollbacks all changes. Lore also introduces a relation for representing `UNIQUE` and `FOREIGN KEY` constraint in an online importable library[1]. The library also contains meta-rules that creates rules that creates errors on constraint violations. The full implementation of this in terms of meta-rules requires a lot of string manipulation and is a bit too technical and involved for this paper, however the interested reader can see the code in the library for implementational details and example use.

7   Lore-Program

Lore is implemented in Scala as a standalone commandline program, and the source code is available at Gitlab[2] under a GPL-license. The program takes flags similar to the standard PostgreSQL-program `psql`[3] for specifying which host, database, user, etc. that should be used for the database connection. The user can also give in one or more files containing Lore-commands to be executed. The following command will execute a Lore-script `taxon.lore` over a database with name `mydb` on `localhost` as user `myuser`:

```
java -jar lore.jar -h localhost -d mydb -U myuser taxon.lore
```

There are also a few other utility commands available listed below:

---

[1] Its URL is https://leifhka.org/lore/library/error.lore.
[2] https://gitlab.com/leifhka/lore.
[3] https://www.postgresql.org/docs/current/app-psql.html.

--debug: Prints out all SQL-commands that are executed by the Lore-script

--clean: Used instead of scripts, and executes `DROP RELATION TO TABLE` on all Lore-relations in the database

--cleanAll: Similar to **--clean**, but executes `DROP RELATION` on all Lore-relations in the database

--metarule: Enables meta-rules, as described in Sect. 6

--checkErrors: Checks for errors as described in Sect. 6

--help: Prints usage information with examples

We have also implemented a program called Edbit[4] that works as an interactive terminal (similar to `psql`) for PostgreSQL, that also accepts Lore-commands. This allows user to experiment with Lore interactively.

8   Triplelore: A Triplestore Based on Lore

Triplelore is a triplestore (a database storing and manipulating RDF-graphs) implemented on top of Lore. Triplelore represents an RDF-triple (`s p o`) as simply a row in a binary relation denoting the predicate, that is, `p(s, o);`. Thus, all properties are represented as binary Lore-relations, and each triple is then represented as a row in such a relation. Triplelore supports the following:

- Prefixes and QNames
- OWL 2 RL [12] reasoning by translating OWL-axioms to Lore-rules (all of OWL 2 RL is supported, except `owl:sameAs`-reasoning)
- SPARQL-querying by generating an R2RML-mappings [14] that can e.g. be used by Ontop [9]
- Automatically generating Lore-rules implementing W3C's direct mappings [8] from Lore-relations to RDF

For more details on these features, please see Triplelore's webpage[5]. Triplelore is, just like Lore, a standalone commandline program also written in Scala and the source code is available at Gitlab[6] under a GPL-license.

9   More Examples

In this section we outline some more complex examples illustrating the expressive power of Lore, and how it can interact with the many features of PostgreSQL.

We will start with a more conventional examples, such as computing transitive closures. In our taxon-example we may wish to be able to query over the transitive closure of the `taxonomy`-relation. We can create the transitively closed relation `subtaxon` with:

---

[4] See https://gitlab.com/leifhka/edbit for more information.

[5] https://leifhka.org/lore/triplelore.

[6] https://gitlab.com/leifhka/triplelore.

```
CREATE RELATION subtaxon(sub int, super int);
subtaxon(sub, super) <- taxonomy(sub, super);
subtaxon(sub, super) <- taxonomy(sub, o), subtaxon(o, super);
```

We can then propagate habitat information down through the taxonomy (e.g. if sea birds have as possible habitat 'Coastal', then all subtaxons of sea birds should also have this as possible habitat) with:

```
habitat(id, habitat) <- subtaxon(id, super), habitat(super, habitat);
```

We will now look at how Lore can make use of advanced features from PostgreSQL, such as spatial relations from its geospatial extension PostGIS[7], as well as complex aggregation. For these examples we will extend our running example with the two tables presented in Fig. 2.

```
             observation                                    habitat_loc
.------------------------------------------.  .-----------------------------------------------------.
| id | location          | behavior      |  | habitat  | location                                  |
|----+-------------------+---------------|  |----------+-------------------------------------------|
|  2 | POINT(59.02 11.23) | Eats          |  | Forrest  | MULTIPOLYGON((59.02 11.27, ...), ...)     |
|  9 | POINT(61.28 10.11) |               |  | Urban    | MULTIPOLYGON((58.21 12.09, ...), ...)     |
|  2 | POINT(59.19 10.79) | Breeds        |  | Coastal  | MULTIPOLYGON((58.21 12.09, ...), ...)     |
|  1 | POINT(58.87 11.04) | Hibernates    |  | Arctic   | MULTIPOLYGON((60.37 10.31, ...), ...)     |
'------------------------------------------'  '-----------------------------------------------------'
```

Fig. 2. Relations of locations for habitats and observations of species: `observation` contains observations of individuals where `id` refers to the `taxon` observed, `location` is a point described as a PostGIS `POINT`, and `behavior` is an optional action the individual performed when observed; `habitat_loc` describes the location of the habitat `habitat` as a PostGIS `MULTIPOLYGON`-type.

We will start by adding a new relation that relates an observation directly to the habitat is was observed in:

```
CREATE RELATION observed_in(id int, habitat text, behavior text);
observed_in(id, hname, behavior) <-
    observation(id, oloc, behavior), habitat_loc(hname, hloc)
    : st_contains(hloc, oloc);
```

We will now use this relation to infer new habitat relationships with even more implications. Lets assume that a species only breeds and hibernates in their habitats. This can be expressed as:

```
habitat(id, h) <- observed_in(id, h, 'Breeds');
habitat(id, h) <- observed_in(id, h, 'Hibernates');
```

Finally, lets assume that the two most commonly observed habitats (with more than 100 observations) for a specie is also considered that specie's habitats. This requires more complex computation, such as aggregation and ordering. For this, we switch to the SQL-like syntax where we can express this computation as:

---

[7] https://postgis.net/.

```
CREATE IMPLICATION habitat AS
WITH ranked AS (
  SELECT id, habitat, COUNT(*) AS num_obs,
    ROW_NUMBER() OVER
      (PARTITION BY id, habitat ORDER BY COUNT(*) DESC) AS rank
  FROM observed_in GROUP BY id, habitat
)
SELECT id, habitat FROM ranked WHERE num_obs > 100 AND rank <= 2;
```

Since we can use all functions and datatypes already available in PostgreSQL within Lore-rules and relations, Lore can also be used for more general computation than just Datalog, more similar to Prolog. For example, assume we have a relation/table `flight(source, destination, cost)` where `source` and `destination` is the source and destination of a flight, respectively, and `cost` is the associated cost, e.g. either price or travel time. We can then compute a new relation `travel` that contains the cost and path (as an array) of all multi-flight travels with:

```
CREATE RELATION travel(source int, destination int, cost int, path int[]);
travel(s, d, t, ARRAY[s, d]) <- flight(s, d, t);
travel(s, d, t1 + t2, p || d) <- flight(s, z, t1), travel(z, d, t2, p);
```

Here we assume that the graph formed by `flight` is acyclic, as the execution would otherwise not terminate. However, if the graph can contain cycles (as would be the case for a normal graph of flights), we could amend the final rule as follows:

```
travel(s, d, t1 + t2, s || p) <-
    flight(s, z, t1), travel(z, d, t2, p) : NOT(s = ANY(p));
```

That is, we add the filter `NOT(s = ANY(p))`, which ensures that the new source `s` is not a member of the current travel path `p` (i.e. not equal to any element in `p`).

These examples illustrate the convenience and expressive power of Lore that comes from mixing the SQL-like and Datalog-like implications as well as exposing all of PostgreSQL advanced functionality.

10   Properties of Lore as a Rule Language

In this section we will discuss the properties of Lore as a rule language and how its specification and execution differs from other rule-languages.

Declarative Rules. First, note that the Lore rule language is purely declarative, that is, Lore rules define the logic of computation and not control flow. This follows from the fact that the order of the rules does not matter, and the ordering of the clauses within rules does not matter: For backward rules, all rules are gathered into view definitions, for which the order makes no difference. Within each such view definition, the rules are translated into subqueries and combined using UNION ALLs, which are essentially commutative[8]. For forward rules, all rules are translated into triggers. Triggers always execute in alphabetical order based on the name of the trigger [4]. In the translation from Lore to SQL, the names of triggers are composed of the names of the source and destination relation names, and a hash of the query within the trigger. This means that reordering the triggers does not affect the execution order.

Within each rule, the ordering of literals corresponds to the ordering of the joins in the corresponding FROM-clause in its SQL-translation. However, inner joins are also commutative and the query planner is free to execute the joins in the most efficient order [5].

Finally, there are no extra-logical operators directly affecting the execution, such as cuts, in Lore. These features makes the core Lore rule language declarative. Note however that Lore is an extension of PostgreSQL which supports non-declarative statements and features. For example, PostgreSQL supports different imperative languages, such as PLPGSQL. Functions defined in such imperative languages can therefore be used within Lore rules.

Rule Execution. The execution of Lore rules is determined by PostgreSQL's execution of views and triggers. Backward rules are translated to views, thus non-recursive rules are simply unfolded at query time into a single SQL-query that can be evaluated directly over normal tables and the table-part of Lore relations. Recursive rules are translated into recursive views, which are computed iteratively until fixpoint [7]. This effectively becomes a breadth-first evaluation. For forward rules, the execution is handled by triggers that fire when rows are inserted. The triggers fire recursively in the sense that inserts performed by a trigger can fire other triggers, thereby propagating the consequences of the rules.

Termination. Lore does not guarantee termination, that is, it is possible to write rules which produce infinitely many consequences, e.g. the following Lore-script would not terminate:

```
CREATE RELATION num(n int);
num(1);
num(n+1) <- num(n);
<- num(x);  -- queries for all natural numbers
```

However, there are different methods for ensuring termination. For queries over relations defined via recursive backward rules, one can add a LIMIT-clause to ensure termination, as the LIMIT is then propagated to the evaluation of the recursion. However, in the general case, one needs to encode termination into the rules, like we did in the flight-example above. Note that in the translation of forward rules, the ON CONFLICT ... DO NOTHING-part of the triggers in combination with the UNIQUE-constraint on the table-part of relations removes

---

[8] PostgreSQL typically, but is not guaranteed to, execute the queries of a union in the order they are written [1]. However, since the subqueries of a union are independent, the order of execution does not affect the execution time nor the rows returned.

non-termination caused by rules producing infinitely many equal statements. E.g. the following rule stating that sameAs is symmetric terminates:

sameAs(x, y) -> sameAs(y, x);

Mappings. A mapping is essentially just a rule, where the head, or *target*, is over a different data structure/model than the body, or *source*. As noted above, Triplelore is a triplestore over Lore. This allows us to use Lore rules to define mappings between normal (Lore) relations and RDF (in both directions). In addition, since Lore is built on PostgreSQL that supports storing and manipulating data represented as JSON and XML, we can also have mappings to and from these structures. As these mappings are just regular Lore rules, the mappings can be both forward chaining, thus producing materialized targets, or backward chaining, thus producing virtual targets. We can also have mappings from different sources, with potentially different structures, into the same target, and can therefore use Lore as a data integration layer.

With all the different types of data (tabular, triples, JSON, XML) within the same database system, much of the purely technical difficulties of mapping creation and data integration is removed, and the student can focus on the conceptual difficulties with mapping data between different structures and formats, such as determining good structure in the target, managing identity (e.g. IRI creation from keys), and so on. Once the conceptual complexities of mapping creation and data integration is understood, one can move over to a real mapping language that maps between different database systems, and then tackle the technical difficulties in isolation.

11   Related Work

In this section we will compare Lore with similar tools and systems. To our knowledge, there seems to be only one rule-based system that has education as primary focus, namely DES (The Datalog Educational System) [15]. DES is a full implementation of a database system supporting many query languages, such as SQL, Datalog, and relational algebra, with implemented translations between these, debuggers, a GUI, and much more. However, to our knowledge, DES does not support forward chaining rules[9], and does not have any support for other data representations such as triples, JSON and XML, where rules can be used as mappings between these.

Yedalog [10], and its successor Logica [3], are two systems that supports Datalog over relational databases via translations to SQL. Their main focus is applying Datalog-rules to large databases efficiently. However, these systems also seems to only support backward chaining, and similarly to DES, does not have any support for triplestores. Logica does support many functions and datatypes

---

[9] DES does support tabling of relations, however, this seems to only be an optimization technique, and does not produce proper materialized relations that e.g. can be updated in place. Tabling is also at a relation-level, and not at a rule-level.

from the underlying database system, however, it introduces a special syntax for this that is handled explicitly in their translation, and seems to not support geospatial datatypes and functions, and other similarly advanced types.

There are also many other systems supporting both forward and backward chaining rules over databases, such as Jena, EYE, etc. (see [13] for an overview). However, to our knowledge, none of these translate rules to SQL, expose all features of the underlying database system, nor support an SQL-like syntax.

12   Conclusion and Future Work

This paper has introduced Lore, a system that extends PostgreSQL with logical relations and implications, as well as a Datalog-like rule language, and support for RDF and OWL via Triplelore. These features allow students and researchers to study different aspects of rules, such as forward and backward chaining, mappings, rules over complex types and functions, combining rules and SQL, and comparing rules and traditional relational constructs like views and triggers.

There are many features that is planned to be implemented in the future. In particular, support for removing and modifying implications and rules directly, and truth maintenance of forward chaining rules when deleting or updating rows. It would also be interesting to perform an experimental evaluation of the efficiency of Lore, compared to other deductive databases.

References

1. Combining Queries (UNION, INTERSECT, EXCEPT). https://www.postgresql.org/docs/15/queries-union.html. Accessed 01 June 2023
2. DBMS popularity broken down by database model. https://db-engines.com/en/ranking_categories. Accessed 16 June 2023
3. Logica. https://logica.dev. Accessed 16 June 2023
4. Overview of Trigger Behavior. https://www.postgresql.org/docs/15/trigger-definition.html. Accessed 01 06 2023
5. Planner/Optimizer. https://www.postgresql.org/docs/current/planner-optimizer.html. Accessed 01 June 2023
6. TIOBE Index for June 2023. https://www.tiobe.com/tiobe-index/. Accessed 16 June 2023
7. WITH Queries (Common Table Expressions). https://www.postgresql.org/docs/15/queries-with.html. Accessed 01 June 2023
8. Arenas, M., Bertails, A., Prud'hommeaux, E., Sequeda, J., et al.: A direct mapping of relational data to RDF. W3C recommend. **27**, 1–11 (2012)
9. Calvanese, D., et al.: Ontop: answering SPARQL queries over relational databases. Semant. Web **8**(3), 471–487 (2017)
10. Chin, B., et al.: Yedalog: exploring knowledge at scale. In: 1st Summit on Advances in Programming Languages (SNAPL 2015). Schloss Dagstuhl-Leibniz-Zentrum fuer Informatik (2015)
11. Kappel, G., Kramler, G., Retschitzegger, W.: TriGS debugger - a tool for debugging active database behavior[1]. In: Mayr, H.C., Lazansky, J., Quirchmayr, G., Vogel, P. (eds.) DEXA 2001. LNCS, vol. 2113, pp. 410–421. Springer, Heidelberg (2001). https://doi.org/10.1007/3-540-44759-8_41

12. Motik, B., Grau, B.C., Horrocks, I., Wu, Z., Fokoue, A., Lutz, C., et al.: OWL 2 web ontology language profiles. W3C Recommend. **27**(61) (2009)
13. Rattanasawad, T., Saikaew, K.R., Buranarach, M., Supnithi, T.: A review and comparison of rule languages and rule-based inference engines for the semantic web. In: 2013 International Computer Science and Engineering Conference (ICSEC), pp. 1–6. IEEE (2013)
14. Rodriguez-Muro, M., Rezk, M.: Efficient SPARQL-to-SQL with R2RML mappings. J. Web Semant. **33**, 141–169 (2015)
15. Sáenz-Pérez, F.: DES: A deductive database system. Electron. Notes Theor. Comput. Sci. **271**, 63–78 (2011)

Comparing State of the Art Rule-Based Tools for Information Extraction

Domenico Lembo and Federico Maria Scafoglieri[✉]

University of Rome La Sapienza, Rome, Italy
{lembo,scafoglieri}@diag.uniroma1.it

Abstract. In this paper, we present a comparative analysis of the leading rule-based information extraction systems in both research and industry, focusing on their main characteristics and their performance. Our evaluation was performed on a dataset of text documents about financial product descriptions from a real-world application scenario. In this study, we demonstrate that, while the considered tools share similarities in terms of expressiveness of their extractors and produce results of comparable quality, the implementation choices of their engines have a substantial impact on their overall execution time. Moreover, we emphasize that some of the considered tools offer seamless support for writing extraction rules, effectively addressing one of the common challenges associated with rule-based approaches.

1 Introduction

Information Extraction (IE) is the process of converting unstructured text data into structured information, so that it is suited for further analysis. To tackle this challenge, two primary approaches are commonly employed: machine learning algorithms [7], which learn identification patterns from training datasets, and rule-based extraction methods [3]. In Rule-based IE, extractors are created using rules to identify and annotate relevant portions of the text. This method proves particularly useful in certain scenarios. For instance, when a detailed explanation of the IE results is needed, when documents adhere to a specific format, when there is a lack of available datasets to train statistical algorithms, or when a very high level of accuracy is needed. In such cases, rule-based IE emerges as the most practical and effective approach [4].

This article focuses specifically on this form of IE and provides a comparative analysis of the most advanced tools that employ this methodology. The comparison evaluates both the features and performance of these tools.

To this aim, we conducted tests in the financial domain, and analyzed the so-called Key Information Documents (KIDs). KIDs contain information about financial products, organized according to a specific format mandated by European regulations, and distributed as pdf files. This domain serves as suitable test scenario for several reasons: *i)* it is derived from real-world business requirements; *ii)* since KIDs must adhere to precise rules, concerning both the nature of the content and the way in which it is formatted, extraction rules can be naturally defined based on these regulations; *iii)* financial domains are not commonly explored in the field of natural language processing (NLP),

A. Fensel et al. (Eds.): RuleML+RR 2023, LNCS 14244, pp. 157–165, 2023.
https://doi.org/10.1007/978-3-031-45072-3_11

given their technical nature and lack of benchmarks [11]; *iv*) IE from KIDs must reach excellent accuracy levels, since extracted data are intended to be used for monitoring tasks, and, in case they highlight some violations of the rules, may trigger sanctions for product manufacturers or distributors.

In this paper, we first discuss how the reference financial datasets used in our evaluation have been constructed (Sect. 2). Then, we provide an introductory overview of the tools considered in our study (Sect. 3), and next we offer a comprehensive comparison of the features available in such tools, evaluate the computational performances of their rule engines, and present the outcomes of our tests (Sect. 4). We conclude the paper by summarizing the findings and suggesting potential areas for future research (Sect. 5). To ensure the reproducibility of our experiments, all the material created for this study, including the datasets, which can be useful even for other purposes, can be accessed at the following repository: https://github.com/Scafooo/RuleMLRR2023.

2   Scenario and Datasets

As anticipated in the introduction, in compliance with European regulations[1], financial product creators are obligated to clearly describe the characteristics of the products they sell (stocks, insurance, obligations, etc.) in documents called KIDs (Key Information Documents), that must be formatted according to precise guidelines. KIDs are two-page PDF documents with an average size of approximately 200 KB. The regulations not only govern the document's content but also dictate its presentation and methods of sharing. Each KID must contain specific mandatory sections where particular information is required to be reported using standardized phrases, forms, or specific vocabularies. For instance, one essential piece of information included in KIDs is the International Securities Identification Number (ISIN), a unique twelve-digit code used to identify the product, with the first two digits being letters. The ISIN must be located in the second section of the document titled "Product". The list of information items (fields) extracted from KIDs in our experiments is given in Table 1[2].

It has to be noted, however, that financial product creators (i.e., financial institutions) often deviate from the precise guidance provided by the European regulations. Therefore, some variants do actually exist for the formatting of the KIDs, typically depending on their author. Another requirement imposed by European regulations is the sharing of KIDs via email with the market authorities of individual European countries. We collected these documents through the authority responsible for regulating the Italian financial market (CONSOB), and created two datasets for our evaluation. KIDs considered in our study are in Italian language. Nonetheless, many of our findings are general and not strictly related to the input language. The first dataset, referred to as KID-Q, consists of 656 documents that exhibit heterogeneity in terms of authorship and presentation style, thereby impacting the complexity of rule-based extraction. Data from this dataset were manually and automatically extracted and then verified by domain experts. KID-Q serves as a valuable resource for evaluating Precision, Recall, and F-measure.

---

[1] PRIIPs Regulation n. 1286/2014.

[2] Note that in various cases we had to realize more than one extractor for a single field.

Table 1. Information to be Extracted

ID	Extractor Name	Description
1	Product Name	The name of the financial product
2	Manufacturer	The producer of the financial product
3	ISIN	The unique code that identifies the financial product in the market
4	Production Date	The date of when the financial product was placed on the market
5	Compression Alert	A phrase indicating that the product may be difficult to understand for those who are not experts in the field
6	Website	The manufacturer's website
7	Currency	The currency used to give quantitative information about the product contained in the KID
8	SRRI	Synthetic risk and reward indicator given on a scale of 1–7
9	RHP	Recommended Holding Period for the financial product

The second dataset, named `KID-P`, comprises 7,717 randomly selected documents, and has a size of 4 GB. This dataset was created specifically to measure execution time, memory usage, and CPU utilization.

3 Rule-Based Information Extraction Tools

In this section, we provide an overview of each tool included in our comparison study. We briefly describe their key features, delve into their rule-based engines, and showcase an example of an ISIN extractor implemented using their proprietary language. For more in-depth information regarding the tools, including syntax and semantics of the rules, we recommend referring to the following sources [3,5,8,10].

StanfordNLP. [10] is a comprehensive natural language processing suite developed by Stanford University. It was initially released in 2010 and since then it has undergone continuous refinement and expansion, including the addition of new features and support for various natural languages. The rule-based system employed by StanfordNLP, known as *TokensRegex*, utilizes a framework for applying cascading regular expressions to token sequences. The rule language used by *TokensRegex* is based on the Common Pattern Specification Language (CPSL) [2]. Below, we give an example of a *TokensRegex* rule used for extracting the ISIN:

```
$code = "/([A-Za-z]{2}[0-9]{10})/"

ruleType: "tokens",
pattern: (
    (?$CodeISIN [{word:$code} &
    {SECTION:"PRODUCT"}]+?)),
action: ( Annotate($CodeISIN, ISIN, "ISIN"))
```

General Architecture for Text Engineering (GATE). [5] is a suite of tools developed by the University of Sheffield since 1995 to facilitate information extraction from text. Its core components are integrated into a modular subsystem called A Nearly-New Information Extraction System (*ANNIE*), which provides essential extraction function-alities. The *Java Annotation Patterns Engine* (*JAPE*) is the component responsible for executing extraction rules in GATE. These rules operate on annotations generated by the *ANNIE* system. The JAPE rules, inspired by CPSL as the TokensRegex rules of StanfordNLP, are executed sequentially through a cascade of finite state transducers over annotations. In 2018, an optimized version of the JAPE engine, called *JAPE Plus*, was introduced. GATE remains actively used in various international projects. Here's an example of a JAPE rule for extracting the ISIN:

```
Phase: ISIN
Input: Token Lookup
Options: control = appelt

Rule: ISIN
({Token.string =~ "[A-Za-z][A-Za-z][A-Z0-9]{10}"})
:match
-->
:match.ISIN = {rule = "ISIN" }
--------------------------------------------------
Phase: ISINProduct
Input: sectionProduct ISIN
Options: control = first

Rule: ISINProduct
({ISIN within sectionProduct})
:match
-->
:match.ISINProduct = { rule = "ISINProduct" }
```

SystemT. [3] is a commercial information extraction system developed by IBM. It oper-ates based on database principles, aiming to overcome the limitations of grammar-based and CPSL-based extraction methods. SystemT has been successfully applied in various industrial projects. In SystemT, extractors utilize a user-friendly declarative language with a syntax similar to SQL, known as the *Annotation Query Language* (AQL). This language allows for concise and efficient rule definitions. An example of AQL extractor for ISIN is given below:

```
module ISIN;
import view _Document from module IEWTDocument
  as _Document;
import view secProd from module section
  as sectionProduct;

create view ISINToBeConsolidated as
  extract
  regex /([A-Za-z][A-Za-z][A-Z0-9]{10})/
  on sP.sectionProduct as isin
  from sectionProduct sP;

create view ISIN as
  select Min(i.isin) as isin
  from ISINToBeConsolidated i;
```

UIMA Ruta. [8] is a rule-based information extraction system designed for text analysis. It is integrated into the Unstructured Information Management Architecture

(UIMA) framework, developed by the Apache Foundation. UIMA Ruta provides a streamlined CPSL-based syntax for rule definition and is supported by a comprehensive development environment called UIMA RUTA WORKBENCH, which is an extension for the Eclipse IDE. Below, there is an example of UIMA RUTA rule for extracting the ISIN:

```
SCRIPT uima.ruta.emnlp.sectionProduct;

DECLARE ISIN, ISINProd;

ANY+{REGEXP("[A-Za-z][A-Za-z][A-Z0-9]{10}")
  ->MARK(ISIN)};
ANY{-PARTOF(ISINProd),PARTOF(ISIN),
  PARTOF(sectionProduct) -> MARK(ISINProd)};
```

We conclude this section by mentioning other rule-based IE tools proposed over the years. The **Finite State Automata-based Text Understanding System (Fastus)** [1] served as an inspiration for modern rule-based IE tools but is no longer actively maintained; similarly, **TextMarker** [9], a rule-based information extraction toolkit based on UIMA, is no longer supported or maintained; additionally, the relatively new systems **Odinson** and **Odin's Runes** [12] are still in early stages of development and require further time to assess their continued support and usage. For the above reasons, we did not include such tools in our comparative analysis.

4   Comparison

In the first part of this section, we compare the features offered by the different tools. In the second part, we discuss the performance of rule-based systems, evaluating both the extraction quality and the computational resources utilized. Finally, we dedicate the last part of this section to the maintainability of extractors and their expressive power.

4.1   Features Comparison

Table 2 presents a summary of the comparison of key features among the analyzed tools. Below we list the features considered for our comparison:

- **UI**: Graphical interface for result checking, inspection, and component management.
- **Debug Environment**: Tools to debug extraction results, including explanation, provenance, and rule induction.
- **Cloud Ready**: Capability to deploy the solution directly through cloud services without local configuration.
- **Library Support**: Support for custom implementations and advanced components injection without coding.
- **Programming Language**: The programming language and its version used to implement the tool.
- **Coding Features**: This parameter refers to the available support for writing extraction rules, classified as follows:
  - *Strong Coding*: No support.

- *Supported Coding*: Facilitated code supported by auto completion, syntax-highlighting, and error-highlighting.
- *Graphical User Interface (GUIs)*: User-friendly environments providing drag & drop or annotation facilities to build rules without coding.
– **License**: License regarding code distribution and usage.

In terms of features, SYSTEMT offers the most comprehensive system, allowing the creation of rules using a block graphical system with refining and inspection capabilities during execution. Among the open-source tools, UIMA RUTA is the most feature-rich, providing explanation and timing of rule execution, introspection, automatic validation, and rule induction through UIMA RUTA WORKBENCH. Instead, STANFORDNLP lacks native support for creating TOKENSREGEX rules, while GATE only allows checking annotations on text created with JAPE.

Table 2. Features Comparison

Tool	UI	Debug Env.	Cloud Ready	Library Support	Program. Language	Coding			License
						Strong	Support	GUI	
StanfordNLP				✓	Java 1.8+	✓			GPL v3+Comm
GATE	✓	✓	✓	✓	Java 1.5+	✓			LGPL
SystemT	✓	✓	✓	✓	Java 1.8+			✓	Comm
UIMA Ruta	✓	✓		✓	Java 1.8+			✓	Apache v2+Comm

4.2 Performance Comparison

To evaluate quality of information extraction for each tool, we conducted experiments using the KID-Q dataset and computed Precision, Recall, and F-measure relative to the extraction of the fields defined in Table 1. Table 3 presents the overall average results, as all systems demonstrate similar performance in terms of these metrics.

Table 3. Quality Results

Precision	Recall	F-Measure
~96%	~89.0%	~92.3%

To assess the computational performance of the tools, we conducted tests on the KID-Q dataset. In order to ensure a fair comparison, we excluded components such as the POS tagger and sentence splitter from the overall computation time and RAM/CPU usage, as they are not part of the main engine being analyzed. Our experiments were conducted on a late 2019 MacBook Pro with 16 GB of RAM and a quad-core Intel i7 CPU, with each core operating at 2.9 GHz.

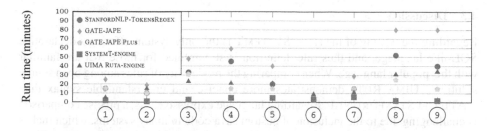

Fig. 1. Performance of Information Extraction (individual extractions).

Figure 1 shows the performance of each extraction listed in Table 1 when executed individually. Additionally, Figs. 2 and 3 present the overall performance, including run time and CPU usage, when all extractors are executed together and optimized in execution by each tool's engine as a whole.

In all the conducted tests, SYSTEMT consistently outperforms the other systems. This outcome is not surprising, considering that SYSTEMT is a commercial tool that incorporates an optimizer inspired by query plans commonly utilized in relational databases. On the other hand, the other engines experience slower performance due to the sequential execution of rules. Within the realm of open-source tools, JAPE demonstrates the poorest performance, whereas its enhanced version, JAPE PLUS, yields better results but at the cost of increased memory usage.

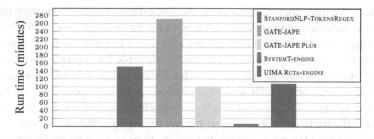

Fig. 2. Performance of Information Extraction (whole extraction).

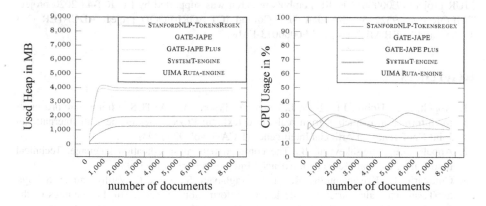

Fig. 3. Memory and CPU Usage

4.3 Discussion

Regarding the writing of the rules, SYSTEMT is the only system offering a declarative SQL-like language, and thus rule definition is streamlined for those that are familiar with this popular language. When comparing the readability of rules among open source solutions, UIMA RUTA demonstrates more concise and understandable syntax than GATE and STANFORDNLP. Regarding language expressiveness, a precise comparison is challenging due to the inclusion of custom Java code in many systems, which makes them Turing-complete. Nonetheless, studies have indicated that SYSTEMT's AQL is more expressive than code-free CPSL grammar at the base of all the other analized languages, as illustrated in Theorem 1 of [3]. AQL has also undergone a formal study known as Document Spanners [6], which defines its expressiveness and computational complexity. From a practical perspective, we have observed that SYSTEMT's AQL language offers numerous native features that are lacking in other tools, often necessitating the use of custom code. An example of this is SYSTEMT's *Max* clause, used to retrieve the last match of a given extractor, which has no direct counterpart in the other languages. Additionally, SYSTEMT avoids potential intricacies related to priorities on the execution of extractors. These priorities are instead heavily used in all the other systems.

5 Conclusion and Future Works

In this study, we have analyzed four prominent rule-based information extraction tools, offering a comprehensive overview along with an analysis of their performance and features. Our evaluation was carried out in a real-world financial scenario, and we have made the dataset and materials used in the study available for experiments reproduction or other purposes. An intriguing direction for future research would involve comparing rule-based approaches with statistical methods, focusing specifically on the effort required for solution development. Such a comparative analysis would yield valuable insights into the trade-offs associated with these two approaches and would assist practitioners in selecting the most suitable method for their specific requirements.

Acknowledgments. Scafoglieri's research was entirely and exclusively supported by PNRR MUR project PE0000013-FAIR. Lembo's research was supported by EU ICT-48 2020 project TAILOR (No. 952215), EU ERA-NET Cofund ICT-AGRI-FOOD project ADCATER (No. 40705), and PNRR MUR project PE0000013-FAIR.

References

1. Appelt, D.E., Hobbs, J.R., Bear, J., Israel, D., Tyson, M.: FASTUS: a finite-state processor for information extraction from real-world text. In: Proceedings of the 13th International Joint Conference on Artificial Intelligence (IJCAI), vol. 93 (1993)
2. Appelt, D.E., Onyshkevych, B.: The common pattern specification language. Technical report, International Menlo Park Artificial Intelligence Institute (1998)
3. Chiticariu, L., Krishnamurthy, R., Li, Y., Raghavan, S., Reiss, F., Vaithyanathan, S.: SystemT: an algebraic approach to declarative information extraction. In: Proceedings of the 48th Annual Meeting of the Association for Computational Linguistics (ACL) (2010)

4. Chiticariu, L., Li, Y., Reiss, F.: Rule-based information extraction is dead! Long live rule-based information extraction systems! In: Proceedings of the 2013 Conference on Empirical Methods in Natural Language Processing (EMNLP) (2013)
5. Cunningham, H., Maynard, D., Bontcheva, K., Tablan, V.: GATE: an architecture for development of robust HLT applications. In: Proceedings of the 40th Annual Meeting of the Association for Computational Linguistics (ACL), pp. 168–175 (2002)
6. Fagin, R., Kimelfeld, B., Reiss, F., Vansummeren, S.: Document spanners: a formal approach to information extraction. J. ACM (JACM) 62(2), 1–51 (2015)
7. Freitag, D.: Machine learning for information extraction in informal domains. Mach. Learn. 39(2/3), 169–202 (2000)
8. Kluegl, P., Toepfer, M., Beck, P., Fette, G., Puppe, F.: UIMA Ruta: rapid development of rule-based information extraction applications. Nat. Lang. Eng. 22(1), 1–40 (2016)
9. Klügl, P., Atzmüller, M., Puppe, F.: Test-driven development of complex information extraction systems using textmarker. In: Nalepa, G.J., Baumeister, J. (eds.) Proceedings of the 4th Workshop on Knowledge Engineering and Software Engineering (KESE), vol. 425 (2008)
10. Manning, C.D., Surdeanu, M., Bauer, J., Finkel, J.R., Bethard, S., McClosky, D.: The Stanford CoreNLP natural language processing toolkit. In: Proceedings of 52nd Annual Meeting of the Association for Computational Linguistics (ACL): System Demonstrations (2014)
11. Skalický, M., Šimsa, Š, Uřičář, M., Šulc, M.: Business document information extraction: towards practical benchmarks. In: Barron-Cedeno, A., et al. (eds.) CLEF 2022. Lecture Notes in Computer Science, vol. 13390. Springer, Cham (2022). https://doi.org/10.1007/978-3-031-13643-6_8
12. Valenzuela-Escárcega, M.A., Hahn-Powell, G., Surdeanu, M.: Odin's runes: a rule language for information extraction. In: Proceedings of the 10th International Conference on Language Resources and Evaluation (LREC) (2016)

A Case Study for Declarative Pattern Mining in Digital Forensics

Francesca Alessandra Lisi[1(✉)] 🔟, Gioacchino Sterlicchio[2] 🔟, and David Billard[3] 🔟

[1] DIB & CILA, University of Bari Aldo Moro, Bari, Italy
FrancescaAlessandra.Lisi@uniba.it
[2] DMMM, Polytechnic University of Bari, Bari, Italy
g.sterlicchio@phd.poliba.it
[3] University of Applied Sciences in Geneva, Geneva, Switzerland
David.Billard@hesge.ch

Abstract. In this short paper, we briefly describe the application of a declarative AI approach to a case study concerning the analysis of real-world phone recordings. In particular, we summarize the general results obtained for a couple of mining tasks, one being sequential pattern mining and the other contrast pattern mining, reformulated within the framework of Answer Set Programming.

Keywords: Declarative Pattern Mining · Digital Forensics · Answer Set Programming

1 Introduction

Digital Forensics (DF) [4] is a branch of Forensic Sciences concerned with evidence acquired from computers and other digital storage devices. DF is used in the investigation of a variety of cybercrimes in which the collected evidence, subject to the same practices and guidelines as any other digital evidence, will be used in prosecution. Its purpose is to examine digital devices by following forensic analysis procedures in order to identify, retrieve, preserve, analyze and present facts or opinions regarding the information collected through different methodological stages. In particular, during the *Evidence Analysis* (EA) phase, experts (I) collect, classify and review evidences; (II) examine them for finding the possible existence of a crime and perpetrators and (III) obtain evidence and present them to, *e.g.*, lawyers and judges. However, the absence of decision support systems leads to undesirable uncertainty about the outcome of the EA phase. Already a decade ago, Garfinkel [9] predicted the end of the golden age of DF in the face of the exponential increase in capacity of storage devices, evidence sources and the spread of cloud computing and cryptography. While nowadays there are different tools to acquire data from the various possible sources of evidence, the EA phase lacks of specific software to analyze data quickly and provide support during investigations. For these reasons, logic-based Artificial Intelligence (AI) techniques, especially from the area of *Knowledge Representation and Reasoning* (KR&R), have been proposed as a means for achieving the objectives defined for the EA phase. Costantini *et*

A. Fensel et al. (Eds.): RuleML+RR 2023, LNCS 14244, pp. 166–174, 2023.
https://doi.org/10.1007/978-3-031-45072-3_12

al. [6,7] were the first to apply *Answer Set Programming* (ASP) to DF. Their seminal work inspired the COST Action CA 17124 "Digital forensics: evidence analysis via intelligent systems and practices" (DigForASP)[1], a project ended in March 2023 which aimed to contribute to the development of new AI tools for DF.

Among the many EA activities, analyzing phone data can be particularly time consuming especially if done manually. The automation of this task can be done, e.g., by looking for *sequential* and *contrast* patterns. In short, the sequential pattern mining problem consists in finding frequent and non-empty temporal sequences from a dataset of sequences, called sequential patterns [19]. Instead, the contrast pattern mining problem is about detecting statistically significant differences (contrast) between two or more disjoint datasets [8]. In this paper, we describe a case study concerning the analysis of real-world mobile phone calls that have been made available within the Dig-ForASP project. The proposed methodology combines pattern mining and ASP which is used for the stream of research known as *Declarative Pattern Mining* (DPM) covering several tasks such as sequence mining [10,13,20] and frequent itemset mining [12,14]. Because EA requires verifiable evidence, our declarative approach turns out to be useful because it provides a broad range of proof-based reasoning features. In addition, the correctness of results can be formally verified, while Machine Learning (ML) approaches or other "black box" methods can be regarded as having the same value as human witness' suspicions.

This paper is organized as follows. In Sect. 2 we provide a brief summary on ASP and Pattern Mining. In Sect. 3 we describe the case study considered for the analysis of phone records. In Sect. 3.1 and Sect. 3.2, we describe the sequential and contrast pattern mining task respectively and how we used them in our DF case study. We conclude this work in Sect. 4 with final remarks.

2 Preliminaries

2.1 Answer Set Programming

ASP is a declarative and expressive programming language, based on the *stable model semantics*, that was introduced at the end of the 90 s to solve difficult research problems (e.g. security analysis, planning, configuration, semantic web, etc.) [3]. Every ASP programs is made up of atoms, literals and logic rules. Atoms can be true or false and a literal is an atom a or its negation *not a*. The *not* statement is not the standard logical negation but it is used to derive *not p* (i.e. p is assumed not to hold) from failure to derive p. An ASP general rule has the following form:

$$a_1 \vee \ldots \vee a_n \leftarrow b_1, \ldots, b_k, not\ b_{k+1}, \ldots, not\ b_m$$

where all a_i and b_j are atoms. The previous rule says that if $b_1, \ldots, b_k$ are true and there is not reason for believing that $b_{k+1}, \ldots, b_m$ are true then at least one of the $a_1, \ldots, a_n$ is believed to be true. The left hand side and the right hand side of the $\leftarrow$ are called *head* and *body* respectively. Rules without body are called *facts*. The

---

[1] DigForASP: https://digforasp.uca.es/.

head is unconditionally true and the arrow is usually omitted. Conversely, rules without head are called *constraints* and are used to discard stable models, thus reducing the number of answers returned by the ASP solver. There are different ASP systems, the most important of which are Clingo [11] and DLV [15].

2.2 Pattern Mining in a Nutshell

Pattern Mining is about the extraction of regularities from data that might take several forms, e.g., transactions and sequences. For example, pattern mining can be used to find malicious code in Android apps [1]. The basic formulation of the problem is known as *frequent pattern mining*. It is the process of identifying patterns or associations within a dataset that occur frequently. A pattern p is interesting if given a threshold k and set of data $\mathcal{D}$, p occurs at least in k examples in $\mathcal{D}$. In this paper we consider two variants of the problem, known as *Sequential Pattern Mining* and *Contrast Pattern Mining*.

Sequential Pattern Mining is concerned with finding statistically relevant patterns between data examples where the values are delivered in a sequence [19]. It is usually presumed that the values are discrete within a time series. Given a sequences dataset $\mathcal{D}$ the *cover* of a sequence s is the set of sequences of $\mathcal{D}$ which includes s: $cover(s, \mathcal{D}) = \{t \in \mathcal{D} \mid s \subseteq t\}$. The number of sequences that includes s in $\mathcal{D}$ is called *support*: $support(s, \mathcal{D}) = |cover(s, \mathcal{D})|$. For an integer k, frequent sequential pattern mining means discovering all sequences s such that $support(s, \mathcal{D}) \geq k$, where s is called *frequent sequential pattern* and k *minimum support threshold*.

Contrast Pattern Mining [5,8], involving the concept of contrast, can describe the significant differences between datasets under different contrast conditions. It applies to a transaction dataset $\mathcal{D}$, i.e., a multi-set of transactions. A *transaction* t is a non-empty set of items with associated a *transaction identifier TID* and the TIDs are unique and can occur multiple times in $\mathcal{D}$. A dataset $\mathcal{D}$ may be associated with classes. In this case, some number $k \geq 2$ of class labels $C_1, ..., C_k$ are given, and $\mathcal{D}$ is partitioned into k disjoint subsets $\mathcal{D}_1, ..., \mathcal{D}_k$ such that $\mathcal{D}_i$ is the subset labeled with the C_i class. The problem of contrast pattern mining concerns the enumeration of all frequent patterns with *absolute support difference*, e.g. for C_i against the other classes, that exceeds the user-defined minimum support threshold *minDiff*.

3   The Case of Phone Records

In this paper we want to describe our formal and verifiable approach to *call pattern analysis*, an intelligence technique used to identify patterns in telephone call traffic such as timing of events and actions, possible causal correlations and contexts in which suspicious actions have occurred. As a case study, we considered the analysis of the real-world mobile phone recordings made available under non-disclosure agreement to DigForASP members for academic experimentation. Data in the DigForASP dataset is anonymised to preserve privacy and confidentiality and does not allow tracing back of real users. So, for example, there are not real telephone numbers but only ficti-tious names - analogously for geographic locations and time periods. The dataset is made up of four phone records, each referring to a suspect: "Eudokia Makrembolitissa"

(8,783 rows), "Karen Cook McNally" (20,894 rows), "Laila Lalami" (12,689 rows), and "Lucy Delaney" (8,480 rows). Phone records in this dataset have the following features: incoming/outgoing call or SMS (*Type*), who makes the call/SMS (*Caller*), who receives the call/SMS (*Callee*), the place of the operation (*Street*), when the operation took place[2] (*Time*) and the date of the day (*Date*).

From the interaction with DF experts inside the DigForASP project, it turned out that it would be useful to automate the acquisition of information (e.g., relationships between two or more telephone numbers) to answer questions such as: "When X calls Y, do always Y calls Z shortly afterwards?" or "What is the day/time of day when there are the most calls?". This information can be obtained by applying pattern mining algorithms to phone calls.

In the following subsections we will briefly describe our ASP-based declarative approach to call pattern analysis: sequential pattern mining (Sect. 3.1) and contrast pattern mining (Sect. 3.2). As an ASP solver we have used Clingo.

3.1 Mining Sequential Patterns in Phone Records

As said before, sequential pattern mining can reason about sequences of events in a given time frame. We encoded this in ASP by exploiting temporal information to create the suspects' relationship network, to identify associations between individuals and to highlight the patterns or "lifestyles" of the suspects [16, 17]. Our goal was to find frequent communication patterns between suspects.

To better understand the following example, we provide some clarifications regarding the syntax and the semantics. Each answer set returned is a sequential pattern represented by means of the *pat/2* predicate. Listing 1 shows one of the 15 patterns discovered in 100 instances from the DigForASP dataset, with maximum pattern length equal to 3 and minimum support threshold equal to 25%. It represents the sequential pattern which consists of three communication events (Line 1). The first is between Karen Cook McNally and Margaret Hasse, the second is between Joan Aiken and Karen Cook McNally, finally between Lucie Julia and Karen Cook McNally. For example, considering the day 08/09/2040, we know that Karen, the subject of the phone records, sent a text message to Margaret at 1:1:34 (Line 5). Later, Karen received a incoming call from Joan at 8:19:53 (Line 6) and once again Karen received an incoming call from Lucie at 8:53:18 (Line 7). The same type of information is obtained by analyzing the other day (September 11th, 2040). Patterns can be graphically presented by means of the Clingraph tool[3] to better clarify the semantics of each answer set as in Fig. 1. Figure 2 shows the behavior of our approach in time and space considering frequent, closed and maximal sequential patterns. The last two are defined as condensed representations allowing to reduce the number of patterns found without loss of outstanding information. The reader can find a complete discussion of all the experiments carried out in [17] and our ASP implementation in the external report[4].

---

[2] ISO8601 format, HH: MM: SS.
[3] https://clingraph.readthedocs.io/en/latest/.
[4] External report to ASP encoding.

Listing 1 An example of sequential pattern

```
 1: pat(1,(karen_cook_mcnally,margaret_hasse)) pat(2,(joan_aiken,karen_cook_mcnally))
    pat(3,(lucie_julia,karen_cook_mcnally))
 2: support((8,9,2040)) support((11,9,2040))
 3: pat_information((8,9,2040),(1,(karen_cook_mcnally,margaret_hasse)),
    out_sms(simple),(1,1,34))
 4: pat_information((8,9,2040),(2,(joan_aiken,karen_cook_mcnally)), in_call(simple),(8,19,53))
 5: pat_information((8,9,2040),(3,(lucie_julia,karen_cook_mcnally)), in_call(simple),(8,53,18))
 6: pat_information((11,9,2040),(1,(karen_cook_mcnally,margaret_hasse)),
    out_call(simple),(13,21,47))
 7: pat_information((11,9,2040),(2,(joan_aiken,karen_cook_mcnally)),
    in_call(simple),(15,21,36))
 8: pat_information((11,9,2040),(3,(lucie_julia,karen_cook_mcnally)),
    in_call(simple),(15,44,14))
 9: pat_information((11,9,2040),(1,(karen_cook_mcnally,margaret_hasse)),
    out_sms(simple),(16,20,32))
10: len_support(2)
```

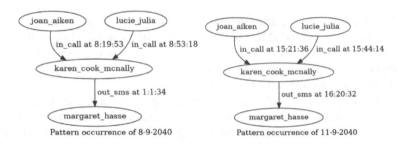

Fig. 1. The two occurrences of the sequential pattern corresponding to Listing 1.

3.2 Mining Contrast Patterns in Phone Records

Contrast pattern mining is an interesting class of pattern mining problems halfway between discrimination and characterization of a data set, thanks to the use of classes to guide the search for regularities. It could exploit background knowledge to extract less but meaningful patterns.

In this case study, we applied the contrast task to find the characteristics and habits of outgoing/incoming calls/SMS (from now on, referred to as *classes*) of each suspect [18]. A single pattern is associated with each answer set and, in our approach, represented by means of the *in_pattern/1* and *absolute_diff/1* predicates. The latter expresses the difference in support of the pattern between the class under consideration and the complementary class. Each pattern conveys information that allows to characterize the considered class. In Listing 2, as an illustrative example of the potential usefulness of contrast pattern mining in the DF field, we report the results obtained on Karen's phone records for the class "incoming call". Here, we have set the minimum support threshold to 10% and the maximum pattern length to 3. Overall, the five contrast patterns returned by the algorithm provide a rich information about the habits of Karen as regards incom-

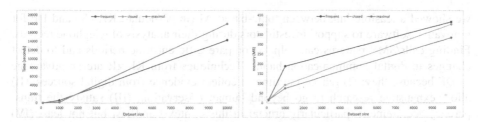

Fig. 2. Comparison between frequent, closed and maximal pattern mining on input of increasing size (100, 1 K, 10 K) as regards (left) execution time and (right) memory consumption. The minimum support threshold is 25% and maximum pattern length is 5.

Listing 2 Example of contrast patterns found for the incoming calls

1: in_pattern(callee(karen_cook_mcnally)) absolute_diff(216)
2: in_pattern(callee(karen_cook_mcnally)) in_pattern(time(afternoon)) absolute_diff(106)
3: in_pattern(time(afternoon)) absolute_diff(130)
4: in_pattern(time(morning)) absolute_diff(43)
5: in_pattern(callee(karen_cook_mcnally)) in_pattern(time(morning)) absolute_diff(72)

---

ing calls in contrast to other types of communication. Notably, they tell us that incoming calls of Karen are mainly received in the afternoon (Answer 3) and less in the morning (Answer 4). Figure 3 shows the trend in time and space of our approach on input of increasing size. The complete discussion of all the experiments performed can be found in [18], while in this report[5] our implementation is presented.

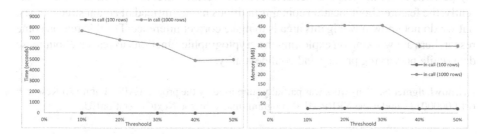

Fig. 3. Comparison wrt (left) execution time and (right) memory consumption for the "incoming call" class by varying the dataset size.

4   Final Remarks

Pattern mining can find useful information that is not visible in simple data browsing as well as interesting associations and correlations among data items. In this paper

---

[5] External report to ASP encoding.

we showed a feasible link between logic-based AI (in particular, KR&R) and DF for innovative software to support investigators during their analysis of telephone records. Finding calls/SMS patterns can help to compare different time periods and to detect changes in digital communication habits. Techniques from KR&R are an advantage in DF because they: (I) reduce the time to collect evidence from digital sources, (II) allow exhaustive research to go beyond human observation, (III) satisfy the transparency requirement (particularly crucial in this context) and last but not least (IV) enable the development of decision support systems for law enforcement investigators, intelligence services, criminologists, prosecutors, lawyers and judges, which can help make judicial proceedings clearer and faster. As shown in Sects. 3.1 and 3.2, these tasks can answer the questions posed in Sect. 3 as when the relationship between one or more referents must be ascertained: mafia association, principal and executor, drug dealer and supplier, etc. In cases of harassment and stalking by telephone, they are crucial for verifying the number, frequency and times of contact between the suspect and the victim.

For the future there are various ways to improve over the proposed methodology. One way is to consider other variants of the sequential pattern mining problem like the discovery of outlier patterns by looking for so-called *rare sequential patterns* [21]. Enhancing knowledge with actions done or not done by a suspect in a time series can be explored by means of so-called *negative sequential patterns* [2]. Pattern mining can generate a large number of patterns and with high dimensionality, thus making it difficult to interpret the results but also degrading efficiency and scalability. For these reasons, we would like to improve our encoding with new DF and pattern constraints. For the contrast pattern mining task, experiments could be replicated with other ASP solvers, such as DLV2 [15], and high-performance hardware. Last but not least, finding patterns about geographic locations is an interesting direction for future work. Currently, the feature about location contains fictitious names instead of actual street names, but we do not know how big this area is to make correct inference. For this reason some researchers are working on exploiting the cryptographic functions to reason about these data while preserving privacy and confidentiality.

Acknowledgments. This work was partially supported by the project FAIR - Future AI Research (PE00000013), under the NRRP MUR program funded by the NextGenerationEU.

References

1. Alam, S.: Applying natural language processing for detecting malicious patterns in android applications. Forensic Sci. Int.: Digit. Invest. **39**, 301270 (2021). https://www.sciencedirect.com/science/article/pii/S2666281721001888
2. Besnard, P., Guyet, T.: Declarative mining of negative sequential patterns. In: DPSW 2020– 1st Declarative Problem Solving Workshop, pp. 1–8 (2020)
3. Brewka, G., Eiter, T., Truszczynski, M.: Answer set programming at a glance. Commun. ACM **54**(12), 92–103 (2011). http://doi.acm.org/10.1145/2043174.2043195
4. Casino, F., et al.: Research trends, challenges, and emerging topics in digital forensics: a review of reviews. IEEE Access **10**, 25464–25493 (2022)
5. Chen, Y., Gan, W., Wu, Y., Yu, P.S.: Contrast pattern mining: a survey (2022). https://arxiv.org/abs/2209.13556

6. Costantini, S., De Gasperis, G., Olivieri, R.: Digital forensics evidence analysis: an answer set programming approach for generating investigation hypotheses. In: Calimeri, F., Ianni, G., Truszczynski, M. (eds.) LPNMR 2015. LNCS (LNAI), vol. 9345, pp. 242–249. Springer, Cham (2015). https://doi.org/10.1007/978-3-319-23264-5_21

7. Costantini, S., De Gasperis, G., Olivieri, R.: Digital forensics and investigations meet artificial intelligence. Ann. Math. Artif. Intell. **86**(1), 193–229 (2019)

8. Dong, G., Bailey, J.: Contrast Data Mining: Concepts, Algorithms, and Applications. CRC Press, Boca Raton (2012)

9. Garfinkel, S.L.: Digital forensics research: the next 10 years. Digit. Invest. **7**, S64–S73 (2010). https://www.sciencedirect.com/science/article/pii/S1742287610000368

10. Gebser, M., Guyet, T., Quiniou, R., Romero, J., Schaub, T.: Knowledge-based sequence mining with ASP. In: IJCAI 2016–25th International Joint Conference on Artificial Intelligence, p. 8. AAAI (2016)

11. Gebser, M., Kaminski, R., Kaufmann, B., Schaub, T.: Clingo = ASP + control: preliminary report. arXiv preprint: arXiv:1405.3694 (2014)

12. Guns, T., Dries, A., Nijssen, S., Tack, G., De Raedt, L.: MiningZinc: a declarative framework for constraint-based mining. Artif. Intell. **244**, 6–29 (2017)

13. Guyet, T., Moinard, Y., Quiniou, R., Schaub, T.: Efficiency analysis of ASP encodings for sequential pattern mining tasks. In: Pinaud, B., Guillet, F., Cremilleux, B., de Runz, C. (eds.) Advances in Knowledge Discovery and Management. SCI, vol. 732, pp. 41–81. Springer, Cham (2018). https://doi.org/10.1007/978-3-319-65406-5_3

14. Jabbour, S., Sais, L., Salhi, Y.: Decomposition based SAT encodings for itemset mining problems. In: Cao, T., Lim, E.-P., Zhou, Z.-H., Ho, T.-B., Cheung, D., Motoda, H. (eds.) PAKDD 2015. LNCS (LNAI), vol. 9078, pp. 662–674. Springer, Cham (2015). https://doi.org/10.1007/978-3-319-18032-8_52

15. Leone, N., et al.: Enhancing DLV for large-scale reasoning. In: Balduccini, M., Lierler, Y., Woltran, S., et al. (eds.) LPNMR 2019. Lecture Notes in Computer Science(), vol. 11481. Springer, Cham (2015)

16. Lisi, F.A., Sterlicchio, G.: Declarative pattern mining in digital forensics: preliminary results. In: Calegari, R., Ciatto, G., Omicini, A. (eds.) Proceedings of the 37th Italian Conference on Computational Logic, Bologna, Italy, June 29 - July 1, 2022. CEUR Workshop Proceedings, vol. 3204, pp. 232–246. CEUR-WS.org (2022). http://ceur-ws.org/Vol-3204/paper_23.pdf

17. Lisi, F.A., Sterlicchio, G.: Mining sequences in phone recordings with answer set programming. In: Bruno, P., Calimeri, F., Cauteruccio, F., Maratea, M., Terracina, G., Vallati, M. (eds.) Joint Proceedings of the 1st International Workshop on HYbrid Models for Coupling Deductive and Inductive ReAsoning (HYDRA 2022) and the 29th RCRA Workshop on Experimental Evaluation of Algorithms for Solving Problems with Combinatorial Explosion (RCRA 2022) co-located with the 16th International Conference on Logic Programming and Non-monotonic Reasoning (LPNMR 2022), Genova Nervi, Italy, September 5, 2022. CEUR Workshop Proceedings, vol. 3281, pp. 34–50. CEUR-WS.org (2022). http://ceur-ws.org/Vol-3281/paper4.pdf

18. Lisi, F.A., Sterlicchio, G.: A declarative approach to contrast pattern mining. In: Dovier, A., Montanari, A., Orlandini, A. (eds.) AIxIA 2022 - Advances in Artificial Intelligence. Lecture Notes in Computer Science(), vol. 13796, pp. 17–30. Springer International Publishing, Cham (2023). https://doi.org/10.1007/978-3-031-27181-6_2

19. Mooney, C., Roddick, J.F.: Sequential pattern mining - approaches and algorithms. ACM Comput. Surv. **45**(2), 1–39 (2013). https://doi.org/10.1145/2431211.2431218

20. Negrevergne, B., Guns, T.: Constraint-based sequence mining using constraint programming. In: Michel, L. (ed.) CPAIOR 2015. LNCS, vol. 9075, pp. 288–305. Springer, Cham (2015). https://doi.org/10.1007/978-3-319-18008-3_20
21. Samet, A., Guyet, T., Negrevergne, B.: Mining rare sequential patterns with ASP. In: ILP 2017–27th International Conference on Inductive Logic Programming (2017)

Semantic Role Assisted Natural Language Rule Formalization for Intelligent Vehicle

Kumar Manas[1,2(✉)] and Adrian Paschke[1,3]

[1] Freie Universität Berlin, Berlin, Germany
{kumar.manas,adrian.paschke}@fu-berlin.de
[2] Continental AG, Hannover, Germany
[3] Fraunhofer Institute for Open Communication Systems, Berlin, Germany

Abstract. This paper proposes a novel pipeline to translate natural language rules and instructions for intelligent vehicles into temporal logic. The pipeline uses semantic role labeling (SRL), soft rule-based selection restrictions, and large language models (LLMs) to extract predicates, arguments, and temporal aspects from natural language rules and instruction. We then use the language understanding capability of LLMs to generate temporal logic rules from unstructured natural language text and additional information provided by SRL. We envision our model as a human-in-the-loop system that can facilitate the automated rule formalization for planning and verification systems in automated driving and drone planning. We demonstrate that our method can generate semantically correct temporal logic formulas from natural language text and provide implicit explanations of the output by showing the intermediate reasoning steps involved. This paper illustrates the integration of additional semantic knowledge and LLM and its application for the intelligent system domain of automated driving and drone planning. Our generalizable pipeline can easily extend to new logic formalization types, traffic rules, drone planning instructions, and application domains.

Keywords: Intelligent Vehicle · Semantic Natural Language Processing · Language Model · Knowledge Representation · Rule Formalization

1 Introduction

Intelligent Vehicles such as Autonomous driving (AD) and drones need to ensure safety by following user-defined rules and instructions. As AD systems become more capable, they will need to deal with increasingly complex and diverse situations on the road. Human drivers use traffic rules, regulations, and expert knowledge to make decisions, which often need to be more specific and straightforward to translate into machine-readable form. Current methods for evaluating AD systems do not measure how well they comply with rules or handle rule-exception. Moreover, different countries have different legal and technical traffic law standards, making applying the same AD model everywhere challenging. Similarly, drones need to understand natural language instructions to operate autonomously. We need to convert the rules and instructions into a formal language that machines can understand and execute. However, this process is challenging and requires domain and logic expertise, and often a complex hierarchy of rules and instructions is involved. This restricts the ability of the intelligent system to adapt to various rules and instructions in a logical way.

Text-to-logic conversion is challenging for large language models (LLMs) due to the inherent uncertainty in natural language. We propose a divide-and-conquer approach that decomposes the task into sub-problems of extracting predicates, entities, and arguments from the textual traffic rules using the semantics of the text and then using them as a soft constraint for the LLM models. Due to such an approach, LLM outputs are more aligned with the user requirements and focus on the semantics and rules needed for our use case of rule formalization. In this paper, we have established a soft rule outlining the types of semantic roles that can serve as predicates, arguments, and temporal aspects within the temporal logic (TL) rule translation framework. Nevertheless, we integrate these rule-based recommendations as soft constraints within the LLM model, ensuring that we can leverage the advantages of semantic role labeling (SRL) without compromising the broader language understanding capabilities of the LLMs. Adding external knowledge has been shown to increase model performance [18] usually. In summary, we added extra knowledge to the LLM model through SRL and rule-based selection as soft-constraint derived from manual traffic rules, world knowledge, and drone instruction planning formalization.

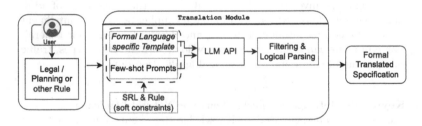

Fig. 1. Architecture of SRL assisted Translation Module for Rule Specification.

Figure 1 illustrates our model pipeline. It has a translation module that converts legal or planning rules from natural language to formal language. The translation module applies a formal language-specific template consisting of information about that formal logic grammar. Additionally, some examples of natural language text and its corresponding formal logic (shown as few-shot prompts) are provided to the LLM. The prompts and template also get access to the additional knowledge, which includes semantic roles and additional rules as soft constraints for the LLM. The LLM module then uses this information, which generates a formal logic expression. Lastly, we parse the LLM output using a parser for the formal language of choice and obtain the final formal language specification.

Using this approach, we aim to improve the accuracy and robustness of text-to-logic conversion, enabling a more comprehensive range of applications in natural language programming, automated theorem proving, rule monitoring, and semantic parsing. Our approach can pave the way for more effective and efficient communication between humans and machines, bridging the gap between natural language and formal logic. Our main contribution can be summarized as follows:

- We present a new framework that transforms natural language driving and planning rules for intelligent vehicles into temporal logic, using SRL and rule-based selectional restrictions as extra knowledge to LLM.
- We demonstrate that the method can generate semantically correct temporal logic formulas from unstructured natural language text and also provides implicit explanations of the output by showing intermediate steps involved in the final formalized rule output.
- Our generalizable framework can be easily extended to new logic formalization types, traffic rules and instructions, and application domains.

Section 2 introduces related work followed by methods and technical background for this work in Sect. 3. Section 4 discuss dataset creation, model selection, and evaluation setup, followed by the results and discussion in Sect. 5. Finally, we wrap up with a conclusion and discussion about our work extension in the future.

2   Related Work

Several works have codified and formalized traffic laws and regulations for automated driving and planning instruction for other intelligent systems. Selected traffic rules from German Road Traffic Regulation (StVO)[1] and Vienna Convention on Road Traffic (VCoRT)[2] are manually formalized for intersection [19], interstate [20], safe distance [27], uncontrolled intersections [11], and overtaking situation [28]. Traffic rules are considered implicitly by the motion planning module so that autonomous vehicles (AV) comply with driving rules. Similarly, natural language planning instructions for drones are formalized in [22].

Traffic rules can be formalized in different ways. [11] used First-order logic (FOL) to formalize traffic rules and incorporated time as a parameter, but FOL does not have an inherent notion of time. Propositional logic [35] can also represent traffic rules, but they do not handle temporal aspects directly. Instead, they use tricks like hiding time information in the predicate or atomic propositions. Another option is to use different temporal logic, such as signal temporal logic (STL) [1,9], linear temporal logic (LTL) [3], co-safe LTL (scLTL) [26], and metric temporal logic (MTL) [19,20]. Temporal logic is more suitable as they

---

[1] https://www.gesetze-im-internet.de/stvo_2013/.

[2] https://unece.org/DAM/trans/conventn/crt1968e.pdf.

have native support of temporal information. However, LTL and scLTL cannot model the duration of the temporal operator well. Therefore, MTL and STL are better choices for traffic rule modeling, which requires relatively more precise time information for temporal operators. We used MTL and LTL in this work. We chose MTL for traffic rule formalization because it suits our final goal of assisting the trajectory verification system we envision. However, our approach can be easily adapted to other temporal logics and FOL. Moreover, STL is more appropriate for continuous dense signals, while MTL is more discrete and useful for verification [19,20]. Formalized rules and instruction can be used in trajectory planning [12,16] and trajectory monitoring [19,20]. However, the manual creation of these rules can limit adaptation. Unlike previous work, we aim to automate the formalization process of traffic rules and drone planning instructions and affect multiple use cases mentioned above.

Before the rise of deep learning, a grammar-based approach [13] was used to convert the natural language to formal or temporal logic. Semantic parsing and SMT solvers were employed to generate LTL specifications from natural language for robotics planning [5]. Lately, LLMs have been applied to such tasks because of their broad abilities in text generation, coding, question-answering, and reasoning tasks. LLMs are neural networks with billions of parameters. They are pre-trained models on a large amount of data gathered from the internet, and the state-of-the-art LLM [2] for natural language processing uses Transformers [32]. Transformers-based models are utilized in verification, planning, and reasoning tasks in the robotics domain [10,34].

Previous work on text-to-temporal logic conversion has used different methods, such as based on a restricted template of the LTL formula [4], fine-tuning [7] for LTL and FOL generation, model training [8] for STL formula generation, and in-context learning [17] for LTL specification in robotics. However, these methods either need a dataset for fine-tuning or training or require rules or instructions to be simplified and structured for in-context learning or prompting. Our approach differs from them in that it uses in-context learning with the help of SRL instead of classical prompting. This enables us to introduce knowledge about the semantic structure of sentences for the automated formalization of traffic rules and planning instructions. Moreover, our approach can handle legal traffic rules as unstructured specifications, which assume a lot of world knowledge and are challenging to fine-tune without the dataset needed for fine-tuning. We also focus on more complex logic that requires time constraints over operators, such as MTL, rather than only LTL, which has been the focus of previous work with very pre-processed datasets [7,10,25] and fine-tuning LLM. In summary, our work differs from others in terms of catering to multiple forms of temporal logic with very few data requirements and unstructured natural language rules due to an in-context learning approach and semantic understanding.

SRL is helpful for language understanding, question-answering, and machine translation [24] because semantic roles and relationships capture the meaning and structure of sentences better than just parts-of-speech tagging based on grammatical relationships. However, their application to text-to-formal logic translation and integration with in-context learning has yet to be thoroughly investigated to the best of our knowledge.

3   Method

3.1   Metric and Linear Temporal Logic Representation

In the following, we informally introduce the operators used in MTL and LTL based on [31]. MTL specifications considered in this paper can be written with grammar:

$$\varphi :: = p \mid \neg p \mid \varphi_1 \wedge \varphi_2 \mid \varphi_1 \vee \varphi_2$$

where $p \in P$ and P is a set of possible atomic propositions; φ is the task specification, φ_1 and φ_2 are MTL formula. We also have the following temporal operators that utilize time intervals.

$$\varphi :: = G_t(\varphi) \mid \varphi_1 U_t \varphi_2 \mid X_t(\varphi) \mid F_t(\varphi) \mid P_t(\varphi)$$

where G, U, X, F and P are temporal operators, and the subscript t represents an interval $[t_1, t_2]$ expressing time constraints when these operators are active. If the interval is not specified for an operator, then it means until the end of the trace, which we assume to be finite. In addition, the logical connectives *negation* ($\neg$), *and* ($\wedge$), *or* ($\vee$) and *implication* ($\Rightarrow$) are used to write formulas. The future globally operator G specifies that φ holds within a time interval for all future states. The until operator U specifies that φ_1 holds until φ_2 becomes true within the time interval specified by t. The next state operator X, specifies that φ holds for the next state within the time interval specified by t. The future operator F, specifies that φ holds within a time interval for some future state, and the past operator P, specifies that φ holds within a time interval for some past or previous state. LTL formalization is similar to MTL but without the time subscript t in temporal operators. MTL is more expressive than LTL and can satisfy more safety properties for cyber-physical systems.

3.2   SRL and Rule as Soft Constraint

SRL analyzes texts concerning predicate-argument structures such as *"who did what to whom, and how, when and where"* [24]. Semantic role representations provide richer linguistic analysis than syntactic parsing and the grammatical role of the sentence alone. SRL is better than Parts-of-speech tagging for our purpose as we are more interested in the meaning of rather than only role of each word in the sentence. SRL provides information about the entity performing an action, the entity of the object affected by the action, the temporal modifier, location, etc. A predicate is the main verb that expresses an action or a state, and an argument is a word or a phrase that modifies or completes the meaning of the predicate. Figure 2, shows a sentence and its SRL based on the PropBank [23] (explained later in this section). As seen here, words in the sentence are

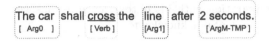

Fig. 2. SRL of sentence based on PropBank.

given roles based on the complete semantics. Here Arg0, and Arg1 represent the argument for the predicate (shown with verb here), and temporal aspects can also be extracted and shown with ArgM-TMP.

PropBank and VerbNet [29] are the resources used in this work for the SRL generation of the sentence, and these two resources provide different kinds of information about predicates and their arguments. These are the different methodologies to achieve the SRL. PropBank is a corpus that is annotated with verbal propositions and their arguments. It captures predicate-argument structure by annotating the predicate and the semantic role of its arguments. It is a verb-oriented resource that reflects the relationships between syntax and semantic role labels more strongly than VerbNet. VerbNet is a lexical resource that links verbs to their syntactic and semantic patterns, and in this way, verbs are grouped as classes based on shared syntactic behavior. VerbNet is more informative and generalizable than PropBank regarding semantic roles, but it does not cover all verbs in English. In this work, our focus is on PropBank due to greater verb coverage, but our methodology is easily extendable to both PropBank and Verbnet styles of SRL.

In summary, the SRL module takes the sentence and produces the output of the words with their semantic roles in terms of the predicate, argument, location, direction, temporal aspects, etc., as shown in Fig. 2. All these pieces of information can be used in formal logic, as our formalization also consists of predicate, arguments, and temporal aspects. Thus, SRL can bridge the gap between natural language and formal logic. However, we found that the predicates used in our MTL and LTL formalization have broader definitions than the predicates defined in the SRL, based on our experience with the traffic rules and planning instruction dataset. Unlike SRL, which only considers the action element or verbs as a predicate, our use case also treats location and direction as semantic roles that form predicates in temporal logic. Therefore, we defined a rule that specifies what constitutes a predicate list and what constitutes an argument. The rule serves as a selectional restriction, restricting the semantic content of the arguments and predicate. However, these are used as extra knowledge along with the LLM knowledge for formal logic conversion, and we applied them as soft constraints for the model.

Predicate Selection Rule: Predicate=[Verb, Location, Direction]

Argument Selection Rule: Argument=[Arg0, Arg1,..., Arg5]

Temporal: Temporal aspect = [ArgM-TMP]

3.3   LLM and Prompting

Language models, or LLMs, are powerful tools that use deep learning to understand and create natural language. They can figure out the context and meaning of a text and produce coherent responses. One type of LLM architecture that performs particularly well in natural language tasks is the Transformer. Transformers use a self-attention mechanism to learn how words and tokens (parts of words) are related in a text. This helps LLMs to capture the meaning and context of a word. By learning the patterns and rules of natural language, LLMs can understand the syntax, semantics, and sometimes the world knowledge of the language. In "in-context learning", the model learns to do a task from some examples or prompts. Prompts consist of an instruction and some input-output pairs. This kind of learning is also called *few-shot learning*. If there are no examples, only an instruction, then it is called *zero-shot learning*. In this work, we used *two-shot learning* for traffic rule formalization, which means we have two examples along with the instruction for the model. For drone instruction planning formalization, seven-shot learning is used. As the number of shots (or examples) increases, the model's accuracy also improves [2]. Figure 3 shows our basic prompt for two-shot learning. Prompt in Fig. 3 starts with an instruction for the model followed by two input-output pairs of natural language traffic rule and MTL translation. Optionally, we can inject additional external knowledge into the prompt (SRL-based knowledge) to enhance model performance.

Translate the following natural language traffic rule into MTL formula based on the semantic role label (SRL) information and rule as soft constraints, and think step-by-step using chain-of-thought.
The MTL formula should contain temporal and logical operators |, &, ~, ->, <->, X, I, G, F, O, P, U, and if the interval is not specified for a temporal operator then its till the end.

① **Natural language traffic rule:** Ego vehicle will not exceed the speed limit of the lane it is driving on, and it will not exceed the maximum velocity allowed for its vehicle type, and ego will not exceed the speed limit such that it can no longer react to traffic regulations and restrictions.
Additional SRL and Rule Knowledge: ''Obtained from external pre-trained SRL module and soft rule constraints.''
MTL translation: G(keep_lane_speed_limit(ego) ∧ keep_vehicle_type_limit(ego) ∧ keep_braking_speed_limit(ego)).

② **Natural language traffic rule:** If an ego vehicle wants to overtake the other vehicle, then it should use turn signals beforehand for t seconds.
Additional SRL and Rule Knowledge: ''Obtained from external pre-trained SRL module and soft rule constraints.''
MTL translation: G(overtake(ego,other) -> P[0,t] turn_signal(ego)).

Fig. 3. Prompt with instruction for using additional rule-based SRL as soft constraints and external knowledge. Prompts used in our experiments have two input-output pairs for two-shot learning. Illustrations are added for better understanding, not part of the actual prompts used in the experiment. A template for the specific formal language is provided in the prompt (shown in blue color). *Additional SRL and Rule Knowledge* shown above will fetch information from the external pre-trained SRL and rule module, so complete input is not shown here, just a placeholder (shown with green color). (Color figure online)

By incorporating SRL and the rules outlined in Sect. 3.2 into the prompt template, it transforms from a hard constraint to a more flexible soft rule. We only show traffic rules examples because they are relatively complex, and drone planning prompts can be written similarly. The model will start translating new traffic rules based on these two prompts, even if it has not seen some operators in the prompts. This generalization is because LLMs have learned about LTL, MTL, or other formal languages during pre-training [2]. Training the LLM is expensive and time-consuming, but creating the prompts as shown in Fig. 3 for in-context learning is fast and cheap [2]. However, in-context learning struggles with unstructured and reasoning-intensive tasks and unstructured input data, such as text-to-formal logic translation. To overcome this limitation, we added extra information based on our rules and SRL so that the model can perform better in text-to-formal logic translation with few-shot learning by integrating additional semantic knowledge into the translator module.

4   Evaluation

We evaluate our SRL-assisted external knowledge module on a traffic rule (ours) and drone plan dataset [22]. Algorithm 1 shows our evaluation pipeline, the procedure involved in traffic rule and drone planning dataset to temporal logic translation using our SRL and soft-rule assisted approach. We experiment with multiple models and two types of in-context learning prompts: classical without SRL and with SRL as an external knowledge base. Since the drone planning dataset has textual instruction and LTL pairs, we only create traffic and driving rule-MTL pairs here.

Algorithm 1. Convert Textual Traffic and Drone Rules to Temporal Logic

---

1: **procedure** CONVERTTEXTUALRULESTOTEMPORALLOGIC($Textual\,Rule\,Dataset$)
2:      $results \leftarrow \{\}$
3:      **for all** $rule \in Textual\,Rule\,Dataset$ **do**
4:          $semanticRoleofWords \leftarrow semanticRoleLabelingModule(rule)$
5:          $additionalKnowledge \leftarrow userDefinedRule(semanticRoleofWords)$
6:          $intermediateTranslation \leftarrow LLM(rule + additionalKnowkedge)$
7:          $temporalLogicTranslation \leftarrow LLM(intermediateTranslation)$
8:          $LogicallyParsedTranslation \leftarrow parser(temporalLogicTranslation)$
9:          **if** $LogicallyParsedTranslation \neq error$ **then**
10:              $results.append(LogicallyParsedTranslation)$
11:          **else**
12:              $results.append(temporalLogicTranslation)$
13:          **end if**
14:      **end for**
15:      $finalTemporalLogic \leftarrow majorityVote(results)$
16:      **return** $finalTemporalLogic$
17: **end procedure**

4.1   Dataset: Traffic Rule and Instruction Planning

We used two datasets to evaluate our method, one for translating unstructured traffic rules to MTL and another for translating natural language drone planning instructions to LTL as introduced in [22] and processed in [25]. To the best of our knowledge, there is no open-source dataset for evaluating LLM for traffic rules with MTL formalization, unlike the drone planning instruction dataset (text instruction- LTL pairs). Existing datasets and metrics [7] [10] [22] are not suitable for us because they do not reference legal traffic and driving rules, and they use LTL data, which is different from MTL. Some datasets for robotics and drone motion planning [22] use LTL data. However, they have straightforward and structured rules that do not need complex reasoning or unpacking complex semantics of complex sentences like traffic rule formalization. Previous works, [19] and [20], have used MTL to formalize traffic rules for intersection and interstate driving in detail, but we cannot use their MTL rules directly. They condensed rules by combining multiple rules of a specific subtype into one rule. They relied on the legal interpretation of various sources of rules (StVO, VCoRT) and court rulings for specific situations. Also, there is no direct mapping of the MTL rule and the corresponding exact text of the rule. These sources are helpful for the manual approach, but they are not enough for evaluating the automated translation of unstructured traffic rules to MTL, unlike language model targeted datasets developed for other domains (robotics and drone). Therefore, we used our dataset of traffic rules and MTL pairs that can work with LLMs and preserve the original structure and wording of the legal traffic rules without much preprocessing or condensation. We also included some traffic rules from previous works [15,16] LTL traffic rules for planning and predicting AV maneuvers.

Our in-house dataset[3] (snapshot in Table 1) comprises 32 traffic rules and MTL pairs based on the MTL syntax as in Sect. 3.1. Natural language textual traffic rules from VCoRT and English translation of StVO[4] are used. Some preprocessing to define vague terms and remove ambiguity is performed, but we kept it minimal. For example, in StVO §(7)(5), we have legal rule *Any change of lane must be signaled clearly and in good time*. For formal logic and automated system, we need to define vague terms such as *clearly* and *good time*. Such terms are open for multiple interpretations, so we preprocess them with more concrete terms, such as change of lane must be signaled beforehand for t seconds.

4.2   Evaluation Setup

We conducted two sets of experiments to test our hypothesis about SRL: one with SRL-assisted prompting and one without. SRL-assisted prompting yielded better results, so we focused on it. Figure 1 illustrates how we apply filter and logical parsing to the LLM output. This enhances the quality of the TL formula and alerts the user about grammar mistakes for a specific TL. The prompt template also limits the TL formula grammar (Fig. 3). We can switch to other logic, such as STL, by changing the MTL parser and filter module. We use modified py-metric-temporal-logic[5]and LTLF2DFA[6] as parsers for MTL and LTL respectively, but

---

[3] https://github.com/kumarmanas/TR2MTL.
[4] https://germanlawarchive.iuscomp.org/?p=1290.
[5] https://github.com/mvcisback/py-metric-temporal-logic.
[6] https://github.com/whitemech/LTLf2DFA.

Table 1. Overview of traffic rules and MTL pairs dataset

Natural Language Traffic Rule	MTL Representation
At intersections and junctions, if there is another vehicle on the right of the ego vehicle, then the ego vehicle must yield to the other vehicle, provided there is no traffic sign number 306 in front of it.	$G\Big(\big((\text{at\_intersection(ego)} \lor \text{at\_junction(ego)})$ $\land \text{in\_right\_of(other, ego)}$ $\land \neg\text{in\_front\_of(ego, sign\_306)}\big)$ $\Rightarrow \text{yield(ego, other)}\Big)$
If ego vehicle wants to change lanes, turn, or overtake, they should use their turn signals beforehand for t time units.	$G\Big(P_{[0,t]}\text{turn\_signal(ego)}$ $\Rightarrow (\text{change\_lane(ego)} \lor \text{turn(ego)}$ $\lor \text{overtake(ego)})\Big)$

we can use other parsers without affecting the model. The generated formula has a confidence score (0–1, 1 being the highest). This score is helpful for the end users as feedback. A less confident model indicates that more human intervention or checks are needed before accepting the final translation. We run our models for each traffic rule five times with *temprature* value as 0.3 for all models and pick the translation by majority vote among model runs.

4.3 LLM and SRL Model Selection

We used [30] and [6] to extract PropBank-based and Verbnet-based SRL from the natural language textual rule, respectively. Then we used SRL and rule as extra knowledge to the prompts, as described in Sect. 3.2 and Algorithm 1. Besides SRL, we also need LLM as a backbone to translate the textual rule. As mentioned in the introduction, we chose the "in-context learning" approach. We provided LLM with a *prompt* that contains a list of input-output pairs with optional extra knowledge that illustrates the task. We used five different LLM as a backbone in this work: *GPT-3.5-turbo*[7], *text-davinci-003*(See footnote 7), *StarCoder* [14], *StarCoderBase* [14] and *Bloomz* [21]. We selected these models based on their performance, relevance, accessibility, and openness. GPT-3.5-turbo and text-davinci-003 were state-of-the-art models that were accessible but not open-source. StarCoder, StarCoderBase, and Bloomz models were open-source with public API. Bloomz was optimized for various tasks that require following human instructions. StarCoder models were optimized for code generation tasks and were state-of-the-art among open-source models [14]. We considered natural language to MTL conversion a code generation task based on instructions. We did not use the Codex[8] model, as GPT-3.5-turbo now replaced Codex.

---

[7] https://platform.openai.com/docs/models/gpt-3-5.
[8] https://platform.openai.com/docs/models/codex.

5   Results and Analysis

We present our framework's performance on the traffic rules dataset using various LLM backbones and SRL styles in Table 2. We compare the models with SRL and rule assistance (denoted as **with SRL**) and without them. Bold numbers indicate the best models for each category. The results show that GPT-3.5-turbo with SRL performs significantly better than the other models, and our approach of using extra knowledge with SRL is effective. We used nl2ltl as a baseline by ignoring the time constraints over the temporal operator, as MTL can be approximated as LTL formulas by ignoring the temporal value for the operators. However, we used the MTL formula to evaluate the other model backbone. We classified the translations as incorrect if they missed the temporal operator or had incorrect predicates, arguments, logical connectives, or MTL grammar. We used *semantic accuracy* as the evaluation criterion, as there can be multiple MTL formalizations with the same semantic meaning for the same traffic rules. We did not consider exact match accuracy in this work, as this metric would only measure exact MTL translation without semantic consideration. Our choice of metrics is also based on the work and results of [25] and [7]. We evaluated our framework on a dataset with long and complex sentences (refer Sect. 4.1). Most incorrect translations involved sentences too long for the language model limits. This affected non-GPT models more, as they failed or gave errors. Some rules, such as *ego vehicle enters the icey road then from next time ego must slow down until there is no bad road.*, had a complicated logical structure with the use of multiple temporal operators such as "X" and "U" with relatively complex semantics and that requires more reasoning from the model. GPT variants did much better than other models, possibly because they had more world knowledge. We also noticed that the code generation models, StarCoder and StarCoderBase, struggled when background world information was needed apart from provided traffic rules. Translating natural language traffic rules into formal logic often demanded a deeper understanding of driving and world knowledge, logical structure, and contextual implications. So state-of-the-art non-code LLMs were more suitable than code generation models without enough data for fine-tuning. StarCoderBase did worse than StarCoder because StarCoder had more data and fine-tuning by design.

The main errors were incorrect logical connectives (including implication) and predicates. For example, models generated "yield_to_right(ego)" as subformulas instead of "yield(ego, otherVehicle)", indicating models take the yield to the right side as a complete predicate in contrast to our requirement, where only yield is a predicate. Moreover, our approach and prompting methods provided the step-by-step intermediate output of rule text with a dictionary with textual rule components and propositions, making it more explainable and easy to edit. Editing was easier than creating a new rule from scratch.

Similarly, we experimented with drone planning instruction dataset [22] having 5900 instruction and corresponding LTL formula pairs as designed in [25] to evaluate our methods for LTL formalization. Table 3 shows the results of our approach alongside nl2ltl and state-of-art BART-FT-RAW [25] model. We

Table 2. Translation Accuracy of models for traffic rules MTL translation.
Model is evaluated for two types of in-context learning: with and without SRL for 32 traffic rules. With SRL has two variants: PropBank and VerbNet.

Model Architecture with LLM Backbone	Without SRL	With SRL (PropBank [23])	With SRL (VerbNet [23])
Ours (GPT-3.5-turbo(See footnote 7))	37.50%	**56.25%**	**53.13%**
Ours (Text-davinci-003(See footnote 7))	**40.60%**	53.13%	**53.13%**
Ours (StarCoder [14])	12.50%	18.75%	18.75%
Ours (StarCoderBase [14])	9.38%	15.62%	15.62%
Ours (Bloomz [21])	9.38%	12.50%	15.62%
nl2ltl[a] [4]	28.15%	–	–

[a] nl2LTL with GPT 3.5 backbone without SRL. As *nl2ltl* does not have native support of SRL and MTL. So for evaluation, we ignored time constraints over temporal operator for this comparison.

showed only GPT variants of model results as other models' performances were relatively poor, as demonstrated in Table 2. Our SRL method used only 7 example pairs or 7-shot prompts and achieved relatively good accuracy with fewer data, although lower than the state-of-the-art fine-tuned model [25].

Table 3. Translation accuracy for drone planning dataset [22]: text instruction to LTL translation task.

Model backbone	Fine-tuning	Prompting	Acccuracy
Ours (SRL-PropBank with GPT-3.5-turbo(See footnote 7))	✗	✓	44.06%
Ours (SRL-VerbNet with GPT-3.5-turbo(See footnote 7))	✗	✓	46.00%
Ours (without SRL GPT-3.5-turbo(See footnote 7))	✗	✓	40.01%
BART-FT-RAW [25]	✓	✗	**69.39%**
nl2ltl without SRL with GPT3.5 [4]	✗	✓	24.00%

We chose 7-shot prompts for this experiment because we had enough data available, unlike the traffic rule dataset, which had only 32 test data and could be overfitted by 7-shot prompts. The fine-tuned model usually provides better accuracy due to access to more data for training than in-context learning. As Table 3 shows, our additional knowledge does not yield a significant gain for the drone dataset, unlike the traffic rule dataset. This may be because the traffic rules have longer and more complex sentences, where the SRL information is more helpful, while the drone instructions are simpler and shorter. This result demonstrates the usefulness of our approach for different kinds of formal specification languages. It also gives us confidence that this approach can be extended and used as a human-in-the-loop system for creating various formal languages with few data points across domains. We used few-shot prompts without access to large data, which raises the question of how well our approach can handle different logic structures, temporal operators, and tasks that are out of distribution. We discovered that our model could generalize to different kinds of TL operators, such as "X", "F" and "U", and to traffic and drone planning rules with different sentence structures that are not present in the prompts, even with only two prompts and a thought process introduction.

6   Conclusion and Future Work

We presented an approach that uses a language model with SRL and soft rule assistance to formalize rules and instructions. Due to the semantic role as additional knowledge and prompting, our approach can be easily adapted to new formal rules and specifications creation. It is useful for AVs, drones, and other intelligent systems that need to follow legal requirements and plan actions based on instructions. Our approach makes this process easier and more explainable. We evaluated our method on rules that require reasoning and showed that the language model could leverage its knowledge to generate safety and legal specifications. Moreover, our method can produce different formal rules (STL, LTL, FOL etc.) by changing the rule as soft constraints, prompts, and parsers. We can also enhance our method by adding more semantic context or more prompts [33]. In future work, we intend to use and ground the represented knowledge for the automated planning of autonomous driving. We also want to investigate how the rule as external knowledge affects the LLM and how we can make it more controllable or tunable for the end user so that the user can adjust the rule's influence for LLM translation.

Acknoledgement. This work is partially funded by German Federal Ministry for Economic Affairs and Climate Action within the "KI Wissen" project.

References

1. Aréchiga, N.: Specifying safety of autonomous vehicles in signal temporal logic. In: 2019 IEEE Intelligent Vehicles Symposium (IV), pp. 58–63 (2019). https://doi.org/10.1109/IVS.2019.8813875
2. Brown, T., et al.: Language models are few-shot learners. In: Advances in Neural Information Processing Systems, vol. 33, pp. 1877–1901 (2020)
3. Esterle, K., Aravantinos, V., Knoll, A.: From specifications to behavior: maneuver verification in a semantic state space. In: 2019 IEEE Intelligent Vehicles Symposium (IV), pp. 2140–2147 (2019). https://doi.org/10.1109/IVS.2019.8814241
4. Fuggitti, F., Chakraborti, T.: NL2LTL - a python package for converting natural language (NL) instructions to linear temporal logic (LTL) formulas. In: AAAI (2023). system Demonstration
5. Gavran, I., Darulova, E., Majumdar, R.: Interactive synthesis of temporal specifications from examples and natural language. Proc. ACM Program. Lang. 4, 1–26 (2020). https://doi.org/10.1145/3428269
6. Gung, J., Palmer, M.: Predicate representations and polysemy in VerbNet semantic parsing. In: International Conference on Computational Semantics (2021)
7. Hahn, C., Schmitt, F., Tillman, J.J., Metzger, N., Siber, J., Finkbeiner, B.: Formal specifications from natural language. arXiv:abs/2206.01962 (2022)

8. He, J., Bartocci, E., Ničković, D., Isakovic, H., Grosu, R.: DeepSTL - from English requirements to signal temporal logic. In: 2022 IEEE/ACM 44th International Conference on Software Engineering (ICSE), pp. 610–622 (2022). https://doi.org/10.1145/3510003.3510171

9. Hekmatnejad, M., et al.: Encoding and monitoring responsibility sensitive safety rules for automated vehicles in signal temporal logic. In: Proceedings of the 17th ACM-IEEE International Conference on Formal Methods and Models for System Design. Association for Computing Machinery (2019). https://doi.org/10.1145/3359986.3361203

10. Huang, W., Abbeel, P., Pathak, D., Mordatch, I.: Language models as zero-shot planners: extracting actionable knowledge for embodied agents. arXiv preprint: arXiv:2201.07207 (2022)

11. Karimi, A., Duggirala, P.S.: Formalizing traffic rules for uncontrolled intersections. In: 2020 ACM/IEEE 11th International Conference on Cyber-Physical Systems (ICCPS), pp. 41–50. IEEE (2020). https://doi.org/10.1109/ICCPS48487.2020.00012

12. Karlsson, J., Tumova, J.: Intention-aware motion planning with road rules. In: 2020 IEEE 16th International Conference on Automation Science and Engineering (CASE), pp. 526–532 (2020). https://doi.org/10.1109/CASE48305.2020.9217037

13. Konrad, S., Cheng, B.: Real-time specification patterns. In: Proceedings 27th International Conference on Software Engineering, 2005. ICSE 2005, pp. 372–381 (2005). https://doi.org/10.1109/ICSE.2005.1553580

14. Li, R., et al.: StarCoder: may the source be with you! arXiv:abs/2305.06161 (2023)

15. Li, X., et al.: Differentiable logic layer for rule guided trajectory prediction. In: Conference on Robot Learning (2020)

16. Lin, J., et al.: Road traffic law adaptive decision-making for self-driving vehicles. In: 2022 IEEE 25th International Conference on Intelligent Transportation Systems (ITSC), pp. 2034–2041 (2022). https://doi.org/10.1109/ITSC55140.2022.9922208

17. Liu, J.X., et al.: Lang2LTL: translating natural language commands to temporal specification with large language models. In: CoRL Workshop on Language and Robot Learning (2022)

18. Liu, J., et al.: Generated knowledge prompting for commonsense reasoning. In: Annual Meeting of the Association for Computational Linguistics (2021)

19. Maierhofer, S., Moosbrugger, P., Althoff, M.: Formalization of intersection traffic rules in temporal logic. In: 2022 IEEE Intelligent Vehicles Symposium (IV), pp. 1135–1144 (2022). https://doi.org/10.1109/IV51971.2022.9827153

20. Maierhofer, S., Rettinger, A.K., Mayer, E.C., Althoff, M.: Formalization of interstate traffic rules in temporal logic. In: 2020 IEEE Intelligent Vehicles Symposium (IV), pp. 752–759 (2020). https://doi.org/10.1109/IV47402.2020.9304549

21. Muennighoff, N., et al.: Crosslingual generalization through multitask finetuning. arXiv:abs/2211.01786 (2022)

22. Oh, Y., Patel, R., Nguyen, T., Huang, B., Pavlick, E., Tellex, S.: Planning with state abstractions for non-markovian task specifications. arXiv:abs/1905.12096 (2019)

23. Palmer, M., Gildea, D., Kingsbury, P.: The proposition bank: an annotated corpus of semantic roles. Comput. Linguist. **31**(1), 71–106 (2005). https://doi.org/10.1162/0891201053630264

24. Palmer, M., Gildea, D., Xue, N.: Semantic Role Labeling. Synthesis Lectures on Human Language Technologies. Springer International Publishing, Cham (2010). https://link.springer.com/10.1007/978-3-031-02135-0

25. Pan, J., Chou, G., Berenson, D.: Data-efficient learning of natural language to linear temporal logic translators for robot task specification. arXiv e-prints: arXiv:2303.08006 (2023)

26. Ren, X., Yin, X., Li, S.: Synthesis of controllers for co-safe linear temporal logic specifications using reinforcement learning. In: 2021 40th Chinese Control Conference (CCC), pp. 2304–2309 (2021). https://doi.org/10.23919/CCC52363.2021.9549746

27. Rizaldi, A., Immler, F., Althoff, M.: A formally verified checker of the safe distance traffic rules for autonomous vehicles. In: Rayadurgam, S., Tkachuk, O. (eds.) NFM 2016. LNCS, vol. 9690, pp. 175–190. Springer, Cham (2016). https://doi.org/10.1007/978-3-319-40648-0_14

28. Rizaldi, A., et al.: Formalising and monitoring traffic rules for autonomous vehicles in Isabelle/HOL. In: Polikarpova, N., Schneider, S. (eds.) IFM 2017. LNCS, vol. 10510, pp. 50–66. Springer, Cham (2017). https://doi.org/10.1007/978-3-319-66845-1_4

29. Schuler, K.K., Palmer, M.S.: VerbNet: a broad-coverage, comprehensive verb Lexicon. Ph.D. thesis, University of Pennsylvania, USA (2005)

30. Shi, P., Lin, J.: Simple BERT models for relation extraction and semantic role labeling. arXiv preprint: arXiv:1904.05255 (2019)

31. Thati, P., Roşu, G.: Monitoring Algorithms for metric temporal logic specifications. Electr. Notes Theor. Comput. Sci. **113**, 145–162 (2005). https://doi.org/10.1016/j.entcs.2004.01.029

32. Vaswani, A., et al.: Attention is all you need. In: Proceedings of the 31st International Conference on Neural Information Processing Systems, NIPS'17, pp. 6000–6010 (2017)

33. Wei, J., et al.: Chain-of-thought prompting elicits reasoning in large language models. In: Advances in Neural Information Processing Systems (2022)

34. Yao, S., et al.: ReAct: synergizing reasoning and acting in language models. In: International Conference on Learning Representations (ICLR) (2023)

35. Zhang, Q., Hong, D.K., Zhang, Z., Chen, Q.A., Mahlke, S., Mao, Z.M.: A systematic framework to identify violations of scenario-dependent driving rules in autonomous vehicle software. Proc. ACM Meas. Anal. Comput. Syst. **5**(2), 1–25 (2021). https://doi.org/10.1145/3460082

FreeCHR: An Algebraic Framework for CHR-Embeddings

Sascha Rechenberger[✉] and Thom Frühwirth

Institute for Software Engineering and Programming Languages, Ulm University,
Albert-Einstein-Allee 11, 89069 Ulm, Germany
{sascha.rechenberger,thom.fruehwirth}@uni-ulm.de

Abstract. We introduce the framework *FreeCHR* which formalizes the
embedding of *Constraint Handling Rules* (CHR) into a host language,
using the concept of *initial algebra semantics* from category theory, to
establish a high-level implementation scheme for CHR as well as a common formalization for both theory and practice. We propose a lifting of
the syntax of CHR via an endofunctor in the category **Set** and a lifting of
the very abstract operational semantics of CHR into FreeCHR, using the
free algebra, generated by the endofunctor and give proofs for soundness
and completeness w.r.t. their original definition.

Keywords: embedded domain-specific languages · declarative
programming languages · constraint handling rules · operational
semantics · category theory · initial algebra semantics

1 Introduction

Constraint Handling Rules (CHR) is a rule-based programming language that
is usually embedded into a general-purpose programming language.

Having a CHR implementation available enables software developers to solve
problems in a declarative and elegant manner. Aside from the obvious task of
implementing constraint solvers [6,10], it can be used to solve scheduling problems [2], implement concurrent and multi-agent systems [20,21,31,32], for applications in music [13,29] and possibly game development [19]. In general, CHR is
ideally suited for any problem that involves the transformation of (multi-) sets of
data, as programs consist of a set of rewriting rules, hiding away the process of
finding suitable candidates for rule application. Hereby, we get a purely declarative representation of the algorithm without the otherwise necessary boilerplate
code.

Implementations of CHR exist for a number of languages, such as Prolog
[28], C [36], C++ [3], Haskell [5,21], JavaScript [23] and Java [1,17,34,35]. These
implementations do not follow a common approach, though, which complicates
and often stops maintenance, altogether. There is also a rich body of theoretical work concerning CHR, formalizing its declarative and operational semantics

© The Author(s), under exclusive license to Springer Nature Switzerland AG 2023
A. Fensel et al. (Eds.): RuleML+RR 2023, LNCS 14244, pp. 190–205, 2023.
https://doi.org/10.1007/978-3-031-45072-3_14

[11,12,30]. However, there is yet no formal connection between CHR as an implemented programming language and CHR as a formalism.

We introduce the framework *FreeCHR* which formalizes the embedding of CHR, using *initial algebra semantics*. This concept which is commonly used in functional programming is used to inductively define languages and their semantics [16,18]. FreeCHR provides both a guideline and high-level architecture to implement and maintain CHR implementations across host languages and a strong connection between the practical and formal aspects of CHR. Also, by FreeCHR-instances being internal embeddings, we get basic tooling, like syntax highlighting and type-checking for free [9].

Ultimately, the framework shall serve a fourfold purpose, by providing

- a general guideline on how to implement a CHR system in modern high-level languages,
- a guideline for future maintenance of FreeCHR instances,
- a common framework for both formal considerations and practical implementations
- and a framework for the definition and verification of general criteria of correctness.

In this work, we will give first formal definitions of FreeCHR, upon which we will build our future work. A follow-up paper will cover first instantiations of FreeCHR. Section 2 will provide the necessary background and intuitions. Section 3 introduces the syntax and semantics of Constraint Handling Rules and generalizes them to non-Herbrand domains. Section 4 introduces the framework FreeCHR. Section 4.1 lifts the syntax of CHR programs to a **Set**-endofunctor and introduces the free algebra, generated by that functor, Sect. 4.2 lifts the *very abstract* operational semantics ω_a of CHR to the *very abstract* operational semantics $\omega_a^\star$ of FreeCHR and Sect. 4.3 proves the correctness of $\omega_a^\star$ w.r.t. ω_a. Section 4.4 gives a short preview of future work, concerning the implementation and verification of FreeCHR instances. Example instances of FreeCHR in Haskell and Python can be found on *GitHub* [24].

An extended preprint of this paper, including complete proofs and additional examples, is available on arxiv.com [27].

2   Endofunctors and *F*-Algebras

In this section, we want to introduce endofunctors and *F*-algebras. Both concepts are taken from category theory and will be introduced as instances in the category of sets **Set**.

We do not assume any previous knowledge of category theory, but to readers more interested in the topic in general, we recommend [22] as introductory literature.

2.1   Basic Definitions

The *disjoint union* of two sets A and B

$$A \sqcup B = \{l_A(a) \mid a \in A\} \cup \{l_B(b) \mid b \in B\}$$

is the union of both sets, with additional labels l_A and l_B added to the elements, to keep track of the origin set of each element. We will also use the labels l_A and l_B as *injection* functions $l_A : A \to A \sqcup B$ and $l_B : B \to A \sqcup B$ which construct elements of $A \sqcup B$ from elements of A or B, respectively.

For two functions $f : A \to C$ and $g : B \to C$, the function

$$[f, g] : A \sqcup B \to C$$

$$[f, g]\,(l(x)) = \begin{cases} f(x), & \text{if } l = l_A \\ g(x), & \text{if } l = l_B \end{cases}$$

is called a *case analysis* function of the disjoint union $A \sqcup B$, and is a formal analogue to a `case ... of` expression. Furthermore, we define two functions

$$f \sqcup g : A \sqcup B \to A' \sqcup B'$$

$$(f \sqcup g)(l(x)) = \begin{cases} l_{A'}(f(x)), & \text{if } l = l_A \\ l_{B'}(g(x)), & \text{if } l = l_B \end{cases}$$

$$f \times g : A \times B \to A' \times B'$$

$$(f \times g)(x, y) = (f(x), g(y))$$

which lift two functions $f : A \to A'$ and $g : B \to B'$ to the disjoint union and the Cartesian product, respectively.

2.2   Endofunctors

A **Set**-endofunctor[1] F maps all sets A to sets FA and all functions $f : A \to B$ to functions $Ff : FA \to FB$, such that $F\,\mathbf{id}_A = \mathbf{id}_{FA}$ and $F(g \circ f) = Fg \circ Ff$, where $\mathbf{id}_X(x) = x$ is the identity function on a set X^2. A signature $\Sigma = \{\sigma_1/a_1, ..., \sigma_n/a_n\}$, where σ_i are operators and a_i their arity, generates a functor

$$F_\Sigma X = \bigsqcup_{\sigma/a \in \Sigma} X^a \qquad\qquad F_\Sigma f = \bigsqcup_{\sigma/a \in \Sigma} f^a$$

with $X^0 = \mathbb{1}$ and $f^0 = \mathbf{id}_\mathbb{1}$, where $\mathbb{1}$ is a singleton set. Such a functor F_Σ models *flat* (i.e., not nested) terms over the signature Σ.

---

[1] Since we only deal with endofunctors in Set, we will simply call them *functors*.
[2] We will omit the index of **id**, if it is clear from the context.

2.3 F-Algebras

Since an endofunctor F defines the syntax of terms, an evaluation function α : $FA \to A$ defines the *semantics* of terms. We call such a function α, together with its *carrier* A, an F-algebra (A, α).

If there are two F-algebras (A, α) and (B, β) and a function $h : A \to B$, we call h an F-*algebra homomorphism*, iff. $h \circ \alpha = \beta \circ Fh$, i.e., h preserves the structure of (A, α) in (B, β), when mapping A to B. In this case, we also write $h : (A, \alpha) \to (B, \beta)$.

A special F-algebra is the *free F-algebra* $F^\star = (\mu F, \mathrm{in}_F)$, for which there is a homomorphism $(\!|\alpha|\!) : F^\star \to (A, \alpha)$ for any other algebra (A, α). We call those homomorphisms $(\!|\alpha|\!)$ F-*catamorphisms*. The functions $(\!|\alpha|\!)$ encapsulate structured recursion on values in μF, with the semantics defined by the function α which is itself only defined on flat terms. The carrier of $F^\star$, with $\mu F = F\mu F$, is the set of inductively defined values in the shape defined by F. The function in_F : $F\mu F \to \mu F$ inductively constructs the values in μF.

3   CHR over Non-herbrand Domains

First implementations of CHR were embedded into the logical programming language Prolog, where terms like 3+4 or f(a,b,c) are not evaluated, as is the case in most other programming languages, but interpreted as themselves. This is called the *Herbrand* interpretation of terms. Since we want to embed CHR in any programming language, we need to generalize to non-Herbrand interpretations of terms. We will formalize this, using initial algebra semantics.

3.1   Host Language

We first define a *data type* in the host language. A data type determines the syntax and semantics of terms via a functor Λ_T and an algebra τ_T. The fixed point $\mu\Lambda_T$ contains terms which are inductively defined via Λ_T and the catamorphism $(\!|\tau_T|\!)$ evaluates those terms to values of T.

Definition 3.1 (Data types). *A data type is a triple* $\langle T, \Lambda_T, \tau_T \rangle$, *where T is a set, Λ_T a functor and (T, τ_T) a Λ_T-algebra.*

We write $t \equiv_T t'$ for $t \in \mu\Lambda_T$ and $t' \in T$, iff. $(\!|\tau_T|\!)(t) = t'$.

Example 3.1 (Boolean data type). The signature

$$\Sigma_2 = \{(n \leqslant m)/0 \mid n, m \in \mathbb{N}_0\} \cup \{(n < m)/0 \mid n, m \in \mathbb{N}_0\} \cup \{\wedge/2, true/0, false/0\}$$

defines Boolean terms[3]. Σ_2 generates the functor

$$\Lambda_2 X = \mathbb{N}_0 \times \mathbb{N}_0 \sqcup \mathbb{N}_0 \times \mathbb{N}_0 \sqcup X \times X \sqcup \mathbb{1} \sqcup \mathbb{1}$$

---

[3] We will generally overload symbols like *false*, *true*, $\wedge$, $\neg$, ..., if their meaning is clear from the context.

the fixed point, $\mu\Lambda_2$, of which is the set of valid nested Boolean terms like $(0 < 4 \wedge 4 \leqslant 6)$. Let $\langle 2, \Lambda_2, \tau_2 \rangle$, with $2 = \{true, false\}$, be a data type. If we assume τ_2 to implement the usual semantics for Boolean terms and comparisons, $(0 < 4 \wedge 4 \leqslant 6)$ will evaluate as

$$(\![\tau_2]\!)(0 < 4 \wedge 4 \leqslant 6) = (\![\tau_2]\!)(0 < 4) \wedge (\![\tau_2]\!)(4 \leqslant 6) = true \wedge true = true$$

For a set T, both Λ_T and τ_T are determined by the host language which is captured by the next definition.

Definition 3.2 (Host environment). *A mapping*

$$\mathcal{L}T = \langle T, \Lambda_T, \tau_T \rangle$$

where $\langle T, \Lambda_T, \tau_T \rangle$ is a data type, is called a host environment.

A host environment is implied by the host language (and the program, the CHR program is part of) and assigns to a set T a data type, effectively determining syntax and semantics of terms that evaluate to values of T.

3.2 Embedding CHR

With the formalization of our host environment, we can define the syntax and semantics of CHR.

Definition 3.3 (CHR programs). *CHR programs are sets of multiset-rewriting rules of the form*

$$[N \,@] \; K \setminus R \iff [G \,[]] \; B$$

For a set C, called the domain *of the Program, for which there is a data type $\mathcal{L}C = \langle C, \Lambda_C, \tau_C \rangle$, $K, R \in LC$ are called the* kept *and* removed head, *respectively. $LX = \bigcup_{i \in \mathbb{N}} X^i$ maps a set X to the set of finite sequences (or lists) over X, with $X^0 = \varepsilon$ being the empty sequence. The optional $G \in \mu\Lambda_2$ is called the* guard. *If G is omitted, we assume $G \equiv_2 true$. $B \in \mathcal{M}\mu\Lambda_C$ is called the* body. *The functor $\mathcal{M}$ maps a set X to the set $\mathcal{M}X$ of multisets over X and functions $X \to Y$ to functions $\mathcal{M}X \to \mathcal{M}Y$. N is an optional identifier for the rule.*

The members of the kept and removed head are matched against values of the domain C. The guard G is a term that can be evaluated to a Boolean value. The body B is a multiset over terms which can be evaluated to values of C. This includes any call of (pure) functions or operators which evaluates to Booleans, or values of C, respectively.

Definition 3.3 corresponds to the *positive range-restricted ground* segment of CHR which is commonly used as the target for embeddings of other (rule-based) formalisms (e.g., colored Petri nets [4]) into CHR [11, Chapter 6.2]. *Positive* means that the body of the rule contains only user constraints (i.e., values from C) which guarantees that computations do not fail. *Range-restricted* means that instantiating all variables of the head (K and R) will ground the whole rule. This also maintains the *groundness* of the segment of CHR which requires that the input and output of a program are ground. $\mathbf{PRG}_C$ denotes the set of all such programs over a domain C.

Example 3.2 (Euclidean algorithm). The program GCD = \{*zero*@..., *subtract*@...\}

$$zero \ @ \ 0 \ \Leftrightarrow \ \varnothing$$

$$subtract \ @ \ N \ \backslash \ M \ \Leftrightarrow \ 0 < N \wedge 0 < M \wedge N \leqslant M \mid M - N$$

computes the greatest common divisor of a collection of natural numbers. The first rule removes any numbers 0 from the collection. The second rule replaces for any pair of numbers N and M greater 0 and $N \leqslant M$, M by $M - N$. Note that we omitted the kept head and guard of the *zero* rule.

Definition 3.4 (C-instances of rules). *For a positive range-restricted rule*

$$r = R \ @ \ k_1, ..., k_n \ \backslash \ r_1, ..., r_m \ \Leftrightarrow \ G \mid B$$

with universally quantified variables $v_1, ..., v_l$, and a data type $\mathcal{L}C = \langle C, \Lambda_C, \tau_C \rangle$, we call the set

$$\Gamma_C(r) = \{ \ R \ @ \ k_1\sigma, ..., k_n\sigma \ \backslash \ r_1\sigma, ..., r_m\sigma \ \Leftrightarrow \ G\sigma \mid \mathcal{M}(\!|\tau_C|\!)(B\sigma)$$

$$\mid \sigma \ instantiates \ all \ variables \ v_1, \ ..., \ v_l,$$

$$k_1\sigma, ..., k_n\sigma, r_1\sigma, ..., r_m\sigma \in C,$$

$$G\sigma \in \mu\Lambda_2,$$

$$B\sigma \in \mathcal{M}\mu\Lambda_C \ \}$$

the C-grounding of r. Analogously, for a set $\mathcal{R}$ of rules, $\Gamma_C(\mathcal{R}) = \bigcup_{r \in \mathcal{R}} \Gamma_C(r)$ is the C-grounding of $\mathcal{R}$. An element $r' \in \Gamma_C(r)$ (or $\Gamma_C(\mathcal{R})$ respectively) is called a C-instance of a rule $r \in \mathcal{R}$.

A C-instance (or grounding) is obtained, by instantiating any variables and evaluating the then ground terms in the body of the rule, using the Λ_C-catamorphism $(\!|\tau_C|\!)$. The functor $\mathcal{M}$ is used, to lift $(\!|\tau_C|\!)$ into the multiset.

Example 3.3. Given a body $\{M - N\}$ and a substitution $\sigma = \{N \mapsto 4, M \mapsto 6\}$, the body is instantiated like

$$\mathcal{M}(\!|\tau_C|\!)(\{M - N\}\sigma) = \mathcal{M}(\!|\tau_C|\!)(\{6 - 4\}) = \{(\!|\tau_C|\!)(6 - 4)\} = \{2\}$$

With Example 3.3, we can also easily see that, if we use a data type $\mathcal{L}\mu\Lambda_C = \langle \mu\Lambda_C, \Lambda_C, \mathbf{in}_{\Lambda_C} \rangle$, we get the Herbrand interpretation of terms over C. Hence, f.i., an expression $3 + 4 \in \mu\Lambda_{\mathbb{N}_0}$ is evaluated to itself, as is the case in Prolog.

Example 3.4 (C-instances). If we instantiate the rule

$$r = subtract \ @ \ N \ \backslash \ M \ \Leftrightarrow \ 0 < N \wedge 0 < M \wedge N \leqslant M \mid M - N$$

with $\sigma_1 = \{N \mapsto 4, M \mapsto 6\}$ and $\sigma_2 = \{N \mapsto 0, M \mapsto 6\}$, respectively, we get the $\mathbb{N}_0$-instances

$$r\sigma_1 = subtract \ @ \ 4 \ \backslash \ 6 \ \Leftrightarrow \ 0 < 4 \wedge 0 < 6 \wedge 4 \leqslant 6 \ | \ 2$$
$$r\sigma_2 = subtract \ @ \ 0 \ \backslash \ 6 \ \Leftrightarrow \ 0 < 0 \wedge 0 < 6 \wedge 0 \leqslant 6 \ | \ 6$$

Both instances are elements of the $\mathbb{N}_0$-grounding $\Gamma_{\mathbb{N}_0}$ (GCD) of the program in Example 3.2.

Classically, the guard G contains constraints which are defined w.r.t. a constraint theory $\mathcal{CT}$. We typically write $\mathcal{CT} \models G^4$ to denote that the guard is satisfiable w.r.t. $\mathcal{CT}$ and $\mathcal{CT} \models \neg G$ otherwise. Since in our case $G \in \mu\Lambda_2$, $\mathcal{CT}$ is essentially τ_2, as it determines the semantics of Boolean terms. We thus write

$$\tau_2 \models G \Longleftrightarrow G \equiv_2 true \qquad\qquad \tau_2 \models \neg G \Longleftrightarrow G \equiv_2 false$$

Note that we always need a data type $\mathcal{L}2$. In Prolog, f.i., 2 corresponds to the set $\{true, false\}$, representing successful, or failed computations, respectively.

Finally, the operational semantics of CHR is defined as a state transition system, where the states are multisets[5] over the elements of C.

Definition 3.5 (*Very abstract* operational semantics of CHR). *Figure 1 shows the very abstract operational semantics ω_a for CHR programs $\mathcal{R}$ over a domain C. With $\uplus_C : \mathcal{MC} \times \mathcal{MC} \to \mathcal{MC}$ being the union of multisets over elements of C, the inference rule* APPLY *reads as follows: if we have a C-instance*

$$R@c_1, ..., c_n \ \backslash \ c_{n+1}, ..., c_{n+m} \Leftrightarrow G|B \in \Gamma_C(\mathcal{R})$$

of a rule $r \in \mathcal{R}$ and the guard G evaluates to true, we can replace the subset $\{c_{n+1}, ..., c_{n+m}\}$ by the body B. We write

$$\mathcal{R} \vdash S_0 \mapsto^* S_l$$

if there are rules $R_1@r_1, ..., R_l@r_l \in \mathcal{R}$, with $1 \leqslant l$, such that

$$\mathcal{R} \vdash S_0 \mapsto_{R_1} S_1 \wedge S_1 \mapsto_{R_2} S_2 \wedge ... \wedge S_{l-1} \mapsto_{R_l} S_l$$

where S_i are multisets over ground elements of C.

$$\frac{R@c_1, ..., c_n \backslash c_{n+1}, ..., c_{n+m} \Leftrightarrow G|B \in \Gamma_C(\mathcal{R}) \qquad \tau_2 \models G}{\mathcal{R} \vdash \{c_1, ..., c_{n+m}\} \uplus \Delta S \mapsto_R \{c_1, ..., c_n\} \uplus B \uplus \Delta S} \text{ APPLY}$$

Fig. 1. *Very abstract* operational semantics for ground and pure CHR

---

[4] As we only work with ground values, we do not need to quantify any variables.

[5] There may be some additional decoration in more refined operational semantics.

Rules are applied until no more are applicable to the state, i.e., we have reached a *final* state.

Example 3.5 (ω_a-transitions). Intuitively, both

$$\tau_2 \models 0 < 4 \wedge 0 < 6 \wedge 4 \leqslant 6 \qquad \text{and} \qquad \tau_2 \models \neg(0 < 0 \wedge 0 < 6 \wedge 0 \leqslant 6)$$

hold. Hence, we can prove the transition GCD $\vdash \{4,6\} \mapsto_{subtract} \{4,2\}$, but not GCD $\vdash \{0,6\} \mapsto_{subtract} \{0,6\}$.

The following example shows the execution of the Euclidean algorithm as a final example of the operational semantics of CHR.

Example 3.6 (Euclidean algorithm (cont.)). The rules of GCD are applied until exhaustion, leaving only the greatest common divisor of all numbers of the input. For an input $\{4,6\}$, the program will perform a sequence

$$\{4,6\} \mapsto_{subtract} \{4,2\} \mapsto_{subtract} \{2,2\} \mapsto_{subtract} \{2,0\} \mapsto_{zero} \{2\}$$

of transformations.

4   FreeCHR

The main idea of FreeCHR is to model the syntax of CHR programs as a functor CHR_C. We then use the *free* CHR_C-algebra to define the operational semantics of FreeCHR which we can directly use to verify instances of FreeCHR.

4.1   Syntax

We now present the fundamental definition of our work which allows us to view CHR-programs over a domain C.

Definition 4.1 (Syntax of FreeCHR programs). *The functor*[6]

$$CHR_C D = L2^C \times L2^C \times 2^{LC} \times (\mathcal{M}C)^{LC} \sqcup D \times D$$
$$CHR_C f = \mathbf{id} \sqcup f \times f$$

describes the syntax of FreeCHR programs.

The set $L2^C \times L2^C \times 2^{LC} \times (\mathcal{M}C)^{LC}$ is the set of single rules. The kept and removed head of a rule are sequences of functions in $L2^C$ which map elements of C to Booleans, effectively checking individual values for applicability of the rule. The guard of the rule is a function in 2^{LC} and maps sequences of elements in C to Booleans, checking all matched values in the context of each other. Finally, the body of the rule is a function in $(\mathcal{M}C)^{LC}$ and maps the matched values to a multiset of newly generated values.

---

[6] That CHR$_C$ is indeed a functor can easily be verified via equational reasoning.

The set $D \times D$ represents the composition of FreeCHR programs by an execution strategy, allowing the construction of more complex programs from, ultimately, single rules.

By the structure of CHR_C, a CHR_C-algebra with carrier D is defined by two functions

$$\rho: \; L2^C \times L2^C \times 2^{LC} \times (\mathcal{M}C)^{LC} \longrightarrow D \qquad \nu: \; D \times D \to D$$

as $(D, [\rho, \nu])$. The free CHR_C-algebra $\text{CHR}_C^\star$ provides us with an inductively defined representation of programs which we will later use to lift the very abstract operational semantics ω_a.

Lemma 4.1 (Free CHR$_C$-algebra). *With*

$$\mu CHR_C = L2^C \times L2^C \times 2^{LC} \times (\mathcal{M}C)^{LC} \sqcup \mu CHR_C \times \mu CHR_C$$

and labels/injections

$$rule: L2^C \times L2^C \times 2^{LC} \times (\mathcal{M}C)^{LC} \longrightarrow \mu CHR_C$$

$$\odot: \mu CHR_C \times \mu CHR_C \longrightarrow \mu CHR_C$$

$CHR_C^\star = (\mu CHR_C, [rule, \odot])$ *is the* free *CHR_C-algebra.*

Proof sketch. From the specialized homomorphism property

$$([\rho, \nu])([rule, \odot]\,(p)) = [\rho, \nu]\,((\text{CHR}_C([\rho, \nu]))(p))$$

we construct the CHR_C-catamorphism

$$([\rho, \nu]): \mu\text{CHR}_C \longrightarrow A$$

$$([\rho, \nu])(rule(k, r, g, b)) = \rho(k, r, g, b)$$

$$([\rho, \nu])(p_1 \odot p_2) = \nu(([\rho, \nu])(p_1), ([\rho, \nu])(p_2))$$

for any CHR_C-algebra $\alpha = (A, [\rho, \nu])$.

The free CHR_C-algebra corresponds to the definition of abstract syntax trees of programs, while the catamorphism (α) corresponds to an interpretation that preserves the semantics of α.

Also, we can easily see that $\odot$ is associative up to isomorphism[7]. We thus will not explicitly write parentheses and generally use chained expressions like $p_1 \odot \dots \odot p_l$ for some $l \in \mathbb{N}$.

Example 4.1 (Euclidean algorithm (cont.)). The program $gcd = zero \odot subtract$ with

$$zero = rule(\varepsilon, (\lambda n.n = 0), (\lambda n.true), (\lambda n.\varnothing))$$

$$subtract = rule((\lambda n.0 < n), (\lambda m.0 < m), (\lambda n\ m.n \leqslant m), (\lambda n\ m.\{m - n\}))$$

implements the euclidean algorithm, as defined in Example 3.2. λ-abstractions are used for ad-hoc definitions of functions.

---

[7] By $\mathbf{assoc}(a, (b, c)) = ((a, b), c)$ and $\mathbf{assoc}^{-1}((a, b), c) = (a, (b, c))$.

4.2   Operational Semantics

We now lift the *very abstract* operational semantics ω_a of CHR to the very abstract operational semantics $\omega_a^\star$ of FreeCHR. We assume that our programs are defined over a domain C, where there is a data type $\mathcal{L}C = \langle C, \Lambda_C, \tau_C \rangle$. Like ω_a, $\omega_a^\star$ is defined as a state transition system, where states are multisets over elements of C.

Definition 4.2 (*Very abstract* operational semantics $\omega_a^\star$). *Let $S, S' \in \mathcal{MC}$ and $p \in \mu CHR_C$. We write*

$$p \vdash S \xmapsto{\omega_a^\star} S'$$

if we can derive a transition from state S to S' with the program p. Figure 2 shows inference rules, defining the very abstract *operational semantics $\omega_a^\star$ of FreeCHR.*

$$\frac{}{p \vdash S \xmapsto{\omega_a^\star} S} \text{ PASS/FINAL} \qquad \frac{p_i \vdash S \xmapsto{\omega_a^\star} S' \quad p_1 \odot ... \odot p_i \odot ... \odot p_l \vdash S' \xmapsto{\omega_a^\star} S''}{p_1 \odot ... \odot p_i \odot ... \odot p_l \vdash S \xmapsto{\omega_a^\star} S''} \text{ STEP}_i$$

$$\frac{k_1(c_1) \wedge ... \wedge k_n(c_n) \wedge r_1(c_{n+1}) \wedge ... \wedge r_m(c_{n+m}) \wedge g(c_1, ..., c_{n+m}) \equiv_2 true}{rule(k, r, g, b) \vdash \{c_1, ..., c_{n+m}\} \uplus \Delta S \xmapsto{\omega_a^\star} \{c_1, ..., c_n\} \uplus b(c_1, ..., c_{m+n}) \uplus \Delta S} \text{ APPLY}$$

Fig. 2. *Very abstract* operational semantics of FreeCHR

The rule PASS/FINAL states that a program is always allowed to do nothing to a state. STEP$_i$ states that we can derive a transition from S to S'', if we can transition from S to S' with the i-th program in the composition $p_1 \odot ... \odot p_l$ (for $1 \leqslant i \leqslant l$) and from S' to S'' with the whole composition. The idea is that, w.l.o.g., p_i is a rule that is applied to the current state, whereafter execution is continued. APPLY is the translation of the original APPLY-rule of ω_a. k_i and r_j denote the i-th and j-th elements of the sequences k and r.

4.3   Soundness and Completeness of $\omega_a^\star$

To prove the soundness and completeness of $\omega_a^\star$ w.r.t. ω_a, we first need to embed FreeCHR into the *positive range-restricted ground* segment of CHR. This is a common approach to relate rule-based formalisms to CHR [11, Chapter 6].

Definition 4.3 (Embedding FreeCHR into CHR). *Let*

$$\Theta : \mu CHR_C \longrightarrow \mathbf{PRG}_C$$
$$\Theta\left(rule\left(k, r, g, b\right)\right) = \{R@v_1, ..., v_n \setminus v_{n+1}, ..., v_{n+m} \Leftrightarrow G | b\left(v_1, ..., v_{n+m}\right)\}$$
$$\Theta\left(p_1 \odot ... \odot p_l\right) = \Theta\left(p_1\right) \cup ... \cup \Theta\left(p_l\right)$$

be the function embedding FreeCHR programs into the positive range-restricted ground segment of CHR, with universally quantified variables $v_1,...,v_{n+m}$, R a uniquely generated rule name and

$$G = k_1(v_1) \wedge ... \wedge r_m(v_{n+m}) \wedge g(v_1, ..., v_{n+m})$$

We now prove soundness, up to the embedding Θ, of $\omega_a^\star$ w.r.t. ω_a, i.e., if we can prove a derivation under $\omega_a^\star$ for a program p, we can prove it under ω_a for $\Theta(p)$.

Theorem 4.1 (Soundness of $\omega_a^\star$). $\omega_a^\star$ *is sound w.r.t. ω_a, i.e., for $S, S' \in \mathcal{MC}$ and $p \in \mu CHR_C$,*

$$p \vdash S \xrightarrow{\omega_a^\star} S' \implies \Theta(p) \vdash S \mapsto^* S'$$

Proof sketch. We prove soundness by induction over the inference rules of $\omega_a^\star$. As induction base cases, we show

$$p \vdash S \xrightarrow{\omega_a^\star} S \implies \Theta(p) \vdash S \mapsto^* S \qquad \text{(PASS/FINAL)}$$

and

$$rule(k, r, g, b) \vdash S \xrightarrow{\omega_a^\star} S' \implies \Theta(rule(k, r, g, b)) \vdash S \mapsto^* S' \qquad \text{(APPLY)}$$

As induction step, we show, for $p = p_1 \odot ... \odot p_l$

$$p \vdash S \xrightarrow{\omega_a^\star} S'' \implies \Theta(p) \vdash S \mapsto^* S'' \qquad \text{(STEP}_i\text{)}$$

assuming the induction hypotheses

$$\forall i \in \{1, ..., l\} . p_i \vdash S \xrightarrow{\omega_a^\star} S' \implies \Theta(p_i) \vdash S \mapsto^* S'$$

$$p \vdash S' \xrightarrow{\omega_a^\star} S'' \implies \Theta(p) \vdash S' \mapsto^* S''$$

We established that we can prove any derivation we can prove with a program p under $\omega_a^\star$, with a program $\Theta(p)$, under ω_a. We also want to prove completeness up to Θ, i.e., we can prove any derivation with a program $\Theta(p)$ under ω_a with a program p under $\omega_a^\star$.

Theorem 4.2 (Completeness of $\omega_a^\star$). $\omega_a^\star$ *is complete w.r.t. ω_a, i.e., for $S, S' \in \mathcal{MC}$ and $p \in \mu CHR_C$,*

$$\Theta(p) \vdash S \mapsto^* S' \implies p \vdash S \xrightarrow{\omega_a^\star} S'$$

Proof sketch. We prove completeness by induction over ω_a transition steps. As the induction base case, we show

$$\Theta(p) \vdash S \mapsto^* S \implies p \vdash S \xrightarrow{\omega_a^\star} S$$

As the induction step, we show

$$\Theta(p) \vdash S \mapsto_R S' \wedge S' \mapsto^* S'' \implies p \vdash S \xmapsto{\omega_a^*} S''$$

assuming the induction hypothesis

$$\Theta(p) \vdash S' \mapsto^* S'' \implies p \vdash S' \xmapsto{\omega_a^*} S''$$

With Theorem 4.1 and Theorem 4.2, we have established that, up to Θ, FreeCHR is as expressive as CHR. Analogously to classical CHR, we are now able to define more refined operational semantics for FreeCHR and prove their soundness w.r.t. ω_a^*.

4.4 Instantiation

State transitions can be modeled as functions that map a state to its successor. Hence, an instance of FreeCHR defines a CHR_C-algebra

$$((\mathcal{M}C)^{\mathcal{M}C}, [\text{RULE}, \text{COMPOSE}])$$

by providing the functions

$$\text{RULE} : L2^C \times L2^C \times 2^{LC} \times (\mathcal{M}C)^{LC} \longrightarrow (\mathcal{M}C)^{\mathcal{M}C}$$

$$\text{COMPOSE} : (\mathcal{M}C)^{\mathcal{M}C} \times (\mathcal{M}C)^{\mathcal{M}C} \longrightarrow (\mathcal{M}C)^{\mathcal{M}C}$$

The function RULE transforms a single rule into a multiset transformation. COMPOSE implements the execution strategy which defines how two programs are composed[8]. A function

$$\text{COMPOSE}(\text{RULE}(...), ..., \text{RULE}(...)) : \mathcal{M}C \longrightarrow \mathcal{M}C$$

then needs to be applied to a state repeatedly, until a fixed point is reached. Simple example implementations in Haskell and Python can be found on *Github* [24].

To prove that a FreeCHR instance $((\mathcal{M}C)^{\mathcal{M}C}, \phi)$ is correct w.r.t. ω_a^* (or another operational semantics), we use the catamorphism $(\!|\phi|\!)$. In particular, we show that, if applying $(\!|\phi|\!)(p)$ to a state S yields S', we must be able to prove a derivation from S to S' under ω_a^* using a program p, i.e.,

$$(\!|\phi|\!)(p)(S) \equiv_{\mathcal{M}C} S' \implies p \vdash S \xmapsto{\omega_a^*} S'$$

Vice versa, we show that, if we can prove a derivation from S to S' using a program p, we need to be able to compute S' from S by a finite number of applications of $(\!|\phi|\!)(p)$, i.e.,

$$p \vdash S \xmapsto{\omega_a^*} S' \implies ((\!|\phi|\!)(p) \circ ... \circ (\!|\phi|\!)(p))(S) \equiv_{\mathcal{M}C} S'$$

---

[8] We generally assume that COMPOSE is associative. Hence, we will not nest COMPOSE-expressions.

5   Related Work

First work concerning the implementation of CHR systems introduced specific embeddings of CHR into different languages. This included first implementations for Prolog by Holzbaur and Frühwirth [15] and the Java Constraint Kit by Abdennadher et al. [1]. The operational semantics used up to this point were ad-hoc refinements of the *abstract operational semantics* ω_t [11], which was first formalized by Duck et al. [8] with the *refined operational semantics* ω_r. This was a major step towards standardizing implementations, by formally capturing the necessary practical aspects of real-life implementations. Further progress was made by introducing more general implementation schemes based on ω_r, for logical and imperative languages by Duck et al. [7] and van Weert et al. [33], respectively, which are now the basis of most modern CHR systems, like the K.U. Leuven System [28] or CHR.js [23].

First approaches to embed CHR as an internal language, i.e., by implementing CHR programs using constructs of the host-language [9], were introduced by Ivanović for Java [17] and Hanus for Curry [14]. The main inspiration for FreeCHR was introduced by Wibiral [35]. It first implemented the idea of explicitly composing CHR programs from single rules and the use of anonymous functions to model the functional dependency of the guard and body of rules on matched constraints.

Although we consider FreeCHR a framework for new implementations of CHR, the question, of whether it may be applied to existing implementations arises. Aside from the JavaCHR by Wibiral [35], CHR(Curry) by Hanus [14] seems to be a promising candidate for a possible future reframing in FreeCHR, as they are implemented as internal languages.

6   Conclusion

In this paper, we introduced the framework FreeCHR which formalizes the embedding of CHR, using initial algebra semantics. We provided the fundamental definition of our framework which models the syntax of CHR programs over a domain C as a **Set**-endofunctor CHR_C. We defined the *very abstract* operational semantics $\omega_a^\star$, using the free CHR_C-algebra $\mathrm{CHR}_C^\star$ and proved soundness and completeness w.r.t. the original *very abstract* operational semantics ω_a of CHR.

Ongoing work is first and foremost concerned with the introduction of formal and practical instances of FreeCHR, including the formalization in proof assistants like *Lean*, *Agda*, or *Coq*. We further plan to lift more definitions and results concerning CHR to FreeCHR, especially more refined operational semantics, as they are crucial for actual implementations (see, e.g., [25,26]). A future step is to generalize the CHR_C functor and the accompanying definitions to more general definitions. The ultimate goal is to be able to model CHR in the context of arbitrary side-effects which are caused by effectful computations, including the addition of logical variables and failure of computations.

Acknowledgments. We thank our reviewers for their helpful comments. We also thank our colleagues Florian Sihler and Paul Bittner for proofreading and their constructive feedback.

References

1. Abdennadher, S., Krämer, E., Saft, M., Schmauss, M.: JACK: a java constraint kit. In: Electronic Notes in Theoretical Computer Science, vol. 64, pp. 1–17 (2002). https://doi.org/10.1016/S1571-0661(04)80344-X
2. Abdennadher, S., Marte, M.: University course timetabling using constraint handling rules. AAI **14**(4), 311–325 (2000). https://doi.org/10.1080/088395100117016
3. Barichard, V.: CHR++ (2022). https://gitlab.com/vynce/chrpp
4. Betz, H.: Relating coloured petri nets to constraint handling rules. In: CHR 2007, vol. 7, pp. 33–47 (2007). https://dtai-static.cs.kuleuven.be/projects/CHR/papers/chr2007/betz_petri_nets_chr07.pdf
5. Chin, W., Sulzmann, M., Wang, M.: A Type-Safe Embedding of Constraint Handling Rules into Haskell (2008). https://www.semanticscholar.org/paper/A-Type-Safe-Embedding-of-Constraint-Handling-Rules-Chin-Sulzmann/ea47790fc268710d73b2a6be0305e3f3453682e3
6. De Koninck, L., Schrijvers, T., Demoen, B., Fink, M., Tompits, H., Woltran, S.: INCLP(R) - interval-based nonlinear constraint logic programming over the reals. In: WLP 2006, vol. 1843-06-02. Technische Universität Wien, Austria (2006). https://lirias.kuleuven.be/1653773
7. Duck, G.J.: Compilation of constraint handling rules. Ph.D. thesis, University of Melbourne, Victoria, Australia (2005)
8. Duck, G.J., Stuckey, P.J., de la Banda, M.G., Holzbaur, C.: The refined operational semantics of constraint handling rules. In: Demoen, B., Lifschitz, V. (eds.) ICLP 2004. LNCS, vol. 3132, pp. 90–104. Springer, Heidelberg (2004). https://doi.org/10.1007/978-3-540-27775-0_7
9. Fowler, M., Parsons, R.: Domain-Specific Languages. Addison-Wesley, Upper Saddle River (2011)
10. Frühwirth, T.: Complete propagation rules for lexicographic order constraints over arbitrary domains. In: Hnich, B., Carlsson, M., Fages, F., Rossi, F. (eds.) CSCLP 2005. LNCS (LNAI), vol. 3978, pp. 14–28. Springer, Heidelberg (2006). https://doi.org/10.1007/11754602_2
11. Fruehwirth, T.: Constraint Handling Rules. Cambridge University Press, Cambridge; New York (2009)
12. Frühwirth, T.: Constraint handling rules - what else? In: Bassiliades, N., Gottlob, G., Sadri, F., Paschke, A., Roman, D. (eds.) RuleML 2015. LNCS, vol. 9202, pp. 13–34. Springer, Cham (2015). https://doi.org/10.1007/978-3-319-21542-6_2
13. Geiselhart, F., Raiser, F., Sneyers, J., Frühwirth, T.: MTSeq: multi-touch-enabled CHR-based Music Generation and Manipulation (2010). https://www.uni-ulm.de/fileadmin/website_uni_ulm/iui.inst.170/home/raiser/publications/Geiselhart2010.pdf

14. Hanus, M.: CHR(Curry): interpretation and compilation of constraint handling rules in curry. In: Pontelli, E., Son, T.C. (eds.) PADL 2015. LNCS, vol. 9131, pp. 74–89. Springer, Cham (2015). https://doi.org/10.1007/978-3-319-19686-2_6

15. Holzbaur, C., Frühwirth, T.: Compiling constraint handling rules. In: ERCIM/COMPULOG Workshop on Constraints, Amsterdam (1998)

16. Hudak, P.: Modular domain specific languages and tools. In: ICSR 1998, pp. 134–142 (1998). https://doi.org/10.1109/ICSR.1998.685738

17. Ivanović, D.: Implementing Constraint Handling Rules as a Domain-Specific Language Embedded in Java (2013). https://doi.org/10.48550/arXiv.1308.3939

18. Johann, P., Ghani, N.: Initial algebra semantics is enough! In: Della Rocca, S.R. (ed.) TLCA 2007. LNCS, vol. 4583, pp. 207–222. Springer, Heidelberg (2007). https://doi.org/10.1007/978-3-540-73228-0_16

19. Karth, I., Smith, A.M.: WaveFunctionCollapse is constraint solving in the wild. In: FDG 2017, FDG 2017, pp. 1–10. Association for Computing Machinery, New York (2017). https://doi.org/10.1145/3102071.3110566

20. Lam, E., Sulzmann, M.: Towards Agent Programming in CHR (2006). https://www.semanticscholar.org/paper/Towards-Agent-Programming-in-CHR-Lam-Sulzmann/43277216bafb824d651c802ad487dbce8f7f7478

21. Lam, E.S.L., Sulzmann, M.: A concurrent constraint handling rules implementation in Haskell with software transactional memory. In: DAMP 2007, Nice, France, pp. 19–24. ACM Press (2007). https://doi.org/10.1145/1248648.1248653

22. Milewski, B.: Category Theory for Programmers. Lightning Source UK, Milton Keynes (2019). https://github.com/hmemcpy/milewski-ctfp-pdf

23. Nogatz, F., Frühwirth, T., Seipel, D.: CHR.js: a CHR implementation in JavaScript. In: Benzmüller, C., Ricca, F., Parent, X., Roman, D. (eds.) RuleML+RR 2018. LNCS, vol. 11092, pp. 131–146. Springer, Cham (2018). https://doi.org/10.1007/978-3-319-99906-7_9

24. Rechenberger, S.: Example Instances of FreeCHR (2023). https://gist.github.com/SRechenberger/739683a23f8a9978ae601c6c815d61c4

25. Rechenberger, S.: FreeCHR-Haskell (2023). https://github.com/SRechenberger/free-chr-hs

26. Rechenberger, S.: FreeCHR-Python (2023). https://github.com/SRechenberger/freechr-python

27. Rechenberger, S., Frühwirth, T.: FreeCHR: An Algebraic Framework for CHR-Embeddings (2023). https://doi.org/10.48550/arXiv.2306.00642

28. Schrijvers, T., Demoen, B.: The K.U. Leuven CHR system: implementation and application. In: CHR 2004, pp. 1–5 (2004). https://lirias.kuleuven.be/retrieve/33588

29. Sneyers, J., De Schreye, D.: APOPCALEAPS: automatic music generation with CHRiSM. In: BNAIC 2010 (2010). https://lirias.kuleuven.be/1584193

30. Sneyers, J., Weert, P.V., Schrijvers, T., Koninck, L.D.: As time goes by: constraint handling rules: a survey of CHR research from 1998 to 2007. TPLP **10**(1), 1–47 (2010). https://doi.org/10.1017/S1471068409990123

31. Thielscher, M.: Reasoning about actions with CHRs and finite domain constraints. In: Stuckey, P.J. (ed.) ICLP 2002. LNCS, vol. 2401, pp. 70–84. Springer, Heidelberg (2002). https://doi.org/10.1007/3-540-45619-8_6

32. Thielscher, M.: FLUX: a logic programming method for reasoning agents. TPLP **5**(4–5), 533–565 (2005). https://doi.org/10.1017/S1471068405002358

33. van Weert, P.: Efficient lazy evaluation of rule-based programs. IEEE Trans. Knowl. Data Eng. **22**(11), 1521–1534 (2010). https://doi.org/10.1109/tkde.2009.208

34. Van Weert, P., Schrijvers, T., Demoen, B., Schrijvers, T., Frühwirth, T.: K.U.Leuven JCHR: a user-friendly, flexible and efficient CHR system for Java. In: CHR 2005. Department of Computer Science, K.U.Leuven (2005). https://lirias. kuleuven.be/1654703
35. Wibiral, T.: JavaCHR – A Modern CHR-Embedding in Java. Ph.D. thesis, Universität Ulm (2022). https://oparu.uni-ulm.de/xmlui/handle/123456789/43506
36. Wuille, P., Schrijvers, T., Demoen, B.: CCHR: The fastest CHR implementation, in C. In: CHR 2007, pp. 123–137 (2007). https://lirias.kuleuven.be/retrieve/22123

Explaining Optimal Trajectories

Celine Rouveirol[2], Malik Kazi Aoual[1,2], Henry Soldano[1,2,3(✉)],
and Veronique Ventos[1]

[1] Nukkai, Paris, France
[2] UMR CNRS 7030 Institut Galilée - Université Sorbonne Paris Nord, LIPN,
Villetaneuse, France
soldano@lipn.univ-paris13.fr
[3] UMR CNRS 7205 Museum National d'Histoire Naturelle, ISYEB, Paris, France

Abstract. We propose a definition of *common explanation* for the label
shared by a group of observations described as first order interpretations, and provide algorithms to enumerate *minimal common explanations*. This was motivated by explaining how performing some action,
for instance a card played during a card game play, results in winning a
maximum total reward at the end of the trajectory. As there are various
ways to reach this reward, each associated to a group of trajectories,
we propose to first build groups of trajectories and then build minimal
common explanations for each group. The whole method is illustrated
on a simplified Bridge game.

Keywords: Abductive Explanation · Inductive Logic Programming ·
Markov Decision Process

1 Introduction

We are interested here in explanations for the classification of an observation by
a logical classifier when the observation is a tree of possible future actions and
resulting states whose branches are called *trajectories*. The work is motivated by
a scenario in which a machine plays a simplified bridge game and must answer
at any point in the gameplay queries of the type "How does the chosen action
leads to winning a maximum number of tricks?".

Expected explanations for choosing action a in state s then refer to a set of
possible optimal trajectories starting from (s, a). For that purpose, we need a
way to group trajectories in a limited number of groups, each made of trajectories
whose optimality may be explained in the same way. Then, we have to define
and search for *common explanations* of optimality for a group of trajectories.

Our definitions are in line with previous works on abductive explanations of
the label assigned to a single observation by a logical classifier [2,3,6,10] that we
have adapted or extended for our purpose in several directions. First consider
that any (state, action) pair (s, a) is associated to the set of all the *possible*
trajectories starting from (s, a) and called the *universe* associated to (s, a). We

© The Author(s), under exclusive license to Springer Nature Switzerland AG 2023
A. Fensel et al. (Eds.): RuleML+RR 2023, LNCS 14244, pp. 206–221, 2023.
https://doi.org/10.1007/978-3-031-45072-3_15

also consider a classifier D that labels the trajectories as optimal or non-optimal. Explanations are then adapted in the following ways:

- A trajectory is described in first order logics as a set of ground literals and an explanation for a single trajectory is a subset of these literals.
- An explanation depends on the universe, introduced as a formula U whose set of models is the universe.
- A *common explanation* for a set of trajectories is defined as an existentially quantified conjunction of literals [13], we call a *relational motif*.

We also need a way to select groups of trajectories guaranteed to have at least one common explanation. We propose to build such groups by learning a rule-based classifier concluding on the optimality, or not, of any trajectory starting from (s, a). To explain a tree of optimal trajectories, the method consists in learning a rule based classifier, consider the coverage O of each rule, building for each rule the most specific relational motif $lgg(O)$ that holds for all trajectories in O, and extracting from $lgg(O)$ the minimal common explanations for O.

Technically, we solve the problem of enumerating minimal common explanations by addressing two sub-problems; i) Computing a least general generalization (lgg) under θ-subsumption for a group of observations O and ii) Searching for all minimal subsets of $lgg(O)$ that do not θ-subsumes any observation with a label different from the label shared by the observations in O. These problems have been studied in different contexts. Since [17] the construction of lggs has been widely used in particular in ascending ILP methods. To limit the lgg size, which is mandatory for our practical purpose, we rather consider building an approximated lgg satisfying a set of declarative constraints. The search for minimal subsets satisfying covering constraints has been studied in many contexts, in particular in data mining (see for instance [22]) but not often when considering relational data in which various useful algorithmic properties are lost [9].

In Sect. 2 we describe the scenario of our case study in which an artificial player has to explain its actions. After presenting some standard notations in Sect. 3, we introduce and discuss in Sect. 4 minimal common explanations for a group of observations together with their use in explaining a set of optimal trajectories. We propose in Sect. 5 algorithms that enumerate them and illustrate the whole method on our case study in Sect. 6. We discuss then related work in Sect. 7 and conclude in Sect. 8.

2   Scenario

We consider a simplified bridge card game with a single color in which 13 cards (with values from 2 to 14) are distributed among the players in a *deal*. The number of cards in each player's *hand* is not fixed. We consider the bidding has ended by a contract requested by South and which opposes the North-South pair (the declarer NS) to the West-East pair (the defender WE).

In the scenario below, we call our artificial player *Noo* and his interlocutor *M. X. M. X* asks for explanations of the decisions taken by *Noo* during the game.

In this scenario *Noo* plays the declarer role, and knows the *WE* hands. We also suppose that in any current state *e Noo* also knows for each possible action *a* which card the defender would play. *Noo* then solves a MDP: *Noo* computes for any (state *s* action *a*) pair accessible from the starting state, the maximum total reward $q(s, a)$, i.e. the maximal number of tricks, the declarer wins by playing *a* in state *s* and further playing an optimal action all along the trajectory. Action *a* is optimal in state *s* if it maximises $q(s, a)$. This scenario is as follows:

1. *Noo* chooses an optimal action *a* in current state *s*
2. *M. X* asks ow playing *a* may result in winning $q(s, a)$ tricks
3. *Noo* then builds a rule-based model *D* for optimality of trajectories and uses *D* to build groups of optimal trajectories sharing common explanations.
4. *Noo* proposes minimal common explanations to answer the request.
5. *Noo* plays *a* which leads to a new state and the scenario goes on at step 1.

3   Notations in Relational Representations

We handle in this paper Datalog languages (i.e. First Order Logics with no function symbols other than constants). The only terms are *constants* and *variables*. Constants are either numbers or atoms starting with a lowercase letter. For instance, cards can be represented by integers in the range [2..14] and players by the four constants *west, north, east, south*. Other terms are variables, identified by symbols starting with an uppercase letter (X, Y, *Card*, ...). The vocabulary $\mathcal{V}$ of a Datalog program P is the set of its constants and predicate symbols. A *literal* is a predicate applied to terms. A *fact* is a ground literal (without variables). For instance, the literal *small_card*(C) states that variable C is a small card (i.e. between 2 and 10), whereas *honor*(12) is a fact stating that 11 (representing a jack) is an honor. In the following, we use the usual notation p/N where p is a predicate symbol and N is its arity (i.e. *small_card*/1 is the predicate symbol *small_card*/1 with a single argument).

In the context of Inductive Logic Programming, two types of formulas are handled : *definite clauses* and *existentially quantified conjunctions*. A *clause* is a disjunction of literals universally quantified $\forall[h_1 \lor \ldots \lor h_m \lor \neg b_1 \lor \ldots \lor \neg b_n]$ or equivalently $\forall[(h_1 \lor \ldots \lor h_m) \leftarrow (b_1 \land \ldots \land b_n)]$ where $h_1, \ldots, h_m$ is a disjunction of positive literals (refered to as the *head* of the clause) and $b_1, \ldots, b_n$ is the conjunction of literals forming the *body* of the clause.

A *definite* clause is a clause with exactly one positive literal. If the head of the clause is a literal without argument, the body of this clause, refered to as a *relational motif* in the following, is an existentially quantified conjunction of literals. We omit the $\forall$ (resp. $\exists$) quantifier when it is clear from the context that we deal with a clause (resp. a relational motif). In the rest of this section, we will adapt definitions initially introduced by [17] for clauses to relational motifs that we mainly study in this paper.

Given a vocabulary $\mathcal{V}$, the *Herbrand universe* of $\mathcal{V}$ is the set of ground terms built on $\mathcal{V}$, the *Herbrand base* is the set of ground facts built on the Herbrand universe and predicate symbols of $\mathcal{V}$. A *Herbrand interpretation* of a set of FOL formulas P built on $\mathcal{V}$ (here a Datalog program or a set of relational motifs) is a subset of the Herbrand base of $\mathcal{V}$.

The generality relationship between two clauses classically used in ILP [15] is θ-subsumption [17] that we adapt here to relational motifs.

Definition 1. *A relational motif G θ-subsumes a relational motif S (denoted $G \preceq_\theta S$) if and only if (iff) there exists a substitution θ such that $G.\theta \subseteq S$.*

Plotkin also introduced the notion of *maximally specific* or *least general* generalisation denoted *lgg* of two clauses, that we reformulate hereafter for relational motifs.

Definition 2. *A relational motif S is the most specific generalisation of a set of relational motifs O (denoted by $S = lgg(O)$) iff $S \preceq_\theta o_i$ for all $o_i \in O$ and for all G_j such that $G_j \preceq_\theta o_i$ for all $o_i \in O$, $G_j \preceq_\theta S$. The lgg of two relational motifs C and D is unique and computed in time $\mathcal{O}(|C| \cdot |D|)$ [16].*

In the following, an *observation* is a Herbrand interpretation of the vocabulary $\mathcal{V}$ (see the learning from interpretations framework [4] or from multiple interpretations [9]). The *coverage* relationship between a relational motif C and an observation o, denoted $covers(C, o)$ holds iff there exists a substitution θ such that $C \preceq_\theta conj(o)$ where $conj(o)$ is the ground relational motif corresponding to o (the conjunction of all facts in o). For the sake of simplicity, we identify in the following the observation o and the corresponding conjunction $conj(o)$. The *lgg* of a set of observations O is defined by $lgg(\{o_i | o_i \in O\})$ (and in particular, $lgg(\{o\}) = o$).

Example 1. *Let $\mathcal{V}$ be a vocabulary with four constants $\{1, 2, 3, 4\}$ and three predicate symbols $\{p/2, r/1, q/1\}$. Let us assume that we have two observations o_1 and o_2, $o_1 = \{p(1,2), p(2,3), r(2), q(3)\}$ and $o_2 = \{p(1,3), p(2,4), r(4), q(3)\}$. The lgg of o_1 and o_2 is: $\exists$ $p(1, X_1), p(X_2, X_3), p(X_4, 3), p(2, X_5), r(X_3), q(3)$ with matching substitutions $\theta_1 = \{X_1/2, X_2/1, X_3/2, X_4/2, X_5/3\}$ and $\theta_2 = \{X_1/3, X_2/2, X_3/4, X_4/1, X_5/4\}$. This formula is reduced. Note that the lgg of o_1 and o_2 is longer (in number of literals) than both o_1 and o_2.*

4   Explanations

We consider *abductive explanations* investigated in recent works to explain the label assigned to some observation entered as input of a decision tree or a random forest [2,3,6,10]. In these works an observation o is represented by the values taken by a set of attributes. An abductive explanation for classifying o into label c with classifier D is then a minimal subset of o which is sufficient to classify o into c. For our purpose we need to extend and adapt this definition.

In a relational context, an observation o is described as a Herbrand interpretation of some datalog language (see Sect. 3) that we represent as a conjunction of literals. The classifier D is as well a first order formula of this language and an explanation for assigning the class label c to an observation may be defined as a ground clause [19] whose head is the label or, as we do hereunder, as the body of such a clause, i.e. a ground relational motif. However when turning to an explanation common to a group of observations, we rather consider general relational motifs, following the definition of abductive explanations in first order logics first proposed by P. Marquis [13] and then further investigated from an operational point of view [8,12].

In what follows, an observation is the subset o of positive literals, excluding its class label in C, that hold for this observation and that we may also represent as a ground relational motif. Furthermore, the set of possible observations in the problem at hand, we refer to as its *universe*, is only part of the whole set of interpretations and is represented below as a formula U that does not mention labels and whose set of models is the universe. A classifier D is then a formula that assigns to o one label c from C and we write $o, D \models c$. Our knowledge U, D on the problem at hand is then divided into a part U, the universe, restricting which observations o are allowed and a part D allowing to infer the label of any observation. This leads to the following definition, adding U to the usual definition:

Definition 3. *An explanation of the assignation of label c to an observation o with respect to a classifier D and an universe U is a subset t of o such that:*
$t, U, D \models c$
If for any $t' \subset t$ we have $t', U, D \not\models c$ then t is a minimal explanation of assignation of c to o w.r.t D and U.

In the example below we illustrate minimal explanations and see that by adding as a formula U the universe of possible observations, we obtain different explanations from those obtained when omitting U.

Example 2. *We consider labels $+$ and $-$. D is a set of definite clauses concluding on $+$ and we consider that whenever $o, D, U \not\models +$ then o is classified as $-$.*

Let p and r be two unary predicates and $\{p(1), p(2), r(1), r(2)\}$ be the Herbrand basis. Consider observation o_1 and classifier D defined as follows:

- $o_1 = \{p(1), r(1), p(2)\}$
- $D = \{+ \leftarrow p(X), r(X); + \leftarrow p(2)\}$

Let us first suppose that any description is allowed, i.e. $U = true$. The minimal explanations for classifying o_1 as $+$ are $\{p(1), r(1)\}$ and $\{p(2)\}$. This is because we have $\{p(X), r(X)\}.\{X/1\} = \{p(1), r(1)\} \subseteq o_1$, and $\{p(2)\} \subseteq o_1$.

Now consider $U = \{p(X) \leftarrow r(X); p(1) \vee p(2)\}$. As observations have to satisfy U, from $r(1)$ and U we deduce $p(1)$ and from $p(1), r(1)$ and D we deduce $+$. As a consequence though $\{p(1), r(1)\}$ still explains the $+$ label for o_1, it is not minimal anymore as $\{r(1)\}$ also explains the label. The set of minimal explantations is therefore $\{r(1); p(2)\}$.

We now define a *common explanation* of the assignation of a same label c to a set of observations O as a relational motif. For that purpose we first search for what is common to these observations, then considering candidate explanations as part of what is common to these observations.

Definition 4. *A* common explanation *of the assignation of label c to all observations in a group O, with respect to a classifier D and a universe U, is a relational motif $e \subseteq lgg(O)$ such that $e, U, D \models c$. If for any $e' \subset e$ we have $e', U, D \not\models c$ then e is a* minimal common explanation *for O.*

Example 3. *Building on Example 2 we add observation $o_2 = \{p(1), p(2), r(2)\}$ with same label $+$ as o_1. Let $O = \{o_1, o_2\}$, we obtain $lgg(O) = \{p(1), p(2), r(X)\}$ with $lgg(O).\{X/1\} \subseteq o_1$ and $lgg(O).\{X/2\} \subseteq o_2$.*

From U and $r(X)$ we infer $p(X)$ and from $r(X), p(X)$ and D we infer $+$. We also have that from $p(2)$ and D we infer $+$. The set of minimal common explanations for $\{o_1, o_2\}$ is then $\{r(X); p(2)\}$.

The following property relates common explanations to explanations:

Proposition 1. *Let e be a common explanation for O, then for any $o \in O$ there exists a substitution θ such that $e.\theta$ is an explanation for o.*

Proof. By definition of a lgg there exists some θ such that $lgg(O).\theta \subseteq o$ and as e is a common explanation for O we have $e \subseteq lgg(O)$ and therefore $e.\theta \subseteq o$. As we have $e.\theta \models e$ and $e, U, D \models c$ we also have $e.\theta, U, D \models c$ which means that $e.\theta$ is an explanation for o.

In what follows U is known through its set of models $M(U)$ which is partitioned according to the labels assigned by D in $\{U_c \subseteq M(U) \mid c \in C\}$. A common explanation e of assignation of label c to $O \subseteq U_c$ is then such that e does not cover any observation belonging to $U_{notc} = M(U) \setminus U_c$. We may then build the minimal common explanations for groups of observations with label c from the partition $\{U_c, U_{notc}\}$ without using the classifier:

Proposition 2. *A relational motif $e \subseteq lgg(O)$ is a minimal common explanation for O if and only if $\forall u \in U_{notc}$ e does not cover u and $\forall e' \subset e, \exists u \in U_{notc}$ s.t. e' covers u*

Example 4. *Continuing with Example 3, U has 8 models among which only $o_- = \{p(1)\}$ has label $-$. We find back the minimal common explanations for $\{o_1, o_2\}$, namely $\{r(X)\}$ and $\{p(2)\}$, as the minimal subsets of $\{p(1), p(2), r(X)\}$ that does not cover $\{p(1)\}$.*

Note that whenever the classifier D is a set of definite clauses, the lgg of the coverage $O \subseteq U_c$ of a clause $c \leftarrow b$ is by definition less general than b and therefore it covers no observation from U_{notc}, which means that the set of common explanations for O is not empty. By construction any observation in U_c belongs to the coverage of some clause from D, and is therefore explained by at least one common explanation.

To summarize, whenever we have neither a classifier nor a formula U but that we do know the set of possible observations and their labels, we may still build common explanations by first building a classifier D, then computing the lgg of the coverage of each clause of D, and finally computing the associated minimal common explanations. Required algorithms are described Sect. 5.

Minimal Common Explanations in Practice. Note that we have defined minimality of a relational motif in $lgg(O)$ according to the subset inclusion ordering, i.e. minimality means maximal *conciseness* in terms of literals. However, we may still choose, among the motifs of equal size, the most specific ones according to θ-subsumption. This turned out to select explanations easier to interpret in our case study of Sect. 6.

Example 5. *Let $lgg(O)$ be $\{p(1), p(2), p(X), q(X), r(X,Y), w(Y,Z)\}$ and U_{notc} $= \{q(1), w(2,3)\}$. The minimal common explanations are $\{p(1); p(2); p(X); r(X,Y)\}$. The most specific ones among them are $\{p(1); p(2); r(X,Y)\}$.*

5   Building Explanations

5.1   Approximation of the Least General Generalization for a Subset of Trajectories

Exact *lgg* computation [17] for a set of observations O has a prohibitive complexity, in $\mathcal{O}(C)^n$ where C is the size (in literals) of the largest observation of O and $n = |O|$. Considering that in our case study (see Sect. 6), observations have an average number of literals of about 250 and some predicate symbols having an average occurrence number by observation above 5, we had to develop an approximation algorithm for *lgg*.

We have implemented a top-down *generate and test* algorithm that computes an approximation of the $lgg(O)$ referred to as *Bottom* in the remainder of the paper. This algorithm is flexible enough to handle constraints meaningful for our problem and is able to bound the size of *Bottom*.

We first define a language bias $\mathcal{V} \subseteq \mathcal{B}$ as a list of predicate symbols associated to their arguments types. The specialisation algorithm randomly selects a seed $\in O$, and applies the ρ specialisation operator to every literal $l_i \in s$. ρ takes as arguments the current generalization *Bottom*, l_i, and the current matching substitution θ $(Bottom.\theta = s)$.

In the following, we represent a relational motif as a list of atoms, i.e. $[l_1, ..., l_n]$. If C is a relational motif and l a literal, $[C, l]$ is the relational motif obtained by adding l after last literal of C.

The refinement operator ρ controls the number of generalised literals for each l_i (at most k), the number and types of variables occurring in each generalised literal. More importantly it controls which generalisations are allowed for a constant: does a constant generalize to a variable already occurring in *Bottom* and linked to the same constant in θ – therefore creating a "link" within *Bottom* (see Example 6) – or does it only generalize to a fresh variable. A literal gl_{i_j} is added to *Cands* if $[Bottom, gl_{i_j}]$ covers all observations of O. Still, the cardinal of $\rho(Bottom, l_i, \theta)$ can be high, the algorithm therefore ranks the candidate generalised literals and finally selects the k-best candidates given the *Score* function. The score function uses the number of variables and fresh variables of gl_{i_j}, the maximum degree of variables in gl_{i_j} in $[Bottom, gl_{i_j}]$. It also integrates the coverage of $[Bottom, gl_{i_j}]$ on observations of U_{notc}. Once the k-best generalised literals

---

Algorithm 1. Computes *Bottom*, an approximation of *lgg(O)*

Require: O: observation set, $\mathcal{B}$: language bias, *Score*: score function
Ensure: A relational motif *Bottom* that θ-subsumes all $o_k \in O$, and of size $\leq k * |s|$
 1: $s \leftarrow random\_choice(O)$; $Bottom \leftarrow \emptyset$; $\theta \leftarrow \emptyset$
 2: **for each** $p \in \mathcal{B}$ **do**
 3:   **for each** l_i instance of p occurring in s ($l_i \in s$) **do**
 4:     Cands $\leftarrow$ k-best literals $\in \rho(Bottom, l_i, \theta)$ given *Score*
 5:     **for each** $gl_{i_j} \in Cands$ **do**
 6:       **if** $[Bottom, gl_{i_j}]$ covers all $o_j \in O$ **then**
 7:         $Bottom \leftarrow [Bottom, gl_{i_j}]$
 8:       **end if**
 9:     **end for**
10:   **end for**
11: **end for**
12: $Bottom \leftarrow reduce(Bottom)$
13: **return** *Bottom*

---

for l_i have been identified, they are greedily added to *Bottom* if $[Bottom, gl_{i_j}]$ covers all observations of O (note that literals in *Cands* can share variables).

Bottom is finally reduced [17] to keep *in fine* maximally specific literals only.

Example 6. *From Example 1, let us suppose o_1 is the seed and that ρ satisfies the following constraints : ρ only generates generalised literals that contains at most one variable (fresh or already occurring in Bottom). Let us start with predicate symbol p, the most frequent predicate symbol in both o_1 and o_2. The first instance of p in o_1 is $p(1,2)$. $\rho(Bottom, p(1,2), \theta) = \{p(1,2), p(X_0, 2), p(1, X_1)\}$. $p(1,2)$ does not cover o_2, neither does $p(X_0, 2)$; $p(1, X_1)$ covers both o_1 and o_2 and is added to Bottom, θ becomes $\{X_1/2\}$. Now considering the second instance of p in the seed, $p(2,3)$, $\rho(Bottom, p(2,3), \theta) = \{p(2,3), p(X_1, 3), p(X_2, 3), p(2, X_3)\}$. $p(2,3)$ does not cover o_2, neither does $p(X_1, 3)$; $p(X_2, 3)$ and $p(2, X_3)$ are thus added to Bottom and $\{X_2/2, X_3/3\}$ is added to θ. In further iterations of the algorithm, $r(X_4)$ and $q(3)$ are added to Bottom and $\{X_4/2\}$ to θ. We finally obtain Bottom $= \{p(1, X_1), p(X_2, 3), p(2, X_3), r(X_4), q(3)\}$ with the matching substitution $\theta = \{X_1/2, X_2/2, X_3/3, X_4/2\}$ for the seed o_1 that does not need to be reduced. Bottom is an approximation of the exact lgg of o_1 and o_2, as it does not contain $p(X_5, X_4)$.*

The goal when proposing this approximate lgg algorithm is to be able to bound the size of *Bottom* as well as to parameterize the introduction of "links" (shared variables) in *Bottom*. Once computed, relational motif *Bottom* is the lower bound of the search space for minimal common explanations for O.

5.2   Building Common Explanations

Algorithm 1 builds a relational motif *Bottom* which approximates $lgg(O)$ (i.e., $Bottom \preceq_\theta lgg(O)$). The next algorithm takes *Bottom* as input and builds a set of common explanations of O seen as $\subseteq$-minimal and correct subsets of *Bottom* (see Definition 4). The first algorithm that extends frequent itemset mining to relational motifs in a learning from interpretations framework is Warmr [7], which was relying in particular on a flexible language bias definition. Since then, a number of works in ILP have targeted relational motifs mining, in particular closed relational motifs [9]. We target here a slightly different problem, that of computing the set of all minimal (under $\subseteq$) and correct subsets of *Bottom*. This problem is directly related to that of computing the bound G of a *Version Space* with lower bound *Bottom* [14] in a relational language.

All observations of O are labelled with class c (thanks to classifier D), a correct motif should not cover any observation of U_{notc}, observations of U labelled by a class other than c. Given a relational motif m, the set of observations covered by m and belonging to U_{notc} is refered to as the *critical set* of m, whereas observations belonging to U_{notc} are refered to as *critical* as far as the goal is to explain O.

A close task has been investigated in boolean itemset mining [22]. In this work, the authors propose a top down algorithm in which a current motif mg is iteratively specialised by adding an item l if $[mg, l]$ rejects at least one critical observation of mg. Adding l to mg is validated if none of the subsets of $[mg, l]$ containing l rejects the same critical observations as $[mg, l]$. We upgrade in the following this algorithm for extracting minimal and correct relational motifs from *Bottom*. This adaptation is not trivial for the following reasons. One such reason is that specialising a relational motif mg may require adding several literals at once for rejecting critical observations: it may be necessary to add so-called "bridge" literals that do not allow to reject a critical observation but that introduce new variables necessary to do so (see [18] for one of the first discussions on that point). Mutliple *lookahead* strategies have been proposed in ILP, all of them relying on *ad-hoc* search or language bias. We propose here an original strategy that exploits the structure of *Bottom* in *locales*.

We refer to [5] for the formal definition of a *locale*, but intuitively, a locale of *Bottom* is a maximal set of *Bottom* literals that "share" variables. The possible instantiations of a variable within a motif are therefore only constrained by variables occurring in the same locale. A ground fact is a locale of size one.

Example 7. *The* lgg *of Example 1 has 5 locales* $\{p(1, X_1)\}$, $\{p(X_2, X_3), r(X_3)\}$, $\{p(X_4, 3)\}$ $\{p(2, X_5)\}$, $\{q(3)\}$. *The locales associated to Bottom in Example 6 are the same except for the second locale that reduces to* $\{r(X_3)\}$.

In the following, we denote by $coverage(m, O)$ where m is a relational motif and $O \subseteq U$ a set of observations the set $\{o_i \in O \mid covers(m, o_i)\}$. Algorithms 2 and 3 upgrade the algorithm [22] for building minimal and correct relational motifs. Algorithm 2 explores all possible subsets of locales of *Bottom*. This algorithm succeeds if mg is correct (the critical set of mg is empty), it fails and backtracks if the largest motif that can be built given the unexplored locales is not correct (line 2 of Algorithm 2). In other cases, it calls Algorithm 3 for further specialising mg by exploring yet unexplored locales.

Algorithm 2. $mings(mg, LLK, NCE)$

Require: mg : current minimal motif, NCE: critical set of mg, $LLK = \{LK_i\}$ locales
   of $Bottom$ still to be explored
Ensure: MGF : set of all minimal and correct subsets of $Bottom$
 1: $MGF \leftarrow \emptyset$
 2: **if** $mg \cup LLK$ is correct **then**
 3:     **if** mg is correct ($NCE = \emptyset$) **then return** mg
 4:     **end if**
 5:     $LK \leftarrow head(LLK)$
 6:     $nLLK \leftarrow tail(LLK)$
 7:     **for** all $M_i = maxGen(LK, NCE)$ **do**   ▷ see alg.3
 8:         $emg \leftarrow [mg, M_i]$
 9:         $rNCE \leftarrow coverage(emg, NCE)$
10:         $MGLK \leftarrow mings(emg, nLLK, rNCE)$
11:         $MGF \leftarrow MGF \cup MGLK$
12:     **end for**
13:     $MGWLK \leftarrow mings(mg, nLLK, NCE)$
14:     $MGF \leftarrow check\_min(MGF \cup MGWLK)$
15: **end if**
16: **return** MGF

Algorithm 3 builds for a given locale LK all minimal subsets of LK rejecting at least one critical observation of mg. Such a minimal subset M_i of LK can be handled as a boolean item as in [22] because, as M_i and LK do not share any variables (by definition of a locale), $coverage([mg, M_i], NCE) = coverage(mg, NCE) \cap coverage(M_i, NCE)$.

Example 8. *From Example 6, suppose o_1 et o_2 are labelled with class c and assume observation o_3 has class $c' \neq c : \{p(2, 4), r(2), p(2, 3), q(3)\}$. Three locales of $lgg(\{o_1, o_2\})$ cover o_3, namely $\{p(X_4, 3)\}$, $\{p(2, X_5)\}$ and $\{q(3)\}$, are immediately ruled out. $\{p(1, X)\}$ and $\{p(X', Y'), r(Y')\}$ are both correct and $\subseteq$-minimal. Considering the locales of Bottom, all of them except $\{p(1, X)\}$ cover o_3, yielding a single common explanation.*

Proposition 3. *Algorithm 2 applied to the set of locales of Bottom and to a critical set of observations NCE is correct and complete: it builds all minimal subsets of Bottom that reject all observations of NCE.*

If needed, and as suggested in Sect. 4, the MGF set may then be pruned to keep among explanations of equal size the most specific ones (i.e., the most instantiated ones) according to θ-subsumption.

Algorithm 3. $maxGen(LK, NCE)$

Require: LK : a locale $\in Bottom$, NCE: critical set of mg
Ensure: MG: set of minimal subsets of LK rejecting at least one element from NCE
 1: **if** LK does not reject any critical observation $\in NCE$ **then**
 2:     **return** $\emptyset$
 3: **end if**
 4: $MG \leftarrow \emptyset$
 5: **for** all subsets mg_i of LK **do**
 6:     $rNCE \leftarrow couverage(mg_i, NCE)$
 7:     **if** $|rNCE| < |NCE|$ and mg_i is minimal **then**
 8:         $MG \leftarrow MG \cup mg_i$
 9:     **end if**
10: **end for**
11: **return** MG

---

6   Case Study

A trajectory is a sequence $p = s_0 a_0 \ldots s_t a_t \ldots s_n a_n$ where s_t is the state observed at time t and a_t the action performed in t to progress to state s_{t+1}. Most of the predicates describing the trajectories have a temporal argument: the atoms hold or not depending on the instant t along the trajectory. For part of these predicates, we use a compact representation using time intervals as arguments. When considering the truth value of some atom a, ground except from its time stamp, we divide the timeline into intervals during which a is true. The positive literal $a([b, e])$ is then true whenever a is true for all $t \in [b, e]$ and is false at time $b - 1$ and at time $e + 1$.

Example 9. *Consider a trajectory where a is true at times $1, 2, 3, 5, 6$ and b is true at times $2, 3, 4, 6, 8, 9$. The truth of a and b along the trajectory is written* $a([1, 3]), a([5, 6]), b([2, 4]), b([6, 6]), b([8, 9])$.

We consider now a deal of our game and follow the scenario of Sect. 2. Given a (state, action) pair we build a classifier D made of definite clauses[1] for optimality of the action, then for each clause we search for minimal common explanations for its coverage. The deal is as follows:

W 8 9 11   N 3 4 5 12   E 6 7   S 2 10 13 14

The decision problem faced by the artificial player Noo is seen as a deterministic Markov Decision Process. The actions are the cards played by Noo as the declarer, either as North or South player. The transition from a state s_t to the next state s_{t+1} is fully determined by the action a meaning that Noo knows which card the defender, either East or West, will play as a reaction to action a in state s_t. The reward $r(s_t, a)$ obtained by Noo is 0 except for the last action of the trajectory where its value is the number of tricks won by the declarer along

---

[1] Using the ILP system cLear, developed by NukkAI.

the trajectory. Time t represents the moment in which North or South has to play and s_t is the current state of the game at time t. This means that each trick is associated to two timestamps.

Example 10. *The game starts after West has played 8 and the North hand has been unveiled. Consider a trajectory starting as follows: W8 (t1) N12 E6 (t2) S2 (t3) S13 W9. North plays 12 (the queen) in t_1 with null reward $r(s_1, 12)$. Then South plays 2 and we have $r(s_2, 2) = 1$ as North wins the first trick.*

Whatever North plays in t_1 by playing afterwards optimally the declarer will win the three first tricks ending in t_7 in which the defender has void hands. In what follows we discuss the case in which in t_1 North plays a small card, say 3. We say that two cards $a < a'$ in a player hand in state s are consécutives whenever in s there is no card a'' in the hand of another player or played by another player during the current trick such that $a < a'' < a'$. Consecutive cards may be exchanged during a trajectory starting in s or after without any effect on the total reward at the end of the trajectory. To discuss optimality of the $(s_1, 3)$ pair we will display a tree of *abstract trajectories*, i.e. trajectories in which consecutive cards in a South or North hand are represented as a single action. There are various abstract optimal trajectories starting from W8 N3, displayed in Fig. 1 and ending on leaves numbered from 1 to 10 from the left. Non optimal actions, leading to non optimal trajectories are denoted by an ending arc towards an empty, unnumbered, leaf. We learn four clauses for optimality from the 40 optimal trajectories and the 104 non-optimal ones:

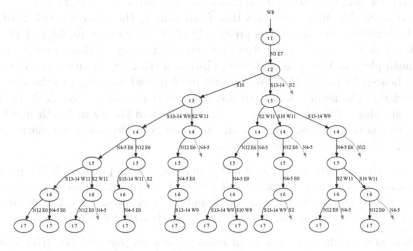

Fig. 1. Optimal abstract trajectories from W8 N3

$$opt \leftarrow playSmallestCard(Card, south, 3), \quad willTakeTrickWith(12, north, T). \tag{1}$$

$$opt \leftarrow action(12, 6), nbSmallCards(1, Player, [1, 3]). \tag{2}$$

$$opt \leftarrow nbHonors(1, Player, [4, 5]). \tag{3}$$

$$opt \leftarrow nbThreats(2, Player, 0, [7, 7]). \tag{4}$$

The abstract trajectories covered by the clauses respectively are leaves 5,6,7 for clause 1, leaves 1,3,9,10 for clause 2, leaves 1,2,4 for clause 3, and leaf 8 regarding clause 4[2]. We focus now on some minimal common explanations for the trajectories covered by clause 3 and give informal proofs of optimality:

1. $nbHonors(1, south, [4, 5])$ grounds the clause 3 body. It says that there is exactly one honor in the South hand between times t_4 and t_5 (and a different number outside $[t_4, t_5]$). This means that i) South plays an honor (either 13 or 14) in t_3, at the beginning of trick 2 and ii) South plays its second honor in t_5 at the beginning of trick 3. From i) we infer that South has won the first trick (with 6 and 7 East cannot win this trick) and wins the second trick (13 et 14 are the highest cards). From ii) we infer that South also wins the third trick, hence the optimality of the trajectories satisfying the explanation.

2. $action(10, 2), action(13, T1), action(14, T2)$ says that South plays 10 in trick 1, then 13 and 14 in tricks 2 and 3, therefore winning the 3 tricks. This explanation proposes a very simple plan to reach optimality.

3. $maxCardHand(2, south, [6, 7]), nextDominant(12, north, [Tb, Te]), Te \geq 4$ is trickier. The first atom says that from time t_6 the highest South card is 2 which means that South has previously played the cards 10, 13 and 14. and therefore i) South has won the first trick (with any of these cards) and ii) South plays at time t_5 and therefore has won trick 2 with an honor (10 would be beaten by the 11 that West would have played according to the defender model[3]). The second and third atoms state that until a time $Te \geq t_4$ there is one player (South) that has cards higher than the 12 in North hand and so 10 has been played before t_4 and as a consequence South necessarily plays its last honor in t_5 and win trick 3.

The value we give to an explanation depends on its purpose. If the purpose is to know which cards to play, explanation 2 is suitable, while if the purpose is about learning to reason on actions and their consequences, i.e. about progressing as a player, explanations 1 and 3 are better. Of course, a request for

---

[2] While most predicates are self-explanatory some are not. $willTakeTrickWith(12, north, T)$ says that at time T and by playing 12 which is the highest card on the board or in hands of players that yet have to play in the current trick, North will win the trick. $nbThreats(2, Player, 0, [7, 7])$ says that at time t_7 card 2 of $Player$ has no threats by cards from its opponents. It also says that such threatening cards exists in t_6.

[3] If possible the opponent plays a card higher than the last card played in the trick.

explanation may include information about this purpose, resulting in selecting for the explanation process only part of the predicates describing the trajectories.

7 Related Work

Many ILP systems indirectly address the explainability issue, because their output – Logic Programs – are explicit, as opposed to black box learning systems. Still, if supervised learning systems provide explicit models, much work remains to be done to provide useful explanations to domain experts: such supervised models may not be concise enough [1, 21] for a human to understand, or may not capture the cause of the classification of an observation, but some of its side effects. As opposed to [1], we do not introduce additional predicates to make the model concise but we fully make use of the vocabulary designed by experts and used for building interpretations as the language for explanations. We use a notion of minimality of explanation, as systems that build abductive explanations do in a propositional logic context [3, 11]. One of our originality is to search for shared explanations by observations of a given subgroup sharing the same label. [19] addresses the problem of finding contrastive explanations for an observed instance as minimal changes to an instance so that its class shifts. The authors rely on the notion of near-miss example introduced by Winston (a negative example closest to a positive one) for defining a near miss explanation.

8 Conclusion

We have proposed a definition for explanations of the label shared by a group of observations described in first order logics. Such kind of explanation is in particular mandatory when we have to explain a decision based on consequences that also depends on further decisions. We also propose to build and use a rule-based model in order to define such groups of observations. Unlike [10, 20], we heavily rely on the observations at our disposal to construct the explanations. Technically this implies building an approximation of the lower bound of the space of common explanations for a group of observations and enumerating the minimal common explanations included in this bound.

By giving informal proofs of optimality of decisions based on minimal common explanations for a simple card game we have emphasized that, as far as the interlocutor understands the semantics of the language and have a sufficient knowledge on the problem in hand, he/she may use common explanations to understand why and how some decision is suitable. One obvious perspective in our case study is to build a formal theory allowing to implement deductions from our explanations. Note that though we use in our experiments a very simple model of the opponent, any deterministic model, in particular one simulating a min-max opponent, is suitable for common explanations. A major perspective is to address the more general cases where the artificial player does not know the opponent's hand, and have then to explain decisions resulting from incomplete information. Definition of explanations in this case remains open.

Acknowledgements. We thank Dr Junkang Li who wrote the program that solves the MDP and Dr Dominique Bouthinon for helping us to apply the ILP program cLear for the simplified Bridge game. M. Kazi Aoual is partially supported by ANRT through a CIFRE agreement.

References

1. Ai, L., Muggleton, S.H., Hocquette, C., Gromowski, M., Schmid, U.: Beneficial and harmful explanatory machine learning. Mach. Learn. **110**(4), 695–721 (2021)
2. Audemard, G., Bellart, S., Bounia, L., Koriche, F., Lagniez, J., Marquis, P.: On preferred abductive explanations for decision trees and random forests. In: Raedt, L.D. (ed.) Proceedings of IJCAI 2022, pp. 643–650 (2022)
3. Audemard, G., Bellart, S., Bounia, L., Koriche, F., Lagniez, J., Marquis, P.: On the explanatory power of boolean decision trees. Data Knowl. Eng. **142**, 102088 (2022)
4. Blockeel, H., Raedt, L.D., Jacobs, N., Demoen, B.: Scaling up inductive logic programming by learning from interpretations. In: DMKD 1999, vol. 3, pp. 59–93 (1999)
5. Cohen, W.W., Jr., Page, C.D.: Polynomial learnability and inductive logic programming: methods and results. New Gener. Comput. **13**(3&4), 369–409 (1995)
6. Darwiche, A., Hirth, A.: On the reasons behind decisions. In: ECAI 2020. Frontiers in Artificial Intelligence and Applications, vol. 325, pp. 712–720 (2020)
7. Dehaspe, L.: Frequent pattern discovery in first-order logic. AI Commun. **12**(1–2), 115–117 (1999)
8. Echenim, M., Peltier, N.: A calculus for generating ground explanations. In: Gramlich, B., Miller, D., Sattler, U. (eds.) IJCAR 2012. LNCS (LNAI), vol. 7364, pp. 194–209. Springer, Heidelberg (2012). https://doi.org/10.1007/978-3-642-31365-3_17
9. Garriga, G.C., Khardon, R., Raedt, L.D.: Mining closed patterns in relational, graph and network data. Ann. Math. Artif. Intell. **69**(4), 315–342 (2013)
10. Huang, X., Izza, Y., Ignatiev, A., Marques-Silva, J.: On efficiently explaining graph-based classifiers. In: Proceedings of KR 2021, pp. 356–367 (2021)
11. Ignatiev, A., Narodytska, N., Marques-Silva, J.: Abduction-based explanations for machine learning models. In: AAAI 2019, pp. 1511–1519 (2019)
12. Inoue, K.: Consequence-finding based on ordered linear resolution. In: IJCAI 1991, pp. 158–164. Morgan Kaufmann (1991)
13. Marquis, P.: Extending abduction from propositional to first-order logic. In: Jorrand, P., Kelemen, J. (eds.) FAIR 1991. LNCS, vol. 535, pp. 141–155. Springer, Heidelberg (1991). https://doi.org/10.1007/3-540-54507-7_12
14. Mitchell, T.M.: Generalization as search. Artif. Intell. **18**(2), 203–226 (1982)
15. Muggleton, S., Raedt, L.D.: Inductive logic programming: theory and methods. J. Log. Program. **19**(20), 629–679 (1994)
16. Nienhuys-Cheng, S.H., de Wolf, R.: Foundations of Inductive Logic Programming. Springer, New York (1997). https://doi.org/10.1007/3-540-62927-0
17. Plotkin, G.D.: A note on inductive generalization. Mach. Intell. **5**, 153–163 (1970)
18. Quinlan, J.R., Cameron-Jones, R.M.: FOIL: a midterm report. In: Brazdil, P.B. (ed.) ECML 1993. LNCS, vol. 667, pp. 1–20. Springer, Heidelberg (1993). https://doi.org/10.1007/3-540-56602-3_124

19. Rabold, J., Siebers, M., Schmid, U.: Generating contrastive explanations for inductive logic programming based on a near miss approach. Mach. Learn. **111**(5), 1799–1820 (2022)
20. Ribeiro, M.T., Singh, S., Guestrin, C.: "Why should i trust you?": explaining the predictions of any classifier. In: Proceedings of 22nd ACM SIGKDD International Conference on Knowledge Discovery and Data Mining, pp. 1135–1144 (2016)
21. Shakerin, F., Gupta, G.: Induction of non-monotonic logic programs to explain boosted tree models using LIME. In: Proceedings of AAAI 2019, pp. 3052–3059 (2019)
22. Soulet, A., Rioult, F.: Exact and approximate minimal pattern mining. In: Guillet, F., Pinaud, B., Venturini, G. (eds.) Advances in Knowledge Discovery and Management. SCI, vol. 665, pp. 61–81. Springer, Cham (2017). https://doi.org/10.1007/978-3-319-45763-5_4

Abstract Domains for Database Manipulating Processes

Tobias Schüler[1]($\boxtimes$)(ID), Stephan Mennicke[2](ID), and Malte Lochau[1](ID)

[1] University of Siegen, Siegen, Germany
{tobias.schuler,malte.lochau}@uni-siegen.de
[2] Knowledge-Based Systems Group, TU Dresden, Dresden, Germany
stephan.mennicke@tu-dresden.de

Abstract. Database manipulating systems (DMS) formalize operations on relational databases like adding new tuples or deleting existing ones. To ensure sufficient expressiveness for capturing practical database systems, DMS operations incorporate as guarding expressions first-order formulas over countable value domains. Those features impose infinite state, infinitely branching processes thus making automated reasoning about properties like reachability of states intractable. Most recent approaches therefore restrict DMS to obtain decidable fragments. Nevertheless, a comprehensive semantic framework capturing full DMS, yet incorporating effective notions of data abstraction and process equivalence is an open issue. In this paper, we propose DMS process semantics based on principles of abstract interpretation. The concrete domain consists of all valid databases, whereas the abstract domain employs different constructions for unifying sets of databases being semantically equivalent up to particular fragments of the DMS guard language. The connection between abstract and concrete domain is effectively established by homomorphic mappings whose properties and restrictions depend on the expressiveness of the DMS fragment under consideration. We instantiate our framework for canonical DMS fragments and investigate semantical preservation of abstractions up to bisimilarity, being one of the strongest equivalence notions for operational process semantics.

Keywords: database manipulating systems · abstract interpretation · labeled transition systems · bisimulation equivalence

1 Introduction

Background and Motivation. Modern software systems intensively interact with diverse environmental components which often includes one or more (relational) databases. Database manipulating systems [1] (DMS) and similar approaches [4,7,8,22] characterize the operational behavior of (relational) database systems by formalizing actions consecutively transforming the current state of databases by adding new tuples or deleting existing ones. The action language supported by DMS-like formalisms must be sufficiently expressive to

A. Fensel et al. (Eds.): RuleML+RR 2023, LNCS 14244, pp. 222–237, 2023.
https://doi.org/10.1007/978-3-031-45072-3_16

capture crucial behavioral aspects of practical database systems. To this end, those actions combine set-based add/delete operations with FOL formulas both defined on databases over (countable) value domains [2]. The FOL part serve as guarding expressions for actions which, if enabled, have the ability to further expand and/or narrow the active domain of databases reached in the subsequent state. However, these distinct features of DMS-like formalisms impose intrinsically problematic properties on the underlying operational semantics. For instance, using labeled transitions systems (LTS) [7], the resulting process model is not only non-regular and infinite-state, but even infinitely branching as arbitrary fresh data may be added to databases in a step. Essential correctness properties of DMS processes like reachability of states are thus not only theoretically undecidable, but also practically intractable by state-of-the-art reasoning tools. As a pragmatic workaround, most approaches consider bounded state spaces and/or narrow down expressiveness of DMS languages to obtain decidable fragments [1].

Contributions. In this paper, we apply the framework of *abstract interpretation* [9,10] to tame the LTS semantics of DMS processes. In the concrete domain, the set of LTS states corresponds to all valid databases of a given database schema over infinite value domains. In the abstract domain, LTS states are constructed by employing different abstraction operators for unifying subsets of databases. This abstract representation enables us to effectively connect the abstract and concrete domains by means of homomorphic mappings. The types of properties of DMS processes being preserved and/or reflected by abstraction depend on the expressiveness of the DMS fragment used in DMS actions as well as the notion of process equivalence under consideration. We instantiate our framework for canonical DMS fragments and investigate behavior preservation of abstractions up to bisimilarity. As bisimilarity constitutes one of the strongest equivalence notions for LTS-based process semantics, our abstraction builds the basis for guaranteeing preservation of essential semantical properties. In this way, our framework provides a sound conceptual basis for building effective model-checking tools for DMS process verification [10].

Extended Version. We omit the proofs for the main results due to space restrictions and instead refer to the extended version [24].

2   Foundations

Databases. We assume a first-order (FO) vocabulary consisting of mutually disjoint (countably infinite) sets of constants $\mathbf{C}$, variables $\mathbf{V}$, and predicates $\mathbf{P}$. Each predicate $p \in \mathbf{P}$ has an arity $ar(p) \in \mathbb{N}$. Terms are either constants or variables, and for a list of terms $\mathbf{t} = t_1, \ldots, t_n$ we denote its length by $|\mathbf{t}| = n$. An expression $p(\mathbf{t})$ is an atom if $p \in \mathbf{P}$ and $\mathbf{t}$ is a term list, such that $ar(p) = |\mathbf{t}|$. An atom is *grounded* if it is variable-free and we call a finite set of ground atoms $\mathcal{D}$ a *database*. The universe of all databases is $\mathbb{U}^{\mathbf{C}}$. A (possibly infinite) set of ground atoms $\mathcal{I}$ is an *instance* with the respective universe $\mathbb{I}^{\mathbf{C}}$. Note that, $\mathbb{U}^{\mathbf{C}} \subseteq \mathbb{I}^{\mathbf{C}}$.

Guards. We consider FOL formulas g to serve as guards as follows:

$$\Phi ::= p(\mathbf{t}) \mid t = u \mid \neg\Phi \mid \Phi \wedge \Phi \mid \exists x.\ \Phi \qquad (1)$$

where $p(\mathbf{t})$ is an atom, t, u are terms, and $x \in \mathbf{V}$. The terms occurring in guard g being variables are referred to by the set $vars(g)$. A variable $x \in vars(g)$ is either *free* or *bound* in g, defining the set $free(g)^1$ of free variables.

Table 1. Guard fragments, their formula shape, and their abbreviation

guard fragment	abbrv.	formula
normal conjuncitve guard	NCG	$\exists\mathbf{y}.\ a_1 \wedge \ldots \wedge a_m \wedge \neg b_1 \wedge \ldots \wedge \neg b_n$
projection-free NCG	pf-NCG	$a_1 \wedge \ldots \wedge a_m \wedge \neg b_1 \wedge \ldots \wedge \neg b_n$
conjuncitve guard	CG	$\exists\mathbf{y}.\ a_1 \wedge \ldots \wedge a_m$
projection-free CG	pf-CG	$a_1 \wedge \ldots \wedge a_m$
conjunction of negated atoms	CNA	$\forall\mathbf{y}.\ \neg a_1 \wedge \ldots \wedge \neg a_m$

Guards as FOL Fragments. A *normal conjunctive guard* (NCG) is a formula

$$\exists\mathbf{y}.\ a_1 \wedge \ldots \wedge a_m \wedge \neg b_1 \wedge \ldots \wedge \neg b_n \qquad (2)$$

where $\mathbf{y}$ is a list of variables occurring in the atoms $a_1, \ldots, a_m, b_1, \ldots, b_n$. For an NCG g of shape (2) we refer to the positive guard part by $g^+ = \exists\mathbf{y}.\ a_1 \wedge \ldots \wedge a_m$ and its negated part by $g^- = \exists\mathbf{y}.\ \neg b_1 \wedge \ldots \wedge \neg b_n$, respectively. Whenever convenient, g^+ (g^-, resp.) identifies the set of atoms occurring within g, meaning $g^+ = \{a_1, \ldots, a_m\}$ ($g^- = \{b_1, \ldots, b_n\}$, resp.). An NCG g with $g^- = \emptyset$ is a *conjunctive guard* (CG). An NCG g is *safe* if $vars(g^-) \subseteq vars(g^+)$. Similarly, the other guard fragments are summarized in Table 1.

Substitution. A *substitution* is a partial function $\sigma : \mathbf{V} \to \mathbf{C}$ mapping variables to constants. The set of all variables for which σ is defined is denoted by $dom(\sigma)$. We call σ a *substitution for guard* g if $vars(g) \subseteq dom(\sigma)$. Such a substitution replaces variables of a guard by constants and, thereby, forms a *guard match*. For convenience, we assume for every substitution σ and constant $c \in \mathbf{C}$, $\sigma(c) = c$, extending the signature of σ to $\mathbf{V} \cup \mathbf{C} \to \mathbf{C}$. If $\mathbf{t} = t_1 \ldots t_n$ is a list of terms and σ a substitution defined for all variables in $\mathbf{t}$, we denote by $\mathbf{t}\sigma$ the term list $\sigma(t_1) \ldots \sigma(t_n)$. A substitution σ is a *match to guard* g *in instance* $\mathcal{I}$ if (a) $free(g) = dom(\sigma)$ and (b) $\mathcal{I}, \sigma \models g$, where

- $\mathcal{I}, \sigma \models p(\mathbf{t})$ if $p(\mathbf{t}\sigma) \in \mathcal{I}$,
- $\mathcal{I}, \sigma \models t = u$ if $t\sigma = u\sigma$,
- $\mathcal{I}, \sigma \models \neg g$ if $\mathcal{I}, \sigma \models g$ does not hold,
- $\mathcal{I}, \sigma \models g \wedge g'$ if $\mathcal{I}, \sigma \models g$ and $\mathcal{I}, \sigma \models g'$, and
- $\mathcal{I}, \sigma \models \exists x.\ g$ if $\mathcal{I}, \sigma[x \mapsto c] \models g$ for some $c \in \mathbf{C}$.

---

^{1} $free(r(\mathbf{t})) = \mathbf{t} \cap \mathbf{V}$, $free(t = u) = \{t, u\} \cap \mathbf{V}$, $free(\neg g) = free(g)$, $free(g \wedge \psi) = free(g) \cup free(\psi)$, and $free(\exists x.\ g) = free(g) \setminus \{x\}$.

Guard Matches. We denote the set of all matches to guard g in instance $\mathcal{I}$ by $g(\mathcal{I})$. We may simply write g to identify a guard. A guard match to NCGs $g = \exists \mathbf{y}.\ \psi$ in $\mathcal{I}$ is tightly connected to the existence of homomorphisms from ψ (viewed as a set of atoms) to instance $\mathcal{I}$. A function $h : \mathbf{C} \cup \mathbf{V} \rightarrow \mathbf{C} \cup \mathbf{V}$ is called a *homomorphism* from a set of atoms $\mathcal{A}$ into a set of atoms $\mathcal{B}$ if (a) $h(c) = c$ for all $c \in \mathbf{C}$ and (b) $p(t_1, \ldots, t_n) \in \mathcal{A}$ implies $p(h(t_1), \ldots, h(t_n)) \in \mathcal{B}$.

Guard Match, Query Answer and Substitution. Guards and guard matches are very similar to queries and query answers in database systems. However, whereas query answers should be *domain independent* (i.e., having finitely many possible substitutions [2]), this does not necessarily hold for guard matches [1]. For instance, query $\neg P(x)$ would have infinitely many answers and is therefore prohibited, whereas the corresponding guard simply checks if, for instance, a to-be-added person is not yet contained in the database.

Example 1. We consider a simplified social network (SSN) with two predicates, (1) a unary predicate $P(name)$ for *persons* currently being members of the network with attributes *name*, and (2) a binary predicate $F(name_1, name_2)$ for a non-symmetric *friendship* relation from person $name_1$ to person $name_2$. We assume all possible strings denoting names to be part of $\mathbf{C}$. A database of our SSN may be $\mathcal{D}_e = \{P(A), P(B), P(C), F(A,B), F(B,A), F(A,C)\}$ (with A, B and C may be Alice, Bob and Charles). Potential guards are

- a symmetric friendship: $g_{sf} = F(x,y) \wedge F(y,x)$,
- a directed friendship: $g_{df} = F(x,y) \wedge \neg F(y,x)$,
- a friendship from x to someone: $g_{af} = \exists y. F(x,y)$, and
- no friendship: $g_{nf} = \neg F(x,y) \wedge \neg F(y,x)$.

On $\mathcal{D}_e$ we obtain the following guard matches:

- $g_{sf}(\mathcal{D}_e) = \{\{x \mapsto A, y \mapsto B\}, \{x \mapsto B, y \mapsto A\}\}$,
- $g_{df}(\mathcal{D}_e) = \{\{x \mapsto A, y \mapsto C\}\}$,
- $g_{sf}(\mathcal{D}_e) = \{\{x \mapsto A\}, \{x \mapsto B\}\}$, and
- $g_{nf}(\mathcal{D}_e) = \{\{x \mapsto B, y \mapsto C\}, \{x \mapsto C, y \mapsto B\}, \{x \mapsto A, y \mapsto A\}, \ldots\}$.

For instance $\mathcal{D}_e, \{x \mapsto A, y \mapsto B\} \models g_{sf}$ holds as Alice is a friend of Bob and Bob is a friend of Alice, whereas $\mathcal{D}_e, \{x \mapsto A, y \mapsto B\} \models g_{df}$ does not hold.

Database Manipulating Systems. Database manipulating systems formalize possible sequences of *actions* consecutively applied to database instances. Syntactically, our formalization loosely follows the canonical notion of actions used in the DMS formalism by Abdulla et al. [1]. An action consists of a *guard* and an *effect* on the current instance. A guard specifies on which instances the action is applicable. The effect might be deletion of atoms from the instance and adding new atoms to the instance. Formally, the effect comprises two finite sets of atoms, Del and Add, such that $vars(\text{Del}) \subseteq free(\mathbf{g})$. Atoms in Del are determined by the match for guard g, while Add is a collection of new atoms. Note that Del and Add may contain variables that will be bound by (a) the guard matches and (b) by arbitrary constants in case of those variables in $vars(\texttt{Add}) \setminus free(\texttt{g})$. The rationale behind case (b) is that an action inserting atoms may depend on external stimuli like sensor data or user input. An action act is a triple $(g, \texttt{Del}, \texttt{Add})$ which forms the basis of a *database manipulating system* (DMS).

Definition 1 (Database Manipulating System). *A database manipulating system (DMS) is a pair* $\mathcal{S} = (\mathcal{I}_0, \text{ACT})$ *where* $\mathcal{I}_0$ *is the* initial instance *and* ACT *is a finite set of actions.*

From $\mathcal{I}_0$, any sequence of actions $act = (g, \texttt{Del}, \texttt{Add}) \in \text{ACT}$ may be performed based on substitutions σ due to matches of guard g. Note that σ specifies all variables occurring in $\texttt{Del}$. We denote by $\texttt{Del}\sigma$ the set obtained by replacing all occurrences of variables $x \in vars(\texttt{Del})$ by $\sigma(x)$. In general, for a set of atoms $\mathcal{A}$ and substitution σ, $\mathcal{A}\sigma$ is the set of atoms in which each variable $x \in vars(\mathcal{A})$ has been replaced by $\sigma(x)$ if it is defined for σ. Set $\texttt{Add}$ may contain variables which are not in $dom(\sigma)$ such that $\texttt{Add}\sigma$ is not a proper database . To facilitate arbitrary external inputs, we expand σ to the missing variables. Substitution σ^* extends σ to $\texttt{Add}$ if $dom(\sigma^*) = \texttt{Add}$ and $\sigma \subseteq \sigma^*$. Extending σ to σ^* completes a step by deletions $\texttt{Del}\sigma^*$ from and additions $\texttt{Add}\sigma^*$ to the current instance.

Definition 2 (DMS Step). *A DMS action* $act = (g, \texttt{Del}, \texttt{Add})$ *is enabled under instance* $\mathcal{I}$ *and substitution* σ, *denoted* $\mathcal{I}[act, \sigma\rangle$, *if* $\sigma \in g(\mathcal{I})$. *If* $\mathcal{I}[act, \sigma\rangle$, *then an* effect *is an extension* σ^* *of* σ *to* $\texttt{Add}$, *producing instance* $\mathcal{I}' = (\mathcal{I} \setminus \texttt{Del}\sigma^*) \cup \texttt{Add}\sigma^*$. *We denote the DMS step from* $\mathcal{I}$ *to* $\mathcal{I}'$ *via* act *and* σ *by* $\mathcal{I}[act, \sigma^*\rangle \mathcal{I}'$.

Example 2. Action $act_{add} = (true, \emptyset, \{P(x)\})$ (adding a new person) is enabled under each instance even if the person already exists in that instance. Thus, σ is empty and σ^* may be, e.g., $\{x \mapsto A\}$. Action $act_{rev} = (g_{df}, \{F(x,y)\}, \{F(y,x)\})$ checks if a directed friendship exists between x and y, deletes this friendship and adds the reversed friendship.

The formal semantics of a DMS is defined as a *labeled transition system* (LTS).

Definition 3 (Labeled Transition System). *A labeled transition system (LTS) is a triple* $\mathcal{T} = (Q, \Sigma, \Rightarrow)$ *where* q *is a set of states (processes),* Σ *is a set of transition labels, and* $\Rightarrow \subseteq Q \times \Sigma \times Q$ *a transition relation. We denote* $(q, a, q') \in \Rightarrow$ *as* $q \overset{a}{\Rightarrow} q'$ *and write* $q \overset{a}{\Rightarrow}$ *if* $\exists q' \in Q : q \overset{a}{\Rightarrow} q'$ *and* $q \overset{a}{\not\Rightarrow}$ *if not* $q \overset{a}{\Rightarrow}$.

LTS $\mathcal{T} = (Q, \Sigma, \Rightarrow)$ is (a) *finitely branching* if for each $q \in Q$, the set $\{q' \in Q \mid \exists a \in \Sigma : q \overset{a}{\Rightarrow} q'\}$ is finite, (b) *image-finite* if for each $q \in Q$ and $a \in \Sigma$, the set $\{q' \in Q \mid q \overset{a}{\Rightarrow} q'\}$ is finite, (c) *finite-state* if Q is finite, and (d) *deterministic* if for each state $q \in Q$ and $a \in \Sigma$, $q \overset{a}{\Rightarrow} q'$ and $q \overset{a}{\Rightarrow} q''$ implies $q' = q''$. Although LTSs may be directly associated with directed edge-labeled graphs, comparison relations based on graph homomorphisms are too strong to capture distinctive features of LTS processes. Instead, *simulation* and *bisimulation* relations on processes are used. Intuitively, process q simulates p if every action that may be performed by p can be mimicked by q and the successor states again simulate each other.

Definition 4 ((Bi-)Simulation). *For an LTS $(Q, \Sigma, \Rightarrow)$, a binary relation $R \subseteq Q \times Q$ is a* simulation *if for all $(p, q) \in R$ and $a \in \Sigma$, $p \overset{a}{\Rightarrow} p'$ implies that $q' \in Q$ exists such that $q \overset{a}{\Rightarrow} q'$ and $(p', q') \in R$. Process $q \in Q$* simulates *process $p \in Q$ if there is a simulation R with $(p, q) \in R$. If p simulates q by simulation R, and q simulates p by simulation R', then p and q are* similar. *Simulation R is a* bisimulation *if, and only if, $R^{-1} := \{(q, p) \mid (p, q) \in R\}$ is also a simulation. If there is a bisimulation R, such that $(p, q) \in R$, then p and q are* bisimilar.

Note, the witnesses R and R' for similarity are not necessarily bisimulations as possibly $R^{-1} \neq R'$.

DMS semantics can be formalized as an LTS DMS $:= (\mathbb{U}^C, \text{ACT}\Sigma, \Rightarrow)$ where $\Rightarrow$ is formed by $\mathcal{I}_1 \xoverset{\langle act, \sigma \rangle}{\Longrightarrow} \mathcal{I}_2$ if, and only if, $\mathcal{I}_1 \lfloor act, \sigma \rangle \mathcal{I}_2$ (cf. Definition 2). In general, DMS is infinitely branching, infinite-state, and deterministic.

DMS builds the basis for investigating desirable properties of all possible processes defining a DMS. For instance, the *reachability problem* asks for a given DMS and a distinguished action act_x, if there is an instance $\mathcal{I}_x$ with $\mathcal{I}_0 \Rightarrow \mathcal{I}_1 \Rightarrow \ldots \Rightarrow \mathcal{I}_x$ such that action act_x is enabled under $\mathcal{I}_x$. The reachability problem is undecidable for DMS [1]. The next example constitutes a semi-decidable reachability problem.

Example 3. Given a predefined set of persons and actions for consecutively adding and deleting friendships between arbitrary pairs of persons, do we eventually reach a database containing a triangle friendship between three different persons (i.e., x a friend of y, y a friend of z and z a friend of x)? To this end, we expand the unary predicate $P(name)$ to a binary predicate $P(name, name)$ and use NCG to define a guard $P(x, x) \wedge P(y, y) \wedge \neg P(x, y)$. $\neg P(x, y)$ (i.e., ensuring that x and y match different persons). This is a standard technique to avoid $\neq$ in first order formulas. Starting from an arbitrary database, we consider two actions: $act_{add} := (P(x, x) \wedge P(y, y) \wedge \neg P(x, y), \emptyset, F(x, y))$ (adding a friendship) and $act_{delete} := (F(x, y), F(x, y), \emptyset)$ (deleting a friendship) and ask for reachability of the action $act_{end} = (\exists x, y, z. F(x, y) \wedge F(y, z) \wedge F(z, x) \wedge \neg P(x, y) \wedge \neg P(y, z) \wedge \neg P(z, x), \emptyset, \emptyset)$.

A finite solution to this problem comprises an *abstract LTS* with four states, where each of those abstract states contains all subsets of databases with (1) no friendships, (2) friendship chains of maximum length ≤ 2, (3) friendship chains of maximum length > 2 without any triangles, and (4) at least one triangle.

In the remainder of this paper, we develop a hierarchy of abstract domains to characterize semantic-preserving abstractions of states of DMS depending on the expressiveness of the guard fragment used. Our approach is based on the formal framework of abstract interpretation.

3 Principles of Abstract Interpretation

Before we present our abstract interpretation framework for DMS, we first describe its basic ingredients. Different processes assembled in DMS may share similar behavior in terms of their enabled actions and subsequent processes. For instance, let us consider a DMS action which inserts a friendship between Alice and Bob, where the guard of this action consists of a conjunction of atoms requiring Alice and Bob to exist in the database. All (i.e., countably infinitely many) *concrete states* matching this guard may be aggregated into *one* single abstract state. The concrete states aggregated in the subsequent abstract state reached after performing this action then all share the inserted relationship between Alice and Bob. The way how the concrete states are aggregated into, and reconstruction from, such an abstract state clearly depends on the guard fragment used. In addition, DMS states are infinitely branching due to the ability of DMS actions to insert any possible new value. However, in many cases, the exact values are often not relevant for reasoning about the subsequent behavior and can therefore be aggregated into one representative abstract value. The following definitions are based on Dams et al. [10] and conceptualize these observations.

Lattice. Abstract interpretation provides a framework for effectively reasoning about computational models over infinite semantic domains modeled as lattices. By $\sqcap$ and $\sqcup$ we denote binary operations on sets S. The operators $\sqcap$ and $\sqcup$ are monotone with respect to a partial order $\leq$ on S (i.e., $x_1, x_2, y_1, y_2 \in S$, $x_1 \leq x_2$ and $y_1 \leq y_2$ implies $x_1 \sqcap y_1 \leq x_2 \sqcap y_2$ and $x_1 \sqcup y_1 \leq x_2 \sqcup y_2$).

Definition 5 (Lattice). *A lattice is a partially ordered set $(S, \leq)$ such that each two-element subset $\{x, y\} \subseteq S$ has (1) a unique least upper bound in S, denoted by $x \sqcup y$, and (2) a unique greatest lower bound in S, denoted by $x \sqcap y$.*

Bounded lattices are not further deployed in the following but are mentioned here only for the sake of comprehensibility. Abstract interpretation aims at establishing connections between lattices modeling different semantic domains.

Galois Connection. By $(\mathbb{C}, \sqsubseteq)$ we denote a concrete semantic domain where $\mathbb{C} = 2^Q$ comprises the set of all subsets of concrete sets of states Q of a computational model (here: DMS). By $\sqsubseteq$ we denotes a partial (semantic) ordering on $\mathbb{C}$ (here: $\subseteq$). By $(\mathbb{A}, \preceq)$ we denote an abstract semantic domain where $\mathbb{A}$ is a set of abstract states and $\preceq$ a partial (precision) ordering on $\mathbb{A}$. It is crucial that the elements of the concrete domain $\mathbb{C}$ are possible *subsets* of concrete states, whereas the elements of the abstract domain $\mathbb{A}$ are *singleton* abstract states. The mutual connection between concrete and abstract domain is shaped by a pair of abstraction function $\alpha : \mathbb{C} \to \mathbb{A}$ and a concretization function $\gamma : \mathbb{A} \to \mathbb{C}$, together forming a *Galois connection*.

Definition 6 (Galois Connection). *The pair $(\alpha : \mathbb{C} \to \mathbb{A}, \gamma : \mathbb{A} \to \mathbb{C})$ is a Galois connection between lattices $(\mathbb{C}, \sqsubseteq)$ and $(\mathbb{A}, \preceq)$ if (1) α and γ are total and monotone, (2) $\forall C \in \mathbb{C} : \gamma \circ \alpha(C) \sqsupseteq C$, and (3) $\forall a \in \mathbb{A} : \alpha \circ \gamma(a) \preceq a$.*

Monotonicity guarantees that more precise abstractions single out fewer concrete states and, conversely, abstracting larger sets of concrete states yields less precise abstractions. Furthermore, (2) requires that concrete states are preserved after reconstruction. Finally, (3) requires a form of optimality of the abstraction thus not decreasing precision.

Bisimulation. Lifting (bi-)simulations to steps $C \overset{a}{\Rightarrow} C'$ between sets of concrete states, as apparent in the concrete domain, amounts to all databases $q \in C$ evolving to $q' \in C'$ via $q \overset{a}{\Rightarrow} q'$. We refer to these as $\forall$-steps and adapt the notions of (bi-)simulations accordingly.

Definition 7 ($\forall$-(bi-)simulation). *For abstract domain $(\mathbb{A}, \preceq)$ and concrete domain $(\mathbb{C}, \sqsubseteq)$, a binary relation $R \subseteq \mathbb{A} \times \mathbb{C}$ is a $\forall$-simulation if for all $(\mathcal{A}, C) \in R$ and $a \in$ ACT, $\mathcal{A} \overset{a}{\Rightarrow} \mathcal{A}'$ implies that there is a $C' \in \mathbb{C}$ such that (a) $C \overset{a}{\Rightarrow} C'$ with a $q \in C$ for each $q' \in C'$ such that $q \overset{a}{\Rightarrow} q'$, and (b) $(\mathcal{A}', C') \in R$ and (c) for each $q \in C$ there is a $q' \in C'$ with $q \overset{a}{\Rightarrow} q'$.*

If $(\mathcal{A}, C) \in R$ and R is a $\forall$-simulation, we say that C $\forall$-simulates $\mathcal{A}$. By reversing the conditions of $\forall$-simulations, we get $\forall$-simulations between the concrete domain and the abstract domain (i.e., $R \subseteq \mathbb{C} \times \mathbb{A}$). Naturally, a $\forall$-simulation R is called a $\forall$-bisimulation if, and only if, R^{-1} is a $\forall$-simulation. We call $\mathcal{A}$ and C $\forall$-bisimilar if, and only if, a $\forall$-bisimulation between $\mathcal{A}$ and C exists.

Abstract Interpretation Framework. The remainder of this paper is devoted to a hierarchy of concrete domains $(2^{\mathbb{U}}, \subseteq)$ for DMS processes shaped by different fragments of FOL as guard language, where the functions γ and α are either based on the supremum or infimum of the corresponding abstract domains. For a guard language $\mathcal{L}$, we call a Galois connection (α, γ) an *abstract interpretation w.r.t.* $\mathcal{L}$ if for each set of databases $C \subseteq \mathbb{U}$ and set of DMS actions ACT using only guards from $\mathcal{L}$, $\alpha(C)$ and C are $\forall$-bisimilar.

4 Abstract Interpretation of DMS

The concrete domain is fixed: $(2^{\mathbb{U}}, \subseteq)$. For (possibly infinite) sets C of databases, we effectively present six different abstractions: The first two very basic ones are based on (set) union and intersection. The third abstraction is a (Cartesian) combination of the two prior abstractions with the benefit of supporting a more practical guard fragment. One caveat about these abstractions is that we have to waive projection (i.e., existential quantification). To gain DMS actions with more expressive guards, and thereby capture more realistic systems, we devise abstractions for more general abstract domains. We expand our abstract domain incorporating so-called *labeled nulls* as terms in abstract instances. The order on the abstract domain is then based on homomorphisms. The three remaining abstractions are complements of the first three, now in the more abstract domain incorporating labeled nulls. Table 2 summarizes our results.

The rest of this section is structured as follows. First, we introduce a naive set-based abstraction based on the set union operator on databases together with a summary of further set-based abstractions. Resolving the issue of neglecting variable projections in guards we introduce instances with labeled nulls, on which CGs can be used without losing precision. Finally, we combine unions and intersections to even support DMS actions with NCGs. Other abstractions are mentioned in results only, whereas our extended paper provides further explanations and proofs [24].

Table 2. Abstract Domains, Interpretations, and Respective Guard Fragments

abstract domain	$\alpha(C)$	$\gamma(\mathcal{I})$	fragment	
$(\mathbb{I}, \subseteq)$	$\bigcup C$	$\{\mathcal{D} \subseteq \mathcal{I}\}$	CNA	Theorem 1
$(\mathbb{I}, \supseteq)$	$\bigcap C$	$\{\mathcal{I} \subseteq \mathcal{D}\}$	pf-CG	Theorem 2
$(\mathbb{I} \times \mathbb{I}, \leq)$	$(\bigcap C, \bigcup C)$	$\{\mathcal{I} \subseteq \mathcal{D} \wedge \mathcal{D} \subseteq \mathcal{I}\}$	pf-NCG	Theorem 3
$(\mathbb{I}^{\mathbb{N}}, \rightarrow)$	$\bigsqcup C$	$\{\mathcal{D} \rightarrow \mathcal{I}\}$	CNA	Theorem 5
$(\mathbb{I}^{\mathbb{N}}, \leftarrow)$	$\bigsqcap C$	$\{\mathcal{I} \rightarrow \mathcal{D}\}$	CG	Theorem 4
$(\mathbb{I}^{\mathbb{N}} \times, \mathbb{I}^{\mathbb{N}}, \preceq)$	$(\bigsqcap C, \bigsqcup C)$	$\{\mathcal{I} \rightarrow \mathcal{D} \wedge \mathcal{D} \rightarrow \mathcal{I}\}$	NCG	Theorem 6

4.1 Set-Based Abstractions: The Case of Union

As a first and very basic abstraction we study $\bigcup C$ of any set $C \in 2^{\mathbb{U}}$ of databases. If C is infinite, $\bigcup C$ is infinite as well, meaning that $\bigcup C$ is captured in $\mathbb{I}$. Henceforth, we facilitate $\bigcup C$ via the abstraction function $\alpha_1 : 2^{\mathbb{U}} \rightarrow \mathbb{I}$ with $\alpha_1(C)$.

$$\alpha_1(C) := \bigcup C \qquad \gamma_1(\mathcal{I}) := \{\mathcal{D} \subseteq \mathcal{I} \mid \mathcal{D} \text{ is a database}\} \qquad (3)$$

The natural choice for the abstract domain is, thus, $(\mathbb{I}, \subseteq)$ because the more databases C contains, the bigger the abstract instance is (cf. Definition 6 item 1). The counterpart concretization function $\gamma_1 : \mathbb{I} \rightarrow 2^{\mathbb{U}}$ is determined by α_1: While α_1 forms the union of all databases contained in a set of databases C, an abstract instance then describes all databases that are (finite) subsets of the abstract instance. $\gamma_1(\mathcal{I})$ is defined in (3).

Databases are finite by definition, implying that if $\mathcal{I}$ is infinite, $\mathcal{D} \subsetneq \mathcal{I}$ for every $\mathcal{D} \in \gamma_1(\mathcal{I})$. The functions in (3) make up for a Galois connection.

Proposition 1. (α_1, γ_1) *is a Galois connection.*

For $C \in 2^{\mathbb{U}}$, we are interested in the behavioral properties of the abstraction $\alpha_1(C)$. Therefore, observe that for every database $\mathcal{D} \in C$, $\mathcal{D} \subseteq \alpha_1(C)$. Thus, guards asking for the absence of atoms will have the same matches on all the databases in C as well as the abstraction $\alpha_1(C)$.

Example 4. We analyze two guards g_{nf} (absence of a friendship) and g_{sf} (presence of a symmetric friendship) from Example 1 on C and $\mathcal{I}$ with $C = \{\{P(\text{A}), P(\text{B}), F(\text{A}, \text{B}), F(\text{B}, \text{A})\}, \{P(\text{A}), P(\text{B}), P(\text{C})\}\}$ and $\mathcal{I} = \bigcup C = \{P(\text{A}), P(\text{B}), P(\text{C}), F(\text{A}, \text{B}), F(\text{B}, \text{A})\}$. If a friendship is absent in each database of C, this friendship is also absence in $\mathcal{I}$ (i.e., the union of all databases of C). If a friendship is absent in $\mathcal{I}$ this friendship is also absent in each database of C. In contrast, the presence of a symmetric friendship like $F(\text{A}, \text{B}), F(\text{B}, \text{A})$ holds for $\mathcal{I}$ but not for each database in C.

The guard $g_{nf} = \forall y.\neg F(x, y)$ ensures the absence of all friendships of a person x through the universal quantifier. g_{nf} behaves similar to g_{nf}. The behavior of the existential quantifier is conversely. For instance, $g_{ex} = \exists x.\neg P(x)$ holds for each database as databases are finite but the set of all constants is infinite. In contrast, if set C is infinite and for each constant c, $P(c)$ is contained in some database in C, $\mathcal{I} = \bigcup C$ does not satisfy g_{ex}.

As the examples show, $\alpha_1(C)$ may enable DMS actions with conjunctive guards that are not enabled by some, or any, of the concrete databases in C. Thus, $\alpha_1(C)$ captures the behavior of all databases in C if we choose CNA guards.

Theorem 1. (α_1, γ_1) *is an abstract interpretation w.r.t. CNA guards.*

Similarly, we obtain an abstraction framework based on intersection of all the databases contained in set C of concrete databases.

Theorem 2. *Galois connection* (α_2, γ_2) *with* $\alpha_2(C) := \bigcap C$ *and* $\gamma_2(\mathcal{I}) := \{\mathcal{D} \in \mathbb{U} \mid \mathcal{I} \subseteq \mathcal{D}\}$ *is an abstract interpretation for pf-CGs.*

This is a special case of Theorem 4 (cf. next subsection). Furthermore, combining both former abstractions allows us to cover projection-free normal conjunctive guards in DMS actions. The rationale behind this abstraction is that for an NCG g, g^+ is evaluated on the intersection component while g^- is simultaneaously evaluated on the union component of the abstraction.

Theorem 3. *For* $\alpha_3(C) := (\alpha_1(C), \alpha_2(C))$ *and* $\gamma_3((\mathcal{I}^{\cup}, \mathcal{I}^{\cap})) := \{\mathcal{D} \in \mathbb{U} \mid \mathcal{I}^{\cap} \subseteq \mathcal{D} \subseteq \mathcal{I}^{\cup}\}$, *Galois connection* (α_3, γ_3) *is an abstract interpretation for pf-NCGs.*

Next, we consider abstractions allowing for projections (i.e., existentially quantified variables in DMS action guards) to fully capture NCGs in DMS actions.

4.2   Abstractions with Labeled Nulls: The Case of Intersection

There are two issues with the abstractions discussed so far: (a) limited expressiveness in guards of DMS actions (no existential quantification) and (b) (still) infinite branching of abstract states. The reason for the latter is that abstract instances resemble their concrete counterparts too explicitly. To resolve both issues we use the well-known *labeled null* abstraction to get a notion of existence of values contained in a database whose exact values are irrelevant. Finite branching is a welcome side-effect of this abstraction as well as a precise abstraction for DMSs using CGs (including projection via existential quantification).

Labeled nulls are introduced in our framework as a countably infinite set $\mathbf{N}$ (disjoint from all other term sets). As labeled nulls are proxies for the existence of values (i.e., constants), a database, in which every occurrence of a null is replaced by a constant (or other null), is certainly related to the instance that uses the null. Let us denote the set of all instances using constants and labeled nulls by $\mathbb{I}^{\mathbf{N}}$ (short for $\mathbb{I}_{\mathbf{P}}^{\mathbf{C} \cup \mathbf{N}}$). The notions of homomorphisms and guard matches naturally extend to databases containing nulls (i.e., constants must still map to constants, but nulls may map to nulls or constants).

Due to the nature of labeled nulls, their identity does not have the same role as constants have. It is natural to consider $\mathbb{I}^{\mathbf{N}}$ closed under equivalence up to homomorphisms. This means, instances $\mathcal{I}, \mathcal{J} \in \mathbb{I}^{\mathbf{N}}$ are equal, denoted $\mathcal{I} \leftrightarrows \mathcal{J}$, if $\mathcal{I} \to \mathcal{J}$ and $\mathcal{J} \to \mathcal{I}$. Note, on $\mathbb{U}$ equivalence up to homomorphisms coincides with set equality. For instance $\{P(A)\} \leftrightarrows \{P(A), P(\mathbf{n_0})\}$ because we can map A on A and $\mathbf{n_0}$ on A. $\{F(\mathbf{n_0}, \mathbf{n_1})\} \to \{F(\mathbf{n_0}, \mathbf{n_0})\}$ but $\{F(\mathbf{n_0}, \mathbf{n_0})\} \not\to \{F(\mathbf{n_0}, \mathbf{n_1})\}$ because we can not map $\mathbf{n_0}$ on $\mathbf{n_0}$ and $\mathbf{n_0}$ on $\mathbf{n_1}$.

$(\mathbb{I}^{\mathbf{N}}, \to)$ forms a lattice and, by duality, $(\mathbb{I}^{\mathbf{N}}, \leftarrow)$, too. The join $\sqcup$ of $(\mathbb{I}^{\mathbf{N}}, \to)$ is simply the union of the instances. Conversely, $\sqcap$ is an intersection of two instances generalizing common atoms with different constants via null assertions. For instance, $\mathcal{I} = \{P(A), P(B), F(\mathbf{n_0}, \mathbf{n_1})\}$ and $\mathcal{J} = \{P(A), P(C), F(A, C)\}$ have $\mathcal{I} \sqcup \mathcal{J} = \{P(A), P(B), P(C), F(\mathbf{n_0}, \mathbf{n_1}), F(A, C)\}$ as least upper bound and the greatest lower bound is $\mathcal{I} \sqcap \mathcal{J} = \{P(A), F(\mathbf{n_0}, \mathbf{n_1})\}$.

The next two definitions describe how an action is performed in $(\mathbb{I}^{\mathbf{N}}, \to)$. Let $\mathcal{I}$ be an instance and $act = (g, \mathtt{Del}, \mathtt{Add})$ a DMS action. Instead of extending guard matches σ to $\sigma^\star$ (involving some constants that are added to the instance through variables in $\mathtt{Add}$), we consider extensions of σ that insert (globally) fresh labeled nulls for all variables in $vars(\mathtt{Add}) \setminus free(\mathbf{g})$.

Definition 8. *Let* $act = (g, \mathtt{Del}, \mathtt{Add})$ *be a DMS action. For abstract instance* $\mathcal{I} \in \mathbb{I}^{\mathbf{N}}$, *if* $\sigma \in g(\mathcal{I})$, *then* $\mathcal{I} \xrightarrow{\langle act, \sigma \rangle} (\mathcal{I} \setminus \mathtt{Del}\sigma^\star) \cup \mathtt{Add}\sigma^\star$ *where* $\sigma \subseteq \sigma^\star$ *and for each variable* $x \in vars(\mathtt{Add}) \setminus free(\mathbf{g})$, $\sigma^\star(x)$ *is a fresh labeled null.*

Example 5. For action $act_{add} = (true, \emptyset, \{P(x)\})$ from Example 2, $vars(\mathtt{Add}) \setminus free(\mathbf{g}) = \{x\} \setminus \emptyset = \{x\}$ and $\sigma^\star(x) = \mathbf{n}$. We obtain $\emptyset \xrightarrow{\langle act_{add}, \emptyset \rangle} \{P(\mathbf{n})\}$.

Note that the action label only contains the match σ and not its extension. The reason is that for instances $\mathcal{I}, \mathcal{B}_1, \mathcal{B}_2$ and action-match pair $\langle act, \sigma \rangle$, if $\mathcal{I} \xrightarrow{\langle act, \sigma \rangle} \mathcal{B}_1$ and $\mathcal{I} \xrightarrow{\langle act, \sigma \rangle} \mathcal{B}_2$, then $\mathcal{B}_1 \leftrightarrows \mathcal{B}_2$. Thus, the different target instances cannot be distinguished in our abstract domain. This notion of steps is similar to what the Chase does in existential rule reasoning [13]. Due to the closure of the domain under homomorphisms, it also resembles the standard chase and the core chase to certain extents [12]. Sets of concrete instances still proceed as originally defined in Sect. 2. To still guarantee a resemblance between the action labels in our abstract domain and the labels used for concrete instances (where no nulls are involved), we introduce a notion of *compatibility* of action labels.

Definition 9. *Action label* $\langle act_1, \sigma_1 \rangle$ *is compatible to action label* $\langle act_2, \sigma_2 \rangle$, *denoted by* $\langle act_1, \sigma_1 \rangle \trianglelefteq \langle act_2, \sigma_2 \rangle$, *if* $act_1 = act_2$ *and* $\sigma_1 \subseteq \sigma_2$.

Note that we could have reduced the action labeling to include only the guard matches for concrete instances already. However, this simplification does not make the branching finite. Even worse, the resulting LTS would become nondeterministic and looses image-finiteness at the same time.

As before, the abstraction mechanisms we study are based on greatest lower bounds and least upper bounds of the abstract domain $(\mathbb{I}^{\mathbf{N}}, \to)$. Next, we study the intersection abstraction of $C \in \mathbf{2}^{\mathbb{U}}$ with $\alpha_4(C)$ in (4). Generalizing from $(\mathbb{I}, \supseteq)$ we get $(\mathbb{I}^{\mathbf{N}}, \leftarrow)$ as the less databases C contains, the bigger the abstract instance becomes (cf. Definition 6 item 1). Conversely, $\gamma_4(\mathcal{I})$ in (4) for abstract instance $\mathcal{I} \in \mathbb{I}^{\mathbf{N}}$.

$$\alpha_4(C) := \textstyle\bigsqcap C \qquad\qquad \gamma_4(\mathcal{I}) := \{\mathcal{D} \in \mathbb{U} \mid \mathcal{I} \to \mathcal{D}\}\} \qquad (4)$$

Proposition 2. (α_4, γ_4) *is a Galois connection.*

Using labeled nulls, abstract DMSs using CGs become precise abstractions of their concrete counterparts.

Example 6. We analyze the guard g_{af} (does there exist a friendship from x to someone) from Example 1 on $C = \{\{P(A), P(B), F(A, B)\}, \{P(A), P(C), F(A, C)\}\}$ and $\mathcal{I} = \bigsqcap C = \{P(A), F(A, \mathbf{n}_1)\}$. In contrast to $\mathcal{I}' = \bigcap C = \{P(A)\}$, we have a friendship with nulls in $\mathcal{I}$. Now we get homomorphisms $h_{\mathcal{I}} : g_{af} \to \mathcal{I}$ and $h_{\mathcal{D}} : g_{af} \to \mathcal{D}$ for each $\mathcal{D} \in C$.

Theorem 4. (α_4, γ_4) *is an abstract interpretation for CGs.*

Generalizing the Galois connection (α_1, γ_1) to $\mathbb{I}^{\mathbf{N}}$ yields (α_5, γ_5) with $\alpha_5 = \alpha_1$ and $\gamma_5(\mathcal{A}) := \{\mathcal{D} \in \mathbb{U}^{\mathbf{N}} \mid \mathcal{D} \to \mathcal{A}\}$. As for all databases $\mathcal{D}$ without labeled nulls, the existence of a homomorphism from $\mathcal{D}$ to $\mathcal{A}$ holds if, and only if, $\mathcal{D} \subseteq \mathcal{A}$, the new domain generalizes the original result (i.e., Theorem 1) slightly, but without further impact. After all, labeled nulls are proxies for the existence of constants, whereas CNA guards account for the absence of atoms.

Theorem 5. *Galois connection* (α_5, γ_5) *with* $\alpha_5(C) := \bigsqcup C$ *and* $\gamma_5(\mathcal{I}) := \{\mathcal{D} \in \mathbb{U} \mid \mathcal{D} \to \mathcal{I}\}$ *is an abstract interpretation for CNAs.*

4.3   Combining Unions and Intersections

Although the former abstractions already capture existentially quantified variables (i.e., projections), they do not jointly support projections as well as negation. A corresponding abstraction capturing both is $\alpha_6 : 2^{\mathbb{U}} \to \mathbb{I}^{\mathbf{N}} \times \mathbb{I}^{\mathbf{N}}$ with respective concretization $\gamma_6 : \mathbb{I}^{\mathbf{N}} \times \mathbb{I}^{\mathbf{N}} \to 2^{\mathbb{U}}$ as defined in (5). The abstract domain is $(\mathbb{I}^{\mathbf{N}} \times \mathbb{I}^{\mathbf{N}}, \preceq)$. $\mathcal{I}_1 \preceq \mathcal{I}_2$ is defined as $(\mathcal{I}_1^{\sqcap}, \mathcal{I}_1^{\sqcup}) \preceq (\mathcal{I}_2^{\sqcap}, \mathcal{I}_2^{\sqcup})$ if and only if $\mathcal{I}_1^{\sqcap} \leftarrow \mathcal{I}_2^{\sqcap}$ and $\mathcal{I}_1^{\sqcup} \to \mathcal{I}_2^{\sqcup}$. The lattice $(\mathbb{I}^{\mathbf{N}} \times \mathbb{I}^{\mathbf{N}}, \preceq)$ is a combination of the two lattices $(\mathbb{I}^{\mathbf{N}}, \leftarrow)$ and $(\mathbb{I}^{\mathbf{N}}, \to)$.

$$\alpha_6(C) := (\textstyle\bigsqcap C, \bigsqcup C) \qquad\qquad \gamma_6(\mathcal{I}) := \{\mathcal{I}^{\sqcap} \to \mathcal{D} \to \mathcal{I}^{\sqcup}\} \qquad (5)$$

Proposition 3. (α_6, γ_6) *is a Galois connection.*

A substitution σ holds for a NCG g and an abstract state $\mathcal{I} = (\mathcal{I}^{\sqcap}, \mathcal{I}^{\sqcup})$ if the following holds: $\sigma \in g(\mathcal{I})$ if $\sigma \in g^+(\mathcal{I}^{\sqcap})$ and $\sigma \in g^-(\mathcal{I}^{\sqcup})$.

Theorem 6. (α_6, γ_6) *is an abstract interpretation for NCG.*

Example 7. With Galois connection (α_6, γ_6) the guard $g_{end} := \exists x, y, z.F(x, y) \land F(y, z) \land F(z, x) \land \neg P(x, y) \land \neg P(y, z) \land \neg P(z, x)$ from action act_{end} (Example 3) holds in the abstract and concrete domain.

5   Related Work

Reasoning about Database-Manipulating Processes. Most recent works consider formal process languages for manipulating relational database in the context of business process modeling [6].

Data manipulating systems (DMS) as considered in this paper are based on Abdullah et al. [1]. The authors use the formalism to study boundaries of decidability of (generally undecidable) reachability of state predicates in DMS processes. Their approach employs a formal semantics of DMS processes based on Petri nets and counter machines in combination with multiset-based abstraction of databases. Thereupon, Abdullah et al. impose bounds on database schemas as well as query evaluation to obtain decidable fragments. Calvanese et al. [7] also consider a DMS-like language for which they define an *LTS-based operational semantics* to support CTL model-checking of such systems. Similar to Abdullah et al., bounds are imposed on the generally infinite state space to enable an effective, yet incomplete model-checking procedure.

Cangialosi et al. [8,11] consider a DMS-like formalism called artifact-centric (service) language to verify process properties expressed in the μ-calculus. To obtain an effective verification procedure, the authors employ, in accordance to our framework, homomorphism equivalence as abstraction and restrict the process language to conjunctive queries, respectively. Bagheri et al. [4] extend the work of Cangialosi et al. by supporting negation within first-order queries serving as preconditions (guards) of transitions. As a consequence, processes must be restricted to be weakly acyclic in order to ensure a finite solution.

Other works use *Petri nets* with data (colored Petri nets) as a DMS-like formalism. Montali et al. [22] propose DB-nets to integrate data- and process-related aspects of business processes. In [21], Montali et al. adopt soundness checks (including reachability) known from workflow nets to DB-nets, where a finite solution is ensured by employing different notions of boundedness. This work has recently been extended by Ghilardi et al. [14,15] to support conjunctive queries with atomic negation and existential quantifiers.

To summarize, most works impose bounds on the state space and/or restrictions of guard/query languages to ensure effective reasoning about semantic properties of DMS-like processes. However, to the best of our knowledge, none of these works provide a comprehensive decomposition hierarchy of guard/query expressions together with a precise characterization of corresponding semantic-preserving abstractions.

Abstraction Techniques for Databases. Halder et al. [16,17] apply principles of *abstract interpretation* in a more practical setting to define fine-grained abstractions for SQL query expressions. For approximating query result sets, query- and database-specific lattice-based abstractions are applied to value ranges of attribute constraints in selection conditions. In other works, abstract interpretation is mostly used to formalize the interface between database languages and programming languages. Baily et al. [5] apply abstract interpretation for termination analysis for a functional programming language performing database manipulations. Similar attempts are proposed by Amato et al. [3] and Toman et al. [25] to reason about the interplay between imperative programming and database manipulating operations. However, using abstract interpretation to characterize an implementation-independent hierarchy of database abstractions as proposed in this paper has not yet been considered.

Besides abstract interpretation, *symbolic execution* techniques are also frequently considered to effectively cope with large/infinite state spaces of database systems. In these approaches, sets of databases instances are symbolically represented using logical constraints, where most recent works employ this approach for test-data generation from/for databases [18–20,23]. In contrast, elaborating a hierarchy of *symbolic* abstractions using different fragments of propositional logics similar to our approach, has not been investigated so far.

6 Conclusion

We proposed a hierarchy of abstract domains for representing (possibly infinite) sets of databases instances in a final way based on the principles of abstract interpretation. The resulting hierarchy is semantic-preserving up-to bisimilarity and is shaped by different fragments of first-order logics serving as guard language of database-manipulating processes. As a future work, our framework can be instantiated in different ways to facilitate DMS model-checking (e.g., considering corresponding fragments of the modal μ-calculus as specification language). To this end, a purely abstract step semantics is to be defined which allows us to explore the abstract LTS (e.g., starting from all possible initial database instances). We further plan to enrich DMS by a formal process language like Petri nets and CCS to investigate effects as induced by constructs like guarded choice and concurrent actions.

Acknowledgements. Stephan Mennicke has been partly supported by Deutsche Forschungsgemeinschaft (DFG, German Research Foundation) in project number 389792660 (TRR 248, Center for Perspicuous Computing), by the Bundesministerium für Bildung und Forschung (BMBF, Federal Ministry of Education and Research) under project 13GW0552B (KIMEDS), in the Center for Scalable Data Analytics and Artificial Intelligence (ScaDS.AI), and by BMBF and DAAD (German Academic Exchange Service) in project 57616814 (SECAI, School of Embedded and Composite AI).

References

1. Abdulla, P.A., Aiswarya, C., Atig, M.F., Montali, M., Rezine, O.: Complexity of reachability for data-aware dynamic systems. In: ACSD, pp. 11–20. IEEE (2018)
2. Abiteboul, S., Hull, R., Vianu, V.: Foundations of Databases, vol. 8. Addison-Wesley, Boston (1995)
3. Amato, G., Giannotti, F., Mainetto, G.: Data sharing analysis for a database programming language via abstract interpretation. In: VLDB, pp. 405–415 (1993)

4. Bagheri Hariri, B., Calvanese, D., De Giacomo, G., De Masellis, R., Felli, P.: Foundations of relational artifacts verification. In: Rinderle-Ma, S., Toumani, F., Wolf, K. (eds.) BPM 2011. LNCS, vol. 6896, pp. 379–395. Springer, Heidelberg (2011). https://doi.org/10.1007/978-3-642-23059-2_28

5. Bailey, J., Poulovassilis, A.: Abstract interpretation for termination analysis in functional active databases. J. IIS **12**, 243–273 (1999)

6. Calvanese, D., De Giacomo, G., Montali, M.: Foundations of data-aware process analysis: a database theory perspective. In: PODS, pp. 1–12. ACM (2013)

7. Calvanese, D., Montali, M., Patrizi, F., Rivkin, A.: Implementing data-centric dynamic systems over a relational DBMS. In: FDM, vol. 1378, pp. 209–212. CEUR-WS (2015)

8. Cangialosi, P., De Giacomo, G., De Masellis, R., Rosati, R.: Conjunctive artifact-centric services. In: Maglio, P.P., Weske, M., Yang, J., Fantinato, M. (eds.) ICSOC 2010. LNCS, vol. 6470, pp. 318–333. Springer, Heidelberg (2010). https://doi.org/10.1007/978-3-642-17358-5_22

9. Cousot, P., Cousot, R.: Abstract interpretation: a unified lattice model for static analysis of programs by construction or approximation of fixpoints. In: POPL, pp. 238–252. ACM (1977)

10. Dams, D., Gerth, R., Grumberg, O.: Abstract interpretation of reactive systems. TOPLAS **19**(2), 253–291 (1997)

11. De Giacomo, G., De Masellis, R., Rosati, R.: Verification of conjunctive artifact-centric services. Intl. J. CIS **21**(02), 111–139 (2012)

12. Deutsch, A., Nash, A., Remmel, J.: The chase revisited. In: PODS, pp. 149–158. ACM (2008)

13. Fagin, R., Kolaitis, P.G., Miller, R.J., Popa, L.: Data exchange: semantics and query answering. TCS **336**(1), 89–124 (2005)

14. Ghilardi, S., Gianola, A., Montali, M., Rivkin, A.: Petri nets with parameterised data. In: Fahland, D., Ghidini, C., Becker, J., Dumas, M. (eds.) BPM 2020. LNCS, vol. 12168, pp. 55–74. Springer, Cham (2020). https://doi.org/10.1007/978-3-030-58666-9_4

15. Ghilardi, S., Gianola, A., Montali, M., Rivkin, A.: Petri net-based object-centric processes with read-only data. IS **107**, 102011 (2022)

16. Halder, R., Cortesi, A.: Abstract interpretation for sound approximation of database query languages. In: INFOS, pp. 1–10. IEEE (2010)

17. Halder, R., Cortesi, A.: Abstract interpretation of database query languages. CLSS **38**(2), 123–157 (2012)

18. Li, C., Csallner, C.: Dynamic symbolic database application testing. In: DBTest (2010)

19. Lo, E., Cheng, N., Hon, W.K.: Generating databases for query workloads. VLDB Endow. **3**(1–2), 848–859 (2010)

20. Marcozzi, M., Vanhoof, W., Hainaut, J.L.: A relational symbolic execution algorithm for constraint-based testing of database programs. In: SCAM, pp. 179–188. IEEE (2013)

21. Montali, M., Rivkin, A.: Model checking petri nets with names using data-centric dynamic systems. FAOC **28**(4), 615–641 (2016)

22. Montali, M., Rivkin, A.: DB-Nets: on the marriage of colored petri nets and relational databases. In: Koutny, M., Kleijn, J., Penczek, W. (eds.) Transactions on Petri Nets and Other Models of Concurrency XII. LNCS, vol. 10470, pp. 91–118. Springer, Heidelberg (2017). https://doi.org/10.1007/978-3-662-55862-1_5

23. Pan, K., Wu, X., Xie, T.: Database state generation via dynamic symbolic execution for coverage criteria. In: DBtest, pp. 1–6 (2011)

24. Schüler, T., Mennicke, S., Lochau, M.: Abstract Domains for Database Manipulating Processes. CoRR abs/2308.03466 (2023)
25. Toman, D.: Constraint databases and program analysis using abstract interpretation. In: Gaede, V., Brodsky, A., Günther, O., Srivastava, D., Vianu, V., Wallace, M. (eds.) CDB 1997. LNCS, vol. 1191, pp. 246–262. Springer, Heidelberg (1996). https://doi.org/10.1007/3-540-62501-1_36

Extracting Interpretable Hierarchical Rules from Deep Neural Networks' Latent Space

Ya Wang[1,2] and Adrian Paschke[1,2(✉)]

[1] Fraunhofer Institute for Open Communication Systems, Kaiserin-Augusta-Allee 31, 10589 Berlin, Germany
{ya.wang,adrian.paschke}@fokus.fraunhofer.de
[2] The Free University of Berlin, Kaiserswerther Straße 16-18, 14195 Berlin, Germany

Abstract. Deep neural networks, known for their superior learning capabilities, excel in identifying complex relationships between inputs and outputs, leveraging hierarchical, distributed data processing. Despite their impressive performance, these networks often resemble 'black boxes' due to their highly intricate internal structure and representation, raising challenges in terms of safety, ethical standards, and social norms. Decompositional rule extraction techniques have sought to address these issues by delving into the latent space and retrieving a broad set of symbolic rules. However, the interpretability of these rules is often hampered by their size and complexity. In this paper, we introduce EDICT (Extracting Deep Interpretable Concepts using Trees), a novel approach for rule extraction which employs a hierarchy of decision trees to mine concepts learned in a neural network, thereby generating highly interpretable rules. Evaluations across multiple datasets reveal that our method extracts rules with greater speed and interpretability compared to existing decompositional rule extraction techniques. Simultaneously, our approach demonstrates competitive performance in classification accuracy and model fidelity.

Keywords: Neural network interpretability · Rule-based explanations · Decompositional rule extraction

1 Introduction

The advent of Deep Neural Networks (DNNs) has brought transformative change to numerous fields, yet their 'black box' characteristics, which obscure the decision-making process within complex layers of computations, raise issues around reliability, interpretability, and traceability in many safety-crucial domains [24]. Conversely, humans demonstrate proficiency in assimilating and

This work has been partially funded by the German Federal Ministry for Economic Affairs and Climate Action within the project "KI Wissen" (19A20020J).

encapsulating knowledge from their experiences, and further translating this understanding into symbolic representations for enhanced comprehension, communication, transfer, and reasoning. Therefore, considering a trained Deep Neural Network (DNN) as a substantial knowledge base [22], the extraction of symbolic rules becomes an extremely meaningful process for human intervention. These extracted rules not only aid explanation, debugging, and regulation but also enable us to leverage the power of these networks more safely and effectively.

Decompositional rule extraction is an approach that extract symbolic rules from Neural Networks (NNs) to explicitly illustrate the relationships between input and output variables [25]. This approach distinguishes itself from pedagogical methods by incorporating the analysis of internal functionalities within NNs [1]. The knowledge obtained by NNs is known to be distributed among various neuron activations within each layer, which enables these representations to propagate to subsequent layers [12,13]. Features and concepts learned are typically embodied by activations across these neurons, thereby increasing the complexity of their interpretability. Most research on decompositional rule extraction was conducted several decades ago [27], targeting relatively shallow NNs. Few studies have attempted to extract rules from DNNs, primarily due to the exponential growth in the number of extractable rules with respect to the network depth and the input size. This growth necessitates a high computational cost, yet it yields low rule interpretability. Recently, studies such as [19,25] have sought to mitigate these challenges by employing efficient substitution, parallel computing, and advanced decision tree learners. Although these approaches have improved extraction efficiency and rule interpretability, the number of extracted rules remains substantial, even for small-scale problems, such as learning the XOR logical relationship. In this paper, we propose a novel approach that extracts significantly fewer rules, enhances interpretability, and maintains competitive model performance. Rather than merely minimizing the number of rules, we pivot towards discovering meaningful concepts within the network and introduce them as auxiliary variables in our rules. This strategy reduces the volume of rules and simultaneously amplifies interpretability. Our principal contributions can be summarized as follows:

- We present a straightforward rule extraction and inference pipeline composed of a hierarchy of decision trees. In this structure, low-level decision trees focus on extracting concepts derived from a trained Neural Network (NN), while the high-level decision tree makes the final prediction by selecting concepts from the preceding layer.
- We demonstrate that our method surpasses current decompositional techniques in terms of rule interpretability, rule extraction and inference speed, while still delivering highly competitive predictive performance.

2 Related Works

The study of symbolic rule extraction can be traced back to the 90s, with the emergence of back-propagation technology which strengthened NNs, triggering their first wave of popularity. Understanding the knowledge obtained by a NN is a challenge for humans, as this knowledge is encapsulated as sets of real-valued parameters within a specialized model architecture. On the other hand, symbolic representation aligns more closely with human cognitive processes, being explicit in nature. Typically, rules extracted from NNs can be represented as a logical rule set (IF-THEN rule [9], MofN rule [22]), a decision list, or a decision tree or table [11]. Despite rule sets offering more expressiveness and flexibility than decision trees due to their ability to accommodate overlapping rules [8], we have still opted to utilize decision trees for representation. This choice was influenced by the presence of numerous advanced decision tree induction algorithms for rule extraction, and we compensate for their inherent disadvantages by training a series of distinct decision trees. In terms of translucency, rule extraction techniques are typically grouped into three categories [1]: decompositional, pedagogical, and eclectic. Decompositional approaches extract rules from each hidden layer and unit, aggregating them to establish a mapping from the input to the output layer. Significant works include those by [2,9,15,23]. Pedagogical approaches [6,16,17,20,21,26] treat the model as a black box, extracting rules that map input-output relationships akin to NN interpretations. Eclectic approaches [18,22], the third category, amalgamate both methods. Given our goal to understand NNs through their internal structure, we focus solely on the decompositional approach in this paper. Most decompositional rule extraction methods come with some limitations, being either only applicable to a subset of architectures or requiring intervention during the training process [25]. The works most comparable to ours are DeepRED [27], REM-D [19] and Eclaire [25], as they are applicable to arbitrary DNNs. DeepRED is an extension of the CRED [15] algorithm for NNs with multiple hidden layers. It employs decision tree induction algorithms to approximate the activation of neurons by considering the incoming activations from the previous layer. This process is recursively implemented, starting from the output layer and proceeding to the input layer by substituting hidden variables with those from its previous layer. Subsequently, the rules are merged to characterize the NN's overall behavior. REM-D is an optimized variant of DeepRED, which improves learning efficiency and memory consumption by replacing the decision tree algorithm C4.5 with C5.0, and promptly substitutes extracted intermediate rules. In 2021, Zarlenga et al. introduced Eclaire [25], which outperforms REM-D in terms of rule extraction efficiency and rule complexity. Eclaire utilizes a clause-wise substitution and parallel computation of mappings between each hidden layer and the output layers, which avoids delays caused by waiting for computational results from previous layers, thereby significantly accelerating the extraction process. However, these methods come with limitations that we have addressed in our work. First, these approaches typically approximate the mappings from the hidden layer to the output layer using a single decision tree, which can easily lead to overfitting or underfitting. Second, they substitute all intermediate rules, which map from the hidden layer to the output layer, even when some rules have minimal coverage or produce incorrect predictions due to underfitting. Lastly, they aggregate all the rules into a final rule set and make predictions based on majority voting, which could reduce both inference speed and rule interpretability. In contrast, our method employs multiple distinct trees and selects only the decisive rules learned for the final rule sets, which can alleviate overfitting and underfitting. Instead of substituting all hidden variables in the intermediate rules, we turn to identify the most informative intermediated variables and introduce them as the auxiliary variables in our rule sets to enhance the interpretability of the rules. Moreover, our inference pipeline relies on a hierarchy of decision trees, which improves prediction speed and aligns more with human cognition.

3   Preliminaries

3.1   Decompositional Rule Extraction

The decompositional rule extraction approach aims to uncover the relationship between the input layer and the output layer by formulating a set of interpretable IF-THEN rules revealing the internal structure and representation of a trained NN. Formally, we consider a dataset denoted by $\mathbb{X} = \{x^{(i)}\}_{i=1}^{n}$, where each sample $x^{(i)} \in \mathbb{R}^m$ represents a feature vector of m dimensions, and n is the total number of samples. Let $\mathbb{Y} = \{y^{(i)}\}_{i=1}^{n}$ denote the corresponding labels for each sample, where each $y^{(i)} \in \{l_1, l_2..., l_c\}$. A neural network, denoted by f_θ, is a function that maps each input vector $\mathbb{R}^m$ to an output probability distribution over c classes. The objective of the decompositional rule extraction method is to create a highly accurate approximation of a trained NN f_θ using a disjunction of Horn clauses. Using a given dataset $\mathbb{X}$ and its predicted labels $\hat{\mathbb{Y}}$, we construct these clauses in the form

$$\bigvee_{i=1}^{n} \left(\bigwedge_{j=1}^{m} P(x_j^{(i)}, t_j) \rightarrow y^{(i)} \right)$$

such that, it can accurately predict a sample's class and mimic the NN's behavior as closely as possible. The predicates P, typically embodied as attribute value tests, can take the form of either $(x_j > t_j)$ or $(x_j \leq t_j)$, where x_j denotes the j-th input feature of sample x and $t_j \in \mathbb{R}$ represents a learned threshold.

3.2   Approximating Neural Network Activations Through Decision Tree Induction

Neural networks and decision trees use different computational units and methods to process data. A neuron is the fundamental computational unit in a NN. It receives activations from the previous layer, computes a weighted sum of these inputs and adds a bias term. A neuron is deemed "activated" when its output value surpasses a specific threshold determined by its activation function. On the other hand, decision trees use a hierarchy of decision nodes, each representing an attribute value test. These tests are determined by the choice of a splitting variable (i.e., feature variable) and a split point (i.e., threshold of feature value). Decision trees are highly interpretable due to their simple method of partitioning the feature space into a series of rectangles and fitting a constant model in each one [10]. In 2001, Sato et.al [15] first proposed a neuron-level approximation using the decision tree, in which each neuron is treated as a binary classifier (see Fig. 1).

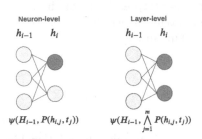

Neuron-level $\quad$ Layer-level

$h_{i-1} \quad h_i \qquad h_{i-1} \quad h_i$

$\psi(H_{i-1}, P(h_{i,j}, t_j)) \qquad \psi(H_{i-1}, \bigwedge_{j=1}^{m} P(h_{i,j}, t_j))$

Fig. 1. A comparison of neuron-level and layer-level activations used for decision tree induction, with activations from the previous layer H_{i-1} as inputs. On the left, a single neuron (shown in red) is activated for $P(h_{i,j}, t_j)$. On the right, a combination of neurons (shown in red) are activated for a conjunction of $P(h_{i,j}, t_j)$.

The neuron accepts activations H_{i-1} from the previous layer and sets the activation of the neuron $P(h_{i,j}, t_j)$ as the target. By feeding a set of training samples, we can use the existing decision tree algorithm to learn a rules set $R_{H_{i-1} \mapsto h_{i,j}}$. One rule could be IF($h_{i-1,0} > t_0, h_{i-1,1} \leq t_1 ... h_{i-1,m} > t_m$), THEN $h_{i,j} > t_j$. Here, in h, the first index i represents the layer number (from 0 to $d+1$), and the second index j refers to the neuron's intra-layer position. Atoms $h_{i,j} > t_j$ in the output layer can be grounded with a predefined threshold, while those in hidden layers can be grounded using the learned threshold from the subsequent layer. The core of this approach is the substitution step, in which each atom in the rule body in i-th layer is rewritten to be a function of activations in the $(i-1)$-th layer using decision trees. By applying decision tree induction to each atom recursively from the output layer to the input layer and eliminating all intermediate variables, we can acquire a final rule set containing only input variables with their threshold $x_j > t_j$ in the rule body, and the predicted class in the rule head.

The issue with neuron-level rule extraction is that it necessitates an exponentially large post-processing step for substitution [25]. Simultaneously, the presence of a large number of neurons results in a high volume of attribute value tests $h_{i,j} > t_j$. A single hidden variable might be associated with multiple thresholds and could appear in several rules, thereby further increasing the computational complexity. To mitigate the aforementioned issue, Mateo et al. [25] proposed the clause-wise substitution, which we refer to as layer-level approximation (see Fig. 1). They set a conjunction of atoms, i.e., a clause, as the target for decision tree learning. To put it more intuitively, this approximation focuses on a specific layer, examining which combinations of inputs result in a particular set of neuron activations in the subsequent layer. This approximation strategy more closely aligns with the characteristics of distributed representation observed in the hidden layer, thereby forming the basis of our approach.

4   Hierarchical Rule Extraction from the Latent Space

Inspired by the hierarchical data processing in NNs-where early layers identify simple, low-level concepts and subsequent layers integrate these to comprehend more intricate, high-level concepts [12,13]-we developed a transparent model consisting of a two-layer decision trees. The first layer focuses on detecting simple concepts, while the second layer selects these concepts to formulate the final prediction. To this end, we introduce two types of decision trees: the Concept Derivation Decision Tree (CD-DT) that learn auxiliary rules for the concept derivation, and the Final Prediction Decision Tree (FP-DT) that learn final rules for the final prediction.

Let's consider an inference process for a classification task as illustrated in Fig. 2. An input sample is initially encoded as a vector, which is then fed into the input layer. Following this, a set of independent Concept Derivation Decision Trees (CDDTs) in the first layer perform multi-classification on the input activations, assigning rule IDs to the sample. The resultant new vector of rule activations can be interpreted as concepts derived from the sample, each corresponding to a decision path within the CD-DTs. Subsequently, a final decision tree performs multi-classification on the rule activations and outputs the class for the sample.

Fig. 2. Decision Trees Inference Pipeline

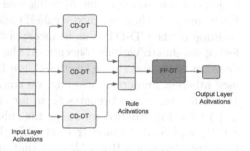

Fig. 3. Decision Trees Training Pipeline

The critical aspect of our design is to effectively train these two types of trees by leveraging the latent representations within a trained NN. To this end, we propose a third type of decision tree: Integrative Activation Decision Tree (IA-DT), which is designed to mine learned concepts across varying hidden layers. The training pipeline is demonstrated in Fig. 3. Consider a trained NN with d hidden layers that processes n input samples, resulting in d distinct hidden layer activations. We then train a set of k distinct IA-DTs-equivalent to a random forest comprised of k tree estimators-on these hidden layer activations, with their output layer activations serving as targets. Every sample represented in the latent space is assessed by the IA-DTs, yielding a unique rule ID (i.e., the decision path) for each tree. When we process n samples through a trained NN with d hidden layers (excluding input and output layers), and train a random forest of k tree estimators, we obtain a $n \times dk$ rule activation matrix. Following this, we train k CD-DTs using the input layer activations as samples and the rule activations as targets.

At last, we train the FP-DT with the rule activations serving as samples and the output layer activations acting as targets.

Our method, as detailed in Algorithm 1, allows us to approximate the trained Deep Neural Network (DNN) f_θ with a corresponding set of decision trees DT_f and a rule set R_f. This approximation utilizes k Integrative Activation Decision Trees (IA-DTs) $\psi_I(\cdot)$, Concept Derivation Decision Trees (CD-DTs) $\psi_c(\cdot)$, and a Final Prediction Decision Tree (FP-DT) $\psi_F(\cdot)$ for rule induction. This process begins by initializing empty sets for the final rules set R_f, final decision trees set DT_f, and an empty array for rule activations C (lines 1–3). In the first loop, we calculate the activations of n samples for each layer (line 5). In the second loop, we configure and train k distinct decision trees for both the IA-DTs $\psi_I(\cdot)$ and CD-DTs $\psi_c(\cdot)$ (lines 7 and 9). At this point, we evaluate the latent representations of the samples (line 8) using rule sets $R_{X' \mapsto \hat{Y}}$ derived from the IA-DT. Each sample is then assigned a rule ID and a prediction confidence. Notably, the training of the CD-DT (line 9) incorporates these confidence scores, giving differing weights to various concepts. At the end of the loop, we assemble the rules, decision trees, and rule activations (line 10–12). As the numeric rule activations lack inherent numerical meaning, we convert them into one-hot encodings (line 15). This conversion prepares them for the training of the final prediction tree $\psi_f(\cdot)$ (line 16). Finally, we merge the rules and decision trees into the final rule set R_f and final decision tree set DT_f (line 17–18). Notice that there may be Concept Derivation Rules ($R_{X \mapsto c}$) that are not selected for the final prediction. These rules are removed from R_f during a post-processing step (line 19).

Algorithm 1. EDICT

Input: DNN f_θ with d layers $\{h_0, ..., h_{d+1}\}$, training data X
Output: Rule set R_f, Decision tree set DT_f
Hyperparameter: Decision Trees $\psi_I(\cdot)$, $\psi_c(\cdot)$, $\psi_F(\cdot)$

1: $R_f, DT_f \leftarrow \emptyset$
2: $\hat{Y} \leftarrow f_\theta(X)$
3: $C \leftarrow list()$
4: **for** hidden layer $i = 1, ...d$ **do**
5:      $X' \leftarrow h_i(X)$
6:      **for** decision tree $j = 1, ...k$ **do**
7:          $R_{X' \mapsto \hat{Y}} \leftarrow \psi_I^j(X', \hat{Y})$ ▷ Train integrative activation decision tree
8:          $c, conf \leftarrow R_{X' \mapsto \hat{Y}}(X')$ ▷ Evaluate hidden layer activations
9:          $R_{X \mapsto c} \leftarrow \psi_c^j(X, c, conf)$ ▷ Train concept derivation decision tree
10:         $R_f \leftarrow R_f \cup R_{X \mapsto c}$
11:         $DT_f \leftarrow DT_f \cup \psi_c^j$
12:         $C \leftarrow C \cup c$
13:      **end for**
14: **end for**
15: $C \leftarrow \text{ONEHOTENCODER}(C)$
16: $R_{C \mapsto \hat{Y}} \leftarrow \psi_F(C, \hat{Y})$ ▷ Train final predication decision tree
17: $R_f \leftarrow R_f \cup R_{C \mapsto \hat{Y}}$
18: $DT_f \leftarrow DT_f \cup \psi_F$
19: $R_f \leftarrow \text{POSTPROCESSING}(R_f)$
20: **return** R_f, DT_f

As we apply our method for the process of rule extraction and rule inference, it is observed that the runtime complexity exhibits polynomial-time growth relative to the size of its input. The computational advantage of our approach over previous decompositional methods is highlighted in Theorem 1 and 2 (detailed proofs are available in an external report[1].

Theorem 1. *(Rule Extraction Runtime Complexity) Let us consider a trained NN with d layers, where each layer (including the input layer) has at most m neurons. Suppose we have n training samples, and we are using top-down impurity-based algorithms, denoted as $\psi(\cdot)$, for constructing k distinct concept derivation decision trees, integrative activation decision trees, and one final prediction decision tree. If the runtime of $\psi(\cdot)$ grows as $\mathcal{O}(n^{p_n} m^{p_m})$ for some $p_n, p_m \in \mathbb{N}$, then the complexity of the training runtime can be upper bounded as $\mathcal{O}(k \cdot dn^{max(3, p_n)} m^{p_m})$.*

Theorem 2. *(Rule Inference Runtime Complexity) Suppose we have k concept derivation decision trees which can be executed in parallel, followed by a final prediction decision tree. Under the same conditions as in Theorem 1, the complexity of the inference runtime commonly grows as $\mathcal{O}(log(n))$, while it can grow as $\mathcal{O}(n)$ in the worst case.*

Compared to the Eclaire [25], which has a proven extraction complexity of $\mathcal{O}(n \cdot dn^{max(3, p_n)} m^{p_m})$, our method improves extraction speed, primarily due to the fact that the quantity of tree estimators k in our case is markedly less than the number of samples n. In practical applications, we set the upper limit of k as the square root of one-tenth the number of samples n. In addition to this, our method also improves upon rule inference speed. This improvement is achieved by relying on a hierarchy of decision trees rather than an assembly of decision rules drawn from all intermediate rules and all hidden layers. It should also be noted that the efficiency of our algorithm can be further enhanced by leveraging multi-processing techniques for layer-specific computations (lines 4–14) and employing vectorized operations for rule evaluations (line 8).

5 Experiments

Our methodology is evaluated utilizing multiple publicly available datasets. This enables us to compare our approach against current rule extraction techniques, in terms of both the performance during the rule extraction phase and the quality of the extracted rules during the inference phase. We take as our foundation the code published by Shams et al. [19, 25], and we adopt very similar experimental settings as they described in their paper.

5.1 Experimental Setup

For all experiments, we conduct a 5-fold stratified cross-validation and present both the mean and standard deviation errors for each metric of interest across

---

[1] https://drive.google.com/file/d/1eU8LUdBueWYI1O2ae_LlqJeqw0EztHB1/view? usp=sharing.

all 5 folds. Additionally, all experiments are executed on a 3.7 GHz Quad-core machine with 32 GB of RAM, running a Windows operating system. We limit each individual experiment to use at most six processes for rule extraction and inference, and we terminate any experiment that exceeds a fourteen-hour completion time.

Datasets. We selected four binary classification datasets: an XOR dataset for capturing logical relationships; two METRABRIC datasets, specifically designed for medical applications; MAGIC, a large dataset from particle physics; and Letter Recognition, a dataset used for multi-classification tasks.

XOR: This is a synthetic dataset composed of 1000 ten-dimensional samples. Each data point $x(i) \in [0,1]^{10}$ is independently sampled from a uniform distribution. A binary label is then assigned to each point by applying an XOR operation on the first two rounded dimensions. Learning this logical relationship is known as a challenge for vanilla rule induction algorithms and pedagogical rule extraction methods without using a large training dataset [3].

METRABRIC [19]: This dataset contains features derived from 1,980 breast cancer patients, is used for two prediction tasks. In task MB-ER, 1,000 mRNA expression patterns are used to predict immunohistochemical subtypes, ER+ or ER-. In task MB-HIST, 1,004 mRNA expression profiles are used to predict histological tumour subtypes, ILC or IDC.

MAGIC [4]: This dataset involves the classification of signals into either high-energy gamma rays or background hadron cosmic radiation, utilizing 10 real-valued features. Compared to the previous three datasets, this is considerably larger, containing 19,020 training samples.

Letter Recognition [7] (hereinafter referred to as *Letter*): This dataset is composed of 20,000 black-and-white representations of English uppercase letters. Each sample in this dataset is categorized into one of 26 classes (from A to Z) using 16 statistical image features.

Baselines and Metrics. In our experiment, we benchmark our method against three existing decompositional approaches: DeepRED, REM-D, and Eclaire. We employ Zarlenga et al.'s [25] implementation of these methods, but replace the intermediate rule extractor C5.0 with Cart (a decision tree algorithm based on the Gini impurity splitting criteria) in Eclaire, which we noted significantly improved rule predictive accuracy for the XOR and Letter Recognition datasets, while delivering comparable results on other datasets (Results including C5.0 are available in the external report). Moreover, we include two non-decompositional baselines: Cart and PedCart, to demonstrate the advantages of decompositional rule extraction. The former is an end-to-end rule induction method, whereas the latter uses a Cart to induce a rule set from a training set, where each sample is labeled based on the DNN's prediction. The evaluation of these methods includes assessing predictive accuracy and AUC of the extracted rule sets. The fidelity metric, defined as the accuracy of a rule set aligned with the DNN's prediction, is used to measure the approximation of the original trained DNN. The methods are also compared in terms of rule extraction and inference time. Interpretability is quantified by the number of rules (i.e., rule set size) and the terms used.

Parameter Settings. Initially, we selected the highest-performing multilayer perceptron (MLP) models for each dataset, which were trained and optimized using grid search over their respective hyperparameters. We configured the MLP models with hidden layer sizes: $\{64, 32, 16\}$ for the XOR dataset, $\{128, 16\}$ for the METABRIC datasets, $\{64, 32, 16\}$ for the MAGIC dataset, and $\{128, 64\}$ for the Letter Recognition dataset. During the rule extraction process, we set up the Cost Complexity Pruning (CCP) [5] option, the minimum number of samples μ required before splitting a node (to manage the growth of Cart trees), and the number of trees k utilized for IA-DTs and CD-DTs. The parameters of the baseline models were determined using the same strategy as described in the original implementations (see [25]). Given the vast number of configurable hyperparameters for decision tree algorithms, and the fact that we have three different types of decision trees, we only vary the parameter k for the number decision trees, and the parameter μ for the CD-DT, leaving all other parameters at their default values. Unless otherwise specified, all CCP options are enabled. The test accuracy of the MLP model and our approach's configuration for each dataset are as follows:

- XOR: MLP test accuracy $96.5\% \pm 0.7$, configuration $k = 2$, $\mu = 2$.
- MB-ER: MLP test accuracy $95.5\% \pm 1$, configuration $k = 2$, $\mu = 3$.
- MB-HIST: MLP test accuracy $89.4\% \pm 4.9$, configuration $k = 2$, $\mu = 4$.
- MAGIC: MLP test accuracy $86.1\% \pm 1.4$, configuration $k = 2$, $\mu = 50$.
- Letter: MLP test accuracy $96.1\% \pm 1.4$, configuration $k = 3$, $\mu = 2$ or $\mu^* = 6$.

Note that, these parameters are configured empirically based on dataset classes and samples to showcase our approach's superior performance in terms of rule extraction speed, interpretability, and predictive accuracy. The performance could be further improved with more optimal parameter configurations.

5.2   Results

Based on our previous analysis of runtime complexity, we expect our approach to outperform the most efficient existing decompositional algorithm, Eclaire, in terms of both extraction and inference speed. By introducing auxiliary variables and rules, there will be a significant reduction in the resultant rule set size and the number of used terms. Furthermore, given that the auxiliary rules are selectively substituted and only the most informative concepts are used for the final prediction, we hypothesize that our method will offer improved predictive performance and fidelity compared to other decompositional methods. As presented in Table 1, the rule sets extracted by our approach, EDICT, achieved the best predictive performance in terms of accuracy, AUC, and fidelity on the XOR, MAGIC, and Letter Recognition datasets, while having comparable results on the two METABRIC datasets. It is worth noting that the extracted rules exhibit even higher accuracy on the XOR and METABRIC-HIST datasets (97.90% and

90.10%, respectively) than the trained DNN (96.5% and 89.4%, respectively), yet they struggle to achieve comparable accuracy on the Letter Recognition datasets (82.7% *versus* the DNN's 96.1%). We attribute this to the inherent characteristics of the hard decision tree learner, which may not be able to fully approximate a learner that selects features probabilistically. It's important to mention that we adjusted parameters k and μ to strike a trade-off between predictive performance and rule size of the model. Greater accuracy could potentially be achieved, albeit likely at the expense of increasing rule size, and vice versa. For instance, we increase μ to 6 for all decision trees on the Letter dataset (as shown the last row in Table 1), the rule size is reduced to 545 at the cost of a 4.5% decrease in predictive accuracy. Hence, further research should explore the development of a unified metric to monitor the rule extraction process, which would provide a comprehensive evaluation considering both rule size and predictive accuracy.

Table 1. The table presents the mean and standard deviation for each metric of interest across all 5 folds for all rule extraction approaches. The best-performing values for each metric and the name of approach are highlighted in bold. AUC is only included for binary classification datasets.

	Method	Accuracy (%)	AUC (%)	Fidelity (%)	Extraction Time (s)	Inference Time (s)	Rule Set Size	Number of Terms
XOR	Cart	81.40 ± 11.10	81.30 ± 11.10	N/A	0.033 ± 0.011	0.338 ± 0.124	51.00 ± 17.48	100.0 ± 34.96
	PedCart	82.00 ± 7.00	82.00 ± 7.00	81.90 ± 7.30	0.115 ± 0.01	0.379 ± 0.128	60.40 ± 11.86	118.8 ± 23.72
	DeepRED	86.90 ± 4.60	86.90 ± 4.70	86.40 ± 5.10	66.31 ± 37.63	14.18 ± 14.59	3321 ± 3194	131.6 ± 68.93
	REM-D	88.80 ± 2.10	88.80 ± 2.10	88.50 ± 1.90	13.80 ± 13.61	5.55 ± 9.41	1306 ± 2220	87.8 ± 64.98
	Eclaire	96.30 ± 1.90	96.30 ± 2.00	95.40 ± 2.00	23.31 ± 1.306	0.232 ± 0.083	41.80 ± 11.34	97.00 ± 28.73
	EDICT	**97.90 ± 1.50**	**98.00 ± 1.40**	**96.20 ± 1.40**	**5.89 ± 0.19**	**0.070 ± 0.01**	**12.60 ± 1.96**	**35.8 ± 10.78**
MB-ER	Cart	90.00 ± 1.60	85.70 ± 2.10	N/A	2.12 ± 0.29	5.77 ± 0.04	22.20 ± 2.48	42.4 ± 4.964
	PedCart	89.50 ± 1.80	87.70 ± 2.50	89.90 ± 2.00	3.10 ± 0.15	5.96 ± 0.12	25.40 ± 2.73	48.8 ± 5.455
	DeepRED	90.40 ± 2.70	87.30 ± 5.80	90.60 ± 4.10	792 ± 888	1.92 ± 1.32	161 ± 131	79.0 ± 34.82
	REM-D	90.00 ± 2.20	87.20 ± 5.10	90.00 ± 3.70	65.22 ± 19.95	1.09 ± 0.54	87.60 ± 68.78	61.4 ± 23.93
	Eclaire	**92.20 ± 1.50**	88.20 ± 3.00	**92.10 ± 0.50**	38.90 ± 3.45	0.52 ± 0.03	24.00 ± 2.19	46.0 ± 3.899
	EDICT	91.40 ± 0.80	**88.40 ± 1.20**	91.10 ± 0.60	13.98 ± 0.44	**0.065 ± 0.002**	**4.2 ± 1.6**	**9.8 ± 3.7**
MB-HIST	Cart	88.50 ± 1.50	63.90 ± 3.00	N/A	2.32 ± 0.46	5.96 ± 0.25	21.20 ± 1.72	40.4 ± 3.441
	PedCart	81.50 ± 4.20	70.40 ± 4.90	84.80 ± 3.00	2.43 ± 0.31	6.00 ± 0.22	24.40 ± 6.56	46.8 ± 13.12
	DeepRED	88.30 ± 3.90	**72.10 ± 8.30**	88.90 ± 3.30	429.1 ± 75.63	1.14 ± 0.49	197.2 ± 83.22	90.0 ± 32.32
	REM-D	89.10 ± 2.60	70.10 ± 4.60	88.40 ± 3.70	116.9 ± 115.1	13.34 ± 25.70	2820 ± 5574	82.8 ± 99.95
	Eclaire	88.40 ± 2.60	71.60 ± 7.20	**89.10 ± 2.50**	38.69 ± 4.08	0.381 ± 0.039	16.80 ± 2.71	29.8 ± 7.83
	EDICT	**90.10 ± 1.80**	69.10 ± 7.10	88.40 ± 3.70	18.39 ± 1.19	**0.063 ± 0.005**	**6.6 ± 3.2**	**21.0 ± 11.05**
MAGIC	Cart	84.40 ± 0.60	81.40 ± 0.80	N/A	0.34 ± 0.02	8.39 ± 0.23	144.40 ± 4.92	286.8 ± 9.847
	PedCart	82.80 ± 1.20	82.50 ± 0.90	89.50 ± 1.00	1.14 ± 0.04	9.46 ± 0.19	176.4 ± 14.56	350.8 ± 29.11
	DeepRED	77.70 ± 2.70	72.50 ± 5.10	78.90 ± 3.30	845.7 ± 389.5	14.35 ± 7.11	502.4 ± 361.3	81.6 ± 35.49
	REM-D	77.70 ± 2.60	72.60 ± 5.00	78.90 ± 3.20	146.7 ± 46.39	31.06 ± 26.59	491.0 ± 357.7	**81.4 ± 35.52**
	Eclaire	82.00 ± 1.60	78.00 ± 1.40	85.40 ± 1.20	56.01 ± 2.31	5.66 ± 0.71	74.40 ± 5.85	224.4 ± 18.12
	EDICT	**82.70 ± 1.70**	**81.40 ± 1.00**	**88.10 ± 1.50**	12.19 ± 0.59	**0.248 ± 0.01**	**46.60 ± 3.88**	212.8 ± 17.77
Letter	Cart	69.6 ± 0.6	N/A	N/A	0.137 ± 0.004	9.623 ± 0.231	150.4 ± 6.28	152.8 ± 4.308
	PedCart	56.90 ± 6.80	N/A	56.70 ± 6.80	3.28 ± 0.06	14.75 ± 0.53	460.4 ± 13.32	157.2 ± 5.154
	DeepRED	3.9 ± 0.2	N/A	3.9 ± 0.2	4495 ± 2041	1755 ± 1641	85877 ± 10726	138.6 ± 9.932
	REM-D	4.1 ± 0.3	N/A	4.1 ± 0.2	1313 ± 759	990.6 ± 623	43626 ± 29956	**134.6 ± 7.6**
	Eclaire	79.60 ± 0.60	N/A	79.30 ± 0.60	140.13 ± 8.87	21.13 ± 0.94	663.4 ± 10.76	456.0 ± 14.63
	EDICT	**82.70 ± 0.80**	N/A	**82.10 ± 1.10**	77.92 ± 1.66	10.22 ± 0.95	862.0 ± 31.98	1228 ± 37.06
	EDICT*	78.20 ± 0.60	N/A	78.10 ± 0.50	**53.62 ± 0.97**	**4.61 ± 0.48**	**545.4 ± 29.32**	837.0 ± 34.96

With regards to rule extraction efficiency and inference speed, our approach significantly surpasses other decompositional methods across all five datasets, which is in line with our earlier analysis. The number of extracted rules is as

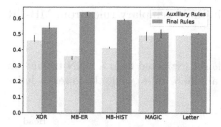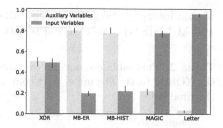

Fig. 4. The Distribution of Rules and Variables across Five Folders: The left represents the percentage distribution of final and auxiliary rules within the rule sets, while the right displays the percentage distribution of unique input and auxiliary variables used in the rule sets on five datasets

hypothesized consistently reduced, thereby enhancing comprehensibility, particularly for the XOR, MB-ER, and MB-HIST datasets, where the number of rules, including both auxiliary and final rules, has been reduced to fewer than 15. Even with the introduction of auxiliary variables, the number of terms utilized in a rule set is still reduced, particularly evident in the first three datasets. These concise rule sets offer insights into how the DNN leverages statistical regularities for prediction, and can be quickly assessed by human analysts. As illustrated in our rule sets' distribution, the count of auxiliary rules is quite similar to that of final rules (shown on the left in Fig. 4) within a rule set. However, for the MAGIC and Letter datasets, the number of auxiliary variables (shown on the right in Fig. 4) is significantly less than the input variables compared to other datasets. This reflects that the extracted rule sizes, as indicated in Table 1, do not significantly reduce for these two datasets; that is, fewer auxiliary variables lead to larger rule sets. This implies that the crucial factor in reducing the size of the rule set, and thereby enhancing its interpretability, lies in the effective identification and selection of informative concepts learned from a trained DNN. We offer, as an illustration, the rules extracted from a trained DNN on the XOR dataset, outlined in Table 2. The first three auxiliary rules, learned by the CD-DTs, yield three conclusions, each signifying a distinct learned concept. Figure 5 demonstrates these rules plotted within the 0-1 range of the first two dimensions, x_0 and x_1. This range was chosen as every data point is sampled from a uniform distribution within it, and a binary label is assigned by XOR-ing the rounding result of these two dimensions. Rule 1 is associated with the lower right square, denoted R_0, and Rule 2 with the upper left square, labeled R_1. Rule 3, denoted R_2, comprises three noisy atoms from x_4, x_6, and x_8, and only the first two dimensions are plotted within the semi-transparent lower right square. Rule 4 states that if a data point does not satisfy R_0 and R_1 conditions, it is classified as 0. Rule 5 asserts that if a data point does not satisfy R_1 and satisfies R_0, it is labeled 1. Rule 6 states that if a data point satisfies R_1 but does not satisfy R_2 conditions, it is labeled 1. Even though the rule set includes noisy terms, the identified auxiliary rules extracted from the trained DNN contribute to enhancing the interpretability of the rule set. For a more comprehensive exploration of rule interpretation, we incorporated additional exemplary rules from MB-ER and MB-HIST in the external report.

Table 2. This table presents an exemplary rule set extracted from a DNN trained on the XOR dataset. The upper part contains the auxiliary rules, while the lower includes the final rules.

	Rule Body	Head
1	IF $[(x_0 > 0.5042) \land (x_1 \le 0.4992)]$	R_0
2	IF $(x_0 \le 0.5207) \land (x_1 > 0.4992)$	R_1
3	IF $(x_0 > 0.501) \land (x_1 \le 0.2809) \land (x_4 > 0.9346) \land (x_6 > 0.2981) \land (x_8 \le 0.9395)$	R_2
4	IF $(R_1 \le 0.5) \land (R_0 \le 0.5)$	0
5	IF $(R_1 \le 0.5) \land (R_0 > 0.5)$	1
6	IF $(R_1 > 0.5) \land (R_2 \le 0.5)$	1

5.3   Discussion

Our experiments conducted across multiple datasets demonstrate that our approach provides substantial advantages in terms of rule interpretability and extraction efficiency. Moreover, it also shows superior performance in rule inference, resulting in a highly competitive predictive output within the rule set. Previous works on decompositional rule extraction focused on creating explicit relationships between input and output variables. They substitute all hidden variables [19,27] or clauses [25], thereby retaining only the input variables in the rule body. However, we argue that enhancing rule interpretability and boosting rule extraction process hinges on

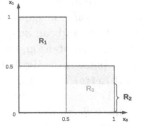

Fig. 5. Visualization of rule sets from Table 2, with distinct colors assigned to areas covered by each auxiliary rule.

introducing informative auxiliary variables, which correspond to the concepts learned by the trained DNN. This is akin to how predicate invention simplifies the structure of the learned program in inductive logic programming [14]. Our method utilizes a set of decision trees (IA-DTs) to mine concepts invented by the trained DNN. Subsequently, we employ an additional decision tree (FP-DT) to select the concepts that yield the maximum information gains. These concepts are represented as auxiliary rules containing conjunctions of atoms that correspond to activations across neurons within a layer. Despite these significant improvements, we acknowledge certain limitations that should be addressed in the future. First, we observed a recurring pattern of similar auxiliary rules, which were differentiated only by slightly varying thresholds. Furthermore, considerably fewer auxiliary rules were learned when we used the MAGIC and Letter datasets. Although we utilized the default bootstrap provided by the scikit library for random forests, more strategies might be required to enhance the diversity of trees. As the final decision tree makes binary selections over concepts, the trees are prone to imbalance and the number of final rules could be significantly reduced through Boolean logic simplification. Secondly, our methodology relied on a simple two-layer architecture, mining concepts across all hidden layers without taking into account the topological order of the DNN. As such, the exploration of a wider variety of architectures would offer further insights into the evolution of concepts between layers. Thirdly, a unified metric for evaluating decompositional rule extraction approaches is absent from current discussions. Such a metric would ideally strike a balance between predictive performance and rule interpretability. Lastly, our study of the DNN's behavior is premised on the observation of activations within layers, thereby implicitly implicating the learned weights. Future research might benefit from a more direct study of weights and appropriate samples. This could reduce dependency on samples and alleviate the sensitivity of decision trees to changes in those samples.

6 Conclusion

As deep learning proliferates across numerous applications, human intervention and understanding become increasingly critical. Extracting symbolic rules serves not only to facilitate the explanation and debugging of models, but also holds important implications for societal regulation. Our approach examines the activations within network layers, extracting the model's learned concepts and introducing them as auxiliary variables in the rule set. This method reduces the rule set size and mines more diverse concepts, thereby enhancing both the efficiency of extraction and the interpretability of the rules. In the context of real-world applications, neural networks trained on large-scale data give rise to vast sets of rules. More high-level rules must be extracted and analyzed, necessitating collaboration and interpretation with human experts. Future work will investigate the scalability of EDICT to larger networks in conjunction with rule visualization techniques, to further bolster interpretability.

References

1. Andrews, R., Diederich, J., Tickle, A.B.: Survey and critique of techniques for extracting rules from trained artificial neural networks. Knowl.-Based Syst. 8(6), 373–389 (1995). https://doi.org/10.1016/0950-7051(96)81920-4
2. Benitez, J., Castro, J., Requena, I.: Are artificial neural networks black boxes? IEEE Trans. Neural Netw. 8(5), 1156–1164 (1997). https://doi.org/10/cr3mjs
3. Blanc, G., Lange, J., Tan, L.Y.: Top-down induction of decision trees: rigorous guarantees and inherent limitations. arXiv preprint arXiv:1911.07375 (2019). https://doi.org/10.48550/arXiv.1911.07375
4. Bock, R.: MAGIC Gamma Telescope. UCI Machine Learning Repository (2007). https://doi.org/10.24432/C52C8B

5. Breiman, L., Friedman, J., Olshen, R., Stone, C.: Classification and regression trees. Wadsworth Int. Group **37**(15), 237–251 (1984). https://doi.org/10.1201/9781315139470

6. Craven, M., Shavlik, J.: Extracting tree-structured representations of trained networks. In: Touretzky, D., Mozer, M., Hasselmo, M. (eds.) Advances in Neural Information Processing Systems, vol. 8. MIT Press (1995)

7. Frey, P.W., Slate, D.J.: Letter recognition using Holland-style adaptive classifiers. Mach. Learn. **6**(2), 161–182 (1991). https://doi.org/10.1007/BF00114162

8. Fürnkranz, J., Gamberger, D., Lavrač, N.: Foundations of Rule Learning. Cognitive Technologies, Springer, Heidelberg (2012). https://doi.org/10.1007/978-3-540-75197-7

9. Fu, L.: Rule generation from neural networks. IEEE Trans. Syst. Man Cybern. **24**(8), 1114–1124 (1994). https://doi.org/10.1109/21.299696

10. Hastie, T., Tibshirani, R., Friedman, J.H., Friedman, J.H.: The Elements of Statistical Learning: Data Mining, Inference, and Prediction, vol. 2. Springer, New York (2009). https://doi.org/10.1007/978-0-387-84858-7

11. He, C., Ma, M., Wang, P.: Extract interpretability-accuracy balanced rules from artificial neural networks: a review. Neurocomputing **387**, 346–358 (2020). https://doi.org/10.1016/j.neucom.2020.01.036

12. Hinton, G.E., Osindero, S., Teh, Y.W.: A fast learning algorithm for deep belief nets. Neural Comput. **18**(7), 1527–1554 (2006). https://doi.org/10.1162/neco.2006.18.7.1527

13. LeCun, Y., Bengio, Y., Hinton, G.: Deep learning. Nature **521**(7553), 436–444 (2015). https://doi.org/10.1038/nature14539

14. Muggleton, S., Buntine, W.: Machine invention of first-order predicates by inverting resolution. In: Laird, J. (ed.) Machine Learning Proceedings, pp. 339–352. Morgan Kaufmann (1988). https://doi.org/10.1016/B978-0-934613-64-4.50040-2

15. Sato, M., Tsukimoto, H.: Rule extraction from neural networks via decision tree induction. In: International Joint Conference on Neural Networks Proceedings, vol. 3, pp. 1870–1875. IEEE (2001). https://doi.org/10.1109/IJCNN.2001.938448

16. Schmitz, G., Aldrich, C., Gouws, F.: ANN-DT: an algorithm for extraction of decision trees from artificial neural networks. IEEE Trans. Neural Netw. **10**(6), 1392–1401 (1999). https://doi.org/10/bzvfs2

17. Sethi, K.K., Mishra, D.K., Mishra, B.: KDRuleEx: a novel approach for enhancing user comprehensibility using rule extraction. In: 2012 Third International Conference on Intelligent Systems Modelling and Simulation, Kota Kinabalu, Malaysia, pp. 55–60. IEEE (2012). https://doi.org/10/gks4jz

18. Setiono, R., Leow, W.K.: FERNN: an algorithm for fast extraction of rules from neural networks. Appl. Intell. 11 (2000). https://doi.org/10.1023/A:1008307919726

19. Shams, Z., et al.: REM: an integrative rule extraction methodology for explainable data analysis in healthcare. medRxiv preprint (2021). https://doi.org/10.1101/2021.01.25.21250459

20. Taha, I., Ghosh, J.: Symbolic interpretation of artificial neural networks. IEEE Trans. Knowl. Data Eng. **11**(3), 448–463 (1999). https://doi.org/10/bpjz4s

21. Thrun, S.B.: Extracting provably correct rules from artificial neural networks. Technical report, University of Bonn (1993). https://dl.acm.org/doi/book/10.5555/895610

22. Towell, G.G., Shavlik, J.W.: Extracting refined rules from knowledge-based neural networks. Mach. Learn. **13**(1), 71–101 (1993). https://doi.org/10.1007/BF00993103

23. Tsukimoto, H.: Extracting rules from trained neural networks. IEEE Trans. Neural Netw. **11**(2), 377–389 (2000). https://doi.org/10/c43brd
24. Wörmann, J., Bogdoll, D., Bührle, E., Chen, H., Chuo: Knowledge augmented machine learning with applications in autonomous driving: a survey. arXiv preprint (2022). https://doi.org/10.48550/arXiv.2205.04712
25. Zarlenga, M.E., Shams, Z., Jamnik, M.: Efficient decompositional rule extraction for deep neural networks. arXiv preprint (2022). http://arxiv.org/abs/2111.12628
26. Zhou, Z.H., Chen, S.F., Chen, Z.Q.: A statistics based approach for extracting priority rules from trained neural networks. In: Proceedings of the International Joint Conference on Neural Networks, vol. 3, pp. 401–406 (2000). https://doi.org/10.1109/IJCNN.2000.861337
27. Zilke, J.R., Loza Mencía, E., Janssen, F.: DeepRED – rule extraction from deep neural networks. In: Calders, T., Ceci, M., Malerba, D. (eds.) DS 2016. LNCS (LNAI), vol. 9956, pp. 457–473. Springer, Cham (2016). https://doi.org/10.1007/978-3-319-46307-0_29

Author Index

A. Fensel et al. (Eds.): RuleML+RR 2023, LNCS 14244, p. 255, 2023.
https://doi.org/10.1007/978-3-031-45072-3

Printed in the United States
by Baker & Taylor Publisher Services